Life Is Hard

D0052419

A CENTENNIAL BOOK

One hundred books
published between 1990 and 1995
bear this special imprint of
the University of California Press.
We have chosen each Centennial Book
as an example of the Press's finest
publishing and bookmaking traditions
as we celebrate the beginning of
our second century.

UNIVERSITY OF CALIFORNIA PRESS

Founded in 1893

Life Is Hard

Machismo, Danger, and the
Intimacy of Power in Nicaragua

Roger N. Lancaster

UNIVERSITY OF CALIFORNIA PRESS
Berkeley • Los Angeles • London

University of California Press
Berkeley and Los Angeles, California

University of California Press, Ltd.
London, England

© 1992 by
The Regents of the University of California

First Paperback Printing 1994

Library of Congress Cataloging-in-Publication Data

Lancaster, Rober N.
  Life is hard : machismo, danger, and the intimacy of power in Nicaragua / Roger N. Lancaster.
    p.   cm.
  "A Centennial book"—P.
  Includes bibliographical references and index.
  ISBN 0-520-08929-4 (alk. paper)
  1. Nicaragua—Social conditions—1979– 2. Nicaragua—Social conditions—1979– —Case studies. 3. Nicaragua—Politics and government—1979– 4. Power (Social sciences) I. Title.
  HN163.5.L36 1993
  306'.097285—dc20   91-45764

Printed in the United States of America

08   07   06   05
9   8   7

The paper used in this publication is both acid-free and totally chlorine-free (TCF).
It meets the minimum requirements of ANSI/NISO Z39.48-1992 (R 1997)
(*Permanence of Paper*). ∞

Para aquellos que han peleado la buena batalla,
Quienes han guardado la fe—a pesar de todo—
Y a ellos quienes acabarán la carrera.

Contents

Acknowledgments

For their encouragement, support, and critical readings of early drafts of this book, I would like to thank Bob Blauner, Mark Colvin, Dan Gunter, Matthew Gutmann, Michael Higgins, Suzanne Neuschatz, Mark Pentecost, Jack Potter, Jim Quesada, Karen Rosenblum, Nancy Scheper-Hughes, Naomi Schneider, Sheila Smith, John Stone, and an anonymous reviewer for the University of California Press. Samuel Colón gave valuable advice at every stage of the writing; he patiently read and productively critiqued several drafts of the manuscript and assisted me with some of the translations.

This book is based on conversations held and observations made during several stints of fieldwork in Managua, Nicaragua: December 1984 to January 1985, May to December 1985, May to June 1986, May to June and August 1988, and July 1991. Funding for my research during these periods was provided by a travel grant from the Center for Latin American Studies and the Tinker Foundation, a Graduate Humanities Research Grant from the Regents of the University of California, three separate small grants from the Lowie Funds of the Department of Anthropology, University of California–Berkeley, a yearlong internship at the Institute for the Study of Social Change (Berkeley), and a 1988 summer stipend from the National Endowment for the Humanities. Support for a final visit with my informants in July 1991 was provided by the College of Arts and Sciences at George Mason University.

Obviously, I owe the greatest debt to my informants themselves. It seems awkward to say merely that the hospitality and candor of my primary informants were instrumental in producing this book; they were that, but also more than that. I am proud to count the people about whom I am writing as friends and compadres. If I have displayed more of myself in these pages than seems properly professional, it is because I feel that I have no right to put other people's personal lives under so much scrutiny without putting something on my own side of the balance at risk. And if I have shown more about my informants than seems meet, or if I have taken some liberties by not just recording our conversations but also offering my own interpretations, it has been with the hope—whether utopian or practical, I cannot say—that all of this might somehow make a difference, if it improves our understanding of just what makes life so hard.

A shorter and rather different version of "Subject Honor, Object Shame" appeared in *Ethnology* (vol. 27, no. 2, April 1988: 111–25), as did "The *Negro* of the Family" (vol. 30, no. 4, October 1991: 339–53).

This Book and Its Title

La vida es dura. In Nicaragua as in the United States, "Life is hard" is a common formula. I first encountered the Spanish phrase in a letter from Alberto Ocampo to his family. Alberto had abandoned his *compañera* (companion, or "wife" of informal union), Celia, and their four children in 1979, just after the revolution. His mistress, a conservative, left Nicaragua immediately after the Sandinistas came to power. Despite his own political radicalism near the end of the Somoza dynasty— he had named his last son "Lenín"—Alberto chose "to be with the other woman," as Celia put it, and followed her to Miami. In 1985, after six years of silence, the Ocampos received this letter from Alberto, which I was invited to read.

> Dear Celia, Gustavo, Marco-Polo, Yolanda and Lenín:
>
> Celia, I know you probably don't want to hear from me, and I know that you probably hate me. I don't blame you. You might not even read this letter, but I hope you won't just throw it away before opening it. I've been meaning to write you for a long time.
>
> Things have gone badly for me here in Miami. I've been sick. I've been unemployed, and that is why you haven't heard anything from me. Life is hard—I know it is hard for you, but it has been hard for me, too. I went two years without work, owing to sickness, and so we've been living in this little one-room flat with hardly enough income to get by. But my old lady—well, I know you don't want to hear about her, but she got a job, and she's been working in a restaurant, and she got me a job working there. At least I have work now. I think I'm in good with the *patrón,* so God willing things will get better.

I know it's been hard on you, without a man around. But you are a strong woman, and I know that you can take care of your family. I hear that there is a gringo who sometimes lives with you, and that is good. I'm glad that you have someone who will help you out.

Gustavo, I hear that you are in the military now. It's a hard life, I'm sure, but it will make a man out of you. And when you get out, if you want, you can come here to Miami and work. There are good opportunities here for a young man in good health who's willing to work hard.

Marco-Polo, I know we had our bad times, and we never really got along well, but you know that you are my son, and I think of you often.

Yolanda, I imagine that you must be a beautiful little lady now. I know that your mother will give you a proper upbringing, so I don't have to worry about you on that count.

Lenín, you were so small when I last saw you! I wonder if you can even remember your father now. But never doubt that I love you very much, and I miss you all.

Celia, I know I haven't written or sent you anything, and for that I am sorry. Life is hard, it has been very hard, and there was nothing I could do. But I am going to try to make it up to you. For the last year, I've been saving up things, and collecting things, and now I have a mountain of clothes saved up! I'm going to send them to you and the children. I've collected different sizes of pants for the boys, at sales and second-hand stores, and some dresses and blouses for you and Yolanda. I just wanted you to know that I was thinking of you and that my family is still in my heart. So if you know of anyone going to Nicaragua, before they fly have them call me, and I'll send it by them.

The Ocampo children, especially Lenín, were delighted to hear from their father, and they immediately mailed him a collective reply. As it happened, Alberto's gifts never arrived. After several tries, Celia gave up her efforts to secure them and threw the letter away.

In one regard, the family biography of the Ocampos is not atypical. Men in Nicaragua often maintain more than one household, and informal polygamy is a sanctioned aspect of the culture of *machismo*. When life gets harder, however, men often abandon wives, compañeras, and families, burdening them with all the economic and social disadvantages that await households headed by women. In another regard, the Ocampo family is unusual. Few working- or middle-class Nicaraguans, unless they were directly tied to Somoza's Guardia Nacional, emigrated at the time of the Sandinista triumph. Certainly, even fewer radicals did so. (Large-scale emigration occurred later, during the economic crisis of the late 1980s. Many men were actually encouraged to emigrate by their wives, to send dollars back to their hard-pressed families.) But like any history, the Ocampo family biography is a conjuncture of social conditions and personal caprice, fate and idiosyncrasy, and it follows many twists and turns on the way to nowhere in particular.

LA VIDA DURA

"Implicit social knowledge" often takes the form of a proverb or maxim. Life is hard. The rich get richer and the poor get poorer. Pride goeth before a fall. Highly stereotyped and readily quotable, such proverbs distill into the shortest and most memorable form a tentative collective agreement on the nature of reality. A proverb always announces itself as "common sense." To those educated in the modern preference for the aesthetics of neologism, such maxims sound simple, simplistic, conservative, ossified: in short, they sound like clichés. Their cantankerously cliched sound can be deceptive, however. The bluntness of most maxims need not betray any intellectual bluntedness.

The cleverness involved in the use of maxims is the diametrical opposite of the neologism's inventiveness. Because invoking a maxim means borrowing from a preexisting stock of phrases, originality in construction counts for little. Delivery is everything: a maxim's appropriateness and cleverness depend on the tone in which it is invoked and the circumstances about which it pronounces. Where the neologism is textual, the maxim is contextual. Delivered in a variety of contexts, circulated endlessly by a community of speakers, cited in an ironic or self-pitying, defiant or resigned tone, employed to solicit agreement, sympathy, disagreement, encouragement, or advice, a formula like "La vida es dura" can display a lively, extensive, and subtly nuanced range of meanings. It is anything but dead speech. Everything depends on who recites it, to whom, under what circumstances, regarding what events. Like the meaning of a life, the meaning of a maxim lies in the convergence of the social and the individual. Whereas the "politics of neologism" (Clifford 1988, 177) express the values of originality, hybridity, and individuation in a world of rapid, constant change, the politics of the proverb are differently positioned.[1] Traditional and commonsensical, proverbial speech may—at different moments or even simultaneously—express popular resistance to power, resignation to oppressive conditions, or simple survival in the face of great adversity.

Into the later 1980s, and in a variety of Nicaraguan contexts, I heard the maxim "Life is hard" a great deal. The frequency with which it was repeated by my informants could be taken as a reliable index of the times. In the midst of war and economic crisis, with inflation running at surreal rates, its invocation traced the decline of the revolutionary optimism of the early 1980s. "Life is hard" signifies a certain degree of fatalism, it must be admitted. But as an all-purpose saying, "La vida es dura" soaks up a variety of meanings, a range of nuances. The vagueness and abstraction of "life" is set against the concreteness of "hard." Most certainly, such a phrase is the simplest possible strategy for linking the particular to the general, the personal to the social. But is this equation an assertion that things must necessarily be so? Or does it not carry the possibility, the implication, that things might be otherwise? As a coda set to the rhythm of life's frustrations, this maxim can relate the *duress* of social and economic crisis experienced as personal conditions. It marks, too, the *duration* of the crisis that renders life so very hard. Its pessimism, its fatalism, can plainly serve as a sort of alibi, an excuse, that relieves the individual speaker of the consequences of his own actions. Delivered with an arched brow and a sarcastic tone, however, it becomes the ultimate put-down. (Such was Doña Celia's mocking quotation of the proverb when she reflected on Alberto's "hard life" with the other woman.) At the same time, this proverb can bring to light the strength and *endurance* of the people who survive life's hardships. It marks, by turns, the banality of suffering, the intimacy of power, the comfort of resignation, and the resilience of the oppressed.

Consider this book an exploration of the truth that it bears as its title.

THIS BOOK

As its title suggests, this book is often about everyday, even "vulgar" things. In keeping with the problems it addresses, it follows with varying degrees of continuity the lives and problems of three families, each headed by a woman, each in a network of friends and relatives. Some sections keep closely to my journal notes, and the incidents described approximate my fieldwork experiences as closely as possible.

All too often, ethnographic writing removes the ethnographer from the scene of his or her investigations and reduces the real men and women who are its subjects to so many abstractions, themselves carriers of abstract structures or principles. Thus, the authoritative voice of Science establishes an orderly, authorless narrative that either marginalizes or suppresses all that is disorderly, trivial, or personal. In the process, it finds the world exactly as it had imagined the world to be, and when it is finished, it necessarily leaves everything exactly the way it was. Every account becomes a "just-so story": "It was preordained that Doña Jazmina would play out such and such a role within the culture of machismo, just as it was inscribed from the beginning that the revolution would fail to introduce a revolution within the arenas of gender, sexuality, and color, just as it was clear from the start that the Sandinistas would eventually fall." Naturalizing the course of events, a just-so approach both freezes the world into a static conceit and provides an alibi for the powers that set the status quo.

This book is written deliberately against that grain. It is disorderly. It misbehaves. Sometimes it may seem trivial. In working against the grain, I hope that some of the apparently trivial aspects of life in Nicaragua will reveal their real depths. I have tried to keep everything as personal as possible, the better to see the humor, the better to see the tragedy. The better to see people struggling, successfully or otherwise, to change the conditions of their lives or, barring change, to adapt to them. And the better to see the ethnographer in the ethnography: my questioning of real persons, my groping toward generalizations and conclusions that might answer the questions I set for myself.

Because meaning frequently outruns the intentions of a writer, books have a way of outrunning their authors' conceptions. No doubt, this book will produce readings I do not intend. And because social conditions change, no work is ever really "fixed," neither by its author's intentions nor by the structure of language itself. In the case of *Life Is Hard,* history has already intervened. The text is not what it was when I began researching and writing it in earnest in 1988, when the Sandinistas were still in power in Nicaragua.

In writing this book, I wished to consider in what sense the Nicaraguan revolution could be said to have "failed" to address and transform preexisting power relations along a variety of dimensions not normally thought of as "political." Quite apart from whatever shortcomings I perceived, and apart from the disappointments many Nicaraguans felt about this or that aspect of their revolution, U.S. foreign policy systematically undermined the revolution in its totality, by subjecting that impoverished nation to a crippling economic embargo and a "dirty" guerrilla war. Such conditions—uneven change, war, hardship—and such a closure to the revolutionary decade are the plainest backdrop for my investigations; they constitute, in Marx's term, the "material conditions," and in Georges Condominas's (1973), the "colonial preterrain." Thematically, then—and as much by circumstance as by planning—my overall intention is multiple:

Real *Political-position himself*

1. To describe conditions leading up to the Sandinista electoral defeat of 1990 without resort to the political just-so stories about "revolutions betrayed" and "lost innocence" that script in advance the course of every revolution as a tragedy.

2. To trace power and conflict on a variety of terrains through interviews, participant observation, and reasoning (both my own and my informants')—that is, to consider in some detail precisely where the revolution was not succeeding at *being* revolutionary and where, in a real sense, it was also least secure.

3. To interrogate anthropological methods themselves by laying open as much as possible the conditions and the problematics of my own work.[2]

Especially in the later chapters, I have attempted to draw out the theoretical implications of my work, but always along a political line. In a world where the strong overwhelm the weak, it would be irresponsible for me to write about the subjects I am pursuing *without* a political and theoretical imperative. Partisan analysis is the only resistance to power that a writer, as writer, can effectively offer. Classical (mis)understandings of power have largely exhausted their creativity and explanatory capacity, and today we are faced with the task of devising new, provisional, experimental understandings of power. Like many others writing about power and resistance today, I am improvising within a Marxist tradition, in the critical and interrogative spirit of Marx's work. If Marxism is to carry opposition to exploitation and the desire for a better world into the next century, if it is to avoid the reification to which many, calling themselves Marxists, have consigned it, then Marxism and the whole socialist project must be reinvented—as numerous times, at critical historical junctures, they already have been; indeed, as today they are still being reinvented in political struggles throughout the world, including those in Nicaragua.

Without seeing power as a seamless, uniform system, I am attempting to trace out, "read," and deconstruct systems of power, in a variety of domains (international relations, community, family, gender, race, sexuality) and in all their slipperiness, arrogance, decenteredness, and perniciousness. Here, the prosaic is the profound, for if Marxism is to be reinvented in its own critical and interrogative spirit, it must begin again—and always—with the conditions of everyday life and with an examination of power in its most mundane forms.

The systems of power I describe are resilient; no one could deny that. In a sense, machismo got the better of Alberto's political commitments.

Power

Power
Resistance

Machismo also set the conditions for Celia's life as a single mother and her precarious struggle to feed, clothe, and take care of her family. Yet for all its force, the system of gender roles directly determined no one's course of action. People lived in—but they also at every turn resisted— the powers that guided their lives. They capitulated to some power relations, accommodated others, and redefined yet others. Celia's children, like their parents before them, would grow up in a culture of machismo; but they would also grow up at a time when that culture was contested in many forums, both public and private. For the Ocampos, as for Nicaraguans in general, the revolution involved an ongoing, ambiguous struggle, both within and against their conditions of life.

I would not claim that my informants and the particular incidents I record necessarily "embody," "typify," "demonstrate," or "exemplify" an abstract Nicaraguan culture, or that the many-seamed and often ambiguous microstruggles over power I record add up to a given, preexisting, unified system of power. Such a conceit would necessarily require freezing an extensive web of social relations and social conflicts into a determinate and deterministic objective "thing" quite alien to Marxist criticism. It is through just such an escape hatch that power absents itself from the scene (absconding with the goods, as it were). While we content ourselves with attempts to depict power as a closed mechanism, it goes on practicing its sorcery elsewhere and otherwise. My own strategy is always to inquire, What are the really existing materials and the self-defining conditions through which and with which people both exercise power and engage in conflict? What larger, longer-term—indeed, global—alignments of power and resistance do these conflicts imply? Finally, what "weak links" in each chain of oppression indicate the possibility that, through struggle, these multiple and distinct yet interlocking and mutually supporting systems might be radically transformed?

All books have points; some are complex, some are simple. The main point of this book is very simple. As hard as life can be, poverty, injustice, and powerlessness make it doubly hard. It is hard, too, to make, maintain, and extend a revolution. War is hard on everyone whose life it touches. The eradication of poverty, injustice, and powerlessness is a goal that will not be achieved easily or quickly. Justice will not be bought cheaply.

Personas

Explicitly or not, most ethnographies draw on a small network of primary informants—people who have established some rapport with the anthropologist and with whom the anthropologist has come to feel more or less at ease. Much of the material in this book is based on interviews and conversations with three families and their close acquaintances. Unless otherwise noted, the persons listed below are residents of Erasmus Jiménez, a middle-income, working-class barrio of Managua. All three of the families live along the same *andén* (way, walk), within a few doors of each other. Their names and exact occupations, like the names of barrios and other places, have been changed to protect the privacy of my informants; however, the pseudonyms used here are names one might expect to encounter in Managua. Ages given are approximate for 1988.

DOÑA JAZMINA ALVAREZ AND HER FAMILY:

Jazmina, 46

Mario (deceased husband; formerly a construction contractor)

Omar, 28 (Jazmina's oldest son; two-term military volunteer; medical student)

Nora (*La Policía*), 26 (Jazmina's oldest daughter; widow, police officer)

Freddy, 24 (unemployed construction worker)

Sara, 22 (student and secretary)

Virgilio, 20 (student)

Josué-Luis, 4 (Nora's son by deceased compañero)

Augusto César, 1 (Nora's second son, by coworker)

DOÑA CELIA OCAMPO AND HER FAMILY:

Celia, 42

Alberto (Celia's former compañero; resident of Miami)

Marco-Polo, 23 (eldest son; student and member of the military)

Gustavo, 22 (second son; out of service, seeking employment)

Yolanda, 19 (airline flight attendant)

Lenín, 15 (youngest son, sent abroad to Mexico)

Juan, 27 (unrelated resident/boarder of Doña Celia's house)

DOÑA FLORA PÉREZ AND HER FAMILY:

Flora, 40

Rolando, 43 (Flora's former compañero, mechanic, living in New York City)

Aida, 26 (secretary at Telcor, student of accounting; Flora's oldest daughter, by her first compañero)

Osvaldo, 25 (a lieutenant in the Sandinista Army; Flora's oldest son, by her second compañero)

Clara, 19 (student and secretary; she and remaining children by Rolando)

Charlie, 18 (student, in military service)

Guto, 16 (student, apprentice shoemaker)

Miguel, 14 (student)

Ervin, 2 (Aida's son)

Zelmira, 34 (unrelated resident of Doña Flora's house)

OTHERS:

Elvis, 21 (Sandinista Youth activist, student, and close family friend of the Ocampos)

Jaime, 20 (student and longtime friend of Virgilio and Doña Jazmina's family; resident of a nearby *asentamiento,* or shantytown)

Róger, 20 (student and friend of Virgilio; resident of the lower-working-class Barrio Rigoberto)

Máximo, 56 (Sandinista militant; unemployed bank worker)

Esperanza, 25 (a friend of Aida; Ervin's godmother)

Pedro, 26 (Esperanza's husband)

Onix, 33 (a friend and neighbor of Doña Flora)

María-Teresa, 22 (a neighbor of the Pérez family)

Introduction

Life is not determined by consciousness, but consciousness by life.
—Karl Marx and Frederick Engels,
The German Ideology

In Nicaragua, as everywhere, people try to find humor and happiness in life. They do the best they can in whatever circumstances they find themselves. But Nicaragua is a tragic place today. Its people's hopes for a better world have been systematically undermined by a foreign power. This tragedy, which Nicaragua shares with most of Central America, is the tragedy of a long history of colonialism, neocolonialism, and systematic, continuing injustice.[1]

Nicaragua's modern political history is a history of U.S. intervention, of political and economic dependency cultivated by Washington, and of sporadic, usually defeated rebellions against imperialism and exploitation. This history of U.S.-Nicaraguan entanglements was literally extravagant from the beginning. In 1855, playing a game of business plotting and international intrigue, a group of U.S. mercenaries led by William Walker invaded Nicaragua. Before being expelled, Walker actually ruled Nicaragua for two years: he had himself elected president, declared English the country's official language, and attempted to reinstate slavery in a country that had outlawed it in 1822. Driven out by a combination of interests, Walker attempted twice more to seize Nicaragua before he was executed in 1860 by a firing squad in Honduras. The Walker episode is bizarre, but Walker's polemical memoirs (1860; reprinted in 1985), read in the light of the Iran-Contra scandals, prefigure the sham and duplicity that would inform official U.S. foreign policy toward Nicaragua in the twentieth century.[2]

In 1909, jealous of its hemispheric prerogatives in a period of waxing

1

imperial ambitions, the U.S. government encouraged Nicaraguan Conservatives to rebel against the Liberal government of José Santos Zelaya. Zelaya was without doubt a dictator, but it was his modernizing nationalism, his dream of Central American unity, and his independence that offended Washington—especially when he sought German and Japanese financing for a Nicaraguan canal that would have competed with the U.S.-controlled Panama Canal, then still under construction. Washington instigated a rebellion, and the U.S. Marines landed to ensure a Conservative victory. Zelaya resigned, and in 1910 the Liberals turned power over to the minority Conservatives. Civil war ensued, with Liberals and some disgruntled Conservatives joining forces against the U.S.-imposed regime. Again the U.S. Marines landed. They occupied Nicaragua from 1912 to 1925, installing a series of Conservative presidents. When the Conservatives proved unable to govern without U.S. military support, the Marines returned again to occupy Nicaragua, remaining from 1926 to 1933. Obviously unable to secure a stable Conservative government, in 1927 the United States forced Liberal Party leaders and Conservatives to accept a new agreement. One Liberal general, however, refused to sign the pact; raising an irregular army of peasants and workers, Augusto César Sandino waged a patriotic guerrilla war against the foreign occupiers and their collaborators.[3]

Unable to defeat this original Sandinista movement, the U.S. Marines withdrew a final time in 1933, having occupied Nicaragua for twenty years. They left behind a national police force, the Guardia Nacional, which had been organized, trained, and equipped by the United States, with Anastazio Somoza García as its head. On Somoza's orders, Sandino was assassinated by the Guardia Nacional after peace talks with the figurehead president Juan Sacasa. In 1936 Somoza seized power outright; with generous U.S. aid, his family maintained dictatorial control over Nicaragua for more than forty years. The corruption of the Somoza dynasty is legendary. The Somozas eventually amassed a family fortune worth more than $500 million (Booth and Walker 1989, 31) and acquired land holdings equal in size to the state of Massachusetts, although Nicaragua itself is only the size of South Carolina. The Somoza regime was perhaps the United States' most reliable ally; under Somoza, Nicaragua became a staging ground for U.S. and U.S.-sponsored invasions of other Latin American countries. Not until the very last days of the dictatorship did U.S. support for the Somoza government waver.

By the late 1970s Nicaragua was again in civil war, and the Guardia Nacional was terrorizing the civilian population on an unprecedented scale. In early 1979, with the Sandinista triumph only months away, the U.S. government finally suspended military and economic aid to the Somoza regime (LaFeber 1984, 233). Still, the Carter administration worked—in vain—through the Organization of American States (OAS) and behind the scenes to facilitate a nonrevolutionary transfer of power to a coalition of its liking. And almost immediately after the Sandinistas came to power in 1979, the CIA began organizing remnants of the defeated Guardia Nacional into the nucleus of what was to become the *contrarevolución*. For the duration of the 1980s, either covertly or overtly, with or without congressional approval, with both state and private funds, by means both constitutional and unconstitutional, the Reagan-Bush administration continued to fund the contras, whose military operations included terrorist attacks on civilian populations, uncontrolled human rights abuses, and attacks on agricultural cooperatives, health care facilities, school buildings, electrical generators, and industrial plants.

REVOLUTION AND COUNTERREVOLUTION IN NICARAGUA

The Sandinista revolution represented an authentically Nicaraguan attempt to transcend Nicaragua's long history of colonialism, exploitation, underdevelopment, and poverty.[4] Its struggle against the Somoza dictatorship was necessarily, too, a struggle against U.S. domination of the country. Organized in 1961 as a guerrilla insurgency, the FSLN (Frente Sandinista de la Liberación Nacional; Sandinista National Liberation Front) named itself for the radical general who a generation before had organized an "Army of Free Men" to fight for an independent Nicaragua.

By the 1970s the FSLN had moved far from what one might call, with some qualification, its Marxist-Leninist origins. Like many such movements, the Sandinistas aimed not just at "national liberation" or "national autonomy" but also at a more equitable distribution of wealth and power in a broadly socialist vein. Like most such movements, at war against a dictatorship or oligarchy imposed and supported by a foreign superpower, the Sandinistas were organized along Leninist-vanguardist lines, modified by the principles of prolonged guerrilla warfare developed by Sandino, Mao, and Guevara. As a movement, however, Sandinismo was young enough to have been influenced by the ideas of the international New Left, with its aversion to the absolutist and authoritarian precedents of the vanguardist movements.

Like the insurgencies in El Salvador and Guatemala, the Sandinista movement entertained close ties to the increasingly radical Christian base communities. Responding to the charge of the Vatican II reforms ("Go to the Poor"), these base communities carried out a systematic, grass-roots reformation of Christian practice and worship in various urban, working-class neighborhoods. In small meeting houses, Christian lay activists, radical priests, and ordinary working-class people re-read and reinterpreted the Bible from the point of view of the poor. The God they encountered in the Bible was not an abstract, remote, or severe deity, but a down-to-earth God who accompanied the suffering and acted as a partisan on behalf of the oppressed. With this vision of God in mind, base community participants reinvigorated the Catholic liturgy, emphasizing popular over elite forms and concrete experiences over escapist ideas. Ultimately, they arrived at an understanding of the gospel as a many-sided message of hope and deliverance for the poor— a conception of Christianity as a simultaneously social, political, economic, and spiritual redemption. This Nicaraguan variant of liberation theology had appeal far beyond the borders of the base communities proper. Because it grew out of widespread Christian symbols of sin and redemption, liberation theology provided both a powerful language for talking about social injustice and a moral paradigm for those who acted as revolutionaries.

By the late 1970s the FSLN had established the tone of a revolution that was to be simultaneously nationalist, socialist, and Christian. Plainly, the FSLN was the only organization in Nicaragua capable of waging an effective political and military struggle against the dictatorship. In practice, the FSLN also proved to be the only political organization capable of representing the aspirations of the popular classes for social justice and an equitable distribution of wealth, of organizing their active political involvement, and of realizing the national interests of an independent Nicaragua. The Frente itself was a blend of various tendencies: liberal, nationalist, social-democratic, Leninist, Guevarist, and radical Christian.[5] This blend gave it a unique revolutionary vision. It championed significant social change, with broad respect for human rights; social justice, without recourse to wholesale nationalization of private property; popular power, through the FSLN and its mass organizations and in the context of political pluralism and competitive elections embracing a wide political spectrum. Much of the political ferment of the revolutionary period drew on the millennial dreams of both socialism and Christianity, and the success of the revolution depended in no small measure on the collaboration of radical Christians and secular Sandinistas within the revolutionary process.

My first book, *Thanks to God and the Revolution* (1988b), which examines the roles of liberation theology and popular Christianity in consolidating Nicaragua's revolution, reflects the optimism of the mid-1980s. A brutal and corrupt dictatorship had been overthrown, a foreign-inspired war of aggression was being repelled, land and wealth were being redistributed, a new state was being built, and ordinary people could speak with great eloquence about their class position, their political practices, their sacrifices, and their hopes.

The "ethnographic present," as they call it in the jargon of anthropology, is sometimes a very fleeting thing. The broad class solidarity, the self-confident optimism, the structure of authority, the attempts at revolutionary reconstruction that I described in *Thanks to God*—all belong to history. As an anthropologist, I feel privileged to have been able to record that moment, its hopes, its conflicts. As a human being, I am saddened that it is over—or, at any rate, entering a completely different phase, fraught with new dilemmas, on a trajectory that would be very difficult to predict. On 25 February 1990, in Nicaragua's second national elections since the 1979 revolution, the voters elected the opposition candidate, Violeta Chamorro, to the presidency on the UNO (National Opposition Union) ticket, and UNO won a solid majority in the National Assembly. UNO, a crazy quilt of political parties and splinters from the Right, Center, and Left, was sewn together under the tutelage of the U.S. State Department, and so obvious was the electoral interference that George Bush could introduce Chamorro in Washington circles as "our candidate in Nicaragua."[6]

The Sandinista revolution was not defeated overnight, nor did the trajectory of local history suddenly veer to the right. Sandinismo was in decline well before the electoral debacle of 1990. In 1988, when I revisited the neighborhoods where I had conducted fieldwork, I encountered conditions very different from those I had seen in 1984, 1985, or even 1986. The contras, organized, trained, and financed by the United States, had wrought almost unimaginable havoc on Nicaragua's small, underdeveloped economy. The war's direct costs alone were staggering. By 1987 more than 60 percent of government expenditures (and nearly a third of the gross national product) was absorbed by defense. More-over, the U.S. economic embargo had deprived Nicaragua not only of its traditional market for agricultural products but, what is more important, of the spare parts and machinery it needed to keep its American-made farming and industrial equipment running. And Wash-ington's vetoes deprived Managua of any relief it might have received through international lending agencies.

Pursuing time-honored methods for financing war deficits, the Nica-raguan government simply printed more money. Inflation was soaring at nearly 35,000 percent for the year 1988. Unemployment, too, ran high. Shortages of basic goods and foods were more acute than ever. In that year, the stranglehold on Nicaragua forced the Sandinistas to im-pose draconian economic measures not at all in keeping with either the principles of the revolution or its supporters' class interests. In an at-tempt to control inflation, the government issued a new currency, de-vised new monetary policies, eliminated most consumer subsidies, insti-tuted austerity measures, and laid off thousands in the civil service sector. To stimulate production, the government effectively legalized the black market and allowed prices to find their own level. Each of these moves further lowered the standard of living of the poor.

The government struggled to breathe new life into the prostrate economy, but the per capita gross domestic product fell to roughly half its prerevolutionary level (Conroy 1990, 7). War, inflation, and reces-sion ravaged confidence in the revolution. The mass organizations—which once figured prominently in Nicaragua's conception of a popu-lar democracy—had all but disappeared from community life. Atten-dance at the local revolutionary Popular Church declined somewhat, as did activism in Christian base communities. And emigration out of Nicaragua's devastated economy reached the proportions of a mass exodus.

My informants still spoke in dichotomies, dividing history into "be-fore the revolution" and "after the revolution"—implicitly, for it was not even necessary to specify "the revolution" as part of this standard construct. But once, people had spoken of antes/ahora (before/now) to mark positive changes: "Before, there were a lot of human rights abuses"; "Before, there was much delinquency"; "Before, poverty was more se-vere, and poor people could not achieve dignity"; "Now, all of that is different. . . . Things are better for the common people." In 1988, peo-ple spoke of the past in different terms: "Before, there was more food, and in greater variety—meat, fish, eggs. Now, it's just beans and rice—

and sometimes not even that." People's conversations with me turned increasingly away from public, political, and social issues and toward domestic, immediate, and personal concerns. The problems that most affected ordinary people were simple: how to obtain enough cash to feed oneself and one's family; how to weather the crisis with one's family intact.

The cost of the U.S.-sponsored contra war proved catastrophic for Nicaragua's experimental mixed economy. Since 1980, fighting had killed more than 30,000. (Somoza's last stand against the revolution, which included aerial bombardment of densely populated urban neighborhoods, had already cost 50,000 lives by July 1979.) War and crisis displaced more than 500,000 people. Between 200,000 and 400,000 people took up residency abroad. Indeed, the contra war has left Nicaragua's infrastructure in a shambles from which it will not soon recover, even under the best of circumstances: the contras dynamited bridges and power stations, burned schools and clinics, and ruined farms. Direct material damages from the war inflicted between $1.5 billion and $4 billion in losses (Conroy 1990, 16). UNO's economist, Francisco Mayorga, has estimated that the U.S. embargo caused an additional $3 billion in losses (*Miami Herald*, 21 Feb. 1990)—this in an economy whose GNP never much exceeded $3 billion, even in good times. Total economic damages from the war and the embargo were undoubtedly much greater: crops were left unplanted for fear that the contras would destroy them; labor was mobilized not to produce goods but to defend the country; skilled workers and professionals fled the country in large numbers; Nicaragua's capital reserves were depleted, and substantial international loans were unavailable. The Sandinista government has estimated that the cumulative direct and indirect damages from the war and embargo totaled as much as $17 billion. As a consequence, by 1988 real wages had fallen to less than 10 percent of their 1980 level.

Nicaragua's human resources, too, were battered by war, not just in terms of the dead, the wounded, the incapacitated, and the impoverished, but also in terms of those emotionally scarred by the traumas of war, crisis, and dislocation. Against such a backdrop, revolutionary political consciousness simply could not maintain itself. A social, political, and spiritual project was consumed in the daily terrors of a precarious economic existence. The will, the dignity, the resolve, and the *faith* of a people were under attack, and Washington's war inflicted costs that could not be borne.

• • •

Because I frame Nicaraguan history in this manner, I will no doubt be accused of writing an apology for Sandinista misrule. The elections of 1990, some would say, prove the unpopularity of a dictatorial regime, the impossibility of its radical agenda, the futility of dogmatic intransigence, the failure of revolution. I would say, rather, that the elections prove the efficacy of Washington's war and belligerence: they demonstrate the effectiveness of low-intensity aggression, of war by proxy, and of international electoral meddling carried out by a rich, powerful country against a poor, vulnerable one. Although the Sandinistas made ample mistakes, the consequences of their errors pale before the damages caused by war and embargo.

The exercise of power inevitably motivates certain representations and represses others. No system of language is ever readily extricable from some system of power. In the United States today, what best characterizes acceptable speech on international matters is the denial of coloniality. That is, the thing that must never be said is that imperialism exists—unless, of course, one is referring to some empire, past or present, other than our own. In general terms, then, the poverty of the underdeveloped world and the affluence of industrial powers must appear as entirely unrelated developments. In the case of Nicaragua, official speech is marked by feigned amnesia regarding the entire Somoza era. Contra terror occurred within the borders of an official blind spot, and contra origins and funding remain a mystery—even to those whose job it was to organize and fund the counterrevolutionaries.

Those who monopolize power and public speech in the United States are fond of mocking Sandinista politics (and exculpating themselves from Nicaragua's travails) by exaggerating Sandinista claims to the effect that "the United States is to blame for *all* of Nicaragua's problems." This hyperbolic construction satirizes the very simple (and self-evident) proposition that North American colonialism has shaped and constrained modern Nicaraguan history, and that U.S. interference has either created or exacerbated many of Nicaragua's pressing problems. With barbed words and an injured tone, the power establishment thus ridicules anyone opposed to colonialism—and tries to make the facts disappear. Hiding behind the caricature of a proposition that they are loath to state accurately, the architects of modern imperialism thus deny the scope of their own power and obscure the litany of U.S. military and mercenarial interventions that have shaped Nicaraguan history since William Walker sought to impose slavery on a country that had already abolished it. It is as though to offer an alibi, in the literal sense of the term: we were not present when the crimes were being committed.

The tragic fate of Central America today, convulsed with violence and agonized by dilemmas with no end in sight, cannot be meaningfully separated from U.S. hegemony in the region: its history of blocking meaningful social reforms; its intervention against independent, nationalist governments; its support for corrupt military dictatorships; its unwillingness to recognize as "democratic" or "legitimate" any government not to its liking; its perpetual siding with the region's rich and powerful against the poor and disenfranchised. Such U.S. policies have defined Central American history at its critical junctures and continue to do so.

Obviously, my experience in Nicaragua, especially in 1984–85, made a deep impression on me. I came away from my fieldwork having reformulated most of my thinking about class consciousness and religion. And I can say—like George Orwell writing of Catalonia—that for the first time in my life, I really believed in socialism.[7] Not that I hadn't always believed that some form of public control over the economy was preferable to private control. Since I first became politically conscious, I have realized that economic Darwinism is no way to vouchsafe the social good. However, I suspected that an alternative vision of society lay with a disaffected (and largely impotent) intellectual minority. And I feared that constructing socialism might require such suppression and repression that its early phases would prove universally unpleasant. What I never quite believed was that the people themselves were capable of taking their fate into their own hands, of acting collectively for the social good, of constructing a workable, democratic socialism—in short, of participating, as willing actors, in the making of their own history. For a time, Nicaraguans en masse struggled heroically, armed only with class solidarity and collective will, to build the sort of society that would reflect popular interests.

This is not to say that I ever experienced revolutionary Nicaragua as a utopia. It was never that, not even in its finest moments. But the collective mobilizations of the revolution's early years did suggest the possibility—and, for a time, the reality—of a more just society, engineered by the people themselves and resting ultimately on their eternal vigilance and popular participation. That is what my experience taught me. And that is why I struggle in my writing to avoid the alibis and just-so

stories that are the preferred forms of the language of power. The Sandinista revolution really did occur. It was neither a transfer of power
nor a ruse, but a true revolution, and for the bulk of its duration, it
enjoyed not simply broad popular support but the *active* support of a
population willing to mobilize and make sacrifices for various projects.

At the same time, however, many things "went wrong," and we need
a serious accounting of exactly "what went wrong" (Gonzalez 1990)
and why. In power, did the Sandinistas fail to guard against bureaucratism and its ensuing privileges, thus driving a wedge between themselves
and their own supporters? To some extent, yes—and in the context of
a revolution whose ethos was aggressively egalitarian, and against the
backdrop of dire hardship for the masses, this failure contributed to the
erosion of Sandinismo as a political project. Did the Sandinista leadership, as years of war and crisis passed, develop a siege mentality and an
arrogant style of leadership that increasingly estranged them from the
less political and less revolutionary sectors of the popular classes? Most
certainly they did. Notably, neither of these failures is the exclusive
property of vanguardist party organizations. Both self-interested bureaucratism and political arrogance can develop wherever a government exercises power over a long term or wherever a movement feels
encircled and besieged. Were the Sandinistas inept at the nitty-gritty
work of economic management? Again, undoubtedly—although it would
be hard to weigh their blame given the absorption of Nicaragua's resources by war. Although the source of *most* of the problems laid at the
Sandinistas' door seems clear, any complete account of the late 1980s
has to consider these possibilities and draw them into its explanation.
Such factors were present, and they were particularly debilitating given
the egalitarian spirit of Nicaragua's highly politicized working class, the
utopian expectations of the popular classes, and the nature of revolutionary discourse itself, with its ideal of exemplary leadership and shared
sacrifices. But I would argue that those were not the real or ultimate
causes of the revolutionary government's downfall—although in the
context of the economy's downward spiral, they clearly contributed grist
for the mill of people's complaints.

SANDINISTA POLITICAL ECONOMY:
A RETROSPECTIVE

In a state of war, the Sandinistas censored the press; for a time, faced
with an unpopular and divided bourgeois opposition, they exercised, in

effect, one-party rule; and amid war and economic crisis, they intimidated political opponents—those to the left as well as to the right of the regime. Opposition leaders were sometimes even jailed or driven into exile. On occasion, human rights abuses were committed by agents of the state, both the police and the army, working in remote, wartorn provinces. If this is to say that the Sandinistas were not the saints depicted by revolutionary hagiography, neither were they the devils portrayed by Reagan's demonology. It should be pointed out that press censorship, political intimidation, and human rights abuses did not show up in either pre- or postelection polls as significant factors in the Sandinista electoral defeat. One has to conclude that the vast bulk of the population was not greatly affected by these abuses.

By comparison, other governments facing far less compelling emergencies have appropriated and systematized far more sweeping powers of coercion. There were no Sandinista death squads, nor was the civilian population subject to napalm, aerial bombardment, or mass detention. And for the duration of its rule, the Sandinista government was the only Central American government in a state of war to prosecute human rights violations carried out by its own partisans. Most serious human rights offenders in the military were given the maximum thirty-five-year prison sentence. (To establish the humane tone of their revolution, the Sandinistas abolished capital punishment as one of their first acts in power.)

Nicaragua's experimental revolution never planned to make Sandinista rule permanent, neither by means of a formal one-party monopoly on political power nor by means of a command economy. Sandinista strategy, drawing on lessons from abroad and from its own historical conditions, aimed at developing a more egalitarian society in the context of a mixed economy, political pluralism, and international non-alignment.[8] The three-legged strategy, hobbled by dilemmas from the beginning, might best be described in terms of mixture, compromise, and pragmatism. The nature and scope of these compromises were complex. International experience in revolution and subsequent development suggested that a "command economy" might be the best way to achieve greater equality in the short term, but it would not provide the best route for developing the forces of production in the long term. Clearly, the Eastern bloc countries could not be counted on for the levels of economic assistance that might make rapid economic development possible. Not the least of the "limits of the economically possible" were the limits imposed by the United States, with its propensity to intervene militarily in the region.

Nicaragua's unique history and social conditions, its agrarian status, its large class of independent small and medium farmers, the absence of large-scale industry, and the dispersal of production among a class of urban artisans: all these factors pointed to a mixed economy as the most effective strategy for developing the nation's underdeveloped economy. The Sandinistas saw small, medium, and even some large private producers as indispensable elements of national development policy—as sources of what their economic planners, perhaps somewhat hopefully, called "social accumulation." Rather than "liquidating the bourgeoisie as a class" (which was Stalin's favored approach), they attempted to curb its speculating, reckless side and channel its dynamism into projects for the social good. They attempted to reconcile private ownership with social development, entrepreneurship with a significant state role in economic planning. In effect, the capitalist class was guaranteed its right to exist and to generate reasonable profits, but it was denied the power to rule society at large: a modest socialism, Nicaraguan style. The FSLN saw itself as the vanguard of this complex reshaping of Nicaraguan society, and although its members no doubt hoped to govern in perpetuity, the Frente never attempted to impose itself as the sole organized political option.

Critics on the Right ignore these features of Nicaragua's revolutionary polity and misrepresent Sandinista rule as "totalitarian." I never experienced Nicaraguan society as totalitarian or even very strictly "controlled" in the usual sense of the words. During my fieldwork, I lived in an ordinary working-class barrio, traveled wherever I wished, and spoke with whomever I pleased about whatever topics we both found agreeable, whether our conversations validated or questioned official discourse. All these practices would have been impossible in what conservatives call the "democratic" states of El Salvador, Honduras, and Guatemala. Critics on the Left might more justifiably charge that the Sandinistas failed in their efforts to construct a more egalitarian society and to forge a substantial national consensus. As an assessment of reality, these points have merit, especially in regard to the late 1980s. But as policy criticisms, such charges ignore Nicaraguan history and reality as well as the revolution's real accomplishments, made before the country was overwhelmed by war and engulfed in the ensuing crisis.

The early years of the revolution both constructed a more egalitarian society and forged a workable national consensus. Before the revolution, Nicaragua's most pressing social problems were the distribution of land, economic distribution in general (especially the distribution of food), health care, and underdevelopment. Revolutionary policies forcefully addressed each of these issues. A policy of agrarian reform redistributed idle lands to Nicaragua's burgeoning class of desperate, landless peasants, on a mixed basis. The huge, well-equipped, efficient farms belonging to the Somoza family became state farms; other lands were distributed to peasants in a variety of forms: cooperatives, collectives, and small to medium family farms. Some 120,000 peasants received title to land under the agrarian reform. Government banks pumped credit into the countryside to encourage production and modernization and provided incentives for various forms of cooperative farming. By tinkering with the pricing structure, the government sought to stimulate production, especially in beans, rice, and corn. And indeed, in the early years of the revolution agricultural production climbed, especially in the staple foods needed to feed a hungry country (Collins et al. 1982). On the consumption side of the equation, state subsidies held out the prospect that for the first time in recent history, the poorest two-fifths of the population might be able to consume the minimum daily calories recommended by the United Nations for a healthy diet. The establishment of free medical care and the inoculation campaigns rectified decades of neglect under the old regime. In the years immediately following the revolution, such programs greatly reduced infant mortality rates and virtually eliminated early death by preventable infectious diseases. In its foreign trade, economic planners actively sought what they called a "comparative advantage"—higher prices on the international markets for coffee, cotton, beef, and bananas—to generate profits that might be reinvested in industrial development projects making the best use of Nicaragua's resources.

All of these practices naturally involved entanglements and compromises. Fostering private production in a revolutionary state can put both planning and equality in jeopardy. Low levels of inflation set in early on. It is difficult to specify the cause of such inflation: Was it the same burden of foreign debt that afflicted other Latin American countries in the 1980s? Or was it the cost of consumer subsidies? Profiteering by speculation proved a problem from the beginning, and the bourgeoisie—which had a very different version of the good life, resented its loss of power, and never trusted the Sandinistas—resorted to widespread decapitalization rather than participation in the economy.

Pro-Sandinista informants often averred that the bourgeoisie was indeed reactionary, but that it was nevertheless controllable. I doubted then, as I do now, that the bourgeoisie can be even minimally socialized, but perhaps it might have been under more favorable circumstances. Indeed, the revolutionary program called for both the preservation of private property in a socialist mixed economy and the elimination of the exploitation of man by man. Were these two goals compatible? Activists and politicized supporters of the Sandinistas argued that a groundwork could be established wherein both goals could be realized, but they recognized the problematic nature of such a program. (Interestingly, among my informants, rank-and-file Christian base community activists were most opposed to private property and large-scale private business; following biblical texts, they equated capitalist commerce with sin. Among Sandinista party members proper, those whose affiliation had been with the classically Marxist Proletarian Tendency were the least skeptical about the role of private entrepreneurship.) Playing the international market, too, is risky, even with nominal state control over foreign trade: the market gives, and the market also takes away. Into the 1980s, a drop in the world market prices for Nicaragua's principal exports exacerbated that country's economic plight (as it would have under any political system).

It would be difficult to gauge the successes and failures of Sandinismo in Nicaragua or to speculate on the viability of its program. Some sectors of the economy were overcentralized; others suffered from a lack of planning. Some policies worked, others did not. All along, the FSLN was flexible, pragmatic, experimental, and willing to learn from its mistakes. In the end, however, the war and its dislocations overwhelmed even the greatest of the revolution's accomplishments. There was simply no cash and no hard currency for running the economy. What good is a farm without seeds and fertilizer? What good is a school if there is no money for textbooks? What good is a clinic without medicine? Infant mortality crept back up, and although health care was free, hospitals ran short of the supplies and medicines they needed to save lives. By 1988 children living in the poorer barrios showed not just the bulging stomachs that indicate infestation by tropical parasites but also the signs of malnutrition, visible even to an anthropologist who knows relatively little about health and nutrition.

The Sandinistas might have equalized the sufferings of the war more effectively, but not in the context of a mixed economy that included private property. They might have pursued an ideal of greater equality, but not in the context of political pluralism. They might have ensured the position of the party in various ways, but not without sacrificing "popular" power. They might have guarded more effectively against the familiar mechanisms of political privilege, party patronage, and governmental corruption—political spoils constitute a major transfer point for the upward redistribution of wealth in countries across Latin America—but not without imposing a regimen of party purges. Like Castro, they might have more effectively forged a national consensus, but not without sacrificing human rights.

Those who see the revolution as an example of "totalitarianism" or "radical extremism" are trafficking in stereotypes, not facts. Those who see the revolution's vision of a more just society as hopeless from the beginning are simply extrapolating from a universalist theory of human nature as inherently "sinful," necessarily exploitive. For those who argue that, in effect, the revolution was not "radical" enough, their burden of proof would be to show the greater social benefits against the costs of more draconian measures. And it seems clear to me that had the revolution been any more "radical," it would have provided the pretext for direct U.S. military intervention. "We are not stupid," the most radical activists would sometimes tell me. Under ideal conditions, they would have favored an accelerated revolutionary program. "If we confiscated the properties of the rich, for instance, or shut down the counterrevolutionary political opposition, the Yankees would invade."

Because the Nicaraguan revolution was often treated as a Soviet or Cuban beachhead in Central America, and because this was the favorite fairy tale of the conservative ideologues who organized, financed, and directed the war against the revolution, I should observe here that there were never any Soviet or Cuban military bases in Nicaragua. Eastern bloc and Cuban technicians and advisors, including military advisors, were indeed present in Nicaragua; a great many liberal, social-democratic, and socialist *internacionalistas* from Western Europe and North America were also working there. A revolutionary government in a capitalist world, the Sandinistas naturally maintained friendly ties with the USSR and Cuba; at the same time, they maintained good relations with many Western European and Latin American nations and with leftist social-democratic parties in various countries. And although many Sandinista militants favored an accelerated program of popular power, very few visualized their ideals in terms of existing socialist models. Nicaragua's was a nationalist revolution with a broadly socialist goal whose spirit was in many ways radically Christian. The political discourses—of activists and nonactivists alike—typically began by locating the problems "here, in Nicaragua." The political agenda, too, was set "here, in Nicaragua": in compromise with the obvious constraints (international conditions, local history) and in the light of the real aspirations of Nicaraguans themselves. So, although existing examples of socialist development were seen as positive to various degrees, Soviet or Cuban models were never seen as models to be mechanically emulated. Experimentally, and in the face of steep odds, people groped for an authentically Nicaraguan revolution.

FAMILY, GENDER, AND REVOLUTION

A significant front for activist efforts during the revolution involved the family and gender relations. Nicaraguan society has a long history of machismo. Its traditional family structure is both patriarchal and brittle, and under such conditions, women and children suffer the brunt of economic inequalities.[9] At the same time, however, and despite the constraints of machismo, there was a long and substantial history of women's involvement in popular political struggles leading up to the Sandinista revolution (Gould 1990, 225–41; Lancaster 1988b, 65). By the close of the guerrilla period, women constituted some 30 percent of the FSLN combatants (Molyneux 1985, 227). In 1977 AMPRONAC (Asociación de Mujeres ante la Problemática Nacional, Association of Women Confronting the National Problem) organized as a specifically feminist voice in the revolutionary struggles (AMNLAE 1983). Renamed AMNLAE (Asociación de Mujeres Nicaragüenses "Luisa Amanda Espinosa," Association of Nicaraguan Women "Luisa Amanda Espinosa") after the Sandinista triumph of 1979, the organization steered its feminist and Sandinista course under the slogan "No revolution without women's emancipation; no emancipation without revolution."[10] AMNLAE's charter was to advance the cause of women within a revolutionary process that—unlike most other revolutions of the twentieth century—did not define feminism as a diversionary tactic (Molyneux 1986a, 288, 287).

AMNLAE achieved a number of legal and social successes early in the revolution. AMNLAE's membership swelled, and the organization achieved a high degree of visibility and effectiveness. According to some estimates, women were a majority of the participants in the early literacy (60 percent) and health care (75 percent) campaigns (Collinson 1990, 97, 124). And, although still a decided minority in the political leadership of the revolution, women constituted a quarter of party membership in the FSLN, were prominent members of the Frente Sandinista, and held nearly a third of government leadership posts (Dirección Nacional, FSLN 1987, 25).

To promote greater gender equality, new laws were passed immediately after the revolution. The 1979 Provisional Media Law prohibited commercial exploitation of women's bodies in advertising as well as degrading or debasing depictions of women in the media. The Fundamental Statute of Rights and Guarantees (whose language is now codified in the 1987 constitution) outlawed sex discrimination, declared legal equality for women, established equal legal rights for illegitimate children, and specified procedures for establishing paternity. In the interests of children's health, a 1980 law promoted breast-feeding and banned advertisements for powdered milk.

AMNLAE-initiated legislation on the family took as its goal the revitalization and reformulation of the family as an institution not of machismo and patriarchy but of equality, responsibility, and reciprocity.[11] At the time of the revolution, some 34 percent of Nicaraguan families were headed by women, with a much higher percentage of such households in the cities, especially Managua. These families were a socially and economically disadvantaged segment of society (Dirección de Orientación y Protección Familiar 1983; IHCA 1984). Indeed, according to data from the National Institute of Statistics and Census, women made up some 60 percent of the poorest stratum in Nicaragua and in Managua were three and a half times more likely than men to fall below the poverty line (Molyneux 1986a, 298). The strategy of a diverse package of laws, sometimes collectively referred to as "the new family laws," was (1) to enhance the legal, social, and economic position of women and children, (2) to secure the protection, rearing, and overall well-being of children, and (3) to stabilize the Nicaraguan family, seen by many as being "in crisis."

Nicaragua's 1904 Family Code had enshrined patriarchal and classist principles as law. Old laws established the father or husband as the family's absolute authority and made it much easier for men than for women to obtain divorce. Moreover, the old statutes recognized only those marriages cemented by a civil or religious ceremony, not the *uniones de hecho* (unions of fact) or *estados de acompañado* (states of companionship, informal unions) which have long been the primary form of marriage for Nicaragua's poor majority. The 1981 law regulating relations between mothers, fathers, and children systematically revised legal definitions of the family: the father or husband was no longer defined as the "head of the household," and both parents were granted rights over their children. This law also reiterated the principle codified in the Fundamental Statute of Rights and Guarantees: that paternity—in or out of wedlock, within or without an informal union—entails economic and social responsibility for one's children. New laws recognized unions that had the characteristics of stability and permanence as a civil state of *acompañado* (companionship) or common-law marriage. The same year, the cooperatives law granted women the right to hold title to land under the agrarian reform.

All along, there was resistance—from the conservative church, from *La prensa,* and from conservative elites in general—to such reforms. An oft-repeated complaint from conservative quarters was that the Sandinistas and AMNLAE were mounting a communistic attack on the sanctity of the family. On the contrary, such reform efforts simply recognized the Nicaraguan family—in its diversity and as it really existed—as an important basis of society and encouraged a more just and stable family structure. In the spirit of the broad reforms under way, AMNLAE initiated the Law on Nurture (Ley de Alimentos), which specified the obligations of parents and other relatives to children. Parents, siblings, and grandparents—in that order—were responsible for the economic, social, and cultural well-being of children under the age of twenty-one, and children were expected to reciprocate care and nurture in their parents', siblings', and grandparents' old age. The Law on Nurture went further than previous reform laws that barred discrimination against illegitimate children; it eroded any remaining legal distinctions between legitimate and illegitimate children. Finally, the new law stated that in cases where both parents worked, household maintenance and family care—including housework—was the responsibility of both parents.

AMNLAE had marked successes in its legislative efforts. The organization was successful in abolishing legal discrimination against women and establishing equal rights as the law of the land. The legal redefinition of the family dissolved decades of elite and governmental hypocrisy about family matters; these new laws recognized the way most people lived and vastly improved the legal standing of poor and working-class women and children. The 1988 liberalization of divorce laws, too, eliminated patriarchal precedent and equalized the grounds for divorce. But there were failures in AMNLAE's record as well. The Sandinista leadership proved divided on the most ambitious and the most sensitive feminist reforms. The sweeping Law on Nurture passed the legislature, but it was not ratified by the executive branch. AMNLAE's various efforts at legalizing abortion also failed. (However, under the Sandinistas, existing laws banning abortion were not enforced.) Plainly, reforms did not go as far as many activists had hoped. Nevertheless, AMNLAE and the Sandinistas put into effect a broad package of new laws that, on paper, were both radical and far-reaching.

In the end, things went badly indeed. Women no doubt enjoyed increased educational and job opportunities after the revolution, but they did so in a context where real wages declined precipitously, especially after 1985. Early on, women and children—who were disproportionately poor—enjoyed the benefits of consumer subsidies and saw their standard of living rise. But in the late 1980s those subsidies largely disappeared as women and children bore the brunt of hardship in the economic crisis. Despite women's increased political participation and the new laws at their disposal, one of their principal aims was never realized: that is, a more stable family life. Families were in no sense stabilized after the revolution, and it is difficult to see how they might have been, given the disruptions and dislocations of the 1980s. My own census of neighborhoods in two barrios indicates that family structures continued to be fluid and fragile.[12] The war and economic crisis worsened a familiar Nicaraguan dilemma: economic conditions drove many men to leave their families in search of jobs. Now, though, men migrated in large numbers not to another Nicaraguan city or province but abroad: to the United States or Canada, where they were far beyond the reach of new family laws and child-support claims.

The revolution's plans for more stable, egalitarian, and responsible families—like its plans for a more productive, just economy—failed. The transformations envisioned by revolutionaries would have been difficult to achieve even under the best of circumstances. Even in the absence of outside military intervention, transforming an exploitive, underdeveloped, and dependent economy into a more equitable system would be difficult in a world already structured by colonialism, and in a world where the international capitalist market economy has already distributed wealth, allotted values, created deficits and surpluses, and preset the terms to the advantage of some and the disadvantage of others. Machismo, no less than capitalism, is a system. Like racism, homophobia, and other forms of arbitrary power, arbitrary stigma, machismo is resilient because it constitutes not simply a form of "consciousness," not "ideology" in the classical understanding of the concept, but a field of productive relations.

Forms of consciousness are precisely what machismo, as a "field of productive relations," produces. In other words, under machismo, relations between men, women, and children are structured in certain standard ways. Moreover, what it is to properly be a man, or a woman, or a child, is also defined relationally, within the logic of the system. These relations themselves—not their idealized representation or coarse expression—constitute the system of machismo. These relations, which both occupy and define the institution of the family, are always "power relations" in that they structure inequality and differential prerogatives, but they are also "productive relations": appropriating and refining the raw material of the human body, machismo systematically produces values that are realized both "ideologically" (as certain manifest notions about the nature of sex and gender) and "materially" (in the most intimate experience of gender, sexuality, and the body). Machismo's "finished product" is not only an array of gendered bodies but also a world built around its definition of gender and its allotment of power. Above all else, the operation of this system appears "natural," "normal," even "necessary," and the human products of machismo confront the consciousness prepared by it as inevitable.

Because systems function as *systems,* operating by and reproducing their own logic—no less in the personalities of people than in the realm of international commerce—the relations they engender are not easily redefined, even by deliberate, self-conscious efforts. The power of capital is difficult to challenge today because all economic value is set by its products, commodities. The logic of the system overwhelms even those who attempt to change the system, for they have few options other than to try to translate cheap agricultural commodities into more expensive manufactured ones. In a parallel sense, the power of machismo, too, is difficult to contest, for the system has already created products that define, embody, and measure value. Genders, sexualities, and bodies thus produced also silently, imperceptibly *reproduce* the logic of the system—even when its obvious inequalities are under challenge.

I am not convinced that the Sandinista experiment, by mobilizing the political will of the working class, the demands of women, and the euphoric energy of its activists, would have naturally glided along to a blissful state of affairs. The demise of the Eastern bloc as a source of funds and support for revolutionary movements has had and will continue to have significant consequences for movements of national liberation and social reconstruction, whatever their ideological orientation. Restructuring any economy is an expensive proposition. Revolutions in impoverished and underdeveloped countries can scarcely succeed in implementing their agendas without subsidy from some more affluent source. (See Colburn 1986; Vilas 1987; Vickers 1990; Landau 1991).[13] The material necessity for such revolutions is more present than ever; the material and international conditions under which they might succeed are less present than they have ever been in this century.

In an uncontested global market economy, and given Nicaragua's meager resources, the class and development agenda of the Sandinista revolution would have eventually confronted a serious dilemma even without the war of aggression: how to balance development against redistribution—and, indeed, how to achieve either in the actual rather than the abstract. Moreover, in certain areas—especially in the realm of gender and sexuality—the revolutionary vision was sometimes quite myopic; elements of the Sandinista bloc were in serious disagreement over some feminist goals. However, I do believe that, given a chance, the revolution would have improved the lives of most people—especially the most disadvantaged and oppressed people. These efforts failed not so much because failure was inevitable but because U.S. foreign policy would not permit the revolution to make and rectify its own mistakes. That is the tragedy of Nicaragua today, and that tragedy will continue to define Nicaragua's history and struggles until the cycle of colonial power and popular resistance is decided.

PART ONE

Life

In order to understand, it is immensely important for the person who understands to be *located outside* the object of his or her creative understanding—in time, in space, in culture. For one cannot even really see one's own exterior and comprehend it as a whole, and no mirrors or photographs can help; our real exterior can be seen and understood only by other people, because they are located outside us in space and because they are *others*.

In the realm of culture, outsideness is a most powerful factor in understanding. It is only in the eyes of *another* culture that foreign culture reveals itself fully and profoundly. . . . A meaning only reveals its depths once it has encountered and come into contact with another, foreign meaning: they engage in a kind of dialogue, which surmounts the closedness and one-sidedness of these particular meanings, these cultures. We raise new questions for a foreign culture, ones that it did not raise itself; we seek answers to our own questions in it; and the foreign culture responds to us by revealing to us its new aspects and new semantic depths. Without *one's own* questions one cannot creatively understand anything other or foreign (but, of course, the questions must be serious and sincere). Such a dialogic encounter of two cultures does not result in merging or mixing. Each retains its own unity and *open* totality, but they are mutually enriched.

—Mikhail Bakhtin,
Speech Genres and Other Late Essays

CHAPTER I

Junkyards

America has a sort of mythical power throughout the world, a power
based on the advertising image, which parallels the polarization of advertising images around Reagan.

—Jean Baudrillard, *America*

A commodity appears, at first sight, a very trivial thing, and easily
understood. Its analysis shows that it is, in reality, a very queer thing,
abounding in metaphysical subtleties and theological niceties.

—Karl Marx, *Capital*

ERASMUS JIMENEZ AT A GLANCE   (From my journal, May 1988): *The
potholes in the roads continue to widen and deepen. One now commonly sees a sight in Managua that was almost entirely absent in 1984–
85: begging.*

*Although the economy is demonstrably destitute, no one in Barrio
Erasmus Jiménez seems to be visibly suffering from malnutrition or
hunger. Nevertheless, beans and rice are virtually the only foods on
most tables. Many of the economically active younger women in this
neighborhood have continued improving their relative social position
(though usually not their real wages) by working as lower-level white
collar employees, mostly in the state sector. Aida is being sent to study
accounting and marketing (there is a shortage in this specialty); Yolanda has obtained an excellent job as an airline flight attendant; María-
Teresa is working as an assistant in a doctor's office. At the same time,
however, some civil servants have been laid off, and there is talk of
future cutbacks.*

*The pace of emigration is still accelerating. From this andén of forty
households, four entire families have moved to Los Angeles since I was
last here two years ago. Predictably, they were headed by men who
were relatively well-off and relatively skilled (thus the shortage in ac-
countants and business majors); two of them were conservatives, opposed to the revolution from the start; two were simply middle-income
economic refugees. Another pair of families has partially migrated, with*

some of their members staying, others going. And numerous fathers and older sons have made the trip to the United States. What seems alarming is that there are very nearly no working-age men left on this andén. Some have abandoned wives to go to other parts of the country; others have never lived with their children anyway; others have left for the United States. Many young men in the military service now tell me that when they complete their service, they are planning to leave for Costa Rica, Mexico, the United States, or Canada in search of work. Indeed, they also say that everyone they know is talking that way.

The overall impression is one of a string of households headed by women. And that, too, is no doubt the story of how the incomes of this colonia (neighborhood) have remained relatively stable: remittances from relatives abroad is the major means of support for several families on this andén, and such remittances supplement the incomes of many others. The real income difference for most people is this: those who are being supported or supplemented from abroad are doing well; those who have been abandoned are doing poorly. (The distance between these two propositions, however, is not very great, and it varies in inverse proportion to both the distance between Nicaragua and the United States and the length of time one's breadwinner is away. Any family being supported today may find itself abandoned tomorrow.) A walk through lower-working-class Barrio Rigoberto, or a visit with my informants in the Sergio Altamirano shantytown, reveals the real extent of economic dislocation for poorer barrios: fearful unemployment and a visibly decreased standard of living, with all of its concomitants— sickly babies, malnourished children, relaxed hygiene.

The bars going up in front of people's houses in Erasmus Jiménez give the inescapable impression of foreboding, hostility. What used to be a very inviting andén now looks closed off and fearful. Those poorer houses, whose members lack the funds to make security improvements, now appear singled out, left out, vulnerable, and menaced. And across this barrio, the night lights no longer work, giving the entire place a desolate, eerie look.

The bars and fences speak loudly of the situation. The fears are not ungrounded, and by nightfall pandillas (gangs) from Rigoberto circulate in large numbers on the streets that bound and dissect Erasmus Jiménez. With the total destruction of the economy, crime continues to grow. People talk a great deal about robbery, theft, rapes, and murders. And in a remarkable turnaround from the open-door atmosphere that

used to prevail here, most people keep their doors shut and locked, even
in the daytime, even while they're home.

ANTHROPOLOGY INSIDE-OUT

On many occasions it was I who was presenting my country to my
informants, and not vice versa. The families I came to know well in
Erasmus Jiménez asked me all sorts of probing questions about life in
the United States: Is it true what they say about crime and drugs in your
country? What do North Americans think about the aggression against
Nicaragua? Is it true that North American men aren't machistas (or
machos) the way Nicaraguan men are? It was not that my informants
had never spoken with anyone who had made the trip north. Nicaraguans are well-traveled these days—as clandestine laborers and as economic and political refugees. Largely, though, they make the trip speaking no English and live in Spanish-speaking barrios. What I was being
asked for, in Bronislaw Malinowski's parlance (1961, 25), was a picture of the United States "from the native's point of view."

For Nicaraguans, the image of the United States serves two simultaneous roles. On the one hand, it provides a distorted mirror image of
all that they find disturbing about their own society (crime, delinquency, prostitution, substance abuse). This distortion, in thus identi-
fying and magnifying "the antisocial," defines the limits of society. ("Is
it true that in your country it is nothing to see people having sexual
intercourse out in the streets, in plain view and without shame?" "I've
heard that when girls are born in your country, the doctors surgically
remove their hymens, so that there are no virgins in the United States.
Is that true?") On the other hand, Nicaraguan reflections on North
America take on all the resonances of a Disneyland of affluence: a fantasy zone, bloated with commodities, where flights of imagination take
off—an image that draws thought to the outer limits of the materially
possible. (While watching "Auto fantástico" ["Knight Rider"], a U.S.
television series about an intelligent, computerized, flying, armed auto-
mobile, an adolescent asks, "Do you really have cars like that over there?"
I answer no, but as I clarify various points—new cars have computer
chips that regulate the engine; some cars in fact "speak"; manufacturers
are beginning to put air bags into cars—the integrity of my answer
crumbles under the weight of a weird irony: seen from Nicaragua, we
do have cars like that, more or less.)

For a long time I tried to dissuade or minimize too much talk about my native land. I thought these exercises were just part of the price of fieldwork: a necessary but not productive precondition for establishing good relations with my informants. But I was wrong to trivialize such dialogues. These instances of anthropology inside-out communicate information, too (and on both sides of the discussion)—for if interpretive anthropology is an attempt at reading other people's culture-texts, then these sorts of discussions allow us a doubly reflexive proposition: our reading of their reading of us. Indeed, it would be interesting to write an ethnography solely on the subject of Nicaraguan perceptions of the United States: the better to know Nicaragua, the better to know ourselves.

The perception of the United States in Nicaragua is an almost perfectly duplex structure, conforming in most cases to a split between social-cultural and economic-material questions. On the social side, almost everything is negative. "There's a lot of corruption in the United States," many of my informants averred. When questioned, most of them would lay out a relatively accurate picture of urban street crime and delinquency, touch on the evils of racism, and perhaps pass commentary on the supposedly voracious sexual appetites of North Americans. Most of my friends feared that I would be subject to political persecution and perhaps incarceration when I returned to my homeland and often warned me to be careful. One positive trait came up with some consistency: Nicaraguan women were convinced that North American men were not machistas, at least not like Nicaraguan men, and this was good. A North American man would make a fine catch for a spouse (as I, putatively single, was always reminded).[1] Nicaraguan men tended to counter that the United States has more than its share of *cochones*—roughly, "faggots."

On the economic side, though, everything was different, and the image was overwhelmingly positive. America was a vast carnival of creature comforts, a land of plenty. For the young, not only was there more than enough food, but hamburgers could be eaten on a daily basis. For the old, it was a place where one's family could be clothed, shod, and fed without resorting to extraordinary means. Women spoke of modern household appliances; men dreamed of owning a car. The wealth of the United States takes on a mythical quality in Nicaragua's poor neighborhoods. More than anything else, this picture of plenty and opulence motivates migration. That is not to say that Nicaraguans believed the myth of America as the "land of opportunity" where immigrants become millionaires within one generation. None of my informants harbored get-rich-quick schemes; their intentions, when the prospects of emigration came up, were humbler and more realistic. In a land of scarcity, the image of plenty is an absolute good in and of itself.

It was always difficult for me to explain that we have poverty in the United States, too, and that being poor here can be a disorienting and terrifying experience. My ideas simply did not mesh well enough with most of my informants' experiences. "I've seen your television shows," Doña Onix told me while a group of us were talking about these things, "and I saw what were supposed to be poor families. Why, they had televisions, and refrigerators, stoves, nice furniture—all kinds of *cosas lujosas* [luxuries]. How could you call that poverty?" "Yes," I tried to explain, "but those things are all relatively cheap in the United States, and even most poor people can afford them." "Well, then, how can you call them poor?" And there, in very simple terms, lies the disparity between development and underdevelopment. The glut of commodities on the developed side of the equation obliterates any system of reference, on the underdeveloped side, that might allow for an understanding of inequality, powerlessness, and relative poverty.

"Look, it's like this," I finally said. "What's it like being poor in Nicaragua? You have to work hard, and you barely make enough money to feed, clothe, and house yourselves. Right? And in the end, some of you don't make enough money to do that, so you go around hungry or homeless, right? And when you get sick, you can't get good medical attention. Well, it's just like that in the United States. Being poor is the same: You have to work all the time just to pay your bills. And when you can't pay them, you end up homeless. And medicine costs a lot. It's just that in the United States, we have better houses, nicer clothes, and more food. But the powerlessness is more or less the same, and the fear is the same."

The more political people present agreed with me. The less political people did not. Quality is difficult to gauge when quantity is scarce, and Nicaragua's economy is currently one of acute scarcity.

"Well," Doña Flora said, "I've talked to my relatives in the United States, and do you know what they all say? They say that yes, you can make a lot more money in North America than here, and that you can buy televisions, refrigerators, good furniture, and such. But everybody says they have to work harder—a lot harder—than anyone works here. Two jobs, in most cases, with no time for their family. And that's why there's so much delinquency in the United States, because children have nothing better to do than *andar vagando* [go around idle] all day."

My neighbors enjoyed talking about matters of personal economics with me, although I found that I was more likely to be open about mine than they were about theirs. After I secured my first teaching job, someone asked me how much money I made. "Twenty-one thousand a year," I hesitantly offered. "Dollars? North American dollars?" someone asked. "Of course North American dollars," someone else said, "that's what they use in the United States, silly." "Then you must be very rich now," another ventured. So I quickly drew up my expenses, which showed that I really didn't have very much money left at the end of the month: $450 for rent, $200 to pay back student loans, $250 for food, clothes, and other necessary expenses, $200 electric bills in the winter, $150 for my car payment, and a $50 phone bill, for a grand total of $1,300 in expenses against roughly $1,300 in take-home pay. "Ah," Aida interjected, spotting the issue: "you get *paid* in dollars, but you have to *spend* in dollars, too!"

Therein lies a large part—though not all—of the mythology: when dollars cross over into Nicaragua, they become very potent indeed against the virtually worthless córdoba. When a relative abroad sends home a hundred dollars, it equals perhaps three to six months pay in Nicaragua. U.S. dollars constitute the real, effective currency of Nicaragua. And obtaining them, though not a matter of absolute survival, surely determines whether one lives fairly well or very poorly. The anticolonial revolution, then, far from establishing greater autonomy and independence, has left Nicaragua more dependent on the economic superpower to the north. It is a clandestine dependency, to be sure. The córdoba is the "official" currency (although the Sandinista government operated "Dollar Stores" in which manufactured commodities from all over the world could be purchased, but only in U.S. dollars). And the United States maintained an official ban on commerce with Sandinista Nicaragua (although there was little to keep Nicaraguan coffee from finding its way into the United States after being sold and processed in Europe). The black market in dollars, large-scale emigration to the U.S. labor market, dependency on dollars from relatives abroad: these are the threads that bind Nicaragua's economy ever more closely to the United States and define what is for Nicaragua a new (but what is perhaps for Mexico an old) *underground* colonialism.[2]

Black Market Colonialism

THE NEW DEPENDENCY

Doña Flora was talking to me one day about Don Jorge, an older man who lived with his family across from her. "Every year or so, he goes to the United States, on *bidni*." (She said "business" in English, respirating the *s*'s, in Nicaraguan style.) "When he comes back, he has televisions, radios, and electric equipment. Where do you think he gets them?"

I said that I didn't know. "Perhaps he buys them *wholesale*"—which I had to say in English, because I didn't know the Spanish word—"that is, in a big quantity, at a low price."

"No, not that," Doña Flora responded. "These televisions and radios are used. How does he get them?"

I said that perhaps he obtained them at a Goodwill or secondhand store. "That's not what he says. People don't believe what he says. Do you think he steals them?"

I pondered that prospect for a moment: would someone assume the effort and expense of travel to the United States to break into people's houses by night and steal their television sets? No, I mused, that wasn't very likely. "Where does he say he gets them?" I asked.

"He says that in the United States, people throw away perfectly good things when just one little part breaks. So, for example, they throw away a whole television just because one little tube is broken. Don Jorge says he goes to the place where they keep these thrown-away things and gets them either for free or for next to nothing. Then he repairs them, if he can, and sells them here. And if he can't repair them, he can use the parts to repair other people's televisions here."

Suddenly I understood: he scavenges junkyards. Properly speaking, Nicaragua has no junkyards, only garbage piles, where daily refuse is disposed: pineapple skins; banana, orange, and lemon peels; a trace of paper products and plastic bags. Managua's garbage piles spring up in huge, open fields at the city's numerous interstices: rotting, breeding flies and mosquitoes, creating immediate problems of sanitation (whereas our own junkyards create long-range problems of environmental contamination) until, every few days, they are cleared by burning.[3] And in a flash, my own country, especially its economic practices, seemed very exotic to me.

"Is what he says true?" Doña Flora asked. "Do people really throw away a whole television when just one little part breaks? And is there really a place where you can go to get them?"

I struggled to reassert in myself a picture of America that was not exotic, wasteful, mysterious. "Well, yes, it is," I said. She seemed incredulous, so I tried to explain it to her (and myself). "It's not economical to have an old television repaired," I began, haltingly. "Let's say I buy a television for $150. It lasts ten years. That means, in effect, that I pay $15 for every year of viewing. Cheap, no? Are you following me so far?" She nodded. "Now, after ten years, the value of the television has depreciated down to, say, $35. That's probably more than what I could get if I tried to sell it. So it isn't worth very much anymore, right?" Doña Flora nodded. "Let's say a part breaks. The part may cost $20, and the labor to repair it may cost another $40. That means that while the television is worth only $35, it would cost me $60 to repair it. It's just not economical—and the television is so old that it may break again, soon. The television has served me well over the years and has already delivered ample value for the dollar. So instead of throwing good money after bad—which is a saying we have—I just throw away the old set and buy a new one. Does that make sense?"

Doña Flora nodded, but I sensed that she was not following me. After all, her experience ran very strongly in the other direction. In Nicaragua, where labor is cheap and manufactured commodities are dear, no one throws anything away. I have seen Doña Flora stitching rags on top of rags to keep a pair of pants wearable. Her children's underwear, hanging in the backyard, were tattered almost beyond recognition. And most people come by their expensive household items, not second-hand, but fourth-, fifth-, and sixth-hand. With my brief and fragmentary accounting, was Doña Flora having as much trouble following my calculations as I did when I attempted to trace the circulation of goods in Nicaragua: from their often uncertain origins, through a long chain of distributors and peddlers, to a purchaser, and finally through an elaborate network of family members, fictive kin, and friends?

Then, a few moments later, she asked, "Is it really true? That you just throw things away like that? Is that really how he gets those televisions? How do you think he really gets them?"

In Doña Flora's mind, there were only two options, and both seemed rather mysterious: either North Americans (as Nicaraguans refer to citizens of the United States and Canada collectively) were so fabulously wealthy that they threw away television sets, or her neighbor has been making his living all these years as a sneak thief. The latter seemed more credible because the former suggested fabulous wealth—and Flora was a hardheaded realist. And my explanation of the logic whereby one throws away televisions, far from "demystifying" anything, served only to bloat the mythical quality of U.S. wealth.

What better picture of a developed country's economic power than that of the dazzling wealth of America's junkyards? Or what more appropriate metaphor for the new dependency than that of a ragpicker?

Long ago, El Dorado was imagined as a land where the streets were paved with gold. But today it is a land where the junkyards are strewn with television sets.

CHAPTER II

Beating One's Wife

Quien te quiere, te aporrea. (The one who loves you, beats you.)
— An old Nicaraguan proverb

Over the course of my fieldwork in Nicaragua, I heard numerous, casual, everyday references to wife beating.[1] These references came mostly from women and were more often couched as generalizations than as specific anecdotes: "Nicaraguan men are *machistas*. They like to beat their wives, and in the past there wasn't much we could do about it. That's why we have a new law against wife beating; now the police will come and put you in jail for hitting a woman!" Many women felt empowered by such a law, as evinced in the manner with which they sometimes threatened men: "You lay a hand on me, and I'll call the police!" said one young woman to her boyfriend when their playful argument threatened to become more serious.

Although complaints about wife beating were common enough, until 1988 I never came across a case of domestic violence during my fieldwork, and no word of any major incident was relayed to me by my informants. This silence seemed peculiar to me, and at some point I began to question my informants' reports about the frequency of wife beating. My reasoning was as follows: In Managua's close neighborhoods, domestic violence would be difficult to conceal. Somewhat naively, I felt confident that I would either see, hear, or hear about almost any violent incident within the community. After all, people still gossiped about violence that had occurred on the andén years ago—between feuding neighbors or between spouses. And concealing domestic violence within the walls of a house, I reasoned, would be difficult at best: in Erasmus Jiménez, each house joins another and shares a tin roof. Between the concrete wall that separates the units in the duplex and the shared roof is an open space. Noises and conversations carry easily between the units even if the open space has been closed with a wooden partition. Some neighbors even call to each other across the opening in the rafters: "Félida! Can I borrow a cup of sugar?" Moreover, backyards are separated only by fences; if conducted on the patio, loud disagreements and shouting can be heard readily by neighbors on three sides. Finally, every home's windows hold wooden shutters, which are usually left open to ventilate the house: an arrangement that affords very little privacy.

I faced what I took to be a discrepancy: women carried on an ongoing discourse about wife beating, but I could find no physical evidence of it. I toyed with various hypotheses, trying to reconcile this discrepancy:

1. Perhaps Sandinista enforcement of the law prohibiting wife beating had achieved its aim very quickly, bringing levels of domestic violence to minimal levels. The skeptic in me made me doubt this hypothesis: longstanding patterns of domination are not often abruptly suspended by the passage or enforcement of a single law.

2. Perhaps wife beating had never been a terribly common occurrence in the first place; perhaps its key role in the culture of machismo was more ideological than practical. The threat of violence, though rarely carried out, reminded both men and women of their relative positions; the status quo was maintained more by the symbol of violence than by the reality of violence. Of course, the weakness of this hypothesis is obvious enough: a threat that is only a threat is not very effective. Moreover, separating "ideology" or "discourse" from "practice" is a familiar gesture in the social sciences: it reconstitutes classical theories of ideology, giving it an after-the-fact status and a relatively minimal scope of play. And to relegate wife abuse to the status of an "ideology" provides machismo with a convenient excuse: "No real harm done"; "She was just imagining it all." Finally, the structure of the proposition itself is flawed: how common would common violence be? Once a week? Once a year? Once in a lifetime? And who could determine what would constitute a common occurrence? Nicaraguan men? A foreign anthropologist? Surely Nicaraguan women themselves are in the best position to say whether domestic violence is frequent or infrequent.

3. Perhaps the law had partially restrained men, reducing the frequency of violent acts against their wives and compañeras, but perhaps the threat of incarceration had also made the practice far more secretive

than it had been before the revolution. And unless the violence were especially onerous or especially frequent, not even its victim would have a strong interest in jailing her husband, which would eliminate her and her children's main source of income and jeopardize the entire family's viability. In all but the worst of domestic situations, there is a general atmosphere of affection and cooperation between spouses or compañeros. At least one informant said that if her generally kind and sympathetic husband should happen to hit her over some incident or other, it would scarcely seem appropriate to involve the police in the matter. General denunciations of machismo aside, then, the consequences of putting one's husband in jail might militate against publicizing wife beating. Neighbors might also refrain from airing such serious matters, which would explain why people still gossiped about incidents that had happened years before: such events lacked immediacy, and thus they were no longer volatile. In such an atmosphere, it might not be such a difficult matter after all to "conceal" domestic violence. Although the houses of Erasmus Jiménez are very "open," the overall noise level on the street is often quite high. Stereos and televisions play at maximum volume; small parties are frequent; and the noise of children playing and babies wailing is constant.

4. Finally, I reasoned, my presence in Erasmus Jiménez over the years might have shaped some of the things I saw or didn't see. Although many of my informants were more or less open to me on a number of issues, they might well conceal matters that were especially private, especially painful, or particularly volatile. Chance itself could disperse cases of domestic violence out of my view, beyond my social setting, or in my absence from the setting.

"ALL BECAUSE OF MINGUITO"

A pair of connected incidents on the andén brought the question of wife beating into sharper focus for me. In August 1988 I returned to Managua to conclude my summer fieldwork, which had begun in May. I had absented myself from the field for a few weeks to take care of pressing business at home. My airplane landed in Managua on the evening of 1 August, the day of the Coming of Santo Domingo (Lancaster 1988b, 38–51), a festival held for Managua's patron saint. My journal records in some detail two incidents: the first involved the threat of spousal violence; the second involved an exchange of blows between a husband and his wife.

(From my journal, 2 August 1988): *Onix and her husband are fighting, and he has locked her out of the house. She spent last night here, with Doña Flora's family.*

Yesterday was Santo Domingo, and Onix joined Flora, Aida, Esperanza, and Esperanza's husband Pedro here for a small party. Together they drank two and a half bottles of rum, according to everyone present, and then went down to see the procession. When Onix came home drunk after the procession, her husband "ran her out of the house." He himself does not drink, according to Onix, and he was outraged that she had come home drunk. "I have never hit you, but if I hit you now, I might kill you," he told her, gripped with rage. "It's best that you stay out." Onix agreed: it was better to be locked out of the house than to be beaten, especially by a husband as enraged as hers.

Somewhat meekly, she walked across the andén and knocked on her own door this morning, but her husband (who addressed her through the front window) still would not let her return home. "But my son is sick," she protested (and so he was, with a high fever), but her husband would hear none of it. "Your son was sick yesterday, too, but that didn't keep you here." "But who will do the cooking? Who will wash the laundry?" Onix demanded, specifying her own morning chores. "What's there to cooking beans and rice?" her husband responded. "And your daughter can wash the clothes today." Again, Onix protested, loudly: "But it was only chicha! You can't even tell the difference between chicha and rum!" Silence. Her husband wasn't ready to make up yet, and he certainly wasn't buying her version of how she had drunk only some corn beer, in moderation.

During this attempt by Onix to patch things up with her husband, Flora and Aida walked up to the edge of their neighbors' front porch to show Onix moral support; her husband did not acknowledge their presence.

Returning to Flora's house, Onix sighed, looked at me, and said, "All because of Minguito." ("Minguito" is Santo Domingo's nickname.)

Early in the afternoon, Onix's husband finally sent word by way of their thirteen-year-old daughter (who had been calmly intermediating between the two of them since the altercation began): "He says you can come home and stay now, but that he doesn't want to talk about it, and he doesn't want to hear anything about it. He's very firm on that point." Having wanted to go home all night and all morning, Onix now hesitated. "Go on!" everyone said. "I'm nervous," she said. "What if he's still really angry?" "He's not," the daughter said, "and remember, he doesn't want to discuss it." Onix was still afraid that when she returned her husband was going to beat her. Her sick boy, flushed with fever, was absolutely silent and appeared apprehensive. Taking the initiative, Flora went over to their house first, on the pretext of bringing back their sick son. Once the door was opened, Onix followed, with Flora there, just in case. Nothing happened, nothing was discussed, and everything seems to be fine now. Flora made another short visit to her neighbors' house, on some other pretext, a little later in the afternoon, to insure that nothing was amiss.

Everyone seems to be fighting this Santo Domingo. The high level of alcohol consumption is no doubt a trigger; so, too, the fact that on Santo Domingo many women assume the usually male prerogative of drinking. Various stories are circulating about scraps between couples and about husbands who hit their wives yesterday while drinking. Another incident happened yesterday, right here at Flora's house. Esperanza and Pedro were both drinking. Esperanza says that she rarely drinks, and in fact I have never seen her drink. Pedro, by contrast, can consume a prodigious amount of alcohol for his small frame. (A couple of months ago, Guto and Miguel ushered him home, propping him up on either side, after we had consumed a bottle of rum between the two of us in less than two hours. I drank a good deal less of it than Pedro did.) According to everyone present, Pedro, who had drunk a good deal of rum yesterday, began playing too roughly with his daughter. Esperanza warned him to be more gentle and lightly pulled his hair to make him stop. This infuriated Pedro, and very quickly he hit his wife in the jaw with his fist. Enraged, Esperanza picked up a metal pitcher that held lemonade and banged him twice on the head, bending the pitcher completely out of shape. It sits out on the patio, like some garish trophy, and no one has used it since. Miguel says that he will bang it back into shape this afternoon. (Esperanza is actually larger than Pedro, and I am not sure which of them hurt the other most—especially since Pedro will not talk about the incident.)

"Just look at this swelling," she said, pointing to her lower jaw today. "Me hizo verga! [He punched me hard!] If he had hit me in the mouth he could have broken my teeth, and I'd be going around toothless!"

Esperanza says that this is the only time her spouse has ever hit her since they've been together and that it shocked her a great deal. "He's a man, and he should know that men are stronger than women, and that he could hurt somebody that way. Why, he's a Sandinista," she said, "and just because of that alone he should know better than to try beating a woman. He doesn't usually carry on like a machista!"

The special circumstances of yesterday's violence seem clear enough to me: Esperanza was drinking, and she corrected Pedro. Both drinking and disciplining are men's activities, men's privileges. Onix was drinking, an activity that her husband eschews, so under the rule of machismo, she was behaving like the man of the family when her own husband has relinquished that particular display of masculinity. (Locking a drunk out of the house is scarcely machista, but the physical threat accompanying the action—in the context of traditional norms—certainly was.) Moreover, the party was being held at Flora's house, and Flora is a very independent woman: an ominous setting. Neither Onix's husband nor Pedro could accept the combination of events and circumstances.

The threat of violence, as with Onix and her husband; the reality of violence, as with Esperanza and Pedro: both are part of a larger picture of gender relations in which men literally have the upper hand. In both cases, violence comes up when women encroach on what men see as their domain. Until the revolution, it was one of the working assumptions of Nicaraguan culture that men could control and discipline their wives and compañeras with impunity. Community opinion, especially male opinion, would not reproach a man for occasionally beating his wife, unless the level of violence was seen as excessive. Physical violence was perhaps not the means of first resort, but it remained a legitimate option when disagreements between husbands and wives came up. In any dispute between a man and a woman, then, either the threat or the reality of violence tipped the scales in favor of the man's opinion, his demands, his wishes.

The impunity with which a man might physically intimidate and discipline his wife is gone now. Legally, he may not do so, and community opinion, too, has changed. The sectors of opinion that have changed the most, not surprisingly, are the most politically involved and revolutionary sectors of the public, especially urban and educated militants. Certainly, women are able to describe machismo as a political and social system and to delineate its core practices: hard drinking, excessive gambling, womanizing, wife beating. Just as certainly, men—even educated, involved, revolutionary men—have been markedly slower to change their habits. Two sets of values coexist, compete, and more than occasionally blur: the ideals of machismo, with its cult of aggressive masculinity, defined as a mode of sexual and physical conquest;[2] and the ideals of the revolutionary New Man, who is envisioned as hardworking, devoted, and family oriented. The irony of Onix's case is that her husband, a Sandinista militant, reformed his machista behavior for political, social, and moral reasons: that is why he did not drink. But to prevent his wife from drinking, even on special occasions, he was willing to retain the option of a sort of intimidation that is at the core of machismo's values and practices.

Aida commented, "Look, he means well, but he's misguided. Yes, Onix drank too much: she's not used to drinking. Yes, she was silly to be out having a party when her son was sick. But there are other ways of solving problems, and in the end, her husband treated her like a child in need of disciplining. This isn't a very proper way of doing things."

THE VIOLENT ORGAN

The New Man Machista Culture — interntpe [handwritten annotation]

In the more politicized sectors of Managua, young people are very much committed to substantial changes in the conduct of personal life. At all levels, ranging from the discourses of the Sandinista *comandancia* to the discussions of ordinary people in the neighborhood, one hears contempt for "those who behave like revolutionaries in public and reactionaries at home." Such criticism is specifically directed against "machista revolutionaries," who are seen as hypocrites: they understand exploitation well enough in a neocolonial or class context, but not in a sexual one, and not within the borders of the family. Although such hypocrisy is common enough, so is its denunciation; the moral field is very much commanded by a critical approach to machismo.

In pointing out the major difficulties attendant to changing the way people live, I do not wish to cast doubt on the authenticity of people's desire for a better way of living. However, old habits die hard. The habits that die hardest of all are precisely those that are habituated in the body, in pervasive conceptions of the body, and in daily practices that resist the scrutiny of active reflection—a combination of "habit," "habitat," and "inhabit" that Pierre Bourdieu (1977) calls "habitus." Even in those sectors most committed to a new society, a new way of living, what remains of machismo is more than just a residue of the past rule. The rule is preserved: in everyday discourse, in a conventional conception of the body, and in real social practices.

The discourse of violence is itself highly gendered. Violence in whatever form is assigned a *masculine* character. The threat *Te voy a hacer verga*—which is used to mean "I'm going to punch you"—could be translated literally as "I'm going to do you a dick" or "I'm going to dick you" or even "I am going to put my dick into you." Blurring the lines between copulation and violence, *Me hizo verga* (or *Me ha hecho verga*) means "He punched me." Not only is violence thus a masculine affair, and not only is the object of violence semiotically feminized (whatever the violence's real target), but the physical subordination of another is equated with penile intromission. Conversely, at the same time and through the same discourse, one's appropriate gender is defined by and through a practice (sex) that is itself defined as violent and dominating. Thus defined, the penis *(verga)* is necessarily a violent organ. Thus defined, masculinity and femininity are interchangeable with domination and submission, aggressiveness and passivity.[3]

Such a conception plays itself out and is reconstituted in a variety of settings.

(From my journal, 3 August 1988): *Today, Guto was holding Esperanza's and Pedro's daughter, Auxiliadora, while Aida was holding her son, Ervin. Guto decided to have them "fight" a mock battle. He manipulated the smaller girl's hands into lightly hitting Ervin. The boy began to cry. "Vení, cochón [Come on, faggot]!" Guto cajoled, mimicking the voice of a small girl. "Come on, cochón!" The baby in his arms seemed confused by the goings-on around her. Embarrassed by such antics, but responding nonetheless, Aida pushed Ervin forward and began manipulating his hands in mock battle. The four of them played this way for a few seconds until Ervin began to cry again. "Cochón, cochón!" Guto chastised, while Aida soothed her son.*

With events of the other day still no doubt very much on her mind, Esperanza said to me, "Now just look at that. They're teaching him how to beat women." And so they were.

The lesson—an inescapable one, reinforced at every juncture of the child's socialization—is, Show aggressiveness, dominate women, or be deprived of your masculinity.

The overall regimen of childrearing remains highly gendered and is very much designed to instill the core values of machismo in successive generations. The following observations are largely drawn from a half-dozen of the more politicized and educated families of Erasmus Jiménez, where discussions of machismo and criticism of its values are not uncommon; they are supplemented by my observations of childrearing practices in an equal number of households in the lower-working-class Barrio Rigoberto and the Sergio Altamirano shantytown; all are based on the observation of frequent incidents and on subsequent discussions of the standard treatment of children with the families involved.

(1) Male children are typically teased, taunted, and provoked by their older siblings until they display an appropriate rage; once solicited, these rages are tolerated and are punished only when they exceed broadly defined limits. Female children receive no such training; older siblings are more likely to take gentle, doting care of them, and signs of rage from small girls are neither indulged nor tolerated. (2) When male children who are learning to speak pick up profane language from the adults and older children around them, their outbursts are greeted with amused tolerance, even encouragement; punishment ensues only when they direct their invective against adults. Female children receive no such indulgence, and even mild vulgarities from them receive swift punishment. (3) By the age of two, male children still toddling and scarcely able to talk might be sent on various short errands—given a bucket and sent to purchase ice from a house down the andén, for instance—or allowed to play without adult supervision at some distance from the house. Female children are not pushed toward personal autonomy at such an early age; when they wander from the house, they are more quickly retrieved and are frequently punished for doing so. (4) Past adolescence, teenage boys are allowed to roam the andén in the evening and to socialize with their friends in a relatively unsupervised manner; teenage girls absolutely are not allowed to do so. (5) Indeed, boys are given great leeway in ignoring or flouting their mothers' orders; girls are issued many fewer warnings before being whipped. (6) Corporal punishment diminishes and ceases for a boy at a much younger age than it does for a girl. (7) When a teenage boy comes home in the evening smelling of alcohol, his mother is unlikely to make too many inquiries; if a teenage girl comes home smelling of alcohol, her mother is almost certain to beat her with a belt.

It might well be imagined that since a machista society privileges men over women, the socialization of boys would therefore be an easier, less painful, or less problematic experience than the socialization of girls. This is not the case.[4] Although a boy's training is to some extent a training for privilege, it also actively solicits the hallmark traits of machismo. Thus, the taunting and provocation of young boys begins while they are still babies and continues in some form or other throughout childhood. All boys are constantly disciplined by their elders—by parents and siblings alike—with the humiliating phrase *No sea cochón!* (Don't be a faggot!) when their demeanor falls short of the assertive, aggressive, masculine ideal. Any show of sensitivity, weakness, reticence—or whatever else is judged to be a feminine characteristic—is swiftly identified and ridiculed. By adolescence, boys enter a competitive arena where the signs of masculinity are actively struggled for and can be won only by wresting them *away from* other boys around them. Justifiably, the regimen of this socialization might be called "brutal"; its whole purpose is to induce a certain insensitivity—and irresponsibility—in men. That the fate of so many Nicaraguan men is alcoholism, broken health, loneliness, and early death is a direct consequence of this atomizing and isolating socialization.

Although men do not necessarily realize all its consequences, they do understand this basic form of socialization by toughening. One evening I was standing on the andén talking to a young man from the neighborhood. He was due to complete his military service in a matter of weeks, and we were discussing his plans on separation. While speaking to me, he and a younger boy from the same neighborhood were roughhousing. Without warning, the young man delivered a hard punch to the back of the boy's shoulder. The younger boy ran to his porch a few yards away and began crying. The young man continued talking to me as though nothing had happened and eventually commented: "You seem surprised by what just happened here." "It didn't seem necessary," I observed. The young man began to say, "Well, here in Nicaragua, it's good for a man to be tough and brave, so sometimes we hit the boys just to toughen them up—" By this time the boy had recovered his bearings; he carefully crept up beside the young man, who was paying no attention, and punched him as hard as he could directly in his solar plexus. Now whispering and wheezing, the young man concluded his thought: "—so that when somebody attacks them, or pushes them around, or perhaps when the United States invades, they'll come back, just like that: wild, crazy, and fearless, just like that."

A strongly gendered division of the world sets the terms for relations between men and women. But this division occurs *within* a system of contrasts—the man's active, violent penis; the woman's passive, gentle vagina—not along its border. And in this mirror world of gender, the values can be just as easily inverted without altering the integrity of the system: the man's beleaguered, inadequate penis; the woman's demanding, insatiable vagina. This underside of machismo is very much a real and indispensable part of its routine operation, which demands male initiative and male action to reassert the original picture. Which is to say: the system of machismo relegates women to the margins of power, but it by no means excludes women from the operation of a system whose values they carry.

Women do indeed speak ill of men—for excessive drinking, for womanizing, for beating women—but it must also be pointed out that when men gather, it is usually the women who send for liquor and prepare the chasers, and they usually do so without being asked. (So routine and unquestioned is this ritual that I often felt that I was having liquor forced on me, even when I was still recovering from a hangover.) By and large, men who are considered too mild-mannered or too passive in their personal interactions are not considered good prospects for husbands, even if they are demonstrably industrious and hardworking. It is also to some extent women—mothers—who solicit independent, aggressive, even violent behavior in their sons, while keeping their daughters on a far shorter leash: they want their sons to be strong and independent, not soft, and they want their daughters to behave like acquiescent young ladies.

"LIKE A PARROT IN A CAGE":
INFIDELITY, VIOLENCE, AND MARRIAGE

Aida and Eddy had been seeing each other for several months before she became pregnant. After the pregnancy, both began referring to each other, interchangeably, as *compañeros* (companions), *maridos* (marrieds), and *esposos* (spouses). Such a pattern is not atypical in Nicaragua, where church or civil marriages are less common than informal unions are for lower-class couples.[5] After a more or less protracted courtship, a couple becomes "married," in effect, after the first pregnancy—if the couple decides to cohabit and jointly rear the child. Marriage, then, is more often a casual rather than a formal arrangement; the bonds that join compañeros depend on the couple's commitment to each other and to their children rather than on a binding civil or religious agreement.

Both Aida and Eddy are Sandinistas; Aida is a feminist, and Eddy certainly validates the notion of a revolutionary new man and the idea of a new society with a new way of living. Both began their life together with romantic feelings of love, the best of intentions, and the understanding that theirs was to be an equal partnership. Eddy's work, however, took him frequently away from Managua, and—Aida complained—Eddy is a heavy drinker whose baby face makes him very attractive to women. By the time their son, Ervin, was one, Aida complained: "Do you know what they say about Eddy? They say he keeps a woman in Matagalpa, and another one in Chinandega. Another colleague from work says he's also seeing someone in León. I bring this up, and he denies it; he says, 'No, no, you're the only one I love, there isn't anybody else,' but I don't believe it. I don't know what to think or what to do." By the time Ervin was three, Eddy had fathered children by three different women in various parts of Nicaragua, and he was rumored to have impregnated two more women.

"¡*Qué barbaridad!* (It's outrageous!)," Aida exclaimed when my queries about the now-perpetually-absent Eddy revealed this information. "He never stops! He says that it's me he loves, yet there apparently isn't a woman in the world he can say no to! And he isn't supporting any of his children, not really—well, anyway, he isn't supporting mine. Ervin hardly ever sees his father, and we get almost no money at all from him." By this time Aida and Eddy had virtually stopped calling themselves spouses; relations between the two were at best cool and distant, and his visits were increasingly infrequent. "I'm thinking about cutting him out altogether," Aida stated. "Why should I sleep with him once in a while when he comes over for a visit? What good is he for me, for my son—for anybody, for that matter? I could take him to Social Welfare and attach his wages for child support, but I think I'd rather just be through with him altogether."

It might seem that the informal character of cohabitation contributes to the brittleness of unions in Nicaragua, and perhaps that is so. Without a tradition of formal and legal constraints, men do abandon women and children to start new families. It might even be argued that this arrangement facilitates the irresponsible sexual behavior of men. But informal union as an institution occurs in the context of the culture of machismo, not vice versa.

Eddy reflected on his situation: "Women don't understand about men and how we are. And if they do understand it, they don't accept it. Aida is very jealous, and she doesn't understand that a man, especially a young man, needs to see more than one woman. And a woman like her, she'd always be making demands, you know? I suppose it's a good thing we didn't get married."

Aida, of course, saw matters differently: "Men like Eddy are machistas; they drink and womanize and accept no responsibility for the consequences. Well, children are the consequences of irresponsible fucking, so while he runs around, some woman—no, *several* women have to assume the responsibilities he avoids. It's a good thing we didn't get married. Can you imagine how I would feel, trapped in a marriage with a man like that?"

Unlike Eddy, most men I interviewed said that they would prefer a legal ceremony. Their reasons were straightforward enough: a legally married woman would be much less likely to leave her husband. Most women countered that legal marriage tips the balance of power in favor of men and that informal union works to the overall benefit of women. Their reasoning, too, is straightforward enough. Men have a variety of threats at their disposal in the event of quarrels: they might withhold money and child support, or they might resort to violence. By contrast, the main leverage women have is that they might abandon their compañero, thus leaving him alone and humiliated. A legal marriage, then, diminishes the wife's freedom somewhat more than the husband's. Because divorce is difficult, the wife would not be at liberty to leave a bad marriage, and her main threat would thus be diminished. A man, however, would remain free to pursue other women outside of his marriage: convention holds that womanizing is not adequate grounds for divorce (as did divorce law before its 1988 liberalization). And, indeed, in a legal marriage the husband would be at greater liberty to beat his wife in the event of disagreements, for she would have fewer retaliatory options.

Such points were made most emphatically by most of the women I interviewed on the subject of marriage.[6] When I asked older women why they had never married in a legal ceremony, preferring instead an informal union, their responses typically resembled Doña Celia's:

"Because Nicaraguan men are such machistas. They think they can beat their wives and do whatever else they please. And this is a Catholic country, so it's very difficult to get a divorce; it's virtually unheard of. And anyway, most women believe it's a terrible sin to get a divorce: they think you'll go to hell for that. So when a woman marries a man, she's agreeing to put up with whatever he decides to do. This isn't good for women. It's much better, much more sensible, to live with him without a church wedding. That way, if he tries to beat you, you can leave him, or if he takes up with other women, you can get out of it, or at least you can threaten to leave.

"When I started living with my compañero, both my parents and his parents pressured us to get married, but I wouldn't do it. 'What,' I said, 'and be like a parrot in a cage? No.' A married man thinks he owns a woman.

"Some younger girls now have a different opinion on the matter. I can't say whether they're right or wrong. I don't know yet. But they say that with the new laws and with some men trying to be more responsible and less machista, it makes sense to have a church wedding. Well, good luck to them. I hope they're right. If men would live, say, more like the Protestants and less like the Catholics, then that makes good sense.[7]

"My own old man, he never beat me. He tried to hit me once. We were having an argument—over the children, I think it was—and he had been drinking. He got up out of his chair, and made a move to hit me. He pulled back his hand, like this. Some women would have taken it, I imagine, and never said anything about it, but not me. I was cooking beans at the time; the pot was good and boiling hot. So I picked up the pot and threw the beans on him. Scalded him good. I said, 'Don't you ever try to hit me again!' 'You're crazy,' he said, 'completely crazy! I wasn't going to hit you. Shit, these women from Chinandega, they're bad, they're very bad witches.' Well, bad I might be, but he never tried to hit me again."

Flora generalized along the same lines as Doña Celia:

"Look what happens when you get married in a church. Rolando married his first wife, and then he started hitting her. Both daughters of Doña Carmen [a neighbor] were married in the same church, over there, by the same priest, one to a doctor, the other to a man from the neighborhood. It was a grand scandal; both their husbands beat them, and now they're both separated. Doña Carmen says one of them is living with her husband in Mexico, but it is well known that she's living with another man in Costa Rica. Can you imagine? Married in the church, and then separated and divorced! It was a grand scandal! And that is why it is better not to get married."

CHAPTER III

Murdering One's Husband's Lover

He said he knew how to handle dangerous women.
—*Women on the Verge of a Nervous Breakdown*, directed by Pedro Almodóvar

On 17 August 1988 Rosa Esther Tapía Fernández, age twenty-eight, entered the Instituto Mario Narváez, a high school in the small town of Diriá, which is located in the province of Granada. On entering a classroom, Rosa produced a pistol and murdered Margarita Selva Hernández, a fifteen-year-old student. Margarita had been having an affair with Roberto Rivas Guatemala, age thirty-one, Rosa Esther's husband. The murder shocked and scandalized Nicaragua. Throughout the country it was the topic of much commentary and speculation in neighborhood gossip. Indeed, talk about the story went on for so long and with such an intensity that it bordered on a mania. In conversation, it was referred to as "the Margarita case" or simply "the crime in Diriá." The story itself, even in its main outlines, touched many themes of interest: love, machismo, cheating, revenge, murder. Sensationalistic journalism stoked interest in the story, and for more than a week new and sordid details came out in front-page stories in the nation's three daily newspapers. "Margarita Still Dead" would not be much of an exaggeration of the front-page headlines.

"Margarita Was under a Threat," announced the front-page headline in *El nuevo diario* on 20 August. According to Margarita's friends, Rosa Esther had known for a long time that Margarita was seeing her husband; jealousy was consuming her, and she had warned Margarita to stay away from Roberto, cursing her within earshot of others and mocking the younger woman's Protestant faith. Farther down the page, *El nuevo diario* ran a series of person-in-the-street interviews: "People

Think: It's Not Worth It to Kill out of Jealousy." "But the guiltier one is the man, for being engaged with the two of them. You shouldn't do that," commented Rosa Jirón. "It [homicide] is a big temptation, but it doesn't have to come to a situation like that," observed Juan Ramón Lazo. "In matters of love, men, because of machismo, are always conquering, and women are always in love, but they don't know how to look for a dialogue to solve their problems," opined Janett Gutiérez, who also said that it was better to give such an unfaithful man to the other woman than to keep him.

Much of the news coverage was gratuitous. "New Details on the Tragic Outcome: Fateful Hours for Margarita," announced *El nuevo diario* on 21 August, rehashing the story and adding more details. *Barricada* carried two front-page pieces on the case the same day: "Psychiatrist and Psychologist Analyze Crime of Passion: Why Did She Shoot Margarita?" and "Diriá Continues in Commotion." On 22 August *Barricada* interviewed Roberto Rivas Guatemala, featuring a large photograph of the man: "The Romance That Ended Tragically: 'I Loved Margarita.' " In the interview Roberto said, "In Nicaragua, it's natural for a man to have more than one woman." Not to be outdone, on the same day *El nuevo diario* reconstructed the fateful event one more time with Margarita's classmates, who acted out the drama for the reporter: "A Pencil Adorned Margarita's Mouth." *La prensa,* which was also covering the case daily, weighed in politically on 23 August: "Students Demand Punishment for 'School Assassin.' " Finally, on 24 August, in a reflective vein, *Barricada* issued its "Psychological Alert on Diriá Crime: Is the Margarita Case an Extravagance of Yellow Journalism?" So acute was interest in the story, and so sensational had been the coverage, *Barricada* observed, that some Nicaraguan families, especially those in Diriá, were going without bread in order to purchase all three daily newspapers. Still, the story continued, in various registers: "Hatred of Crime and Compassion for the Delinquent" (*El nuevo diario,* 24 August); "Anonymous Voices Break the People's Monotony: Diriá and Perverse Tales" (*El nuevo diario,* 24 August); "Diriá Crime Should Move on to Reflection" (*Barricada,* 25 August). An editorial of 29 August in *El nuevo diario* discussed, one more time, "The Social Roots of the Crime in Diriá."

Journalists, classmates, school officials, psychologists, sociologists, the killer's family, her victim's family, their neighbors, and people on the street—all sorted through the events in Diriá, and the newspapers printed their thoughts. In Erasmus Jiménez, men and women, young and old, told and retold the story of the crime in Diriá, animatedly recounting its details, pointedly arguing over its plot, coolly rehearsing and analyzing its characters' motives, with various degrees of sympathy for the three main characters. A classical love triangle, with a very un-classical turn of events, the story was not only good to tell but also merited repeating and was worthy of disputation. I was more curious about its peculiar appeal than its morbid details. Why the endless traf-ficking in *this* tale, *these* events, when so many other news items of the year bore more directly on Nicaragua's fate?

Five simple elements: love, unfaithfulness, jealousy, murder, punish-ment. The story seems "classical" and "closed," a typical pop tragedy, but the oddity of a woman murdering another woman renders the nar-rative anything but classical. The tale itself was perhaps arresting, but not in a disinterested, closed way. Certainly, part of this narrative's appeal is that, taken up in different voices, it could be used to tell dif-ferent stories representing different morals, different points of view. One informant felt that the Margarita case exerted so much interest "be-cause the story is about the moral depravity of people and what it comes to": in short, it was a tale of passion, crime, and all-around punish-ment. A man commented that women, after the revolution, had become more aggressive, and this was an extreme example of women losing their femininity and behaving more like men. Another—a woman and an AMNLAE activist—argued that the tale had special interest to women and implied a feminist analysis of male irresponsibility: "It is about machismo and its results. That Roberto was a typical machista, and you see what happened." Yet another observed that the story itself was a morbid curiosity: "It is so rare, so strange, and so disturbing for a woman to kill somebody—that gives the story its fascination. You expect women to be wives and mothers, not murderers." Doña Flora, in my view, proved the most reflective of my informants on the subject.

"If a man had killed his woman for cheating on him, it would have been news, but it would not have been a big deal. That would be com-mon enough. If a woman had killed her husband out of jealousy, now that would be something. It would be bigger news, because that doesn't happen very often. But it does happen; there are cases, so I don't think it would be such big news as this. But for a woman to kill the other woman? No one has ever heard of it. It's never been done before. But then, you think about it, and it makes sense. Look how many men died in the revolution, and then in the contra war; how many men are out of the country, working, and on top of that, how many left the country to evade military service. It adds up, it comes to a lot of men. Men today are scarce. Even if you were driven mad with rage, it still wouldn't make sense to kill one, from a woman's point of view. There just aren't enough around, and that would be one less. So there is more competition between women for men. Women have, well, less solidarity in these matters. So this woman, she kills *the other woman* instead of the man. It's a new thing. It's unheard of. But then, it makes sense."

The crime of Diriá thus became a hyperbolized story that Nicaraguans could tell *about* themselves, their families, their culture, and its dilemmas—specifically, as these dilemmas were experienced in the social and economic crisis of the late 1980s, and as they were construed in the context of women's liberation. (For women, the tale implied a feminist analysis of machismo; for men, it justified their fears about unruly women.) The fascination lay simultaneously in the tale's succinct, dramatic illustration of certain common themes—passion, unfaithfulness, jealousy—and in its eerily intelligible novelty. It was a story in which the familiar confronted the new, in which tradition met modernity in the head-on collision of a heinous crime: a crime whose brutality and senselessness made sense in a culture of machismo, not yet changed but under challenge, and in a political economy beset with shortages, where the most acute shortage was in men.

CHAPTER IV

Coping with Less: *Compadrazgo,* Friendship, and Provisioning

> The obligation attached to a gift itself is not inert. . . . Total prestation not only carries with it the obligation to repay gifts received, but it implies two others equally important: the obligation to give presents and the obligation to receive them.
>
> —Marcel Mauss, *The Gift*

As Michael Higgins once asked, What do you do if going to bed with a córdoba in your pocket means waking up the next morning to find that the money has already lost a third of its value?[1] The immediate answer is simple enough: you make sure that you never go to bed with a córdoba still in your pocket. You spend money as quickly as you earn it. You try to convert your income into immediate necessities or durable goods, or you try to convert it into a more stable currency, like U.S. dollars. Living in an economic crisis, Nicaraguans resorted to all of these strategies, and more.

How did families survive when real wages in the late 1980s equaled less than 10 percent of real wages in 1980?[2] Faced with such a catastrophe, you resort to means outside the structure of the formal economy. For instance, you try to produce more of what you consume. Most backyards in Managua sport a variety of impressively productive fruit trees: bananas, coconuts, mangos, lemons, oranges, *mamones.* These resources, carefully used, lower household consumption costs. Most families also store up economic value in the form of chickens, turkeys, ducks, even pigs. Raising chickens is an especially good strategy: they are cheap to feed and provide both meat and eggs. With enough chickens in the backyard, a family might be fortunate enough to have eggs for breakfast every morning. Such reserves regularly supplement people's diets and help families through especially hard times. (Many CDSs [Sandinista Defense Committees] attempted to mitigate the scope of the crisis by extending this principle from private provisioning to the communal level: they sowed public gardens in many barrios across Managua; volunteers planted and cultivated the gardens, and the produce was distributed freely and equally to members of the community.)

Then, too, there is activity on what economists usually call the informal economy. The term *informal economy* is too neutral, too innocuous, to describe the range of activities to which people resort in Nicaragua's long and continuing crisis. The "informal economy" is simply this: People do whatever they have to do to make ends meet.

With the collapse of real wages, followed by the *compactación* of government ministries and the massive layoffs of civil servants, more and more people in the capital have been forced to eke out a meager living in the so-called informal economy. Thus, a family's income may be supplemented by the housewife who bakes goods and discharges her children every afternoon to sell them door-to-door or in the marketplace. Or her family might draw on the reserve labor of its older children: in vending, or in hiring out their labor to artisan-producers or repair shops. A single mother supporting children might canvass the area on a daily basis, washing and ironing the laundry of her neighbors who have slightly more income than she herself commands. Or, by taking a trip to Costa Rica, a family member might purchase certain goods wholesale—shoes, shirts, pants—and then sell them informally out of his or her own house. A family with its own refrigerator might post a sign over its front door advertising *hielo* (ice) or *helados* (frozen fruit desserts). And there is always room in Managua's chaotic, decentralized distribution market. At the lowest end of the chain, peddlers buy small quantities and then resell them door-to-door or in the marketplace; some range far across the city on their preappointed rounds. At the least productive end, some even sell water in the marketplace. An especially effective strategy for the family—although a deleterious one for Nicaragua's economy as a whole—is to send a husband or older son to the United States, where he can work on the clandestine labor market and send home periodic remittances in dollars to his family.

By a variety of such tactics, most families get by, and Nicaraguans have resorted to all of these means in recent years—so much so that the informal economy has eclipsed the formal economy in Managua, according to government statistics. And I have no doubt that income received from family members abroad exceeded income produced in Nicaragua.[3]

AVOCADOS, MANGOS, BANANAS, AND TIN:
THE SIGNS OF FRIENDSHIP

During the economic crisis, Nicaraguans have also turned to networks
of family, friends, and fictive kin to ward off the worst ravages of unemployment, low income, and scarcity. The economic and journalistic
literature on Nicaragua's crisis often mentions barter as a primary
mechanism of the informal economy and as a major means whereby
people have survived the crisis. No doubt this is so, especially in middle-
class or farming communities with access to values and quantities appropriate for bartering. But in Managua's working-class barrios, I witnessed very few transactions that might be called barter proper. Rather,
most Nicaraguans seem to carry out a host of meaningful transactions
in the form of informal gift exchanges.

For example, I once accompanied Doña Flora to the Mercado Oriental to buy groceries. There we found her husband's cousin, who had
come to the market from Niquinohomo to sell avocados from his farm's
prolific trees. (Since he had no market license, his sales were on the
"black market.") After greeting him, Doña Flora inspected the avocados. "They're very pretty," she commented, gently squeezing one in her
hand. "Good and ripe." Her husband's cousin responded, "Ah, yes, but
I've already sold the best ones. These are the ones left over." After a
few more friendly exchanges, he announced that he was through with
marketing for the day and was ready to go home. Would Doña Flora
be so kind as to take these avocados? "Why certainly," she responded.
Thus, she did him a favor by receiving his gift. And having found little
else at the marketplace that was worthwhile or affordable, we went
home with a large burlap shopping bag stuffed full of avocados.

Doña Flora's countergift to her husband's cousin would never be
framed in terms of "repayment" for the gift. Rather, she might keep his
son at her house for an unspecified period of time—as she often did—
or pass along to his wife an assortment of clothes that all of her own
children had outgrown. But unlike a barter arrangement—the immediate exchange of goods of equal value—no one literally "counts" economic value in these exchanges, least of all publicly. For that reason, it
would be impossible to say what constituted "repayment" for what. In
this case, mutual assistance is simply one of the rights and requirements
of kinship, by marriage as well as by descent.

Consider another sort of example. Doña Jazmina's grandson, Josué-
Luis, came to her one day saying, "Mamá, I'm hungry. I want a mango."

"But love," she responded, "we don't have any mangos." "Yes, I know," he responded, "but I'd still like a mango." "Well, then," she instructed him, "go down the andén to your godfather, Marco-Polo, and tell him, 'Padrino, give me a mango.'" The child did, and his godfather went into the backyard and produced a huge, ripe mango; moreover, he sent the child back to the house with enough mangos for his whole family. In this case, the exchange of favors and assistance follows the routes established by *compadrazgo* (coparenting) or fictive kin.

The one transaction I witnessed that came closest to qualifying as outright "barter" was never described as such by any of its participants. Aida, by means that were never clear to me, had somehow obtained a supply of used tin in good shape to reroof the leaking sections of her house's roof. One of her coworkers lived in a house whose roof was entirely improvised from cardboard and newspapers, replaced frequently after rains. The morning in question, a truck, borrowed by her coworker's brother, arrived carrying the load of new tin. The woman, her brother (who had somehow borrowed this work truck during a lull in the work day), and Aida were seated in the front seat. The woman's brother drove, and I helped him haul the long, heavy sheets of tin. The old roofing was immediately loaded up and dispatched to Aida's friend's house. Later that afternoon, the woman's brother returned in the truck, delivering several *cabezas* ("heads" or bunches) of bananas. Aida's family ate bananas for a week, consuming them rapidly, before they spoiled and crawled with worms.

On the surface, this exchange certainly looked like barter: truck use and bananas in exchange for tin roofing. I asked Aida if this were a barter arrangement, if the bananas constituted repayment for tin. "Certainly not!" she insisted. "I gave her the tin because we are friends and they needed it. It's not good to sleep with water falling on your head. She gave me the bananas because we are friends, and my family has no banana trees, and her mother's trees produce more than enough for them to eat." In this case, mutual aid is one of the signs of friendship. Its activity frequently engages not just those persons immediately connected by ties of amity but also their kin and fictive kin.

Such transactions represent the continued functionings—and even the extension—of what might be called a "traditional gift economy." In the short term, goods are occasionally exchanged in a manner that appears to approximate barter—bananas and labor for tin; mangos or avocados for child care or clothes. In the long term, surpluses in one household are leveled off to those households with a temporary deficit. Should deficits overwhelm the original household, what was given in friendship will be repaid in the same spirit. Thus, without actually expanding production, the social security of participants in this gift economy—whose true value is friendship—is secured. These transactions are never depicted as purely economic, and the relationships established are protected by the ideals of friendship, kinship, and compadrazgo. The relative reciprocity in these friendships is secured by two ideas: first, that no one should be stingy and withhold goods that they have and others do not, and second, that one should never try to take advantage of someone else's generosity. If a family is known to be hoarding, its members will be labeled *pinche* (stingy), and everyone in that household will be able to monitor the community's disapproval: in the circulation of hostile gossip, in community speculation about the immoral source of such a household's surplus, and in the escalation of minor confrontations and a generally chilly reception on the andén. Likewise, if a family gets the reputation of taking advantage of others—*aprovechándose*—they, too, will be increasingly shunned and will find a concomitant reduction in the number of favors coming their way. Through these dual mechanisms, the functioning of a subeconomy based on mutual reciprocity is insured.

I would not say that these are really entirely utilitarian exchanges—naked self-interest "masked" or "disguised" by the theme of friendship. Rather, I would say that the concept of amity—of friendship, of kinship, of neighborliness, and of compadrazgo—has a material dimension. And what better measure of friendship and affection than mutual assistance? Such relationships are, then, simultaneously emotional and material. People are aware of their practical side (which they pointedly deprecate when they speak of it), but such relationships are not purely economic: the demand for reciprocity and fairness extends to a range of interactions, material and emotional.

In lateral exchanges—that is, in transactions carried out among equals—the gift itself is not merely a form masking some other content, a means of reifying, fetishizing, disguising, or promoting a false consciousness about the source of value (as is the case in commodity exchange).[4] Rather, there is nothing to be masked, no exploitation to be hidden. The gift neither conceals its essentially social nature nor attempts to pass itself off as an object independent of morality. Two exceptions apply: (1) Participants may attempt to "cheat" the system either by being stingy or by taking advantage of others' generosity in excess of their own real need; in these cases, they are no longer playing by the rules of gift exchange and risk severing the relationship or reducing its warmth by abusing it. (2) In vertical relationships, between nonequals, the poorer participant may attempt to stimulate a flow of goods and favors to his or her advantage, seeing the more affluent participant as "fair game." Here, the logic of the gift tilts over into the logic of *patronage,* with all the calculations and positionings-for-advantage on both sides that the term implies. And although the poorer participant in such a relationship may gain some short-run advantage over others in his or her position, the wealthier participant's gifts cost little but buy much (in service, subordination, political loyalty, and the like). Unsupported by the old rural hacienda system, these relationships today tend to be brittle and are clearly not the same sort of thing as lateral relationships. Indeed, in this case the transactions are masked, however thinly, by the rhetoric of the lateral exchanges.

Within the community of equals and among kin, and against an economy of commodities and exploitation, the gift circulates in its own realm—not as a form for conveying relative advantage but as a medium for cementing social relations. The power it carries is the power to compel reciprocity: that is, it bears a moral and ethical imperative. It establishes something like a long conversation carried out between persons engaged in its friendly network: words, favors, warmth, and goods circulate in an ongoing and reciprocal fashion; they involve participants in a larger and larger network of transactions (as kin and friends of the participants come to participate, indirectly or directly); drawing on the logic of kinship and frequently augmented by ties of compadrazgo, these ongoing transactions are likely to extend over a lifetime. In the sense that these transactions are "economic," they represent a simultaneously friendly and moral economy of the poor, against and within a larger hostile economy marked by scarcity and exploitation.

Even transactions that appear to be purely economic sometimes enter this moral subeconomy. In 1986 Doña Celia was herself hard-pressed for money, having been abandoned by her husband; at the time, her family received no source of support other than her daughter's small salary as a secretary. The only additional source of money for her household of five was a small monthly rent that she collected from the young man who lived in the rear of the house—and, when I was in town, a small and scarcely profitable fee for room and board. She never described her long-term household resident as a "boarder" or a "renter" but rather as a close friend of the family, citing his origin in her own hometown as evidence. When times were especially hard—as they usually were—she would supplement her family's income by taking in neighbors' laundry or by taking lunches to shut-ins across the city, who were too sick to cook for themselves and whose families would pay her a fee for providing them with lunch while they were away at work. One week, after I had paid the rent, I found a neighbor at Doña Celia's house washing and ironing clothes while Doña Celia herself was out washing and ironing clothes at another neighbor's house. When I asked Doña Celia about this apparently baffling practice, she explained it to me as follows: "That poor woman has three small children, not one of them old enough to work, and her husband ran out on her. She needed the money, and she was too proud to take charity. So I hired her to do the laundry."

As if that weren't enough of an explanation, I pressed further. My questions solicited a recitation of the woman's good qualities and the warm tone of the two women's relationship. "Because she's *buena gente* [good people], *muy amable* [very kind, very nice]. She works hard to take care of her children, she's a good Christian, and she's a good friend of mine."

FOOD

For the majority of Nicaraguan workers, just feeding one's family was a constant challenge in the late 1980s. New clothes or other household items were generally out of the question; indeed, most Nicaraguans struggled to obtain the basic necessities of food and shelter. The inventory below indicates the price (in córdobas) of various household necessities for the week of 25–31 May 1988:[5]

	puesto (subsidized)	*mercado* (unsubsidized)
pound of sugar	C$5	C$20
bar of soap	5	100
pound of rice	4.10	40
liter of cooking oil	16	150
pound of beans	18	35

This information was gathered some months after the introduction of the new currency in February. For the first month of the new cur-

TABLE 1.   COST OF THREE STAPLE GOODS FOR
A FAMILY OF SEVEN[a]

	Amount per person per day	Family of seven per day	Family of seven per month	Cost per month
Rice	0.33 lbs.	2.31 lbs.	71.61 lbs.	C$2,864
Beans	0.25 lbs.	1.75 lbs.	54.25 lbs.	1,899
Sugar	0.12 lbs.	0.84 lbs.	26.0 lbs.	520
				C$5,283

[a] Data on prices collected 25–31 June 1988. At this time, $1.00 U.S. = C$13 at the official rate, C$100 on the black market.

rency, most people reported a sharp gain in purchasing power. Within a month, though, the same hyperinflation that had sapped the old currency was already taking its toll on the new. By May, purchasing power had declined to its pre-February level. Although the prices listed above varied a great deal from week to week, the relative prices remained fairly constant for most of the late 1980s.

By 1988 foods at the subsidized prices were routinely unavailable in the state-supported *puestos;* the *mercado* (market) prices were the effective prices.

A simple calculation (table 1) demonstrates the terrible predicament facing working-class families in Managua. In 1988 even the *maximum* basic salary for a worker supporting a family of six would buy only about 60 percent of what government economists called the "basic basket" of forty-six essential products (see IHCA 1988a, 30). Obviously, most workers were not receiving the maximum salary. In the salary range of most workers, even two incomes would prove inadequate. In Doña Flora's family (which included seven family members living in one house), monthly salaries (for May) totaled only 4,000 córdobas (about $40): Aida contributed 1,500 córdobas; Clara, 2,500. Given the prices shown in table 1, Aida's and Clara's *combined* incomes would purchase only 76 percent of the family requirements in rice, beans, and sugar *alone*. At 400 córdobas, a bottle of aspirin would have taken one-tenth of the family's monthly income; a pair of jeans, at 1,600 córdobas, exceeded Aida's income for a whole month.

Under such circumstances, how did people make ends meet? Working-class subsidies played an important role. Occasionally, staple foods

were available at very low prices through workplace commissaries designated as subsidies for productive labor. Thus, when it was available,
Aida could purchase the following package for only 145 córdobas (Clara,
however, was not eligible: her executive secretarial position was classified as management, not labor):

  10 pounds of rice
  10 pounds of beans
   5 pounds of sugar
   1 liter of oil
   4 bars of soap
   1 large can of powdered milk

This package made up much—though not all—of the difference between purchasing power and market prices in beans, rice, and sugar.
Such subsidies plainly had a major impact on consumption in working-
class households. But they were not enough to alleviate the crisis. Such
packages were available in theory only once a month; in practice, their
delivery was frequently late, and their availability was sporadic. And,
of course, a household must have more than beans, rice, and sugar to
survive.

Without additional income, the economic situation of Doña Flora's
family of seven would have been a desperate one indeed. Under the
circumstances, it seems clear that the family would have almost certainly suffered the effects of malnutrition. Additional income was provided by Zelmira, who lived with the family and contributed to household expenses, and by Rolando, who periodically sent money from the
United States.

A typical daily diet in the Pérez house went as follows: the day began
with a breakfast of french bread (two pieces), butter (when it was available), and heavily sugared coffee. Lunch was beans and rice, with perhaps a bit of cheese on the side, and whatever was left of the bread from
breakfast. It was always served with a heavily sugared fruit drink, made
either from oranges and lemons picked in the backyard or from fruits
purchased at the market. Dinner was again beans and rice, usually stirred
together and refried (gallo pinto), with perhaps some fried cheese and a
tortilla for each member of the family. Dinner was invariably served
with a large glass of pinol (a toasted cornmeal drink) or pinolillo (pinol
mixed with ground cacao). Between meals and after dinner, people ate

whatever was available from backyard trees—green, salted mangos, an occasional fruit. The Pérezes were fortunate: they always had beans and rice; they usually had condiments of cheese, butter, milk, or tortillas; and roughly once a week, household income warranted a stew or special dish for variety. Others were not so fortunate. Households whose incomes fell below the national average consumed only beans and rice. And if their incomes fell substantially lower, there was not even enough beans and rice.

Over the course of living in Erasmus Jiménez, and despite the acute shortages which made beans and rice the regular meal, I had the opportunity to observe the preparation of dishes with special, sentimental, or holiday value. *Bajo,* a prized dish, is a hearty pork or beef stew, stocked with indigenous vegetables and tubers. Chop suey, oddly enough, is Managua's preferred dish for birthday parties. *Vigorón* is fried pork skins (*chicharrón*) served on a spicy bed of raw, shredded cabbage and cooked, sliced yucca. *Nacatamales* are a Nicaraguan version of tamales: a cornmeal jacket with pork and vegetables inside, wrapped in a banana leaf and boiled until done.

Nicaraguans prepare such dishes in a mood of generosity and sociability. No one would send beans and rice to her neighbors, but whenever a special meal is prepared, samples are sent up and down the block to neighbors and friends. Ordinarily, Managuan families do not take their meals together; people eat individually when they arrive home or when they are hungry. But when valued or holiday food is prepared, people dine together and commune.

As time passed, I became acutely aware of the generosity that special food mandates. Indeed, I can say that at some level I came to appreciate this mandatory generosity: it was impressed on me often enough by means subtle and not so subtle. I once prepared a banquet of spaghetti and meat sauce for Doña Flora's family: real ground beef—a rarity in Managua—and ample fresh tomatoes for the sauce, flavored with a variety of fresh spices and served on a bed of pasta. As we sat to sup, Doña Jazmina entered forcibly into my mind, and I recalled that she had made a short visit to our house earlier that afternoon and had seen me preparing the meal. She knew that we were eating spaghetti, and we all knew that she and her family had none. It would not go too far to say that Doña Jazmina, or rather my image of her, *demanded* a serving of spaghetti—for I knew that tomorrow she would be pointedly *not* mentioning it, and I knew that there would be hurt feelings and an implicit judgment of my character were she not to receive any. As I finished my plate, enjoying it somewhat less than I had imagined I would, I resolved to take her a large helping immediately. My timing, however, was off. Flora, who had finished before me, absented herself for a moment. Sopping the last bit of sauce off the plate, I looked up and saw that Flora had entered the house with Jazmina. She was serving the latter a large helping of spaghetti and saying that I had invited Jazmina to try my recipe. Doña Jazmina ate heartily but saved enough of the serving to take some back for the rest of her family.

After witnessing several such disbursements of festive, prized, or special food, and in consultation with several female informants (who would in any case be the ones making such decisions), I began compiling a list of general rules for the distribution of valued food items: (1) Whoever helps prepare the food will receive some of it. This includes even neighbors who drop by for a few minutes to chat and end up stirring the pot or throwing in a few spices. Friends and neighbors are far more likely to lend a hand preparing special dishes than cooking routine ones. (2) Whoever lends any vegetables, tubers, or spices to the woman preparing the food will also be offered a serving of the completed dish. This, too, is a not infrequent occurrence, as there is much lending back and forth between neighbors. Chronic shortages, too, imply that at least some assistance will be necessary in preparing a complicated dish. (3) Whoever *sees* the food, while it is being prepared or afterward, is likely to be offered some. Again, with neighbors going and coming on short visits for most of the day, it is almost a certainty that several neighbors will see the food.[6] (4) To a lesser extent, and at the cook's discretion, portions may also be sent to others: to friends and compadres with some regularity; to someone known to know about the meal (by word of mouth), even if they haven't seen it; to friendly neighbors experiencing hard times.

The distribution of food in this manner crescendoes during Purísima, the feast of the Immaculate Conception, which celebrates the Virgin Mary's purity (see Lancaster 1988b, 52–54). A family that "throws a Purísima," or sponsors the feast, invites the entire range of its acquaintances to the house, serving them roast pork, vigorón, nacatamales, candied mangos, and other delicacies. The larger Purísimas occupy much of the house and the front porch and spill over into the andén. At one neighbor's Purísima, as the woman of the house was serving food, two urchins from another neighborhood seated themselves with the group and awaited their servings with plaintive expressions. "Who are you?"

she asked. "We don't know you." The small boys first attempted to con the harried woman into believing that they were distant relations; when that failed, they simply asserted that they were hungry. They were eventually served.

Such formalized sharing does not account for as much in the way of calories as it accounts for in the way of enjoyment. In itself, it probably cannot greatly affect the overall nutrition of a poor population. But it can and does cement mutual ties between friends and neighbors. And, of course, that counts for something.

COMPADRAZGO

Compadrazgo is the traditional ritual practice of coparenting. An infant's parents select a compadre (cofather) and comadre (comother) for the child's baptism; the compadres (coparents) act as sponsors at the baptism and enter into a long-term relationship with the child. The godparents are putatively in charge of the child's religious and moral instruction. They also act as protectors and sympathetic ears in times of distress; they are expected to provide material aid in the child's upbringing, and they are to serve as parents should the biological parents die. In essence, compadrazgo is a spiritual gift: the potential—and sometimes real—gift of a child. And it is not simply godparents who are joined to their godchildren in this relationship, but, as the term suggests, parents to coparents and, indeed, whole families to whole families. Compadrazgo provides a particularly fitting means of extending one's social network. It can supervalidate kin and in-law relationships by redoubling the multiple connections of persons within the compadrazgo relationship; it can intensify existing close friendships by sealing them within a religious and familial context; and it can generate new relationships at a social distance.[7] Through frequent visits and the perpetual exchange of goods and favors, compadrazgo networks circulate emotional support and mutual aid among their participants: advice, food, supplies, clothing, and medicine all change hands in routine fashion. In established working-class neighborhoods, neighbors are linked not just by proximity but by fictive kin relationships. Most households on the andén where I lived in Erasmus Jiménez were linked in this manner to at least one other household on the same andén. If one counts nearby andenes in the same barrio, virtually all the households on the andén were linked to at least one household nearby.

Compadrazgo in Nicaragua is richer than it might appear at first glance, for it engages not just the actual comadres and compadres in a social network with parents and children, but also everyone closely attached to the relationship. I found that the best means of extending my own networks of informants was simply to engage myself—and allow myself to be engaged—in compadrazgo's circulation of goods and favors. Thus, I was introduced to Doña Jazmina and her family because Marco-Polo asked me to take some photos of his godson, Josué-Luis. A little later, when Josué-Luis was overwhelmed with diarrhea, his grandmother stopped by Doña Celia's house to ask if anyone had any advice or medication. Doña Celia, in turn, asked if I had any medicine. I did, and thus I became progressively engaged in regular visits to the Alvarez household. Such examples multiplied over time, and my own networks of informants began to duplicate interlacing networks of fictive kin. My strategy also had the effect, I realized later, of distributing my primary informants disproportionately among households headed by women. Single mothers are especially active traffickers of goods and favors among kin and fictive kin.[8] They—and their fatherless children—were more likely to solicit my assistance and friendship than were either adult men or married mothers. They were also more likely to cooperate in my research by giving forthright answers to my questions—not only as a means of reciprocating my material and medical aid but also, I believe, as a means of discussing their particularly acute social, personal, and economic dilemmas.

In the context of Nicaragua's economic crisis, compadrazgo played a critical role in circulating and allotting resources. Three levels of goods and services correspond to a hierarchy of exchange types. "Plentiful goods" are inexpensive and are circulated with high frequency, largely within one's own neighborhood. Neighbors, friends, and nearby compadres may be called on for small amounts of food (often lent), small favors, information, advice, and readily exchangeable services such as child care. "Intermediary goods" are more expensive and are exchanged with less frequency. These goods include some medical equipment (for example, syringes), used clothing, and farm food in bulk; they usually circulate beyond the immediate neighborhood. Distant compadres and relatives in other towns and barrios are most frequently engaged in such transactions. "Scarce goods" are, by definition, costly and are exchanged less often: U.S. dollars, electric appliances, manufactured goods, expensive or rare medicine. Because these goods are scarce, one can hardly call on one's own neighbors or nearby kin, who face the same scarcity. Distantly located kin, especially close relatives living in the United States, are the most likely sources of aid in these transactions. Although compadres rarely figure directly—as sources—in these transactions, they often figure as intermediaries. That is, gifts or remittances from relatives abroad are often entrusted to compadres living abroad for delivery. Thus, although it is unusual for padrinos living abroad to send a great deal of material aid from the United States to their compadres, it is not unusual for them to carry goods and money from their compadres' blood relatives to their godchild's family members when they come to Nicaragua for family visits of their own. (Indeed, the rules of compadrazgo extend to cities such as New York, San Francisco, and Miami, and such networks of ready-made compadrazgo relationships, along with family connections proper, provide the social fabric that cushions the new arrival in a strange and disorienting land.)

The choice of *padrinos* (godparents) for one's children is, from the outset, strategic. Does it make more sense to choose a couple as *padrino* (godfather) and *madrina* (godmother)? Or to select both godparents from unrelated households, thus doubling the potential social field while perhaps diminishing its intensity? Should one choose padrinos from near kin, neighbors, or associates at a distance? From the same or higher social class? Each option carries its advantages and disadvantages. The closer one is socially to a person—by way of kinship, neighborhood, or class—the more likely the bond of compadrazgo will prove enduring. But the more socially distant a person is, by the same measures, the wider one casts one's net. Most people opt to vary their strategies, building up networks through different children along supplementary routes.

1. Some compadres are selected from within close family relations (parents' siblings, cousins) and in-laws, to tighten preexisting family bonds (and, for the mother, to insure continued aid from the father's family should the father himself exit).

2. Some compadres of equal status are selected from among one's network of friends; these usually live in the same neighborhood or barrio. On the same principle, one might select compadres from among one's coworkers. Such relations can be readily called on for favors, as they live close at hand or are encountered on a daily basis.

3. Naturally, many people maintain compadrazgo relations in their town or province of origin, choosing, for example, their parents' neighbors—people with whom they might want to maintain friendship over the years.

4. Other compadres are selected precisely because they are of higher social status. These compadres often live farther away, and the relation-

ship itself is usually relatively stiff and formal. The advantage of this sort of relationship is obvious: padrinos of a higher social standing can deliver goods normally out of one's own reach. Here, compadrazgo displays the logic of patronage, and it is indeed patronage that is being sought out when one contracts such a relationship. Especially favored are doctors: they cannot refuse their services to their *ahijados* (godchildren). Lawyers, too, make a fine choice should the child or its family encounter legal difficulties. This arrangement functions smoothly as long as the other, more affluent side recognizes the utility of the social contract—which is to say, social compromise, a sense of responsibility to one's subordinates in a system of class stratification, and the long-term value of securing loyalty from one's subordinates (especially one's employees, or one's dependents in the old hacienda system) by binding them into such relationships and providing occasional favors. Logically, whatever one's own social standing, one may be asked to be a padrino to a child of equal or lower social status; one will choose a padrino for one's own child of equal or higher status than one's self.

5. A relatively new strategy seems to be emerging in various households: selecting padrinos from among relatives living abroad. By redoubling an existing kin connection (between, for example, cousins), this strategy maintains family relationships that might otherwise be severed by great geographic distances or political differences; it also provides access to assistance in U.S. dollars, as well as occasional gifts of manufactured items that would be prohibitively expensive in Nicaragua.

In the end, an ideal strategy would be to select compadres from among both social equals and social superiors and from those both close at hand and at various distances. The familiar and friendly relations are engaged in economic, material, and emotional transactions of "generalized reciprocity" (Sahlins 1968, 82–83; 1972, 193–94)—that is, friendly transactions of a sort that are not formally tallied and weighed but that balance out in the long run. From one's social superiors, one seeks material and economic patronage. In thus contracting out compadrazgo relationships, one also constructs a unique social map of the world as a series of pathways and connections between various others: paths along which one might accept, as well as provide, material aid, comfort, friendship, and security.

In this fashion, compadrazgo performs several simultaneous roles. At one end of the scale, its egalitarian system of mutual aid perpetually reallocates resources in lower-class neighborhoods and provides some measure of insurance against disaster and distress. At the other end of the scale, when embodied as patronage, it has the effect of blunting (though certainly not masking) class antagonisms. My informants were quite aware of the patronage involved in compadrazgo between non-equals: they occasionally referred to upper-class padrinos as *patrones;* they self-consciously sought out such relationships for the patronage they might provide; and they speculated about the other's class motivations in participating in such relationships. Despite the egalitarian rhetoric of the gift in this case, no one is actually fooled about the nature of class inequality. Many of my informants also insist that, since the revolution, such relationships have become more brittle and less common, forcing a more "egalitarian" or lateral distribution of padrino choices. During the revolution, large numbers of upper-class professionals abandoned Nicaragua and severed relations with all but their own family members. Godparents who had once been politically choice—because of their connection to the Somoza regime and the political favors they might deliver—fled the country at the time of the revolution, cutting all compadrazgo ties to the lower classes who had removed them from power. Subsequently, too, middle- to upper-class Nicaraguans migrated permanently to the United States more often than did members of the lower classes. Indeed, most people had lost track of their upper-class compadres, and they had lost contact with them precisely in the political earthquake of the revolution. And according to various informants, in an atmosphere of acute class struggle, affluent Nicaraguans were less likely to accept invitations to be godparents, and poorer Nicaraguans were less likely to forward invitations. With the decline of such patronage choices, people increasingly contracted their relations closer to home, within one's circle of kin (whether they lived in Nicaragua or abroad), and among one's own friends.

Finally, a new variant of godparent choice became available and proliferated: the political or ideological selection. Sandinista militants, political organizers, class-conscious coworkers, and neighborhood activists are remarkably interlinked with each other through the bonds of fictive kin. These bonds are generally similar to other compadrazgo relations between equals (although the solicitation of one's superiors for political patronage, too, was present). Every one of my informants who might be described as highly politicized—whether they were lower-ranking members of the Frente or the Youth Organization or just strong Sandinista sympathizers—was entangled with at least one such relationship of what might be called "ideological compadrazgo." Relations who called each other *compañero* ("companion"; in this case, the term bears something of the force of *comrade*) at the beginning of the revolution became, during the decade of the revolution, compadres, which they will remain for life.

This development has remained unreported in the literature on Nicaragua. But if political memories are long in Central America—the Sandinistas named themselves in the 1960s after a nationalist movement that had been wiped out in the 1930s—Nicaraguan cultural practices afford numerous mnemonic techniques for preserving, remembering, and binding people together in the face of adversity. And if the Sandinista position has remained stronger than many analysts predicted in the wake of its electoral defeat, memory and resilience may owe more to compadrazgo than is immediately apparent. A revolutionary decade was more than long enough for leftist political and ideological identifications to acquire the traditional form of an association of fictive kin.

CHAPTER V

Chicken Soup;
or, Gossip, Tradition,
and the Anthropologist

Gossip is a text crafted with many signals of confidence and conspiracy, highlighted with a glance to see if somebody is listening, phrased to titillate with the most savory or unsavory bit reserved for the ending. One could not divorce the inflections of voice, the body posture, the signs of intimacy from all the techniques of storytelling in a gossip's performance of history. We who hear the gossip have a fine sense of its poetics as we separate the snide from the good-humored, commit ourselves or suspend our judgement of its truth, know what friendly relations are damaged or enhanced by it. We produce histories by performing them and we live by being critics of their theatre.

—Greg Dening, *History's Anthropology*

Imagine, if you will, that it is 1978. The revolution is fast advancing. In the wake of the assassination of Pedro Joaquín Chamorro, editor of *La prensa*, by the Guardia Nacional, there have been hunger strikes, labor strikes, protests, and demonstrations. An uprising in Masaya's indigenous barrio, Monimbó, has been put down after a bloody fight, and no other cities have yet followed suit. Instead, the Sandinistas are developing a framework within the working-class communities of Managua, León, Granada, and Estelí, whose organization will eventually culminate in massive, simultaneous urban insurrections across Nicaragua. Students in Erasmus Jiménez are joining Sandinista mass organizations or working as clandestine activists for the Tercerista faction of the FSLN. A few have gone to the mountains, recruited as *guerrilleros* (guerrilla fighters) by the Prolonged Popular War faction. Parents, too, have been participating in the struggle against Somoza's dictatorship through the local Christian base communities and through various political organizations. As quickly as the revolution is gaining ground, so, too, is Somoza accelerating his preventive measures, counterreactions, and methods of violent suppression.

People, especially teenagers, begin disappearing. Often their bodies show up the next day, frequently mutilated—the work of Somoza's Guardia Nacional. Horrible mutilations. Grave signs. Dire warnings.

How do people speak about such obscene events? The Guardia Nacional still comes and goes throughout the neighborhood. Indeed, known and suspected informants live in the community. Who does one trust, and who does one not trust?

Three women sit in a house in rocking chairs. (Most people in Managua prefer rockers to couches or regular chairs, and the living room holds six rockers, all built by Masaya's woodworkers.) The three women are united by long-standing friendships, lending relationships, and fictive kinship. Out back, on the packed-dirt patio, younger women—their daughters—sit and talk. In the street, children play and young men socialize. All are passing between them the information they need under such circumstances—naturally, in inconspicuous cadences. In quiet murmurs, low voices, set to the creaky rhythm of the rocking chairs, the women's talk goes something like this:

First Woman: Did you see what they did to her? Did you see? [*It is not necessary to specify the victim: everybody already knows who she is.*]

Second Woman: Yes.

Third Woman: My niece told me about it.

Second Woman: It was very horrible. [*She pauses.*] Barbaric.

First Woman: Barbaric and cruel. Damn the sons of bitches!

Such discourses were textured into the fabric of commonplace small talk, woven into the cloth of everyday community life. And ten years later, when recounting events leading up to the revolution—especially when discussing Guardia atrocities—the same women still speak in low voices, still exchange a sideways glance, a conspiratorial look, as though to take the anthropologist into their confidences. For how else would one relate such events? And how else would one tell how one told of such events?

Drawing in part on Jacobo Timmerman's account of torture and terror in Argentina, Michael Taussig describes the "culture of terror, the space of death" as "nourished by the intermingling of silence and myth" (1987, 8). Silence is the operative concept: terror aims to produce silence in its victims and in whole communities of people. But this was not the case in Managua's neighborhoods. What resulted was not a silence at all, but the deafening roar of whispers.

Paradoxically, the terror signified by torture would have no meaning were real silence to surround it. Torture, atrocities, and assassination simultaneously command silence and enjoin discourse. Thereby their terror is secured and magnified: in gossip, whispers, rumors, murmurs. By this means, too, terror is committed to the political memory of the community—a way of remembering that sometimes metamorphoses into resistance. The relationship between the clandestinity of gossip, which is the very stuff of community opinion, and the clandestinity of the massing revolution was by no means accidental.

Gossip, too, was the medium of much political discourse under the Sandinistas (Lancaster 1988b, 145–63). Which officials were enriching themselves at the public expense? Which were shielding their sons from military service? Why were there shortages, and what happened to the food? What had the revolution delivered or failed to deliver? So, too, I imagine that many people sensed the impending electoral defeat of the Sandinistas far in advance of the polls and the pollsters. Gossip, as semi-private, semipublic talk, is the most sensitive, most accurate, and least easily monitored index of public opinion; indeed, it is the very dialogical structure of public opinion, which never quite becomes public because it belongs to the community of speakers.

THE PRACTICES OF GOSSIP

Gossip, then, is not a trivial matter. Rarely seen but ever present, it is the means by which people—especially women, but also men—share the information they need to plan meaningfully for the future and to cope with the realities of life. In the Nicaraguan vernacular, *comadre* connotes "gossip," and this is a telling point. Gossip is an ongoing conversation, at once intimate and practical, conducted among people who have long-standing relationships, who share interests, and who pool resources and information. It is the medium that supports a host of institutions: compadrazgo networks, informal lending relationships, and long-term friendships.

The same word of mouth, the same conversations that reveal who is having an affair with whom, who has recently come into money, and who is having marital problems also and quite matter-of-factly carry practical information: whether the gas truck has delivered its weekly supply of propane to the neighborhood store; that chickens are available at such and such a market; and what the price of tomatoes is on a given day in the Mercado Oriental. In the context of acute shortages, hyperinflation, and soaring unemployment, and given the important role of gossip in facilitating a wide range of relationships, such economic applications of gossip are anything but trivial. For ordinary working-class families, being well-connected on the gossip grapevine could mean the difference between a barely adequate diet and malnutrition. Gossip is a flexible and fecund way of talking. It can take up almost any subject and imbue it with significance. It encompasses divergent practicalities and facilitates innumerable practices.

As an anthropologist working in Managua's neighborhoods, much of my information came to me by way of gossip. I imagine that if anthropologists were honest about their sources of information, most of us would have to admit that we work a great deal in and through the medium of gossip. And it is also clear that I was a particularly fertile subject for gossip's ongoing and open-ended negotiation with reality. I was, at least at first, an outsider, about whom very little was known, in a neighborhood where people are accustomed to knowing the most intimate sorts of details about a person's life. I became well aware that, out of view, the most delicate details of my stay in Managua were passing into the public domain: the color of my underwear, roughly how much money I was carrying, where I went on various rounds, how often I ate out. Over time I became sensitive to the sorts of information that could be shared, or concealed, in gossip.

Trinh T. Minh-ha (1989, 67–70) critiques ethnographic method in general terms when she objects to anthropology as "gossip about other people's gossip"; that is, it is gossip being gossiped about. (One might as easily call it "stories about other people's stories" or "talk talked about.") In so doing, she draws a dubious dichotomy: on the one side, legitimate gossip, which lies within a "real" speech community; on the other side, illegitimate gossip, which is carried by the anthropologist across the borders of community, culture, ethnicity, society. Gossip within a community is not always as innocuous—nor is cross-cultural gossip always as malicious—as Trinh's discussion suggests. For cochones, for example, gossip is indeed the prison-house of language. The power of gossip is real, and it can never be entirely "innocent" of the relations in which it is embedded and which it in turn structures.

The real political problem with anthropology is not that it sorts other people's dirty laundry in print, in public, or for other people, nor that it utilizes "their" meanings for "our" intellectual enrichment (or aggrandizement), nor even that it generates "fictions" about other people's "realities." Rather, the intimacy of detail provided by good ethnographic fieldwork carries with it a very real danger: that anthropology will degenerate, by degrees, into eavesdropping, snooping, spying, and thereby integrate its observational powers into the system of colonial and neocolonial power that today dominates the globe. If anthropology really understands anything systematic about the nature of custom, belief, kinship, family, economics, and political power in this or that society, then that understanding can provide the levers whereby marketing, advertising, international business, and foreign governments can pry open, exploit, and dominate the societies in question. Research, like talk, always carries with it a political and moral dimension because no one can hold at bay the real power relations that are always its context (and generally its intention as well). Good, critical, reflexive ethnography at least carries with it certain correctives: an awareness of the dimensions of local and global power; a willingness to treat those power relations critically, antagonistically; an understanding of the role of ideology in producing knowledge of any sort; a recognition that one-way observation is always a power relationship; and, at the most extreme, a willingness to be silent when speech clearly threatens the other.

Trinh's stance is at core a *proprietary* one, in both senses of the term: she is concerned with both *property* and *propriety*. For Trinh, legitimate gossip is the property of some all-encompassing community of otherness (as defined and subjugated by colonialism); when it is appropriated by someone not-other (the anthropologist, the colonialist), this appropriation for her represents a theft, and because it is removed from its community of origin, a distortion approaching the structure of a lie. Nothing, however, could be less in the spirit of gossip than the notion of *propriety*, in the sense of property. The gossiping voice willfully asserts that information is *not* individual property but belongs to us all. Through face-to-face interaction, gossip establishes a true collectivism of language. It is all give-and-take. Nothing truly belongs to anyone; it all circulates in the form of information, speculation, between and among us. Roland Barthes (1982, 430–31), too, misses the point—for gossip is not a closed mausoleum but a free creative form, the very essence of Bakhtinian dialogue. Perhaps its shuffling of pronouns and referents temporarily distorts this or that, relegates him or her to the status of an object of interest, but sooner or later its very mechanisms level all differences, and we all enter its circuitry: as speaker, spoken-to, and spoken-about. In this sense, gossip provides the very model for a reflexive, dialogical, critical anthropology in that it puts everything on the anthropologist's side of the discourse as much at risk as everything on the other side.

Remaining objections to gossip as a form, and to writing about gossip, might best be met (1) by the humility of admitting from the outset limited, partial, and one-sided knowledge; (2) by providing as accurate a picture as possible of the real, circuitous circulation of gossip; (3) by placing the anthropologist plainly *within* the circulation of gossip (as both its subject and its object), and (4) by drawing out as plainly as possible his or her sources of information.

Why do we savor this endless trafficking in the trivia of life? Is it maliciousness? During my stay in Nicaragua, I was rarely exposed to truly malicious gossip. Malicious discourse signifies the failure of gossip in its normal state, which is to say, its existence as a social lubricant. Such malicious gossip no doubt exists, but no one wants to acknowledge it. Everyone denies *hablando mal de la gente* (talking badly about folks; bad-mouthing people) at least in part because malicious gossip carries with it an implicit threat: that we who speak ill of others will appear worse than those about whom we speak.

On the contrary, it is not simple malice that makes gossip so delightful. Rather, gossip provides us with a form of discourse that is at once useful and playful. It is the perfect unity of form and function, aesthetics and utility. Gossip is essentially *tacky,* and this "tackiness" means simultaneously that it sticks to us all (speaker, spoken-to, spoken-about) and that it sticks us together, binds us in tangible ways. Its boundaries are amorphous and undefinable; it is a plastic and malleable form of discourse.

Of course, gossip is always strategic: one tries to advance one's own fortunes through the medium; through this form of discourse one also attempts to gain privileged access to information, secrets, or material resources. There is defensive gossip just as surely as there is offensive gossip; and there is also gossip in which all the participants meet on a common ground of group self-interest. The very structure of gossip (not its subject matter) implies its efficacy. For gossip is a quintessentially open form, an exploratory discourse. People use gossip to provide themselves, their family, and their community with all sorts of experimental assays of the world around them while remaining grounded in some semblance of empiry. The sorts of information it can provide are virtually limitless.

THE PATHS OF GOSSIP

CHICKEN SOUP AND THE CIA

It was a sweltering day in June 1985, and I was walking down the andén in Erasmus Jiménez on my way to the neighborhood *tienda popular* (popular store) to buy a chicken. Part of the CDS (Comités de Defensa Sandinista; Sandinista Defense Committees) system of services, the tiendas populares marketed a variety of basic foods at state-subsidized prices. Perhaps the quality of food available there was lower than what could be found in the marketplace, but Managua's Mercado Oriental and the closer Roberto Huembes were at least thirty minutes away, and haggling could prove both time-consuming and less than economical for an obviously North American patron, so I simply went to the local popular store to make my purchase. A neighbor had already told me that chickens had been delivered that morning, so I was optimistic that I would still find some there.

Doña Celia had come down with a case of dengue—or, at any rate, what she called "dengue"; after the first outbreaks of the epidemic, many people began calling every passing flu "dengue." She might have had either a severe flu or a relatively mild case of dengue. I was going to prepare her some chicken soup, hoping it would make her feel better. I was also planning to record the prices of various goods available in the popular store. Carrying notebook and pen, I must have looked more officious than I thought I did. A drunken old man, staggering down the andén in my direction, stopped to talk to me. We exchanged greetings, and then he uttered a string of vowels and consonants that proved entirely unintelligible. I responded, "*¿Qué? ¿Cómo?*" and he repeated himself, again completely beyond any semblance of intelligibility. "I'm sorry," I said, "I don't understand," and excused myself. I wondered if I had perhaps been too abrupt with him, but the temperature was 105 degrees, we were standing in the sun, and already the perspiration was beginning to stick the shirt to my back.

I went into the store, which conjoins the owner's house, and said, "*¿Hay pollo?*" (Do you have chicken?) "Yes," the proprietor, Don Pablo, told me, "there in the icebox. How many pounds?" I was trying to decide how large the chicken should be when the drunk old man appeared in the doorway, waving his arms and raving that he had caught an agent of the CIA trying to spy on Nicaragua. "*¡La CIA!*" he kept shouting. I turned and realized that he was talking about me.

Drawn by the disturbance, Don Pablo's wife quietly appeared behind the counter. An always serious woman, she now wore an even more concerned look on her face. "What are you talking about?" Doña Carmen gently demanded, as one would of a drunken older man, a mixture of admonishment and respect in her voice. "Him!" the old man shouted. "This one! He's here to spy on Nicaragua, and I caught him. You are the CDS, arrest him!"

Now it was Don Pablo's turn to speak. "Now what makes you think this *joven* [youth] is CIA?" "Because," replied the old man with a flourish of cunning, "I spoke to him in English, and he pretended that he didn't understand what I was saying! Now why else would he do that unless he were trying to conceal his nationality? And why would he conceal his nationality unless he were trying to hide something? He must be CIA. Arrest him!"

I was growing concerned because the old man was now blocking the doorway, and it would scarcely have been appropriate for me to push my way past him. I was trying to figure out how to prevent this from becoming an even more unpleasant scene when Don Pablo's wife walked over to the meatbox, pulled out a chicken, and asked me if it were acceptable. I said that it was, and she put it on the scales. "Two and a half pounds," she observed, and then turned to address the old man. With an air of authority, she announced, "Listen, compañero, this isn't a spy from the CIA. This is Róger Lancaster, a friend of Nicaragua from the United States. He's an anthropology student at the University of California at Berkeley—not Los Angeles, there's another one in Berkeley, which doesn't have a basketball team. He's working on his doctoral dissertation, and he's here studying the role of religion in our revolution, especially the Popular Church. When he goes back, he's going to tell the truth about Nicaragua, and our revolution, and it will be good for us."

I listened with amazement. I had never been inside the popular store before, and I didn't even know either the proprietor or his wife by their names. I had seen them only in passing, and we had never been introduced. Yet here was Doña Carmen, accurately describing my credentials and my research topic. Gossip moves quietly but quickly on the streets of the neighborhoods.[1]

The old man continued to disagree; it had apparently become quite firmly lodged in his mind that I was up to no good, and he was perplexed that he seemed to be the only one who could see it. The proprietor gently positioned himself between the old man and myself, and his wife took me by the arm, making a gesture with her hand to indicate confusion. "*No te preocupe', amorcito. Está picado,*" she said. ("Don't let it bother you, honey. The old man is stung," a euphemism for drunk.) With that, she ushered me behind the counter and through the back door, which led into their house, and out through a side door. "But how much does the chicken cost?" I asked. She told me the price and said, "Pay me later. You can send Lenín with the money. Just get on back home before the old man gets out; he's very agitated." I could still hear him ranting at Don Pablo, apparently enraged at having been delayed on his mission to capture me. I walked back home, quickly.

CHICKEN SOUP? A CURE? WHOEVER HEARD OF THAT?

"You're going to like this soup, Doña Celia. It's my own special recipe." I tried to think of the Spanish for "It's good for what ails you," but I could come up with only "*Es buena para la salud.*" "It's good for your health? Chicken soup?" She had risen from her bed: face drawn, hair disheveled, looking every bit the part of dengue victim. "Whoever heard of such a thing?"

"Yes, yes," I told her. "In the United States, many people believe that chicken soup is a great cure for various sicknesses—colds, influenza. It may or may not be true; I suppose it's popular medicine. Anyway, it'll make you feel better. You won't have to do any cooking today: just relax, there'll be plenty for everybody. See, I've got garlic and chile peppers here, for strength. They might kill microbes, too. Well, I think so, anyway. I've got peppers and celery here for vitamins. Potatoes and spaghetti noodles for carbohydrates—energy food." "And what's the chicken for?" she wanted to know. I was stumped. "Just because . . . well, it's the chicken that's good for whatever's the matter with you," I improvised. "People have believed in chicken soup for hundreds of years. Who am I to say that they're wrong?"

At suppertime Doña Celia sat on the edge of her bed and ate her soup with a tablespoon. "How is it?" I asked. "*¡Riquísimo!*" she replied, making one of her rare appreciative faces. "*¡Pero me pica!*" she exclaimed. "It's spicy." "That proves it's working," I extemporized. I am convinced, after all, that if garlic and red chile peppers don't kill germs, nothing will. I sat at the table and ate my own bowl, breaking out in a healthy sweat.

Housewives from up and down the andén began drifting by and coming in for quick visits shortly after that: it was sunset, when most people go about visiting each other in the neighborhood. Singly and in pairs they came to see about Doña Celia and to investigate a rumor. "How are you feeling today, Celia?" they inquired, and then: "We heard that Róger was fixing you a cure. Imagine that! A man, and he knows how to cook! What is it?" "Chicken soup," she told them. The usual response was something like, "Chicken soup? A cure? Whoever heard of that?" Some were openly skeptical. Various women came up to the pot on the stove and looked in. I invited them to sample it. Two or three of the women began naming what was in it and asked me to explain the reason for including garlic, chile pepper, and the like. I did, reciting my own idiosyncratic rationales for each one. "But garlic and chile pepper, aren't they too strong for someone who's sick?" "Well, they use a lot of that stuff in Mexico, right? Even babies eat it there. And maybe it's strong enough to kill germs." Doña Celia interjected, "That's true. They eat a lot of chile in Mexico, and look how much better their health is than here in Nicaragua." That wasn't exactly the reasoning I wanted to project, but I let it go. Perhaps I was beginning to take my own reasoning a little too seriously. At least one of the visitors nodded appreciatively. "That's true. My son, who is studying at the university, tells me that it is microbes that cause sickness. Now, if you can kill the microbes, you can kill the disease." We were all nodding in agreement now.

Then, while some of our guests were still there, Doña Celia got up out of bed and announced, "I feel much better. Thank you for the cure, Róger."

I subsequently checked with several households on the andén and determined that, indeed, no one had ever heard of chicken soup as a remedy for the cold or flu.

Was it really possible, I asked myself, that nobody had ever heard of the chicken soup remedy before? Or that it could produce results so quickly? As our visitors trickled out that evening, many of them took small samples home—to taste, to eat, no doubt to experiment, and to ponder.

WINDOWS

The day before I departed, I gave Doña Celia the present I had been saving for her as a *recuerdo* (memento) and Christmas gift: several yards of cloth, in different colors and textures, which I had brought from the United States. Enough to make shirts or pants for each of her four children. Or, if she preferred, the cloth would no doubt fetch a hefty sum on the black market. I was hoping she would use the material to make clothing for herself and her children. When Doña Celia realized she was getting a gift, her first act was to walk quickly through the house, slamming shut all the doors and wooden shutters. After we were enveloped in privacy, she opened the gift, cried a bit, and thanked me. Then, she carefully hid the cloth in the rafters before reopening the doors and windows that led outside into the world and the gaze of the community. Over the next year or so, the cloth would materialize in her children's wardrobe: little by little, one article of clothing at a time.

AVOCADOS

The following year (1986), on another trip to Nicaragua, I stayed with Doña Flora and her family. I remember well how diligently she could provide for the family, drawing on all sorts of kin and fictive kin. She was, as we might say, a very active networker. One trip to the marketplace netted us a large sack of avocados, donated by her estranged husband's cousin from the countryside. We had avocados two or three times a day for several days, eating them quickly lest they spoil.

Shortly after that, I had my first bout of dengue. Dengue is the scourge of Central America, and my first case was acute and, I imagine, life-threatening. After a night of headaches and vomiting, I got up in the morning feeling like hell. Doña Félida called across the fence: "Good morning, Róger, and how are you this morning? Do you feel better? I heard you vomiting last night." "No, I feel horrible." "What's the matter?" asked Doña Flora, who was in the kitchen preparing breakfast. She must have been a sounder sleeper than our neighbor, having slept through my persistent heaving. She was watching me now for signs of illness. "Are you sick?" she asked. "No, he's not sick," volunteered Doña Félida from across the fence with an air of certainty, "He was drunk last night, and now he has a hangover." "No, señora," I corrected, "I was not drunk, and I don't have a hangover. I think I have a case of food poisoning."

"Well, just sit down, and let me bring you some juice," Doña Flora advised. "Juice is good for stomach problems." I sat slumped over and, I suppose, looking rather miserable. She brought me some juice with plenty of sugar and salt in it. "Drink it all," she demanded, and watched as I did. "Thank you, that's much better." "Do you want something to eat?" she asked. "Ay, no," I said.

Fifteen minutes later I threw up the juice, and it wasn't simple nausea. For the first time in my life I experienced projectile vomiting. As the nausea caught me suddenly and unaware, I sprayed Doña Flora's kitchen floor.

Miguel got the mop and went to work on my mess; he would hear nothing of it when I offered to clean it up myself. I thanked him and tried to collect myself. Doña Flora produced an oral thermometer; we bathed it in rum and took my temperature: 103 degrees. I became alarmed and swallowed four aspirin with some more juice and ate a bit of bread. Within thirty minutes I had thrown it all up again.

The next several hours were absolutely miserable. My head felt as though it were in a vise. My bones ached mightily: Nicaraguans call dengue *la quebradora* (the breaker, as in bone-breaker). My legs ached more fiercely even than the rest of my aching body. My temperature climbed to 104. My whole body shook with chills. I lay in bed shaking from toe to head, my teeth chattering. The breeze off the lake felt like the frigid breath of a blizzard. I tried frequent showers, intermittent ice-water baths, aspirin in large quantities, and liquids. I even tried standing inside Flora's large rainbarrel, which was full of cold water. Nothing assuaged my symptoms. Nothing brought my fever down. Nothing stopped the vomiting.

Soon the women of the neighborhood came by, singly and in small groups, to see what was wrong and offer remedies. Doña Celia did not come; she did not enter the house of Doña Flora, nor did Doña Flora enter hers (thus the latter had never come by to sample my chicken soup), but she sent her son Lenín to see about me. (As I later discovered, Doña Celia and Rolando's first wife had been very close friends; after Doña Flora moved in with Rolando, the two women were always distant.) Doña Jazmina, Doña Carmen, Doña Félida, Doña Onix, and several women I didn't even know came by. Many of them had their own hypodermic needles, and some had saved up remedies for various sorts of infections. I looked in vain for expiration dates on these medicines, but some were not even stored in their original containers. "How long have you had this?" I asked some of the women. Six months. A year. Two years. And what was it for? A variety of obscure and vague ailments. They all offered me various kinds of shots. I knew that I must be really sick, because by midafternoon I was toying with the idea of letting them inject me with God knows what.

When she got a phone call telling her that I was sick, my comadre Aida came home early from work. I could hear Doña Flora and her daughter Aida out on the patio, discussing my case in low voices. "What do you think it is?" "It looks like dengue, and a bad case." "Maybe we should take him to the hospital if it's dengue." "Maybe so." And then, even more quietly: "People are going to say we didn't take good care of him."

I lay in bed that afternoon, racked with fever and chills, shaking and thinking, detachedly, about the possibility of my own demise. I couldn't seem to get my fever to go any lower than 103, and it kept rising to 104. A couple of times it registered very nearly 105. I knew I was on the verge of delirium and seizures when I started hallucinating geometrical designs on the ceiling of my room, and I remembered a time, when I was three and a half, when I had hallucinated snakes, bears, wampus cats, and Disney cartoon characters all night long. The expression on her face let me know that Doña Flora began to be really concerned when I started laughing for no apparent reason.

Osvaldo, Doña Flora's eldest son, a member of the Frente Sandinista and a lieutenant in the army, came home early from work that day. He sat down on the bed, put his hand on my forehead, and asked me if I was all right. "I feel like shit." Osvaldo called on a neighbor, and the two arranged for use of a truck. "Róger, you ought to go to the hospital," he told me. That was the contingency I had been avoiding all day, but it seemed there was no more avoiding it. It was about five-thirty in the afternoon. The last bout of vomiting had left me feeling especially bad, and my fever was inching back up to 104. "All right," I agreed. Feebly I sat up in bed and stood up. I tried to walk and started to fall. Osvaldo caught me, draped my arm around his shoulder, and walked me out to the truck. Our neighbor joined us in the andén, took my other arm, and led me to the truck. I had the strangest sensation, being led by my two friends that way. I realized that I must have looked rather ridiculously pathetic, almost martyrlike, supported on either side in such a fashion. Such luxurious suffering! Our neighbor kept telling me jokes to keep my spirits up: "Don't worry, Róger. You're not going to die. It's just that we've got some really nasty diseases here in Nicaragua, and you're not accustomed to them. And if you do die, we'll give you the biggest send-off anyone has ever had around here. There'll be women crying, men gambling, and children playing in the streets. We'll set you up down at the end of the andén, next to the obelisk, so everyone passing by can see you." And as we passed each house, I realized that people were standing or sitting out in front of their houses—for me?—as I passed by.

I threw up only once on the way to the hospital. The swerves and bumps made me nauseous. Osvaldo would not let me sit by the door, which was loose, for fear I might fall out. So he had to hold me while I leaned across him, my head lolling out the window. After what seemed like a very long time, we arrived at the hospital. It was everything I had feared.

The hospital was not an impressive building. It looked like a warehouse that had been converted to a public hospital. Osvaldo checked me in at the front door, and we waited outside on the sidewalk with others who had shown up for acute care. Within fifteen minutes, I was inside, in a small examination room, being interviewed by a nurse. "It sounds like dengue," she said. "We'll have to run some tests to be sure. But we can go ahead now and treat the symptoms. We'll give you something to bring the fever down, and something to stop the pain, and you're badly dehydrated, so we'll rehydrate you."

I was sent to another room, where I pulled down my pants and bent over for my first shot, which was administered by another nurse. She seemed to me less professional and less solicitous than the first. I'm not fond of needles anyway, and I had great reservations about those giant, reusable Soviet needles, which seem about three times thicker than our own and have to be conscientiously sterilized. "Ay!" I shouted. She had struck the sciatic nerve. My left leg went numb all the way down to my big toe. As though on cue, I threw up. "I can't feel my leg!" I announced. The culpable nurse scolded me, good-naturedly, as though it had been my fault, "*Todos los gringos son cochones*" (All gringos are faggots).

The rest of my treatment was more pleasant. The nurses set me up in a large room with a cement floor. This chamber was well stocked with locally produced rocking chairs of the sort almost everyone has at home. The room was full of people, perhaps two dozen in all, most of whom were being treated for dengue. A blood sample was taken; I asked if the needle was sterile and was assured that it was. Then I was put on glucose, and I sat, with the others, and waited. Osvaldo came to the window, which was next to me, and we talked for a few minutes. He told me that the neighbor had to take his truck back home, but that he would come to see about me in a couple of hours.

The treatment was very effective. I didn't throw up again. Within an hour my headache was gone. Within a couple of hours I felt pretty well. Every hour or two, someone came through the room, mopping the floor with a strong mixture of chlorine and water. After a while, I noticed the tape and cotton that held the needle in my arm through which the glucose ran: they had bloodstains on them from a previous use. A nurse came by to replace my empty bag of glucose with another bag. A doctor came through and sat with some of the patients to reassure them. I remember one woman in particular; she sat the whole time crying aloud. No doubt her head ached terribly, and she was frightened. The doctor held her hand, assured her that she had nothing to be worried or frightened about, and told her that it was okay to cry if she wanted.

Aida, Doña Flora, and Miguel arrived outside the window and woke me up. It was nine or ten at night, and I felt quite well by then. Aida, who recognized the doctor as a friend of the family from León, insinuated herself inside the hospital. The nurse who had taken my temperature and interviewed me on arrival said, "We ran the blood tests. We can't find evidence of dengue, but we're pretty sure that's what you had. You should be fine now, but you may have mild symptoms for a few days. Get a lot of rest and drink plenty of liquids."

Our truck was gone, so we set out walking for Erasmus Jiménez. It was about a forty-five-minute walk. We arrived around midnight, and everyone retired to bed.

The next morning, various people in the neighborhood came by to visit me. The neighborhood had already formed a consensus on the origin of my illness. "You ate too many avocados," I was told, over and over again. "Mosquitoes give you dengue, not avocados," I insisted. No one would listen; everyone insisted that avocados had been the source of my debilitation. Nicaraguans generally think of avocados as a "strong" food. They are associated with strength and virility, and many people believe them to be an aphrodisiac. Avocado salad is the typical meal of seduction, served to men either by women or by men with a sexual interest in the recipient. By and large, avocados are eaten in moderation. As I had eaten my avocados in private, how was it that people knew I had been eating so many of them? Apparently, someone passing by or through the house had seen the sack of avocados sitting inside the house. We tried to figure out who it had been and settled on Doña Jazmina as the most likely candidate. Such a large sack would have to be consumed quickly, she might have reasoned, or it would spoil. Obviously, I had been eating a lot of avocados, even if no one outside the house had seen it. There was some concern about the propriety of feeding a young, single male so many avocados in such a short space of time, and my hosts' wisdom, motives, and hospitality were the subjects of vigorous community gossip. There was something, well, a bit *im-*

moral about it. Doña Celia announced to the neighborhood that I had never been sick when I was at *her* house, which was a clear insult to Doña Flora's hospitality. And just why were they feeding a young, healthy man so many avocados? The whole business became a touchy subject, and several arguments occurred because of it.

And two years later, people were still warning me not to eat so many avocados and reminding me of what had happened before.

SEX AND MONEY

Some two years later (1988), I was back in Nicaragua working on another project. I was again staying with Doña Flora's family, as her daughter was my comadre, and it would not have seemed right to stay anywhere but with my compadres. In the meantime, Doña Celia's family had enjoyed a dramatic increase in their fortunes. Celia's daughter, Yolanda, had obtained work as a flight attendant with a Central American airline, and was now well paid in U.S. dollars. The whole family was visibly better clothed, better shod, and better fed than they had been before; indeed, they had gone from being the poorest to being the most affluent members of the neighborhood.

Every time I visited Doña Celia, she inquired, "What are they saying about us? What are people saying?" I replied that I had heard nothing in the way of untoward talk and that people were happy for her good fortune. She asked me to report to her any malicious rumors that I heard about her. Now interested in the matter, I set about asking my closest informants, individually, what people might be saying that would give Doña Celia so much cause for alarm. Within the neighborhood everyone played innocent. "What? Talking about Celia behind her back? Of course not. I haven't heard anything bad. People are happy that her family is doing so well." Finally I raised the matter with Jaime, who lives in a nearby barrio and visits Erasmus Jiménez on a daily basis. From his distance and his perspective, I reasoned, he might be willing to be more forthright. "It should be obvious to you what people are saying," he informed me. "They're saying that Yolanda is using her sex to get a good job and that her mother is encouraging her to do that."

THE DANCING WOMAN

My informants often made inquiries about what I was writing about them and how I was presenting their practices, their culture, and their country in my writing. Sometimes their responses to my fieldnotes were defensive. Sometimes they offered to introduce me to various persons who would give me a "true" (i.e., politically correct) picture of this or that aspect of Nicaraguan society. Often they assessed my descriptions and analyses and offered correctives, useful criticisms, or endorsements. I considered this to be a normal and necessary part of fieldwork—a useful practice in any ethnographic work. Entertaining this sort of interaction was not at all difficult. While visitors came and went, I generally sat out on the front porch or near the front of the house and recorded each day's fieldnotes in a large spiral notebook. Later I typed them up and organized them by topic.

"What are you writing about us today?" asked a group of women who had gathered in Doña Celia's house. I looked up from my notebook and responded forthrightly: "I am saying that Nicaraguans are a very religious people but that they are not a very pious people. What do you think? Am I right?" "It depends," came the response, "on how you mean it. How is it that we are religious but not pious?" I recounted an event I had witnessed at San Jerónimo's fiesta in Masaya (Lancaster 1988b, 34–35). In this, Masaya's most solemn religious occasion, a very old woman had been marching and dancing in the procession, paying off a promise to the saint. Her attitude of devotion was undeniable, and she was simultaneously one of the most solemn and animated persons in the procession. However, the cobblestone streets of Masaya are very narrow, and the celebrants at this *fiesta patronal* were very numerous. So every time the band struck up its tune to inaugurate the ritual dance, the crowd pressed into the old woman, or bumped her, or stepped on her toes, at which she would invariably emit a loud cry, "Ay, jodido!" (The force of the verb *joder* lies somewhere between the English verbs "to screw" and "to fuck.")

When I related this story to the gathering, they all laughed. "Yes, our talk here is very vulgar!" One woman commented, with appreciation, "How Nica!" Then someone demanded clarification: "Are you going to put that story in your book?" I said that I was. "No, Róger," I was told, "you mustn't give people the impression that we're vulgar. You'll give people the wrong idea about us." Together we discussed the pros and cons of this tale at some length. Everyone agreed that it was indicative of a certain aspect of the Nicaraguan sensibility, that it represented a certain social *truth;* but no one would assent to its inclusion until I explained that the broader context for this illustration would not cast the old woman, or Nicaraguans generally, in a bad light. And of course, their concerns were legitimate: that a country so ravaged by war and hardship, and so often lied about by those who inflicted the war and hardship, should be subjected to malicious or idle gossip: this, in the vernacular, would be adding insult to injury.

SMALL TALK AND EVERYDAY POWER

One day in 1988, when I was staying with my compadres, Aida's comadre came visiting Aida and Doña Flora; at about the same time Onix, too, showed up for a visit. The women were recounting the details of events that had transpired a few days earlier, on Santo Domingo: how Esperanza's husband had struck her, after which she had delivered him a fierce pounding with the metal pitcher; and how Onix's husband had locked her out of the house later that same day when she came home drunk. In the recounting, the women were also formulating a collective strategy for dealing with such events.

Sitting at the table with my notebook, I began soliciting details: Who struck whom first? How hard did the blows land? How common was this sort of thing? After answering all of my questions, Esperanza looked at Flora and said, "Why is he asking all this?" "Because," answered Flora, "he's going to write it all down in that book of his." Disbelieving, Onix said, "No, you're joking, right?" "Not at all," Aida responded; "It's all going to come out in that book." Esperanza's and Onix's eyes widened at the thought that such dirty laundry would be aired in my fieldnotes and in whatever book I would write from them.

I assured them, first, that their names would be changed and their anonymity protected; that I would try to provide a balanced picture of Nicaraguan society and a sympathetic depiction of the persons who appeared in the text. I even told them that I would not report any incidents they felt were too painful, or too embarrassing, to warrant inclusion.

"No," Aida interrupted, taking charge of the dialogue. "Tell it. But tell it all. Put down in your book that Nicaraguan men are machistas, that they like to beat their wives, and that they are irresponsible toward their children. Put down that despite the New Family Law, and despite the revolution, men are difficult to change. Put down how Rolando left Flora. And while you're writing about machismo, make note of how Osvaldo has a fine salary yet doesn't want to support his daughter, and how that woman had to take him to Social Welfare to attach his salary so she could buy food and milk for their baby."

FLORA'S SURPRISE

Doña Flora was always good at finding sales and getting the best prices on everything. A few times I followed her through the Mercado Oriental on her daily marketing trip. Frankly, she exhausted me, walking at a very fast pace despite the cruel sun. Striding without hesitation past rows of merchants, she brusquely shouted out, "*¿Cuánto vale?*" (How much?) like an accusation until she secured the lowest price for the best produce. As she had received some dollars from her estranged husband, who was living in New York City, Doña Flora was looking to make a more permanent investment in some good furniture and, she hoped, a refrigerator. She had been scouring the ad pages of *La prensa* on a daily basis, looking for good prices. As the exodus from Nicaragua's devastated economy was reaching its peak, good garage sales were not difficult to find. "*Gusanos*" (maggots), she said, in contempt for those who were bailing out. "But they leave behind some nice furniture, and if I can put it in my house, why not?"

One night I was helping her family move some furniture she had bought, in dollars, at a good price from some middle-class Managuans who were selling everything to raise money for their one-way trip to Miami. Aida had secured the services of a Soviet-made Lada truck, through a colleague of hers, who appeared more than a little nervous and reticent about this (mis?)appropriation of what I surmised was a government vehicle. (Our neighbor whose truck had been used to transport me to the hospital was now among those who had left the country, so we no longer had access to a truck in the neighborhood.) Doña Flora got into a heated argument with the people selling their furniture; apparently they had tried to raise the price on her, putting the refrigerator out of her reach. (The refrigerator itself was in doubtful shape; I advised against buying it at any price.) While moving the furniture out of its owners' house, I felt what I feared to be dengue symptoms coming on and was rather light-headed. It started to rain. As we were putting the last item on the back of the truck, I slipped and fell. I threw my hand out in front of me to grab the edge of the tailgate. And then I discovered something. Cheaply produced Ladas are not built like North American trucks. They have sharp edges.

"Shit!" I shouted in English, followed by "*¡Mierda!*" There was a deep, broad gash in the palm of my hand, and blood was spurting out. Doña Flora, Aida, and the kids came running. Looking alarmed, the residents of the house produced a clean towel for compression. After a few minutes, we looked at the damage. "Ay, it's bad," said Doña Flora, "you need stitches." I surveyed the jagged scar on her arm from recent surgery for tumors and opined that I did not much like the idea of getting stitches in Nicaragua. I was still bleeding like a stuck pig and holding the cloth tight when I boarded the back of the truck again. No place to sit. I would have to stand. The rain was pouring down, and midway through the trip back to Erasmus Jiménez, I felt nauseous, light-headed, and dizzy. Great, I thought, self-pityingly, I'm going into shock. I'll probably fall off the truck and die. I tried to put my head between my legs but found I couldn't do it; there was not enough room in the truck. I tried to stand still and concentrate on not falling off the truck.

When we got home, everyone recommended stitches. Muscles and severed tissue were jutting and curling out of the wound in odd patterns. Still, I could not bring myself to brave the needles again at Nicaragua's public health facilities. We poured alcohol into the wound, and rum into me. I got adequately liquored up to numb the pain and fall asleep.

Sure enough, the next morning I awoke with not only a badly cut, throbbing hand but also a case of what I took to be dengue. (Doña Celia could again confirm to her neighbors, "He didn't get sick when he stayed with me, and I certainly didn't get him hurt," thus initiating a fresh round in the debate about who was more hospitable than whom. By this time, even those injuries that clearly resulted from my own incessant clumsiness—a broken toe from a soccer accident and a scarred shin from bad night lighting, too much to drink, and potholes in the andén— were being laid to my hosts' carelessness.) Fortunately, though, this second bout of dengue was far milder than the first. My fever never climbed to dangerous levels, and the other symptoms were much less severe. Home care made more sense than a trip to the hospital. Doña Flora went out marketing, leaving me at the house with a fever, headache, and chills. Miguel was prompt in purchasing ice, and I was impressed by his newfound maturity: he did the daily housecleaning, looked after my godson, and rubbed me down with ice every hour or so to keep the fever down. He kept everything under control and even managed to keep my godson from making too much noise and further irritating my frayed nerves and bad temper.

When Doña Flora returned, she announced that she was preparing me a cure. Delighted to be on the trail of some authentic Nicaraguan folk medicine, I responded, "Good. What are you making for me?" "Chicken soup!" she replied.

A little stunned, I asked, "Chicken soup? Chicken soup?" "Why yes," she explained, "when people are sick here, they make chicken soup. It's traditional. It's good for whatever the problem."

THE SECRET LIFE OF TRADITION

Managuans frequently refer to gossip (*charla*) and small talk (*hablilla*) in the vernacular as *bola* (literally, "ball"), which I take as a reference to its circuitous, circular, and indeed *global* character. Its circularity eventually envelops us all within its compass. In conversation, as in provisioning, what goes around comes around (Stack 1974, 32–44).

Within the space of three years, chicken soup had not only become institutionalized on the andén but had also become ensconced in "tradition," mustering all the authority of a timeless remedy. "*Es tradicional*," Doña Flora had announced, safely relying on the timelessness of collective knowledge.[2] And this comment immediately brings to us the formal character of tradition. Tradition is a form of discourse, not to be confused with its ever-shifting contents. It always appeals to the self-evident, to the perpetual world of common sense: "That's the way it's done here"; "Everybody knows"; "It's well known." How does one know? Through a medium of talk that is continuous with gossip.

Some will say that my circuitous account of chicken soup is an example of neither gossip nor tradition but of folk medicine or, perhaps, the flexibility of popular conceptions of medicine. On the contrary, the chicken soup prescription traveled the same route as did other information on the andén, the route of gossip and small talk. And as is the case with all good gossip, by the time its subject matter had become traditionalized, the author of the discourse had been forgotten. What we call "gossip" is nothing less than discourse in its most "traditional"—or dialogical—form, at once empirical, experimental, imaginative, and moralizing; conversely, it is only in and through this open form that tradition finds its supports, its medium.

One contemporary current of postmodernism maintains that tradition is not only dead but was never really alive anyway. With an air of great revelation, these critics and theorists inform us that "tradition" was "invented" (and, very frequently, imposed); they revel in what they take to be a cacophony of connotations and imagine that they have somehow "undone" or "deconstructed" the hold of the image of tradition in society and culture (for a Marxist version, see Hobsbawm and Ranger 1983; Said 1978 carries something of this force; most explicitly, the point organizes Clifford 1988; see also Hanson 1989). What they have in fact subverted is the juridical model of tradition, which envisions custom as a series of articulate rules, a set of laws not to be broken, an exhaustible inventory of established practices.

Certainly, tradition all too frequently appears to be an empty gesture, if we take it for what it purports to be: old, timeless, authentic, invariant. The whole mode of discourse appears to be something of a fraud once we realize how new most traditions are. But to bring to the fore the ongoing, dynamic, and discursive nature of culture by no means undermines the place of tradition there, its role in anchoring a variety of practices and securing a range of meanings. Most people can cite a repertoire of beliefs and practices, no matter how new, which they maintain to be old. People frequently justify their perplexing behaviors to the anthropologist in terms of tradition and let it go at that. "It's traditional." "It's customary." "That's just the way we do things here." "Everybody knows it." (And the anthropological interrogation, which "produces" tradition by way of explanation, is not so different from various instances of dialogue that also "produce" tradition in the absence of an outsider-observer.)

At the same time, most people employ their customs not as a set of inflexible imperatives but as a set of usefully manipulable tools (see Mintz 1973, 96–97), which they often wield with a bit of cynicism. Everybody knows that sudden exposure to cold water when you are hot or agitated can endanger your health and perhaps even your life; and it is well known that this principle extends to fruits and juices designated as being *muy fresco* (very fresh, or very cold). These things are well known, traditional, and everyone is constantly reminding each other and the anthropologist of the dangers of mixing things hot and cold. Yet at the same time (the occasion for these constant reminders), people routinely write exceptions to these rules—for instance, to provide for the emergency shower before going out at night. And, although everyone acknowledges that some fruits are too "cold" to be eaten when the body is "hot," there is very little agreement on how to classify even the most common household fruits. Thus, every household shares the system of classification, but every household classifies differently—according to experimentation, whim, or taste. Indeed, customs abut each other— for the anthropologist, jarringly; for the native, not so jarringly. Many households classify *mamones* (a citrus fruit) as cold; yet custom has it that the mamón provides an excellent herbal remedy for diarrhea (especially its pit, which, when boiled, produces a constipating tea). What do you do if you have both fever and diarrhea? Only a person who takes custom for what it purports to be would imagine that Nicaraguans become paralyzed in the face of such apparent contradictions. As any native child can tell you, Nicaraguans are supposed to be open, generous, *sencillo,* as custom demands—and indeed they are, when their equally traditional efforts at concealing the sudden windfall of money or goods fail. Only a child or an anthropologist would imagine that there was some sort of contradiction there.

Although the image of tradition evokes a certain rigidity—indeed, it actively traffics in the juridical mode—this image by no means paralyzes its carriers. Rather, custom enters the field of discursive relations as a particularly powerful ordering agent; its underside, gossip, provides the lubrication for its incessant ordering and reordering, signifying and re-signifying. Social relations may be constructed or deconstructed; meanings may be relayed or withheld; codes may be enforced or ignored, as situations warrant. Rather than seeing gossip, then, as a trivial mode of discourse, it would be better to see it simultaneously as the most fluid end of a discursive continuum whose other, less fluid end is "tradition" and as the necessary underside of—and support for—tradition. Rather than seeing tradition as the set of laws it purports to be, it would be better to see it as a certain form of discourse—the commonsensical mode—whereby actors engage themselves in the social world, negotiate their multiple relations with others, formulate and justify their courses of action, and thereby, ultimately, little by little, reconstruct the world every day in the light of self-interest.

gossip as a form of
knoledge travel

CHAPTER VI

Censoring *La semana cómica*

Discourses, sign-systems and signifying practices of all kinds, from film
and television to fiction and the languages of natural science, produce
effects, shape forms of consciousness and unconsciousness, which are
closely related to the maintenance or transformation of our existing systems of power. They are thus closely related to what it means to be a
person. Indeed "ideology" can be taken to indicate no more than this
connection—the link or nexus between discourse and power.

—Terry Eagleton, *Literary Theory*

THE PADRE'S DAY-BEFORE-MOTHER'S-DAY HOMILY AT THE POPULAR
CHURCH   (From my journal, 30 May 1988): *"There was some movie
on TV last night about a woman, and I don't know what kind of mother
this woman was: drinking, partying, running around here and there,
having all kinds of sexual relations with all kinds of men. That is what
it's coming to these days, when people have no shame.*

*"And then there was some woman on a radio talk show the other
night. She was talking about sex, masturbation, contraception, abortion, and whether a young woman ought to come to marriage a virgin
or not. It surprised me to hear such things coming out of a woman's
mouth on the radio. And I wonder what kind of ideas children are
getting, when they hear things like this.*

"Now there are some who say that women should be licenciadas
*[holders of college degrees], that they should be lawyers, and doctors,
and professionals. Well, fine. That is well and good. But the true voca-
tion of woman is to produce new men and new women. I say to you:
the most exalted role of woman is mother, and it always will be."*

Traditional ideas about masculinity in Nicaragua have been labeled
machismo. The term was given general currency by AMNLAE's consciousness-raising efforts and by Sandinista discussions of gender relations. Drawn from a politicized international social science literature,
the term turns the commonplace *macho* (man, or real man) into a
"system of manliness." The aim of the term *machismo* is transparent

enough: it designates a system in order to diagram it and critique it; it elevates to the level of explicitness all that was implicit in the term *macho*.

Interestingly, no corresponding term was deployed in Nicaragua to describe traditional notions of femininity. The complex of images of the ideal woman has sometimes been called *marianismo* in the social science literature; the term draws on the Virgin Mary as the model for appropriate womanhood (Stevens 1973).[1] This femininity, however, is not simply the direct opposite of masculinity: the one concave where the other is convex, the one passive where the other is active. Clearly, that is the way each perspective in the gender system sees and treats the other—as an inverted mirror image of itself—but it cannot simply be said, as machismo might occasionally maintain, that masculinity is active, femininity passive. That is, after all, only the view from within the masculine horizon. The traditional ideal of femininity is not simple "passivity"—working-class Nicaraguan women were never expected to be shrinking violets—but rather an ideal of elevated motherhood. Traditional feminine practice, then, is conceived as a different mode of doing than male practice: feminine action emphasizes planning over risk, self-abnegation over self-promotion, domesticity over worldliness, action in and through networks rather than interpersonal competition. The leitmotifs of the feminine ideal might be summarized as caring, nurturing, and self-sacrifice—which is to say, a form of acting on behalf of others.

The priest's homily points up the persistence of a very traditional view of womanhood, even in the otherwise politically radical Popular Church. The disputes around *La semana cómica* (The Comic Weekly) reflect and refract a different, though related, set of divisions and conflicts. The rub, as I see it, occurs when women become active, not simply in the personalistic sphere of household, family, friends, and kin, but in the larger social and political world. How to interpret this activity? As the waning of nurture from the world? As female encroachment on male territory? As the disappearance of gender itself, as traditionally defined? Or as a scenario for sexual impurity, where the worldly, active woman can only be "up to no good"?

PARODY OR PORNOGRAPHY?

La semana cómica is a tabloid humor magazine—and quite possibly, the publication that enjoyed the largest circulation in Nicaragua during the 1980s. Its late editor, Róger Sánchez, was well known for the political cartoons that regularly appeared in the pages of *Barricada,* the official newspaper of the FSLN. His lampoons routinely mocked the hypocrisy of the conservative faction of the Catholic church, the greed of Nicaraguan businessmen, the duplicity of U.S. policy in Central America—and, increasingly, bureaucratism in Nicaragua. Under Sánchez's editorship, *La semana cómica* provided a bohemian vehicle for left-wing political irreverence and satire. Waggishly subtitled "A Weekly of Humor, Marxism, Sex, and Violence," it was also a forum for sexual humor and photos of nude women.

The 1 March 1988 issue of *La semana cómica,* which was circulated on 8 March, provoked a storm of controversy in Managua. The conflicts, which occurred on the Left and within the ranks of Sandinista partisans, pointedly raised—and left unanswered, undecided—questions of gender, representation, and censorship. What triggered the controversy was the magazine's spoof of AMNLAE militants preparing for International Women's Day. *La semana cómica* ran a photograph of a nude woman apparently shaving her pubic area. Underneath the photograph appeared the caption "On 8 March, things are going to be celebrated with all the law allows, because already the most representative of Nicaraguan women is making preparations."

AMNLAE immediately protested the depiction: it mocked a legitimate revolutionary holiday, and it depicted women in a degrading manner. Both forms of representation had been prohibited by Sandinista law since the early days of the revolution. AMNLAE protests were followed by an avalanche of phone calls to Managua's call-in radio talk shows; radio audiences pointedly condemned *La semana cómica*'s pornographic burlesque of International Women's Day. Publication of *La semana cómica* was suspended by order of the Ministry of Interior. In its reportage on the suspension, *El nuevo diario* (the independent pro-Sandinista newspaper) reproduced the photograph in question and was itself suspended for three days.

Nudity per se was not the issue. *La semana cómica* often ran photographs of nude women. Sánchez's cartoons routinely depicted fully nude women in bedroom situations. *El nuevo diario*'s weekly literary supplement sometimes ran nude art photographs, usually accompanied by poetry, and these composed studies of the female form—soft-focused and bathed in diffuse light—were often quite erotic. Nor was the public depiction of sexuality the issue—at least not for AMNLAE, whose militants had long lobbied for more progressive and more open sex education in the schools and in society at large. "Sex and Youth," a 1988 television sex-education serial inspired in part by AMNLAE and produced by the National Commission on Sex Education, featured frank talk about such topics as sexual intercourse, masturbation, and homosexuality. (The segment on masturbation concluded with a wet, choreographed beach scene: a boy and girl, separately, moved to erotic rhythms with motions that were explicitly autoerotic.)[2] For such efforts, AMNLAE, far more than *La semana cómica,* came under attack by the conservative faction (and occasionally the leftist faction) of the Catholic church. What put leftists at loggerheads and led to the temporary suspension of two leftist papers (while, paradoxically, the conservative daily *La prensa* emerged from a lengthy closure under the state-of-emergency laws) was the *manner* in which women, their bodies, and their sexuality were depicted. Did the photograph and its caption represent a legitimate form of satire, or was it reactionary, *machista* pornography? Did it objectify and debase women? In either case, was censorship warranted? Where does one draw the line on issues of representation?

The April–May 1988 issue of *Pensamiento propio* (Proper thinking or Our own thinking) contained an article by Nick Cooke and Mariuca Lomba entitled "Hay que abrir la Caja de Pandora del sexismo y el machismo" (The Pandora's Box of sexism and machismo has to be opened). An interview of three people involved in the debate, Cooke and Lomba's piece aired a discussion of the political issues in the censorship of *La semana cómica.* In the interviews, the three discussants took three distinct positions. Róger Sánchez asserted that *La semana cómica* was guilty of nothing more than "bad taste" and that such bad taste was satire's license. Marta Munguía, a member of AMNLAE's executive secretariat, argued that the depiction was a clear "violation of the law and of the principles that we established with the revolution." Sofía Montenegro, a *Barricada* editorial chief and AMNLAE militant, argued that the position of *La semana cómica* was "indefensible" and that the parody of AMNLAE was offensive to women in "political terms," but she insisted that censorship in this case was counterproductive. I will quote at length from these interviews, which highlight the sometimes awkward dilemmas of postrevolutionary politics.

"The pornographic," Montenegro reasoned, "if you understand everything that can be offensive as pornography, in this case is offensive in political terms, fundamentally because of the caption accompanying the photo." Munguía elaborated: "People reacted for two reasons: the photo itself as pornography, and on the other side, the caption of the photo, making fun of AMNLAE." Explaining AMNLAE's position, Munguía continued, "We are not puritans about what ought to be humor. More than opposing the photo, we are against the caption of the photo, which was a manipulation of the date. The caption—consciously or unconsciously—came to coincide with a reactionary position, in the sense that the AMNLAE woman, the active woman, is up to no good, or looking to have sexual relations."

Defending *La semana cómica,* and apparently wishing to out-feminist the feminists, Sánchez argued, "It wasn't our intention to ridicule women." The satire "was meant as disrespect for a religious value. . . . On the eighth, all women are pretty. Then, on the ninth, no. They go back to washing dishes, etc. . . . There's a lack of sense in anniversaries. I prefer that they not be 'celebrated' as such, but rather, that people have a more conscious attitude the rest of the time." Then, elaborating his own sense of the sexual "double standard," Sánchez opined: "The women that so indignantly called in to the radio are people who are incapable of publicly questioning the issue of sexual blackmail. There are women who obtain employment by way of the bedroom; there are a lot of women who do that. This happens every day in this country."

"There are situations much more obscene than that photo," observed Montenegro. "For example, in this country the second cause of death is abortion. And until now AMNLAE has insisted on evading focusing on the whole problem of sexuality, which is not only abortion, but also a less hypocritical, less puritanical education. We lack a more direct education on things that are of interest to the population: sexual health and women's access to control of their own reproduction." Of the political storm itself she argued, "AMNLAE's response was too visceral and emotional. . . . [It] ratified the stereotype that we want to dismantle: that we women are too emotional. It feeds that type of idea—that we don't have a sense of humor, that there are a lot of women bent on having a witch hunt."

For Munguía, however, AMNLAE's response was not at all problematic. "If we are struggling to change the role of women, then we are obligated to respond to whatever attack or tergiversation that comes, from wherever it comes."

But, according to Montenegro, in the political context of Nicaragua in 1988, censoring *La semana cómica* was inherently problematic. "One has to look at the political consequences of that action. AMNLAE has been forcing the government to take positions. I ask myself, has AMNLAE thought through what would happen in this little incident if

La prensa, just to create a political problem for the revolution, had decided to reproduce the photo? They would have put the state in an embarrassing position: to censor two prorevolutionary papers, or apply the law also to *La prensa,* with all its consequences on the international plane. It's part of political responsibility to think about these things before acting."

Sánchez depicted AMNLAE as immature, evoking stereotypes of hysterical and infantile women: "The women, instead of discussing the issue—Why didn't they call out their side, their lawyers, their sociologists? And they took the position: 'We're going to mess up this fucker.' Instead of doing that, they went to ask for protection from daddy, asking for repression."

Montenegro ratified and clarified Sánchez's point in less charged terms. "If we really wanted to give a political response, we could have used other means of communication, establishing a debate with *La semana cómica.* It would have been more mature, more productive, and more educational for the population. One cannot simply remember that there exist laws and ask papa state to hit a bad boy on his head."

The fact that men laugh at this type of humor, this "bad taste," which women find offensive, Sánchez argued, indicates something that "is also a question of sexual repression." Now himself fully empowered to play the victim—and evading the whole question of what constitutes humor and why—Sánchez queried: "Who is more sexually repressed in this country? Men or women?"

Munguía attempted to put matters into perspective by talking about the structure of humor and the position of women in society.

> Eight years after the triumph of the revolution, people have another view of women, even though women's subordinate role in society has not totally changed. And with relation to women being used as sexual or commercial objects, there is a position now established, and the population has more or less reached a certain level of education.
>
> *La semana cómica* has had a critical line, and we think that it's a good, correct line, because it puts into perspective things that have never been brought into a wider debate. . . . We can have and we must maintain the debate in different media, discussing things in depth. Not over the photo itself, but around the significance of women's manipulation. Why is it that when we make humor, we talk about women? Why are things funny, things ridiculous, done with women? And effectively, we come to touch on a deep subject: woman as object in society.

Sánchez rejected the contention that *La semana cómica*'s humor was machista and developed his own guerrillero vision of revolutionary humor.

We didn't make jokes about women drivers, or things of that sort, since we didn't intend to reinforce stereotypes. . . . We ridiculed those who are ridiculous, bureaucrats, or whoever they are. . . . We don't use real artillery, it's all firing, little more. We are commandos. We are ideological street fighters. . . . We attack weaknesses, and women's plans of struggle in this country have a mountain of weaknesses, and we jump over them. But if AMNLAE had a strong fighting plan, rational and brilliant, what could we say? What would there be to laugh at?

If the people that brought on this confrontation had ideology, they would have formulated better arguments. We gave ourselves the luxury of putting ourselves in the role of the bad guy. But who has come out worse here, us or AMNLAE?

Montenegro summed up her position: "I have great faith and confidence in the Nicaraguan people, an alert people who want to know new things, including things that can shock them. But if out of fear of touching old values we don't have the courage to talk about things called 'taboo,' we are doing a small favor for the people, and being terribly paternalistic." Cooke and Lomba concluded the piece by observing that "there now exist more mature conditions to take on openly, seriously, and profoundly, once and for all, the question of women in the country."

ALLIANCES AND DISPUTES

Sánchez had, of course, violated an unwritten rule of politics in Nicaragua's tense and conflictive situation: never directly attack your allies in public. In the revolution and during the contra war, the pro-Sandinista bloc had maintained apparent unity by suppressing differences of opinion in public. By 1988 the facade of unity was showing signs of stress on several fronts. That year, for publicly airing a factional dispute within the FSLN, Omar Cabezas was removed from his post in the Interior Ministry and put in charge of the basically defunct Sandinista Defense Committees (CDS)—a remarkable demotion for a comandante with Cabezas's international profile. AMNLAE responded—and certainly overreacted—to La semana cómica's parody by insisting that the law be applied against an element of the pro-Sandinista bloc. AMNLAE no doubt had its reasons, and they are entangled with the organization's mixed record of successes and failures (see Cooke and Lomba 1988, 17). Specifically, women activists were increasingly irritated by the patronizing and demeaning depictions of women in *La semana cómica*. Whether they acted out of strength or weakness, maturity or immaturity, depends on how one looks at the question and how one assesses the general background of the specific case. Plainly, AMNLAE had brought a vigorous discussion of women's issues to a public forum in the early 1980s with its series of town meetings on the New Family Laws, including the Law on Nurture. Such debate peaked when the Council of State passed a far-reaching package of AMNLAE-initiated laws in 1982. The executive branch of government, however, deferred final approval of the Law on Nurture; President Ortega declared that social conditions were "not yet ripe" for the passage of such sweeping reforms. The discussion of gender, sexuality, and family issues was pushed aside. In 1986 AMNLAE again massed its forces to participate in the town meetings on the new constitution. Activists pushed for a constitutional guarantee to a woman's right to abortion. Although such a provision appeared in the FSLN working draft of the constitution, it vanished from subsequent versions, including the final constitution.

Pragmatically and, I think, realistically, AMNLAE placed "defense of the revolution" above all its other concerns because the Sandinista revolution constituted the only imaginable arena where women's social and political demands might be realized. But there was also pragmatism of a different sort in the Sandinista National Directorate, and AMNLAE eventually found even its less aggressively feminist agenda obstructed by realpolitiks, caution, and official trepidation. AMNLAE strategy had paid off, but the results were ambiguous. AMNLAE brought about real reforms early in the revolution, secured a high public profile for the organization, and maintained a good working relationship with the FSLN. At the same time, however, its relationship with the government curbed its grass-roots activism and moderated its militance on women's issues qua women's issues, and ultimately it became clear that the executive branch of the revolutionary government would not support feminist causes perceived as "divisive." After various political debacles and frustrations, AMNLAE's activism declined. Many militant women expressed discontent about the declining emphasis on women's issues, the organization's neglect of its grass roots, and the lack of militant activism. By 1988 the organization needed fresh victories. By taking the dispute with *La semana cómica* to the Ministry of the Interior, run by Tomás Borge—who was known to be sympathetic to feminist concerns and who was identified with a more radical variant of Sandinismo than was Daniel Ortega—AMNLAE militants both achieved a temporary victory and to some extent carved out a more activist, less passive, political profile.

Militants like Munguía clearly favored more direct and more confrontational activism. Perhaps they could not substantively accelerate the feminist agenda by attacking *La semana cómica,* but they could draw the line on public images, public representations, simply by applying existing law. And, fortunately or not, they could win such skirmishes, in part because the issue of "pornography" gave them more clout with a broader sector of the public—including those opposed to the feminist agenda. Others, like Montenegro, continued to prefer public unity on the Left and thus favored less confrontational and less divisive tactics. Although both women advocated a broader discussion of the issues, it is unclear whether conditions actually existed for a productive debate. For instance, there is something peculiar and suspect about Sánchez's depiction of his opponents as "immature." His tabloid's sexual and scatological humor appealed most widely to adolescent males, who would purchase *La semana cómica* and hide it from their mothers; its humor was anything but "mature." Sánchez is indeed noted for his own brand of sexual liberation: the liberation of libido—but in what terms? His portrayal of himself as a hit-and-run comic gangster evades Munguía's interrogation of how eroticism is constructed, what defines humor, and how woman is defined.

Nude, pliant women, always made ridiculous with captions; men, intimidated by women and somewhat fearful of their own and women's sexuality: these were the stock and trade of *La semana cómica,* and they were completely consonant with an unbuttoned and unzipped version of machismo. In the context of machista norms, the journal's nude photographs are erotic because they convey an image of women as inherently ridiculous, as harmless objects of contempt. At the same time, and from another angle, the AMNLAE/International Women's Day photograph proved especially offensive because it conveyed an image of AMNLAE that is completely consistent with machismo's view of the "active" or liberated woman as someone who enjoys and is overly preoccupied with sex. Worse yet, the photograph suggested, and its caption implied, that the woman was a prostitute. This was certainly the way most people understood the image. On radio talk shows and in some print formats, the photograph was simply and without qualification referred to as the picture of a prostitute. Strong insult indeed, to call the most representative of Nicaraguan women, the AMNLAE activist, a whore.

THE QUESTION OF CENSORSHIP

In Erasmus Jiménez, when they discussed such things—usually at my prompting, for the issue cannot be said to have preoccupied working-class Managuans—my informants typically expressed an attitude of amusement toward the dispute between AMNLAE and *La semana cómica*. Most women opined that the tabloid had been *muy vago* (roughly, "way out of line") and deserved a firm reprimand: for some, because its photographs had been "pornographic," depicting nudity; for others, because the paper had been sexist, machista, or sexually reactionary. Sandinistas and AMNLAE militants simply observed that the parody's intention had been to debase women and to mock a revolutionary holiday, that the paper had thus consciously violated the law, and that its suspension, while unpleasant, was by no means severe. Adolescent boys lamented the temporary absence of nude photographs from the marketplace. Most men saw it all as a harmless joke and said that AMNLAE had been too sensitive.

It would be altogether too easy to dismiss AMNLAE's protests or the censorship issues raised by summarily invoking the values of U.S. civil libertarianism, with its unconditional imperative "Thou shalt not censor." I would not argue simply that this North American political and intellectual construct is inapplicable to Nicaraguan reality—a sort of special pleading, with censorship thus good for them, bad for us. I would also argue that it has theoretical defects in its own right. Absolutists of the First Amendment typically make "free speech" sacred by distinguishing "speech" (including writing, representation, and all forms of signification) from "action." This is a reified distinction at best. Speech, too, is first and foremost a form of practice. Only an impoverished and ultimately *impractical* conception of speech (and text) follows from a premature separation of signification from practice. Every act of "signification" is also an act of "production" (in which meaning is produced out of sounds, images, other meanings), connected to an ideology or ideologies (that is, to a code or codes for producing viable meaning)—not simply because "individual speech" is an expression of "social language" but because meaning, and every act that produces meaning, is always already engaged in the world of power and the conflict over it. To name, to depict, to characterize: these are social practices, and they are complicit with power at every level, for the categories they create and the perceptions they structure precede and inform every subsequent way of acting, even as they themselves were preceded and informed by antecedent ways of acting.

To situate "speech" in "ideology," then, and to see representation in its productive role, is to link it at every level to systems of practice, to ensembles of social relations, and to really existing power relationships. "Power" enters into signification not only at the moment of censorship but also at the moment of production. The "free market of ideas" (which is the theoretical expression of absolutist civil libertarianism) all too often entails a mode of production that inoculates some forms of power, exculpates some people's speech from its consequences, and puts ideology itself beyond scrutiny. In the free market of speech, as in the economic free market, one person's freedom is another's absence of freedom.

Advocacy of censorship does not necessarily follow from the political application of this Marxist-semiotic analysis, but neither does a fundamentalist civil libertarianism.[3] If this perspective goes a long way toward reducing the hypostatized distinction between "speech" and "action," representation and practice, it offers no easy solutions to the power struggles that accompany textual production and that animate discursive practices. Those conflicts are no less present in the United States than they are in Nicaragua. In the United States of the early 1990s, speech issues have become increasingly politicized. The furor over flag burning was the Bush administration's first real political issue; the dispute was framed in terms of which was more sacred: a cloth symbol of the nation or the First Amendment. (The Sandinista law stipulating respect for revolutionary holidays seems no more exotic than U.S. congressional attempts to legislate proper treatment for the Stars and Stripes.) And the debate over pornography continues into the 1990s. The puritanical, New Right, religious antipornography position has been joined and complicated by new questions, new positions. For many feminists, the question has become, What are the social effects of debasing depictions of women? What are the implications of violence as entertainment? Some North American feminists favor legislation much like the Sandinista law prohibiting the visual and textual debasement of women. In some cases, they have formed tactical alliances with the New Right fundamentalists who are their most hardened adversaries on most other issues. In a few cases (see Dworkin 1987; Dworkin 1989;

MacKinnon 1983), they propose arguments far more extreme and offer correctives far more sweeping than the simple censorship law drafted in Nicaragua. (See Tribe 1988, 920–28.) A variety of strings have been attached to federal funds for art, strings whose stated aim is to stifle any aesthetic work that offends conservative values and specifically to silence public homosexual discourse and representation. Hateful, incendiary, and bigoted speech appears as comedy, provoking feminist, gay, and minority protests, and various universities have moved to regulate stigmatizing, hateful, or harassing speech on campus and in the classrooms.[4] Positioning itself opposite the American Civil Liberties Union, the Southern Poverty Law Center has had unprecedented success bringing civil suits against hate groups (the Alabama Ku Klux Klan, Tom Metzger's White Aryan Resistance [WAR]) when their propaganda favoring violent racism has motivated and incited the murder of blacks.

The specter of censorship is very much with us, on a variety of fronts and representing a variety of intentions. Again, it is tempting to assert an absolute civil libertarianism, the free market solution: to protect the speech of the Left, of dissidents, of gays, and of the traditionally censored voices, perhaps we should also tolerate hateful, stigmatizing, incendiary, and demeaning speech in public forums. But once one recognizes speech as a form of practice, concretely connected to other practices, there can be no such ready solution to the problems of representation and censorship—neither those in the United States nor those in Nicaragua. I see no inherent reason why "hate speech" designed to terrorize and intimidate minorities—to promote violence—should be protected speech, any more than harassment, slander, blackmail, or libel should be protected speech. Casually or maliciously stigmatizing speech has no place in the classroom because it damages the educational environment for women, African Americans, Hispanics, gays, and other stigmatized groups. Various European countries (as well as Canada) have enacted broad statutes prohibiting public hate speech, or speech that defames, denigrates, or terrorizes a group of people on the basis of their ethnicity, religion, or national origin. Such regulations have not led to wholesale censorship on other fronts. Of course, putting the power to censor in the hands of government and law in the United States *might* constitute a dangerous precedent—if, having minimized the difference between speech and action, the distinctions between "hateful" and "unpopular," "harassing" and merely "offensive," are not maintained.

In sum, we North Americans—Left and Right, women and men, minority and majority—are no less densely engaged in the problematics of

expression and censorship than were the participants in the dispute over
La semana cómica. Such issues are problematic because, while speech
is a practice, it is by no means immediately reducible to other practices:
it is a special case of activity, not just one activity among others. Thus,
on the one hand, few could doubt that the objectification of women—
in speech, text, and representation—both reflects and incubates a broader
objectification of women;[5] that images of sex as conquest have something to do with rape and its prevalence in our society; that casually
stereotyped depictions of ethnic and racial minorities reinforce racism;
that speech that stigmatizes and does semiotic violence to gays and lesbians also promotes physical violence.

In this sense, oppressed people are always the targets of what must
rightly be called linguistic terrorism. On the other hand, connecting
specific and often ambiguous images to an ideological regime is slippery
work at best, and this connection is very frequently made by invoking
fuzzy logic—or by resorting to a terrorist counterterrorism. An image,
a text, can evoke very different meanings for different observers, different readers. Myriad power struggles ensue, dispersing themselves along
the lines of such ambiguities: Does a pliant human form depict submis-
siveness, a sexual invitation, or a celebration of the quiet, hidden power
of the human topos? When are sexual images "erotic," and when are
they "debasing"? Do certain images of urban violence reinforce racial
stereotypes, or do they protest the distorted conditions of twentieth century American life? Is it malicious to depict an oppressed people as
anything but noble, brave, and courteous? And what of Sánchez's contention that he was ridiculing a "religious" value and poking fun at
bureaucrats? No doubt that is one way of reading the photograph. A
clear and perhaps inevitable danger in all such disputes is that wounded
and legitimately angry people can take umbrage at any outsider's depiction of themselves that is not characterized by unambiguous, unctuous
flattery. And when such a terror rules discourse—either through censorship or self-censorship—critical inquiry is likely to be the first casu-
alty of that power struggle.

Regulating public speech, public representation, is one possible tool
for changing ideology—or, at least, for changing *public* ideology. Censorship seizes the "commanding heights" of discursive production. The
assumption is that other practices, other discourses, will follow suit,
sooner or later. But all the pertinent questions remain: Where does one
draw the line on representation? How far is too far? The threat of censorship, as Montenegro argues, undercuts the very grounds on which a

dialogue might establish fair rules of discourse. Censorship constitutes a poor tool for social tinkering. It is easier to repress another's speech than to produce one's own. The connection between lived ideology and public ideology, between social relations and official discourses, is complex, and the connection between social intolerance and hateful speech is not easily severed.

In Nicaragua, the open debate apparently desired by all sides occurred only in the pages of *Pensamiento propio*. Perhaps Sánchez indeed felt that he had come out on top in the controversy. On its return to the newsstands, flush with free publicity, *La semana cómica,* in the style of ideological gang warfare, continued to inflame AMNLAE's sensibilities with similar photographs and captions. AMNLAE continued protesting; calls to radio talk shows ran against *La semana cómica.*

On 5 August 1988 *La prensa* carried an ironic headline: " 'El despertar' Returns, *La semana cómica* Suspended." "El despertar," Radio Noticias's conservative news program, had returned from a fifteen-day suspension. As before, *La semana cómica* had been suspended under article thirty, decree number forty-eight, which prohibited the publication of texts or photographs exploiting or debasing women. However, after this suspension the unreformed *Semana cómica* returned to circulation for good. The tide of government opinion turned against AMNLAE, and *La semana cómica* won the war of positions after all.

La prensa had itself recently returned from a lengthy suspension under the state of emergency. The new *La prensa* proved a far more professional journal than its previous manifestation had been. Gone were yellow-journalist stories such as "Woman Gives Birth to Chicken," accompanied by the documentary photograph of a woman holding a chicken. Gone were its recurrent, shrill editorials claiming that the FSLN intended to abolish religion and establish an atheistic totalitarian society modeled after the Soviet Union and Cuba. On its return, and heavily subsidized by the National Endowment for Democracy, *La prensa* had set about quietly hiring better-trained writers from Costa Rica, and the staff improvements showed.

Most cases of government censorship in Nicaragua, like the closing of *La prensa* and Radio Católica, had been framed in terms of the contra war. The free speech of the business, religious, and political Right had been curbed in the defense of the revolution and against those whom the Sandinistas labeled *vendepatrias* (national sellouts)—those who openly or covertly sided with the U.S.-sponsored aggression, who encouraged draft evasion, and who spread rumors that might be labeled "disinformation." In such cases, the Reagan-Bush administration manipulated the issue of wartime censorship to its own advantage. In congressional debates on contra aid, and in Republican propaganda, government censorship of *La prensa* and the right-wing Catholic press constituted the centerpiece of charges that the Sandinistas were "totalitarian."

The disputes around *La semana cómica* illuminated a different set of divisions in Nicaraguan society, no less political but no longer fitting the pattern of a revolutionary-counterrevolutionary split. With Sandinistas feeling free to take different sides of the question, one could argue that the disputes signaled a certain "maturing" of the revolution: perhaps it was, oddly enough, a freeing of discourse from the constraints of unity, with Sandinista partisans squabbling in public. Or perhaps it signaled a different sort of development: unresolved social and cultural issues eating away at the Sandinista consensus, and growing disunity in the face of an overwhelming outside threat.

PART TWO

Some Lives

Reagan se va,
La revolución se queda.
(Reagan will go,
The revolution stays.)

> —A 1988 slogan, frequently played
> on Sandinista television

La revolución se queda,
Mi papá se va.
(The revolution will stay,
My papa goes.)

> —Miguel's parody

In this part, each chapter follows the life of a particular person within my circle of close informants. The first three—Rolando, Flora, and Osvaldo—are members of the same family; the last two—Jazmina and Virgilio—are mother and son. All save Jaime and Róger are residents of Barrio Erasmus Jiménez. The material herein is based mostly on my conversations and interactions with specific informants between 1984 and 1988 and my observations of their daily household routines, supplemented in some cases by letters.

My methods in these interviews were simple. I discovered early on that the presence of a tape recorder produced a stiff, formal interview, so I worked without one as much as possible. I made daily visits to various informants' houses; we passed time at a leisurely pace, threading our discussion in and out of topics—some of them my choice, others the informant's. In a few of the more formal interviews, I took notes as we talked. This practice, too, proved distracting: like the tape recorder, the notebook stiffened the interviews, so I tried to keep our discussions as informal as possible. In most cases I worked this way: immediately after a discussion, I retired to my room and tried to reproduce the conversation as well as possible in my journal notes. With a little practice, I discovered that I could recollect conversations with a high degree of accuracy. If anything in my notes was vague or unclear, I followed up with specific questioning and clarification either that evening or the next morning. These questions, of course, invariably produced new topics and new questions, in an open-ended process. Living in the neighborhood, recording observations as well as dialogues, and spending time with my informants on a daily basis provided ample checks and cross-checks on my data.

For the most part, then, these interviews are not verbatim translations of the original conversations. I would observe that all interviews—perhaps especially tape-recorded ones—go through lengthy editing, reconstructing, and rearranging. By comparison with tape-recorded transcription and editing procedures, my methods are not especially intrusive or distorting. And I have been careful to avoid that most distorting device of all: the disappearing or absent author/interviewer whose questions are edited out of existence and whose very presence is repressed in the final text. Questions do not ask themselves, conversations do not occur, and interviews do not get written up without more than one participant. I have everywhere tried to keep a sense of what circumstances motivated and what questions prompted a given discussion.

I would not claim that the sketches presented here provide complete depictions of any given person. My aim is not to compile exhaustive "oral life histories" per se, but to follow the impact of the revolution, its hopes, its successes, and its failures through the lives of specific individuals—almost all of them committed, to various degrees, to the goals of the revolution. Nor, given the nature of my fieldwork in a particular community, do these informants in any sense represent a random or representative sample of Nicaraguans, rich and poor, rural and urban, Left and Right. However, these individuals are by no means atypical of a broad sector of the urban working class. Like most poor or working-class Nicaraguans—and certainly like most residents of the militant barrio Erasmus Jiménez—these people were active supporters of the Sandinistas in the early years of the revolution. (Osvaldo and Elvis were members of the Sandinista Youth organization, and Máximo was a member of the FSLN. With the exception of Rolando, the rest, like most urban Nicaraguans of their class, were involved at some point and with various degrees of activism in either a Sandinista mass organization or a labor mobilization.)

At the risk of preempting the material that follows, I will observe that certain general themes emerge with some clarity: the significant impact of gender roles—in addition to class position—on life chances and on the distribution of hardship; the protracted hardship of my informants' motivated sacrifices during the revolution, the contra war, and the economic crisis; and a gradual waning of enthusiasm for the revolutionary project they once had enthusiastically embraced. I would point out that the discomforts, dissatisfactions, and complaints increasingly aired in these discussions had little to do with the antirevolutionary sentiments of ideological conservatives, entrepreneurs, or business elites. Exhaustion, more than reaction, informs the discourses I record—although an antirevolutionary political coalition was ultimately able to mobilize such pains. In the 1990 elections, the vote in Erasmus Jiménez went to the Sandinistas by only the slimmest of margins. If the FSLN could not commandingly carry a former stronghold such as Erasmus Jiménez, it would do even more poorly in less politicized—and more desperate—working-class wards. And without a strong working-class majority, the FSLN certainly could not win a majority in the population at large. In a sense, then, the following chapters narrate a sequence that culminated in the Sandinista electoral defeat of 1990.

CHAPTER VII

Rolando

Here it is so corrupt that I have reexamined my life.

I had casually encountered Rolando in a variety of settings in the neighborhood. An auto mechanic by trade, he was also an excellent general mechanic, and families up and down the andén solicited his aid in repairing things, either for a fee or in exchange for other favors. Rolando repaired electric blenders, radios, televisions. He was a jack of all trades. He was also a famous drinker in a country where most adult men drink a great deal. Weekends would find him sprawled out back behind his house, on a bed that had been moved there for his convenience—the very picture of working-class decadence—consuming bottle after bottle of Flor de Caña, the Nicaraguan rum.

My first real meeting with Rolando was near the end of 1985, on my second trip to Nicaragua. His son, Charlie, was celebrating his fifteenth birthday and had asked me to come over to the house that evening and take some pictures at his party. When he made his request, he called me "compadre"—perhaps to indicate that it was incumbent on me to honor his request. Charlie's sister, Aida, was six months pregnant at the time, and Miguel had already engineered an invitation for me to be the child's godfather. Already, then, we were kin, subject to the mutual favors entailed by compadrazgo.

When I came to the house that evening, I found Charlie dressed in his best clothes and looking somewhat uncomfortable. There was indeed a birthday cake, but where was the party? No one Charlie's age was present in the house: just the family. Rolando was sitting at a table in the backyard with four of his friends, drinking rum and eating turtle eggs. After taking a few pictures, I was ushered out back to drink.

We sat, drinking and talking. Rolando offered me a turtle egg. I said that I had never eaten one before and puzzled over its rubbery shell. Intrigued at the prospect of someone who had never sampled this delicacy, my host insisted, "It's good for you. It'll put hair on your chest!" Rolando demonstrated the technique by tearing off a small piece of the egg, putting the hole against his lips, then squeezing the contents into his mouth. He followed this demonstration by draining a shot glass, which he slammed down on the table, and then laughingly proclaimed, "Makes a man of you!" A bit more cautiously, I followed this procedure. When I sucked the yolk, my face must have betrayed my surprise: it was a warm, gooey, salty liquid. Waves of good-natured laughter. "It makes a man of you!" "*Chu-pa*" (Suck it down)! I drained my shot glass and slammed it down, to applause and laughter.

After five or six more shots, I took a few pictures of this gathering (wondering whether they would be properly focused and framed). After a while, Rolando took me aside and told me of his plans: he was preparing for a trip to the United States, to work for a couple of years and bring back U.S. dollars to refurbish the house, buy a refrigerator, and improve his family's lot in life. He walked me into the house's new addition, which was almost complete: a wooden room tacked on behind the kitchen. "You can stay here when you come back to Nicaragua. You can stay with your compadres from now on, when you return."

Then, looking straight into my eyes and speaking in a quiet voice that I did not quite understand at the time, he said, "Take good care of my family while I'm gone." We returned to the party and had a few more drinks. Eventually I excused myself, staggered back to the Ocampo house, and collapsed.

When I returned in the summer of 1986, Rolando was gone. I stayed in the new room out back, we baptized my godson, Ervin, and I tried to catch up on events in everyone's lives. Rolando had crossed the U.S. border via Mexico, en route to a job as an auto mechanic that was waiting for him in New York City. In southern Texas he was captured by the Immigration and Naturalization Service (INS). His family was vague about exactly what had happened—perhaps because they did not understand the intricacies of immigration or perhaps because they wanted to conceal the potential scandal. Doña Flora said that La Migra (INS) kept him in a prison for a few days, which was something like paying a fine for entry without permission, and then released him because he had paid the penalty. As I pieced the story together, it seemed clear to me that, after being captured, Rolando had asked for political asylum. At that time, INS was granting asylum on demand for Nicaraguans if they said that they were fleeing Sandinista persecution.

At first, Rolando's phone calls back home were numerous and expensive. No doubt he was afraid and lonely and sought the comfort of his family. After a few weeks, however, the phone calls and letters stopped. Only rumors carried news of Rolando's doings.

Some letters, some money, eventually came. I reproduce the letters below and will let Rolando speak for himself.[1]

New York 5 March 1987

Hello my sweet I hope this finds you in good health surrounded by All Your Children well I, thanks to God, am well and Working and I repeat to you that I don't know what it is that happened with the letters that I sent well you told me that you haven't received a single one of them I will tell you that this is very strange, Sweet with respect to the money that I'm sending you I want you to do the following change only the money that you need and whatever's left keep it safe and don't tell anyone what I sent you because I'm going to be sending you [money] so you can save it for example you can stop by again on the 21st of March to pick up the money I'm going to send you Also I want you to buy clothes for yourself and I want you to go to the right just before the La Reynaga bridge and find out how much it costs to build a three-door wardrobe and when you have this information write me immediately so that I can give you the okay to get it Also you can go to Altagracia and ask my uncle juan-jose if he too can build it and see which of the two makes them cheaper by the way give them my regards Also if you can buy a bed of the same sort that we bought or if not give him the old one to fix whatever you think is best sweet wednesday I went to Lucy's [Flora's cousin, who also lived in New York City] because she was waiting for me to give me the letters that they brought to me that were from Clarita and Aida the ones where they sent me those newspaper clippings where the story came out about the train accident and the names of Eusebio and Xiomara where I took account of what bad shape they were in Out of the money I am sending you I want you to change ten dollars and give half of it to Ariel to help him get Xiomara and Eusebio through their illness and give the other half to my aunt vilma The money that you're giving to Ariel, give it to him in front of my aunt vilma and tell them that the money I'm giving him is for Xiomara and Eusebio Sweet I am also sending you some photos that you can take to show at the farm and afterwards give Jamile [Rolando's sister] whichever ones have something written on the back Also I am sending some earrings you take a pair the other to Clarita the other to Aida and send a pair to Jamile and Aurora [Rolando's other sister] Well love that's all I can tell you your sweetness that loves you very much Say hello to all my children and family especially to my grandmother, Goodbye and see you soon Also say hello to Zelmira Note: I want you to send me the papers that I put along with this letter Also tell my uncle Perfecto that he never sent me the address that I asked for and if he writes give him Lucy's address

tell clarita and Aida that I am going to write them or that on the 21 of march I will write to them

[Written along the side of the letter:] Sweetness it slipped my mind to tell you that now I am not drinking I quit drinking at the beginning of the new year and every sunday I go to mass and light a candle to the blood of christ.

New York 12 August 1987

Dear Love it's my best wishes that this letter finds you in good health and surrounded by Your Children after greeting you I want to tell you the following, that about me I'm doing fairly well I say fairly because I was sick with the flu and high blood pressure but that's going to be over soon Also I burned my neck at work with a hot rod but I'm all right because I used a burn cream but that is not all I'm also sick because of how much I think of you even though you don't believe it but it's true Every day I remember you thinking what you do where you go and with whom you go out when you go to the street, it's for that reason that I want to leave because truly truly I miss you very much even though I think that maybe you don't miss me the same way I miss you I'm telling you this because you don't write me but I hope that now that Lucy's back [visiting Nicaragua] you send me a long letter telling me everything I know what you think of me but I want to tell you that you are wrong because now that I don't drink I realize a lot of things Also I am telling you that if I was drinking perhaps I wouldn't send you what I am sending you because here it is so corrupt that I have reexamined my life in time to become responsible the way I am now, also I want you to know that I go for a walk on sundays that's true but after going to mass because I think I have the right because you know spending all week working in a factory but I will always have you in my thoughts I hope you do it but in a clean way when we are together again I am going to tell you a lot of things that I was thinking here but I tell you one thing that I have faith in you and it's for that [reason] that I believe you won't cheat on me, Going on to something else I was talking with Lucy with respect to you coming here I think it can be done but only if you get your American visa because it couldn't be done any other way for example going through mexico because I had a bad experience crossing the border and that's the reason I wouldn't like it but if you want try it I also think that the kids can't be left alone so it's better you wait for me We'll see how we have our life there, Going on to other things I will tell you that of the things I've sent you I can't remember what I've sent because I was buying them little by little what I was going to send and there were so many things that I can't remember exactly what I sent but I can tell you that there were a lot of things that you can sell for example some purses with a value of $11.00 dollars I sent a lot of deodorant worth $2 dollars apiece and I sent some scented creams that cost $4.00 dollars but let's do something whenever you open the suitcases write on a paper what you received and whatever you see that you can sell and send it back to me with Lucy's daughter who is coming back on the 26th of August and I'll give you the prices so you don't lose anything when you sell the things, Now you know that the things with a name I wrote them down just to go through customs only so you won't think it's for the person whose name is on that article also the money I'm sending save it and I want you to change $100 dollars and put it in the bank where you say you have the account but don't put it in all at once but in three installments I was thinking of sending you enough but I think I have to find a lawyer to go to immigration to get a working permit and also I have to pay excess weight for the suitcases that Lucy is taking Well sweet I want you to send me some *pinolillo rosquillas* [hard cookies, often pretzel-shaped, made from toasted ground corn, cacao, and butter] and try to send me about 5 pounds of dry cheese and when you go to the farm tell my aunt juanita to send me *jocotes* [a tropical fruit] you know that you can send them with Lucy's daughter or with Lucy if you can't find *cacao* you can make it stewed [*sancochado*] or the way I taught you to do it well sweet greet all my Children tell them how much I remember them and what I wouldn't give to have them here Sweet it slipped my mind that I've sent some dresses that are for Jamile's girl Do me the favor of sending them to her with a letter that I'm sending to Aurora tell Charlie to take them to them Well sweet that's all I have to say and I am awaiting your answer Say hello to everyone who asks about me also say hello to Zelmira even though she never answered the greetings that I always send her because I think she's always at the house Well love one sends you farewell your sweet that loves you so much and who wants more to see you than to write to you goodbye and see you soon

Your sweet

Rolando

[Note:] Flora I couldn't write to Aurora I'll write her later on

New York 3 August 1988

My well remembered sweet It is my best wishes that at the receipt of this letter you are in good health surrounded by your Children After greeting you I want to tell you the following sweet don't think I've forgotten you what happened is that I've had bad luck this year Well I'll tell you that I've lost a lot of things you know who I came with you know the old lady that you mentioned in one letter that by the way you told me that she sold her business to come to here with me well that old lady took up and left one day while I was working and took everything that I had in the apartment even my Clothes she only left me with two pairs of pants and those because I had them in my car among the things she took there was even a box of Clothes that I was going to send you that box alone was worth 200 Dollars at the same time I was laid off work and winter was beginning however I could I started buying my clothes and my shoes that I didn't have So now I am planning to do like before start buying things one at a time and give them to Lucy so when she goes back she can take them to you Now it's not too much what I'm sending but something is something, you know I know you're upset with me but I'm more with you because of all you've told Luzy you didn't have to tell her anything, not even that you didn't want to talk to me like as if I didn't have any right or maybe I don't have it now to talk to you like this but I want you to know one thing but even this far away you are the woman that I love the most in spite of all the things that have happened between us that you well know I'm going to do everything possible to put together some money to see if I can go next year that's why I told you that I'll be sending you once in a while and also that I'm scared to go because you know I'm here as a political refugee [*yo estoy aquí como asilado*] but any way I want to go I'll go sweet tell clara [Aida?] that I'm not sending the children's clothes for the baptism that she asked me for but tell her to send me a letter with Lucy's Son telling me more or less how many months or better yet how old the baby is also tell her to send me the box number and the phone number where she works because I'll send the kid's clothes in the mail Also I want you to know that if I haven't written anybody it's because I also lost my Addresses and telephones of everybody that I had sweet I want you to do me a favor that if you're going to keep this letter only where you know or if not tear it up or burn it because what I want with this is that you and me are more private [*reservado*] even when we're away from each other well send my regards to charlie Guto Miguel Clarita Aida and if she's still living there la Zelmira give her my regards too sweetness if you will I want you to send me a jar of pickled chile [*un chilero*] with onions and some sweets [*cajetas*] of the sort they sell in Masaya, I'm sending you 100 Dollars and the rest I'm sending is to buy me 2 liter bottles of Ron Oro [rum] You know I'm sending some boy's and girl's clothes the boy's clothes are for your grandson and the rest if you can sell them, sell them I don't want anybody to notice this and tell the kids they don't have to say anything to anybody sweet if I'm not mistaken your birthday is going to be the sixth of august I send you my congratulations well sweet that's all your sweet has to say goodbye and see you soon

Rolando

CHAPTER VIII

Flora

The lords have gone; they live in Miami.

Although I usually referred to her as "Doña Flora," she insisted that I call her simply "Flora." *Don* and its feminine form, *Doña*, are formal, polite terms. Roughly equivalent to "Mr." and "Mrs.," these terms harken back to the archaic Spanish for "Lord" and "Lady." Historically in Nicaragua, people addressed both those higher in status and their elders with such polite forms. The wealthier, higher status, or senior party was under no obligation to reciprocate; instead, he or she would address the poorer, lower status, or younger person informally, using familiar terms of address. After the revolution, in the spirit of egalitarianism, many Nicaraguans abandoned polite terms for most social circumstances. The colloquial, familiar *vos* was preferred to the formal *usted* (you), and most forms of address approached the plane of egalitarian and reciprocal discourse. So whenever I would call her "Doña Flora," she would correct me: "Flora. Los dones se fueron; viven en Miami" (The lords have gone; they live in Miami). I tried out her formula on more than one occasion, but I discovered that, although many people spoke in an egalitarian mode across the boundaries of class and status, most continued to use polite forms when addressing their elders. When in her absence I referred to her simply as "Flora," I was frequently corrected. Ultimately, I tried to duplicate what seemed to me the rule: I used *vos* and informal address when speaking with or of people my own age; I used *Doña* out of politeness when speaking with or of any woman who was more than a few years older than myself; and I employed *Don* with men who were visibly senior. With Flora, I

117

resorted to various forms of code switching: I always used the egalitarian pronouns *tú* and *vos;* when we were alone, I generally conceded to her wishes and called her Flora; when others were present, I often called her Doña Flora.

I never heard Doña Flora refer to anyone by a polite term of address—neither her seniors nor persons of superior wealth or social standing. Her forms of address were aggressively egalitarian. Although she could not be described as particularly political in the usual sense of the word—she attended few meetings, for instance, and she was actively engaged in no mass organization—her insistent egalitarianism was deeply rooted in her own experience and her own intimate knowledge of the weight of social class. Before the revolution, she had worked as a cook; she was a very good cook, and eventually she found employment as a domestic for one of Somoza's family lawyers.

In one of our first conversations, Flora put the lessons of Nicaraguan history into a terse synopsis: "*Los ricos* [the rich] do not care one bit about the fate of the poor people or of their country. All they care about is their own riches." She went on to explain her conclusion—not quoting from political tracts or historical lessons but by drawing on her observations as a cook in a privileged household. "I saw the way they thought and acted. And because I came and went in my employer's neighborhood, and in the houses of his associates, I saw the way other rich people lived, too. Let me tell you, they looted this country. They lived like parasites, off the work of other people. They took out all the wealth they could, and then they fled to Miami.

"After the earthquake [1972], the United States sent a lot of aid here to Nicaragua—the United States, and Europe, too. . . . Aid came from all over. Money. Food. Huge boxes of food. Bread. Potatoes. Cans of vegetables. All kinds of things. Times were hard after the earthquake, and we needed help, so everyone was glad to hear that help was coming. That aid never got to the poor people, who were left homeless and hungry and hurt. After Somoza took his share, the other rich people divided up what was left among themselves. Some of it they sold in the marketplace for a profit: cans of food were everywhere, but who could afford it? The rest they took for themselves. It wasn't just the money. They unpacked huge crates of food and took these home for themselves—they, with enough money that didn't even need it! Oh, they ate all they could. But they couldn't eat it all. I saw huge boxes of food spoil in the houses of these rich people. But that's the way they are. They would rather the food spoil than that it get to the poor and hungry people who needed it. They would rather it go bad than go into the mouths of the hungry.

"I don't understand that. The people needed the food. They didn't. I can only say that they hated the poor people and wanted to keep us as weak and dependent as possible."

As we sat on the porch and talked, a teenage boy wearing plastic pants and a plastic jacket walked past the house—a neighbor from down the andén. Such plastic clothes were considered very fashionable among Managua's teenagers at the time; a whole terminology had sprung up around them: *chicos plásticos* (plastic boys), whose plasticity resonated with the Ciudad Plástica (Plastic City), their favorite haunt. A modernistic, sprawling, mall-like complex at the south end of Managua, Ciudad Plástica sported a range of diversions: boutiques, restaurants, discotheques, and a bowling alley. "Look at that. *Plástico, puro plástico* [plastic, pure plastic]," Flora remarked as the youth walked past us. "Boys are out fighting and dying in the mountains today, and all some of these kids want to do is wear plastic and go to discotheques. What a disgrace."

After the revolution, Doña Flora went to work for a time as a cook at the Sandinista police station. When two of her children were old enough to start working, and after her whole family had moved in with Rolando, she felt secure enough to quit her job and take up housekeeping full time. Now, like many other grandmothers in Managua, she spends much of her day taking care of her daughter's son. When Ervin was still a drooping-headed infant, she bathed him in the large cement sink behind the house, where babies are bathed and laundry is washed. The water is invariably cold, which provokes the screaming and resistance of any healthy baby. Her movements in these early morning encounters registered much of her personality in gestural form: she was gentle, but remarkably quick and efficient. Ervin's protestations made not the slightest difference; a bath had to be taken, and it would be done as quickly as possible. Then, the finale: somehow, in a move that never failed to amaze me, she could hold her grandson with one hand and sling a towel completely around him with the other. Only *after* the bath was completed and the boy had been swathed and dried did she begin consoling him: "Now, now, little baby, it's all right, it's over, don't cry."

Doña Flora had been Rolando's "other" woman for more than a decade. She and her four children fathered by Rolando (Clara, Charlie,

Guto, Miguel) had constituted his second family. Living at some distance in León while Rolando remained with his wife in Managua, they received occasional monetary support from Rolando.

As we discussed family matters, Doña Flora produced a photograph album and showed me a yellowing black-and-white picture of Rolando when he was in his twenties, not long off the farm and still an apprentice mechanic. Before years of hard drinking had overwhelmed him, he had been a strikingly handsome man. Doña Flora pointed this out and told me that she moved into Erasmus Jiménez in 1980, after Rolando's first compañera left him, taking her four children with her. I asked why the woman had left him, and Doña Flora explained, matter-of-factly, "Because he beat her. They were having a lot of problems, the two of them, and arguing all the time. She put up with a lot from him. She always warned him that if he ever struck her, that would be the end of it. One day he got drunk and beat her. So she left him."

I went ahead and asked the obvious question: "Did Rolando ever try to beat you?" Doña Flora laughed at the thought—deep, sonorous laughter. "That he should try such a thing with me!"

"You should have been here when he first left for the United States," she said. "He was scared. He called here all the time. Sometimes he cried and said he was coming back right away. He talked about how much he missed me. Then the calls got further and further apart. Then they stopped altogether. I knew what was going on, and that he had found another woman."

She showed me his latest letter. I read it and commented, "Poor thing."

"Poor thing!?" she demanded. "How so?"

"Well, look, he's been sick, and his old lady not only left him, she took everything he had with her."

"It's just," she remarked, with some apparent satisfaction. "It's good enough for him. She should have done worse."

She mulled the situation a while, then continued, anger and frustration in her voice, making sharp gestures with her hands to underscore her points.

"*¡Qué baboso! ¡Qué estúpido! ¡Qué bruto!* [What a fool! How stupid! What a brute!] He goes all the way to the United States to work, and he finds another woman. I expected as much, because I know him. It didn't surprise me. He's helpless by himself, and he needs someone to take care of him. But what surprised me is this: he actually goes to the church and gets married. And who do you think he marries? A North

American woman, who would give him citizenship? No. That's what an intelligent man would do. He marries a Nica! A Nicaraguan woman! He goes all the way to the United States to marry a Nicaraguan! It's not just that you can't trust him; he doesn't even know what he's doing when he cheats on you. And you say 'poor thing.' I say, it's good enough. That, and worse . . .

"*Qué baboso. Estúpido. Bruto . . .*"

I eventually followed up this line of discussion and asked what I imagined to be the obvious question. "Which would it be better to send to the United States to work? A husband or a son?" The question was too obvious, and from the look she gave me—which already carried the answer—I imagined that she was weighing my own intelligence in the balance and finding me as thick as she had gauged Rolando to be. When finally she answered, she simply said, "A son."

Continuing my line of questioning a few days later, I asked Flora which it was better to *have* (not to send), sons or daughters. Very quickly she responded, "Daughters." Why? "Because daughters are more faithful. They'll stay with you. They'll help you out. Sons leave when they grow up, and you can't count on them." Which, then, did she think most women preferred to have? "Sons, most probably." Again, why? "Machismo. They think boys are better than girls."

With my return to the United States in the fall of 1988 only a few days away, I began packing my things and rounding up the letters my informants wished to send to their relatives, who were distributed to the extreme coastal points of the United States: Los Angeles, San Francisco, Seattle, New York, and Miami. Rolando's mother had received a Mother's Day card from New York, a card of the sort that proved very popular in Nicaragua: when the card was opened, a small computer chip played a tinny, sentimental tune. The slight, gray-haired woman came to Flora's house for a visit, bringing a letter she wanted mailed to her son. I was not home at the time, so she left the letter with Flora, who subsequently opened and read it. Flora showed it to me. The letter proved to be mostly an inventory of crops on the farm: a lengthy description of which fruits, vegetables, and tubers had produced well, which ones showed promise, and which ones looked poorly. The old woman wanted her son to know that his mother was eating well and that the farm (tended by his brother) was running smoothly. Crops, rain, and weather made up the bulk of the letter. In a somewhat shorter section, Rolando's mother briefly discussed the well-being of her son's siblings, near kin, in-laws, and neighbors from Niquinohomo. "Look at that," Flora remarked, pointing to this section. "She has a word for everybody in the world—except us! That foolish old woman, not one word about us. Don't send him this letter. I'll keep it."

And so she did, and the move was not atypical in the game of inter-personal relations. When information—no less than goods—passes through anyone's hands, the intermediary occupies a node in a web of transactions. He or she is generally aware that withholding as well as giving are both options, and that information, like goods, signifies power. Flora withheld information that might flow to Rolando while passing on to me Rolando's letters—the last of which expressly requested that their problems remain confidential. Perhaps Flora wished to punish her estranged husband even more than fate had punished him: by depriving him of word from his mother and by publicizing his poor treatment of her. No doubt, too, she was genuinely angry that his mother had not included word of her and her children in the letter and perceived this omission as an attack on her. (And perhaps it was. Or perhaps Rolan-do's mother wished to steer clear of subjects about which her son might not want to hear.)

I have received dozens of letters from my informants in Nicaragua over the years and many more phone calls. Generally, it is women who write. (I have received only one letter from a male informant.) After Flora disposed of Rolando's mother's letter (and forwarded me his own private letters to her), I became acutely aware of the sort of information that comes my way. Women do not discuss men—neither their hus-bands, nor their brothers, nor even their older sons—in these commu-niqués. What is left out seems to me sometimes glaring in its omission. I receive detailed word of sisters, mothers, and female friends, but never of men. My questions about male informants receive vague answers at best. In controlling and modulating the flow of information, my infor-mants effect a sort of power relationship, both with me and through me: This will be known; that will not be known. These relationships will be enhanced; those will not be. Information, and sometimes goods, will flow through these channels, and not others. By means of their control over personal information, women carve out a sphere of trans-actions that is largely under their control—and that can, when properly leveraged, translate into limited power or stimulate a flow of goods in the direction of themselves and their dependents.

Doña Flora did not expect much from men in the way of support, con-stancy, fidelity, or intelligence. She was not unique in her opinion. Per-

haps she was more forceful than many Nicaraguan women in expressing her impressions. Perhaps she was more independent than other women
living in and coping with the culture of machismo. But most women
her age expressed similar attitudes toward men: that they were basically
irresponsible and childish; that they drank too much; that they couldn't
be trusted. Certainly, Doña Flora cultivated her own, mostly female,
networks of aid and mutual support: among relatives, friends, fictive
kin, even in-laws. In this, too, she was not atypical. Perhaps the scope
of her independence vis-à-vis men was atypical—the thought that Rolando might try to beat her she found amusing—and perhaps the degree
to which she relied on other women was extreme, but the motifs are
hardly uncharacteristic of Nicaraguan culture.

Zelmira had lived with Doña Flora and her family longer than any
of the children save the very oldest could remember. A quiet, unexpres-
sive, businesslike woman, she had taken up residence with them in León.
When Flora's family moved to Managua to live with Rolando, Zelmira
moved in, too. On my stays with Doña Flora's family, Zelmira was
seldom around: by day she worked—she was a petty officer in the Sandinista military—and by night she went to school, earning college credit
toward a technical degree. My most extensive interactions with her arose
around her English homework, late at night, when I assisted her with
grammar and translations.

Zelmira took an active hand in rearing the children. She issued mild
warnings when their antics got out of hand, and they responded to her
understated suggestions. She contributed to the household expenses. After
an operation for benign tumors left Flora with a gaping, infected inci-
sion on her arm (out of which worms sometimes crawled), Zelmira
helped change the bandages and treated the wound with an antibiotic
ointment (locally made and of dubious quality). When Zelmira came
home from work and school, supper was always waiting for her in a
covered plate on the stove; Flora would put it back before her own
children depleted the beans, rice, and tortillas that were the staples of
everyone's diet. When Zelmira purchased a late supper from the vendor
who every weekend set up a grill down the street, she either shared her
plate with Flora or purchased her friend a meal as well. Sometimes the
two women stayed up together, late into the night, sitting side by side
in their chairs: slowly rocking, quietly talking, and watching television.

Neighbors sometimes commented—approvingly—on the two wom-
en's strong friendship. I never heard any untoward gossip about their
relationship, never any suggestion that there was anything illicit, sexual,
or unwholesome about it. "It's a good thing to have a friend like that,"

Doña Jazmina once remarked. "It's good to have someone who'll always help you out." (Rolando's letters acknowledged the importance of the two women's relationship and complained, indirectly, that he felt left out by Zelmira's refusal to acknowledge his letters.) I paid the matter less attention than I might have until I got around to the business of classifying household residents. Was Zelmira a relative? (I had always assumed that she was a cousin.) No, Doña Flora responded. An in-law? No. A boarder? "Certainly not. I would never charge her rent! She's a friend, a good friend of mine, and a dear friend of the family."

Other than her children, the only permanent fixture in Doña Flora's household was Zelmira, another woman. Most likely, Zelmira will remain long after most of Flora's children have left the house. It might even be said that Zelmira, more than Rolando, was Flora's "primary relationship," if we define primacy in terms of security, constancy, predictability, and endurance rather than romantic interest or sexual activity. Indeed, although Rolando fathered most of Flora's children, the two women together performed most of the work of rearing and providing for those children. In many ways, Zelmira was more their "parent" than Rolando was.

Carroll Smith-Rosenberg (1985, 53–76) describes how Victorian-era gender roles and sexual segregation provided the space for an intimate world of lifelong, committed, loving friendships between women. Because of the wide acceptance of this subculture of female intimacy and the prevailing assumption that women were not sexual beings per se, no sharp boundary was drawn between friendship and romance during the Victorian period in North America. Nicaragua's culture of machismo duplicates the logic of the Victorian situation in several regards: women often find their intimate emotional (and sometimes even much of their *material*) support and mutual aid in the company of other women more than in the company of men. The structure of work, and the division of the day into various gendered labors, means that women spend most of their time socializing with other women, and men spend most of their time with men. Indeed, from the point of view of women, traditional male gender roles make men a dubious investment in terms of emotional and material security. And from the point of view of men, traditional gender roles still assign activity (sexual and otherwise) to the masculine temperament and passivity to the feminine—although two decades of political ferment have clearly undercut any assumption that women are uniformly passive.

Were the two women also lovers? I think not. I have no reason to believe that they were, and I don't think a Nicaraguan would even raise the question. A sexual relationship between two women living together could undoubtedly be concealed from one's neighbors, but it would be difficult to conceal within one's own cramped household, bustling with children, relatives, husbands, and assorted guests. Were such a relationship to be discovered, it would without doubt provoke family and community consternation. At the same time, however, close female friendships are scarcely seen as cause for alarm, and even should these relationships occasionally tilt over into sexual intimacy, there does not exist in Nicaragua the cultural atmosphere or the package of assumptions that would mandate ferreting out a woman's sexual indiscretions with another woman.

But intimacy? Caring? Responsibility? Commitment? It is simply assumed that these are part of the community of women and their children—a community in which some women achieve relationships like that of Flora and Zelmira. From one angle, this community forms a line of resistance against machismo—a refuge for women and their children, a means of mobilizing women and their resources apart from and even against men. From another angle, it is a product of machismo—an allocation of expectations in which physical intimacy is heterosexual, emotional intimacy homosocial. From yet another angle, this female world is also a necessary prerequisite for the ongoing reproduction of the male world of machismo—for the package of assumptions it carries, the efforts and resources it allots, even the spheres of relative autonomy it grants for women, are part and parcel of a deeply gendered division of the world, where gender remains defined in terms of male dominion over women and children.

CHAPTER IX

Osvaldo

Life is hard.

In Sandinista ideology, the imagery of the guerrillero is largely beatific. One renounces one's relatively comfortable life to pursue a difficult calling, a dangerous passion, in the mountains. The political lore relates many such stories—of middle-class university students who became heroes and martyrs. Osvaldo's is another sort of story. His was a different—and undoubtedly more common—path to the mountains.

I first saw Osvaldo in late November 1985. He had not been in the neighborhood when I began my fieldwork. One day I passed a young man on the andén. He was wearing military fatigues and greeted me when I passed. I nodded and said, "Adiós." A few days later, I saw the same man courting Doña Jazmina's daughter, Sara; he was standing out on the sidewalk, she was inside the porch on the other side of the waist-high wall, and they were discussing Lenin's tract on imperialism.

A couple of days later, while I was doing some last interviews before my return to the States, someone asked me if I had met Osvaldo yet. "Osvaldo?" I asked. "Doña Flora's oldest son," I was told. "I didn't know she had another son." "Yes. Osvaldo. He was away in Cuba, studying. He's a Sandinista, a member of the Frente, and a lieutenant in the army. [It later turned out that he was not a member of the FSLN but an advanced member of the youth organization.] He was a guerrillero when he was still just a little boy. You should talk to him. He knows a lot about the revolution."

The next day I wandered over to Doña Flora's house at dusk. Doña Flora and Aida were out back, making preparations for Purísima. Just as I had hoped, Osvaldo was home and greeted me with some enthusiasm. We introduced ourselves, and I asked him if we could talk for a while. He agreed.

We sat out on the front porch while the sun set. Osvaldo spoke in hushed, secretive tones, frequently looking around him to see if he were being overheard—as though we were entering some sort of conspiracy. There was a lot of background noise: Miguel was watching television inside the house, and radios were blaring in the houses on either side. I am somewhat hard of hearing, so I had to ask Osvaldo to repeat almost everything he said. He later explained that he felt inhibited by the setting: "Most of the people around here don't know me very well. That's why I speak so softly."

We discussed various issues: Cuba, the Soviet Union, Chile. "Chile was a big lesson for us," he explained. "Here, we're not going to go like that. Allende attempted to bring socialism to Chile in much the same way we're trying to do here in Nicaragua—gradually, and by democratic means. It was a beautiful experiment. But Allende had no way of protecting himself, and he laid himself open for the CIA. He thought Chile's democratic traditions would protect him, I imagine, or that the United States would do nothing as long as he didn't align with the Soviet Union. He was very wrong, and he paid the price."

Was Osvaldo a Leninist? "Well, more or less," he equivocated. "I believe in the class struggle, and I believe in the national liberation movements. And I believe in vanguard leadership, but with all the new lessons of guerrilla warfare that Lenin could not have imagined. I suppose in some ways that makes me a Leninist, in a Latin American sense. I've read a lot of Lenin, especially while I was in Cuba. He was a very intelligent man. We all need to read Lenin, to understand what is going on in the world today, and to know how to fight against imperialism."

"Then why don't you call yourself a Leninist?" I wanted to know. "Because this materialism thing—it's not too clear to me. It's very difficult, and I'm not sure I understand it. I believe in God, and on occasion I go to Mass. The Cuban officers who trained me said that if you believe in God, you're not a real Leninist. So that's why I say more or less."

When I asked him where he attended Mass, I was surprised by his answer: he went to Don Bosco, the conservative church. "Not the Popular Church, which is nearer?" "No, I go to Don Bosco. I know that the Popular Church is full of good people and good revolutionaries. Every day their work helps us realize a better society. And their Mass is a beautiful thing. Yes, I know that the church hierarchy is very reactionary and perhaps even dangerous, but they're controllable. Really, I just prefer the old Mass. It's what I knew when I was a child, and it seems more like Mass to me.

"I know, in your country, the government tells a lot of lies. They say that we're going to prohibit religion here in Nicaragua. But how could we? Good Christians make good revolutionaries. Our experience shows that. And in a country where 80 to 90 percent of the people are religious, how could we, in good conscience, prohibit religion? We couldn't, and we have no intention of doing that. I'm a good example. Why, I don't even go to the liberation Mass; I go to the old Mass, and I'm a Sandinista."

Osvaldo had been favorably impressed by what he saw in Cuba. "In Cuba, they have accomplished a lot in a short period of time. They have big industry there, now, and all the houses have electricity and running water. You'd be surprised at the quality of medicine and machinery they produce. Health care is free and of good quality. People are relatively equal, and everyone receives an education. I am impressed by the socialism I saw in Cuba. Someday, perhaps, Nicaragua can achieve as much. But it is clear that we won't get there quickly. We can't follow the Cuban road or the Cuban model. It's not appropriate for Nicaragua. Things here are different. Large-scale expropriations, for instance, are unthinkable here. We don't have the industries to nationalize! And what good would giant state farms do here? We don't produce that much sugar cane, and for what we do produce, small farms and collectives are better. And we want more democracy than they have in Cuba. So don't ever let anyone tell you that Nicaragua is another Cuba. We are Nicaraguans, and we don't take any other country's experience as our model. Our task, over the long run, will be to develop production within the confines of a mixed economy, political pluralism, and international nonalignment. And we will do so with as much social equality as possible, so that everybody has work, food, and dignity. That's the Nicaraguan path to socialism."

I made a final call on Osvaldo just before my departure in December 1985. He and I were set to have a few drinks that evening, and when I arrived, he and Rolando had already polished off a bottle of Flor de Caña. The two of them were sprawled out in their jockey shorts to escape the hot, dry December heat, and I, too, had shown up with nothing on but a pair of shorts. Over the second bottle we talked of politics, plans, and adventures. After a while, Osvaldo got up and put some sad, slow music on the stereo. To my surprise, he took my hands, invited me out of my seat, and began dancing with me. A bit nervous, I looked around the room. Rolando was in a beatific daze and could have scarcely registered scandal had there been any. It was late at night, and everyone else was in bed. I protested, "I don't dance very well." "Don't worry. That's not important." Osvaldo put his hand on my hip, held me within inches of his own body, and swayed. Was I being romanced? Probably not, I decided. I took it as a matter of friendship, different from my own culture's assumptions about friendship, that two men could get drunk and dance with each other.

Later that night, Osvaldo saw me to the door. His arm around my shoulder, his parting words were: "When you go back to the States, tell the truth about our revolution. And always remember to fight imperialism, which is the enemy of humanity."

Osvaldo's commitment had faded somewhat after only seven months had passed. The now rapidly declining economy was taking its toll on everyone, and Sandinistas were scarcely shielded from the hardships. He complained of his work: "They work me like a slave—and pay me like one, too. There just isn't any money left in Nicaragua, I suppose."

Rolando had left the country sometime earlier, and on my 1986 visit to Nicaragua, Osvaldo informed me that he, too, was considering going to the United States. "Would I be arrested," he wanted to know, "because I'm an officer in the Sandinista Army?" I said that I didn't know, but that the current policy toward Nicaraguan immigrants was very generous provided that they ask for political asylum. "No, no," he stressed. "I don't want to do that! I don't want to live in the United States. I just want to work there for six months or a year so I can bring some money back and make a better life here, in my own country." I told him what he already knew: that it was a long journey, through Mexico, and that he ran the risk of being captured by INS.

"I still believe everything I ever believed," Osvaldo said. "Our revolution is a just revolution, it is a correct revolution, and this is the only way forward for our country. But right now, because of the war, and the embargo, we're not moving forward at all. We're moving backwards. And things are very, very difficult."

In the summer of 1988, when I returned again to Nicaragua, much had changed in Osvaldo's life. I heard that he had had his first child, a daughter, by the same woman he had been seeing on my last stay. And some time before my arrival, he had wed—a different woman—and moved into her parents' house, a few blocks away from his own mother's home. The couple were expecting their first baby in September.

I noticed after a few weeks had passed that Osvaldo almost never visited his mother's house. It appeared that relations were strained, and Doña Flora almost never brought up the subject of her son. When he finally did stop by the house, it was only for a brief visit. He exchanged greetings with Doña Flora and Aida and then spent some time with me in the patio. He said that it was difficult, at times, living with his wife's family, but he seemed excited at the prospect of having a baby.

We talked about the continuing war. "War is hard," he said. "It's a horrible thing to see a friend die. I've seen many friends die, and I've killed a lot of guardsmen. I've seen war since I was a little boy. War is hard."

Changing the subject, I asked him which he preferred in September, a boy or a girl. He said, "Whatever. It's not important. But I hope it comes out a boy." And then, with what seemed to me a matter-of-fact delivery, not a joking one: "He can be a soldier, and go to the mountains."

Osvaldo told me that he had to go and invited me to stop by his house and see him. "Miguel knows the way, he'll take you there. Please do come by and see me. Oh, I know what—we can go out shooting together at the firing range where I practice. Would you like that? I can bring you an extra pair of earplugs. It would be fun."

I visited Osvaldo's house a few days later, and we sat together talking in front of his house. He brought out an album of wedding pictures, and I leafed through them. Noticing a discrepancy, I said, "But Osvaldo, look. Your family is not here at the wedding. Why not?" What ensued shed a whole new light on the man. He told me that he had been abandoned by his mother when he was just a boy. We talked about his life for hours that evening, and I tried to piece the story together. It was clear that resources had been very scarce when Osvaldo was growing up. And he also thought that perhaps his mother had vented her rage on him when his father abandoned her.

"It's a hard thing to be rejected and abandoned by your mother. I couldn't understand what I had done wrong to be rejected by this woman who had given me life. I thought I must have been a terrible, horrible person, because I loved my mother, but she had no affection at all for me. Even today, you've seen the way she speaks to me. It's 'Hello, good-bye,' very formal and distant.

"She gave me to another woman to keep when I was just a little boy. That señora didn't have any children of her own, and she wanted a boy. I couldn't understand why my mother gave me away. That was why I went to the mountains when I was still very young. I tell you, I cried every night in those mountains, when I was a guerrillero. I felt so alone, so lost. It was painful, and I still hurt because of it. Life is hard. Do you know she never asked about me the whole time I was a guerrillero? Not once. It would have been easy to ask or to send word to me. She knew people in the movement. She could have sent word for me. I waited, and waited, and cried myself to sleep at night, just a little boy carrying a gun. But nothing. Never anything. Not a word.

"And then when they sent me away to Cuba for three years, I wrote her all the time. I sent her letters telling her how I was doing and what I was learning. Not once did I ever receive a letter from her. Ah, life is hard.

"I lived with her only one year when I got back from Cuba. She didn't even wash my clothes. I had to wash and iron my own clothes, like I was a tenant in my own mother's house. Can you imagine how I felt? She never had any affection for me, and she still doesn't. And no-body in that house treated me well. What do you think it was like, living with brothers and sisters who didn't know me and hardly even spoke to me? And Rolando, he never treated me well, either. I think he didn't like having me around. Why do you think I got married? Just because I love my wife? That's not the only reason. No, not really. I married and moved out of the house to get away from her, to get away from all of them. She never loved me, and she loves me even less because I'm mili-tary, and she doesn't like that. And that's why she didn't come to my wedding, neither she, nor Aida, nor Clara, nor Charlie, nor Guto. Mi-guel. Miguel was the only one who came, only Miguel. He's the only one who has any feelings for me. And Miguel is the only one who comes around here to visit me, too. Every few days he comes to see me. He even comes and eats with us sometimes.

"But the señora my mother gave me to, *she* came to the wedding. Here is her picture. She treated me right all these years. I send her money, now that she's older, and I try to look after her. I suppose my real mother did come to my wedding.

"And even my father came to the wedding, too. He was never much of a father for me, but at least he came to my wedding. Here's a picture of him."

Osvaldo came by to see me about a week later and asked me if I could change six dollars for him. Sure, I said. "Good. Now I have the ten dollars I need to buy a bottle sterilizer at the Diplo-Tienda [the dollar store]." "For your daughter?" "Yes, for her. But listen, don't tell anyone what I'm doing." "Why not?" I asked. "Because I don't want them to know." As usual, Osvaldo was clandestine.

The next night, when I stopped by to visit him, he showed me the bottle sterilizer he had bought, and we went for a walk around the barrio. I kept stepping into puddles, which Osvaldo artfully avoided. Once he grabbed my arm to steer me away from a particularly deep hole. I marveled that he could see in the dark and said that he must have cat's eyes. "In the mountains," he said, "it's dark all the time. You learn to see in the dark. I learned a lot of things in the mountains: how to see in the dark, because you're in the dark most of the time. How to be very quiet, because the Guardia Nacional was all around. And how to be clandestine."

We passed some teenage boys hanging out on the street between Erasmus Jiménez and Rigoberto. "Be careful now when you go out at night," he warned me. "There are a lot of gangs in Managua now, and some of them are quite vicious. War is hard, and the economy has collapsed. Delinquency is a result of that." I asked if he thought it was safe for us to be walking around so late at night. "Well, there are two of us." As we turned a corner into darkness, he added, "And I have this," producing a small pistol from his pants. "Here, you carry it for a while if you like."

A little later, as we rounded another corner, someone turned on car lights, and at the same moment a boy started running behind us, playing with his friends. Osvaldo whirled and crouched, his face deadly serious. After a few seconds had passed and he had regained his sense of place, he explained that in the mountains the Guardia Nacional had used giant lamps to illuminate the jungle before making its assaults on guerrilla camps. Then he broke into a grin, and we both laughed.

CHAPTER X

Elvis

I believe in worshiping God by right living.

It was 1984, and I was interviewing Doña Celia on her beliefs, especially her religious beliefs. A young man who frequently came by the
house joined us. I had asked Doña Celia, "What is a true Christian?"

She began: "A true Christian is someone who follows the laws of
God and keeps his commandments. It has nothing to do with going to
church and everything to do with how one comports oneself in everyday life. The people across the street, for instance, go to Mass all the
time [she crossed herself vigorously and affected an attitude of great
faith, eyes uplifted], but when they come home, they're the basest, most
vulgar people in the neighborhood. She has a filthy mouth, and he drinks,
bothers all the young girls who pass by on the street, and beats his wife
whenever he pleases.

"A true Christian is not like that. A true Christian follows God's
commandments. These are: Don't have any other gods . . . Don't bear
false witness . . . Honor your father and mother . . ."

Doña Celia faltered; she was obviously having difficulty recalling all
ten commandments. Elvis—our visitor—prompted her. "Don't steal what
belongs to your neighbor . . ." "Don't steal what belongs to your neighbor," she repeated, and waited a moment. "Don't fuck his wife," Elvis
again prompted. "Don't fuck his wife," she repeated, then paused, realizing what she had said. She had used the verb *coger*, which means
literally "to grab" or "to hold," and figuratively "to fuck." In Nicaragua, *coger* is much stronger than the commonplace verb *joder*, which is
equivalent to our "to screw" or "to fuck."

"Oh, you!" she laughed, gesturing for Elvis to stop teasing her. And instantly I took a liking to Elvis.

Elvis was the only person I met in Nicaragua who refused to classify himself religiously. Was he a Christian? He would not say. Catholic? No. Evangelical? Certainly not. At least as far as his own self-classification went, Elvis was uniquely secular in his orientation. His formulative intellectual experience was with the Sandinista Proletarian Tendency, which, when he was younger, was relatively "purist" (by comparison with the Prolonged Popular War and Tercerista [Third Way] factions) in its Marxist interpretation of the struggle against Somoza, its agenda for reconstructing Nicaraguan society, and its analysis of religion.

"For the most part, the church is irredeemably reactionary," he said to me. "Yes, some of the clergy became radicalized, in the last days of Somoza, and these people were an intermediary force in the revolution. That is because this section of the clergy was middle-class, and represented a middle-class position. That is all, nothing more. In fact, some of the Frente, too—the Terceristas—have the same middle-class politics. So these aren't finished questions yet. But some of the members of the church, and even some of the clergy, became genuinely revolutionized by the experience of the struggle against Somoza. They reread the Bible from the point of view of the poor. They sided decisively with the working class. These are good people.

"But I don't know much about it, because I don't go to Mass, and I don't care for church. It's mostly fake, mostly boring. Take life after death. How do we know that there's life after death? Because somebody said so, or because the Bible said it. But how did they know? Because someone else said it, or because someone says God told him. What's the proof? You have to take somebody's word for it—and that's when they all start jabbering about 'faith.' I prefer to believe in things I can see and touch. If I were to go to Mass, I suppose it would be to the liberation church. At least they have lovely political paintings . . . and a rock and roll Mass."

Despite his apparent contempt for things religious and his relatively orthodox Marxism, Elvis would never describe himself as an atheist or even an agnostic. "I believe in God, in my own way," he said. "Not the God of the rich, worshipped by the church hierarchy. They have distorted and perverted the idea of God—whatever that is. I'm not sure. Not the God of the church—I don't think any church has a monopoly on God."

"Then what do you believe in?"

"Right living. I believe in worshiping God by doing right." Why? "Because right living is real. You can see and touch its results." And what was his conception of right living? "Be honest, be humble, don't exploit people." His vision of God and morality was not so very different from Doña Celia's after all.

Despite his love of jest, Elvis was a very serious young man. In 1985 I talked with him about the state of youth in Managua and consumerism. "Many people my age are interested only in things like how they look, dressing up in strange-looking clothes to be fashionable, going out to discotheques every night," he said. "This is rarer among working-class children—for one thing, it costs two or three hundred córdobas just to get into a discotheque, and few proletarian children can afford such diversions. But it is increasingly common among middle-class youth. You may have seen them, wearing shirts and pants made out of plastic. *Chicos plásticos*, we call them. Well! Who would want to wear plastic? *Why* would anyone want to wear plastic? And in this climate? It's just stupidity, foolishness, that's all it is.

"It is because these kids are interested only in the impression they make when they are seen. They want to scandalize public opinion with their expensive and strange clothes. These new values aren't good. They keep people from being interested in study, hard work, sacrifice, or the good of the country—much less the duty of military service. Just appearances and impressions, that's all these new values are about.

"Many such youth dream of going to the United States, because they are more fond of the pleasures of capitalism than of building a free and independent country. I have a cousin like that. He fled to Miami to avoid military service. Mind you, he doesn't have close relations with my family or anything; he is from a higher social station than we are. Well, he has written back to his parents that he likes it just fine there in the United States, among all the crime, vice, and delinquency of capitalism. I don't understand it. His parents are upset now because they say he's not coming back, and they've lost him. Of course, it's their own fault. They sent him away. They were also the ones who spoiled him.

"They do it for the plastic clothes and the Walkmans. Luxuries have some sort of power over people. These expensive things are like drugs that intoxicate the middle-class youth and lead them off to the United States and into vagrancy, delinquency, or drug addiction.

"Look, I don't want to sound like I'm no fun at all. I'm not saying that it's bad to have good things. I like blue jeans. That's a fine type of clothes: practical, convenient, sturdy. A pair of blue jeans lasts forever. I like having a good time with my friends. There's nothing wrong with joking, and laughing, and having a few beers. But it comes down to this: Nicaragua is a poor, Third World country. Our economy is under-developed. We cannot produce our own clothes yet, much less stereo headphones. If the people of our country develop the tastes and the habits of the North Americans, then we'll never develop our economy. All the work will go, and all the money will go, to buying plastic clothes and Walkmans and other things we can't really afford. So for now we should enjoy the things we can afford, we should be content to enjoy the things of Nicaragua. And we have a long road ahead of us: a path of studying, hard work, and planned investment, if we are ever going to reach even the lower stages of industrial development."

"Why is it that whenever you see a gringo walking, they're always walking fast, like they're in a hurry to get somewhere? I've watched them, a lot of times, walking"—Elvis made a Nicaraguan gesture with his hand, something like finger snapping, slapping thumb into index and middle finger in a gesture that denotes a range of possible meanings: haste, fear, pain, threat, or violence—"almost running."

I thought about his question. "Well, remember, the United States is a very developed country—overdeveloped, if you will, the opposite of underdeveloped. Everyone has to be punctual, for instance, at work, because everything is automated. The workplace is very much on a time clock, because the managers know exactly how much work can be done within a given time period, if everyone works and moves efficiently. United Statesians [*Estadounidenses,* a common way of referring to U.S. citizens in Nicaragua] are usually in a hurry, because—well, we have a saying: time is money."

"Time is money?"

"Right. And it really is, in an overdeveloped economy. So we just get used to walking in a hurry, compared to Nicaraguans, and to walking past people without saying hello."

Elvis pondered my response to his question. "I'm for developing the economy, but it would be a tragedy if Nicaragua developed into a so-ciety where time is money."

"A lot of kids want to join the Sandinista Youth today because it seems like a good way to get ahead in the world," Elvis observed over beer one evening. "I'm sorry to say it, but that's the way it is. You have more job and educational opportunities if you're a member of the Sandinista Youth. The organization tries to screen people carefully. It requires a lot of community service work, but the selfish appeal is still there.

"Back during the days of clandestinity, the appeal was different. I joined the Sandinista Youth back in 1978, when I was twelve. It seems to me that there were two reasons why anyone would want to join in those days. Many kids became involved, back when we were clandestine, for the thrill of military engagement and armed robberies. They liked to shoot, and hold up liquor stores, and throw gasoline bombs, and it was all very exciting. Then there were others, like myself, who were attracted to the Sandinista Youth by the political aspect, even though we were not yet fully conscious of it at the time.

"I was thrown in jail four times by the Guardia Nacional and released each time. I was twelve, and moreover I was very small for my size—about like Miguel today. When they captured me, they thought I was only seven or eight years old. They kept saying, 'What can a little boy like this do?' and they let me go."

I asked, "What were you actually doing at the time?"

Elvis laughed. "I was assisting with armed robberies, manning the barricades, passing messages, and helping with a clandestine Sandinista Youth press doing propaganda work. Things like that."

In the summer of 1985 Elvis had just returned from his third tour of duty in the mountains. He was preparing to go to Bulgaria sometime later that year, he said, for a six-year program of university study, to be financed by a full scholarship from the government of Bulgaria.

"Six years is a long time," I ventured.

"I know," he said. "I think about that a lot—not seeing my family for six long years."

"When you come back, your younger brothers and sisters, your nieces and nephews, will be young adults. You might not even recognize them."

"It will be hard, I know. But it's the best thing. The schools here are very weak, and I can get a better education abroad. The program gives a year to learn the language and then five years of study. I am going to study electronics. Nicaragua needs electronic technicians, electronic engineers; we need all sorts of technical expertise. Employment looks good in that field, too, so I won't be wasting my time. I'll be useful. The war won't go on forever, and when it ends, we will need the specialists that can do the planning and the work of developing this country. Right now, much of our expertise comes from abroad—internacionalistas from Cuba, Bulgaria, the Soviet Union, even volunteers from the United States. We need our own expertise. We don't want to be too dependent on other countries."

Politics was never very far removed from conversations with virtually all of my informants. Political talk, political analysis, was an everyday occurrence—naturally so, in such a politicized situation. More than most, Elvis talked politics; moreover, Elvis sometimes wished to talk *theory*, especially after I explained that one of my specializations as an anthropology student was in Marxism.

"You study Marxism in the United States?" he asked, a bit baffled.

"Why, yes. At my school, it isn't so rare."

"Well, then, you be careful," he warned. "Here, they used to put you in jail for reading Marx. And your government is persecuting our whole country now for even thinking about Marx. How do you get away with coming to Nicaragua and writing about us?"

Elvis was not alone in his impression. Many of my informants worried that I might go to jail for my work. "The government isn't much worried about us because it thinks we're harmless," I reasoned to Elvis. "They like to allow free speech and free opinion—up to a point. And Western Marxism—critical Marxism—doesn't tend to be very engaged politically, at least not on *class* issues, so perhaps they're right about that. Oh, they probably keep lists with names of people like myself on it, but I don't think I'll go to jail, because the Constitution guarantees free speech. Of course, if there were a leftist political movement in the United States, things might be different, and the government might view Marxist intellectuals in a different light. They've put people in jail in the past because of what they believed, and not so long ago. For now, as I see it, my whole problem is this: as a Marxist, and as a sympathetic student of the Nicaraguan revolution, my politics are very definable. I'm not writing about something that happened five hundred years ago, and I'm not talking about something that's very obscure. Because of that, it could be that when my thesis is written I'll have a great deal of difficulty finding academic work. Some people say that there are informal blacklists at the universities, and I imagine there are, in this sense: leftists are regarded as not being quite academically sound."

As 1985 wore on, Nicaragua's economic situation began to deteriorate visibly. The first and hardest hit were the most vulnerable families—

those households headed by women whose male breadwinners had abandoned them. Doña Celia and her family were in just such a position. Government subsidies could no longer moderate the effects of inflation on Doña Celia's family, and few additional means of increasing the family's income were available to them: two children already worked at poorly paid bookkeeping jobs in the Ministry of Agrarian Reform; one son was in the military; the youngest son was not yet old enough to work. As the year 1985 went by, and as times got harder, Doña Celia's family increasingly began voicing dissatisfaction with their plight. Why had things not gotten better for the poor? Where was the equality and peace that had been promises of the revolution? By engineering a war and an economic crisis, the U.S. policy of bleeding Nicaragua into despair and submission was already beginning to produce its results. The years 1985 and 1986 registered a rapid decline in rank-and-file activism by Sandinista supporters who were not members of the Frente or its youth organization. Indeed, ordinary working-class people began voicing complaints that were sometimes sharply critical of the Sandinistas and the revolution. Sandinista activists like Elvis were placed in the difficult position of defending the revolution, upholding Sandinista leadership and policies, and trying to explain the nature of the deepening crisis to their sometimes skeptical neighbors and friends.

María-Teresa and Yolanda had been teasing Elvis on political subjects for some time—telling him, for instance, that he was being tricked into going to Bulgaria, where they would make a slave of him for six years, impressing him to pick cotton and work in the mines and things of that sort. One evening when we were seated in the Ocampo living room and the electricity went out, drenching us in darkness, Yolanda upbraided Elvis: "*Los Sandinistas son jodidos*" (The Sandinistas are fuck-ups); "*A los Sandinistas les gusta jodernos*" (The Sandinistas like to fuck with us). One night, as we were sitting on the front porch, the teasing became intense, and an argument ensued.

Elvis: "You surprise me, Yolanda. I think you're losing your convictions. You didn't talk this way before."

Yolanda: "That's because the revolution has fooled us. It's a hoax. Nothing has changed."

Elvis: "How can you say that, when we're building a more just society?"

Yolanda: "A more just society? How can you talk about equality and socialism in the New Nicaragua? People still don't have enough to eat. Before the revolution, there were rich and poor. After the revolution, it's just the same. Tell me, what has changed?"

Elvis: "A lot has changed! Yes, we still have rich and poor—because we are a long way from developing socialism in Nicaragua. You know better than that. Justice is still something we work for, we fight for. You do it every day at the Ministry of Agrarian Reform, which gives land to the peasants. You know how hard the rich are fighting to preserve their privileges. And certainly, you know that in Nicaragua today, we are a country with human rights. Nobody has to be afraid for their lives any more!"

Yolanda: "Yes? At my school last week, the teacher told us how Somoza's Guardia used to come through the city and kill young men and boys, and that we should be glad this can't happen now. But it *does* happen now. The government comes and takes youths off the streets, drafts them, and gets them killed in the mountains. What has changed?"

Elvis: "You know very well why we have obligatory military service. We are fighting a just war against the counterrevolution. If *they* come back to power, then *nothing* will have changed, and we really will go back to the days when people were grabbed off the streets and had their throats cut. It's because of Yankee imperialism, and the Guardia, and the rich, and their supporters, like Cardinal Obando, that we have a war—"

María-Teresa: "Don't go dragging the church into this. All the cardinal wants is an end to the slaughter. He's a man of peace. There has been enough killing."

Elvis: (*With scorn*) "Right. All of a sudden, the church hierarchy has discovered pacifism and preaches a message of love and reconciliation. Where was their pacifism, back in the days of Somoza? Where was there love, back when the rich were eating the poor? Where were their Christian principles, back when the bourgeois like themselves could get rich and fat off the work of other people? We're in a fight for our country right now, and this talk by the church is just a pretext. They're not for peace, they're for exploitation and imperialism! They're pacifists now because they don't want to kill their friends, who want to kill *us*."

Yolanda: "Well, I'm a pacifist. It is better to be killed than to kill."

(*All three of us look disbelievingly at Yolanda.*)

Elvis: (*Eventually*) "You don't even believe that! Why, the irresponsibility of it! How can you talk like that, with your own brother, tonight, in the mountains . . . ?"

Yolanda: "Don't bring my brother into it! My brother would be here, tonight, in his own house, if not for the Sandinistas. The Sandinistas are all in it for the money and power. Why, they are just parasites, living off the people! Parasites!"

The last characterization left Elvis speechless. *Parasite* is a strong insult—one of the few insults that I have seen children come to blows over. Responding to the noise of argument, Doña Celia intervened, suggesting it was time for her daughter to come inside and prepare for bed. Our little group made a sort of peace, said good night, and disbanded.

I walked Elvis home that evening; he was still visibly upset. He volunteered to talk without my prompting.

"This is very bad, very bad. Yolanda is very young to be talking this way—talking so very contra! I know a lot of people are tired of the war, but they know why we have a war. You should have seen Yolanda six years ago, in the Plaza, on the Triumph, carrying a placard and shouting, '¡Viva el Frente! ¡Viva el Frente!' But now . . . this is bad, it is very bad.

"Many of the youth of Managua before the revolution spent all their time dancing, going to fiestas or discotheques. Even many of the Sandinista Youth were very frivolous: they knew how to throw a gasoline bomb; they didn't know how to carry arms. They knew how to rebel, but they lacked discipline. And a lot of kids in Managua are still like that, and they resist military service, and hide from the army. But people like that are very young. They can change. The military changes people, too, for the better, usually. They learn how to work together with other people, how to make sacrifices.

"And Yolanda is still very young: you know young people can change very rapidly.

"Like her, some people think the Sandinistas are in it for the power and the money. They are suspicious of our motives, and I am no Sandinista, strictly speaking. I am still just a Sandinista Youth, and still a long way from party membership, although I am a Sandinista, figuratively speaking. But they don't understand, we are not interested in personal power, but in popular power, not personal wealth, but social wealth."

I didn't expect to see Elvis when I returned to Nicaragua in the summer of 1986. I imagined that he was already in Bulgaria. I visited his family to inquire after him and follow up some interviews with his mother, who was a CDS member active in health-care campaigns. I found Elvis seated in his family's living room, studying Russian. His plans had been changed: not Bulgaria, but the Soviet Union was his destination, and the date had been moved back to late 1986, or perhaps some time in 1987.

Seated with him, I surveyed his progress with the language. A host of mystifying signs, copied over and over again, covered his notebook as Elvis set out first to master a new alphabet and basic Russian terms. "I'm having a lot of trouble with this Russian," he said. "These letters are hard to make, and the pronunciation is difficult." He showed me a few terms and told me what they meant: *I, you, man, woman, boy, dog.*

"How did you learn Spanish?" he wanted to know.

"Practice, mostly," I replied. "But I didn't have to learn a new alphabet."

As we were talking, a tragic sort of thought occurred to me. "What if you go to the USSR to study for six years, but in the meantime the Sandinistas lose the war?" (I did not imagine, at the time, a different turn of events: that the Sandinistas would lose elections in 1990, or that the Warsaw Pact and the Soviet Union would collapse, stranding hundreds of Nicaraguan students so far away from home: without scholarships, without income, and without return fare home.)

"It won't happen," Elvis assured me. "We're winning the war, decisively now. We're going to win the war. The contras—really, we're mowing them down this year. We're cutting up their supply lines and uprooting their support networks. When I come back, the war will be over, and things will be better."

On another visit to Elvis's house, it occurred to me to ask if he were well prepared for the change of climate. "You've never known really cold weather," I warned, "and it gets very cold where you're going. A Nica in the Russian winter—man, your ass is going to freeze. Are you packing warm clothes?"

"I think I'm prepared," he told me, then shouted out, "Mamá, show Róger the jacket I'm taking to the USSR." From his grammatical text, Elvis produced a map of the Soviet Union and pointed to his likely destination: a town near the geographical center of the Russian republic. His mother appeared from the back of the house bearing a light cloth jacket with a thin cloth lining. "See," she said, "we've already prepared. But we were wondering: do you think it's heavy enough?"

I looked at the jacket, considering how to frame my answer respectfully yet indicate the cloth's inadequacy. "It's going to be very cold in the middle of Russia—below freezing all winter, and snow everywhere.

That won't keep him warm. [To Elvis:] You should wear that underneath a heavier jacket, with two pairs of pants. [To his mother:] He'll need something with a thick lining. I prefer a leather jacket with a heavy lining. Cold can't cut through leather the way it can cloth. If not, some sturdy cloth with a very thick lining."

Obtaining such a jacket would be no easy matter, and Elvis and his mother began surveying their options: they had made friends with an internacionalista from the United States; perhaps she would send them one. Or relatives abroad—perhaps they could be called on. Elvis's mother announced that she would go down to Telcor (the telecommunications and mail service center) the following day to begin making phone calls. I volunteered that I would be happy to send a proper jacket if Elvis were still in Nicaragua when I returned to the United States.

As it turned out, the family's internacionalista connection paid off quickly: long before I departed, a very appropriate jacket arrived, with an amply padded down lining and a detachable hood. Elvis was preparing to take a language test, and it looked like things were moving along well.

When I visited Elvis's house in May 1988, his mother greeted me at the door, and I could see the recognition dawning on her face after my two-year absence. "Róger!" she shouted. "Come in, come in!" I walked inside, out of the blazing midafternoon sun. "How happy to see you!" she exclaimed. I asked her how things were going for her family. "Ay, times are hard," she sighed. "Prices just keep rising and rising. The war goes on and on. But we're getting by."

"Elvis," she ventured, "is still here. He didn't go to the USSR. He's very disappointed, as you might imagine. Why don't you come and talk to him when he gets out of school this evening? He'll be glad to see you."

I returned later that evening and invited Elvis out for a soda. We walked and talked. Of the fellowship, Elvis said only, "They changed the plans and didn't send me." I found it difficult to inquire further: Had he failed some entrance examination—a language test, perhaps—whose importance he had minimized two years before? Or had his overall grades proven inadequate? He had been so certain of the fellowship: with reason? Or was his certainty just wishful thinking? Or had the Soviet program seen cutbacks, reducing the total number of international fellowships allotted to Nicaragua. (Soviet largesse toward Nicaragua was never evident, and Soviet international aid to that besieged country—in all its forms—was becoming increasingly meager.) All of that was left unclear to me, and Elvis seemed sensitive about the issue, so I did not press the point. Apparently it was also unclear to Elvis's friends, among whom I made inquiries.

"It's not important. It would have been grand to study in the Soviet Union, and I think I could have made a contribution to national development. And I would like to see the Soviet Union, to see for myself how its socialism works and whether we can learn anything from it. All of that would have been very fine. But it wasn't to be. And it's not the most important thing. What's important is that Nicaragua survive, that our revolution survive, and that we go on to rebuild. And why should this preoccupy me when there is so much more tragedy all about us? Really, I have both my arms, both my legs, I'm in good health, and my family is well. I'm doing better than a lot of people. I am working at Telcor, now, in international communications. Then, at night, I study accounting at UNAN." (He used the abbreviation for the Nicaraguan Autonomous National University—a decided demotion from his previous track.)

Eventually, hesitantly, I raised some current political questions: Had Elvis noticed the change of tone in *Barricada*'s and *El nuevo diario*'s editorials and news articles? Was Sandinista rhetoric becoming less leftist and more Third Worldist—if that was a meaningful distinction? Certainly, the party organ's analysis of U.S. internal politics was now far more sophisticated than I had ever seen it. What did all of this mean about the direction of the revolution, Sandinista policies, international politics? "I don't really know," Elvis responded. Resignedly: "I had a lot of time for politics before, but not so much now. I'm working to help support my family and going to school, and that doesn't leave me a lot of time for politics. It's strange, but it just seems that everything important is out of our hands. The only thing we can do is to maintain our position the best we can: defend the country, stand our ground, try to get through the crisis, and wait." As we walked the andenes of Erasmus Jiménez, it seemed to me that Elvis had the strange dignity of a man who was trying very hard to maintain his dignity.

CHAPTER XI

Róger

The crisis, man, the crisis! I can't stand living in crisis anymore.

For a time, Róger and I had a special rapport. Its source proved difficult to describe. Sometimes we discussed it: perhaps, we reasoned, it was because we both shared some sort of artistic temperament. Or maybe it was because we were both brought up Protestant, and, although we had rejected the hardened theologies of our respective churches, we retained more than a little of that training in our personalities. Perhaps he was the younger brother I never had. Or maybe it was just that we shared a name. Whatever its source, we cemented a fast friendship and initiated a vigorous traffic in little favors. I would solicit his aid in translating and understanding the poems of Rubén Darío or in understanding Nicaraguan culture from the point of view of its urban youth, and he would solicit mine in helping him with his English homework or lending him little household items. In this manner, Róger became a fast fixture around the house where I was staying, and we would visit out on the front porch. Or, as was often the case, he, Virgilio, Jaime, and I would go out drinking together, or we would all hang out on the andén late into the night when all the lights were out, talking politics and discussing the vagaries of life.

Even by Nicaraguan standards, Róger was a very proper young man, from a protective and conservative family of Jehovah's Witnesses. When his mother learned that Róger was friends with an older North American visitor, she insisted that I meet her. And so Róger took me over to his house one evening, somewhat blurry about the details or the reasons for my sudden visit. He lived in the lower-working-class barrio Rigo-

berto, and his house was typical of others in the neighborhood. From a
large living room in front, it ambled backwards, its rooms randomly
added on in mazelike fashion one at a time, until all that remained of
the backyard was a narrow strip of dirt that hosted a few chickens.
The house had wooden walls, a cement floor, and a rusty tin ceiling that
was forever springing leaks. When we arrived, it had just stopped rain-
ing, and most of the house's meager furniture was stacked against one
wall to keep it dry; several chickens and a cock had decided to roost
there for the evening. Róger hastily mopped the little puddles of rain-
water off the floor, scattered the chickens into the backyard, and arranged the furniture—several rocking chairs and a small table—in what
I took to be their normal constellation. There was still no sign of his
family. Róger informed me that his mother and several of his sisters
were in the back of their rambling house, sewing and reading the Bible.
He served me pinolillo with an air that was simultaneously gracious
and formal, and then I was summoned to the back of the house, where
I was confronted by a very stern, maternal woman. Feeling scrutinized,
I was careful to use proper forms of address and show every sign of
politeness.

"I don't let my son go around with just anybody," she told me. "I
like to know who his friends are, and what they're like. I won't have
my children going around with vagrants, picking up bad habits. A lot
of bad things can come from hanging around the wrong crowd. We're
a Christian family, in this house. I imagine Róger has told you. Are you
a Christian?" she demanded. "Yes," I lied. "What denomination?"
"Baptist—actually, Free Will Baptist." She pondered this answer a moment, and I conjectured that she was thinking, Well, it's not Jehovah's
Witness, but at least it's Protestant. Then the interrogation resumed:
"Do you drink, or take the Lord's name in vain?" Again, I did not have
to be cued on my responses and lied with what I supposed was a straight
face. I had already seen that Róger could consume far more beer than
either Jaime or Virgilio could without wobbling, and foul language was
no stranger to his lips when he was sufficiently agitated. I was sure that
his mother would disapprove of such behavior in either her son or his
friends. "Do you study?" she wanted to know. Yes, I explained to her,
I was a graduate student at a North American university, where I stud-
ied anthropology. "Good," she responded, and then: "So why are you
here in Nicaragua? Are you here just idling around, or are you working?" I explained that I was doing fieldwork, studying Nicaraguan culture. "And I hear that you love the Lord's creation, too," she observed,

commenting on the trip to Masaya's volcanoes that Róger and I were planning. "That is good. It is a fine thing, to be able to enjoy God's handiwork." At last she initiated what I took to be a proselytizing routine, enumerating all the fine points of the Jehovah's Witnesses. Gently, respectfully, Róger broke into her monologue and said that we had to go.

Seventeen years old, Róger had clear memories of the revolution, and we sometimes discussed his experiences. "The Guardia didn't much enter Rigoberto; they couldn't. The people were all against them, and we were armed. Even the prostitutes stopped having anything to do with the Guardia Nacional, that's how much everyone hated them. So instead of trying to take the barrio by force of arms, they bombed us with airplanes. I was eleven at the time and remember it well. The loud noises, the explosions, and afterwards the fires, and people screaming. I served as a firefighter, and sometimes I helped build barricades. That's where I got these burns." He showed me a series of little scars on both his arms.

"In retrospect, the barbarisms committed by the Guardia seem almost unbelievable. Every morning I used to get up at the crack of dawn and walk down to the marketplace for my mother. All along the way, I would count the corpses of teenage boys whose throats had been cut by the Guardia the night before. Indiscriminately, and just like that, they slaughtered the teenage boys and left their bodies by the roadside. And the worse things got, the more bodies I could count.

"Their tortures were ingeniously sadistic. Pins under the fingernails. Gang-raping women. Sometimes they would feed a victim's castrated sexual organs to dogs in front of him. And now the same Guardia Nacional is still torturing, raping, and killing, committing atrocities along the border and in the mountains. Really, Róger, I know Christians are supposed to believe in love and forgiveness, but it would have been better to have killed them all in the insurrection, if we could have."

Róger spoke of the revolution's accomplishments in mixed terms. "When we made the revolution, it was an insurrection of workers and students, and we had a socialist ideal. We wanted to build a new society, peopled by men and women made new, where the humble people ruled. But I cannot say that all power has passed to workers and students. I feel this very strongly, despite the official position that the working class holds power in Nicaragua. The bourgeoisie persists. It is very powerful, and it continues to vigorously oppose all collectivist ideas.

"At the same time, there is no 'New Man'—only talk of him, and little pieces of him here and there. We are no doubt closer to this collectivist idea than before. But the egoist remains very strong. Many kids my age are concerned about nothing but shirts, pants, how they look, and a lot of them just want to breakdance all day.

"To elaborate a New Man, we need order, discipline, work, and good language. Yet we still have a lot of delinquent gangs in the city, and a whole generation is being beckoned by plastic, delinquency, breakdancing, and drugs.

"And when I raise such points at school," he continued, "do you know what they call me? A contra. A reactionary. I, a son of the poor, a contra! All I care about, politically, is building this revolution along its proper collectivist lines.

"I think there are two kinds of souls, one bourgeois, the other proletarian. That boy we met, the Nicaraguan who is my age and who grew up in the United States: he has a bourgeois soul. He is a hedonist, always thinking about this party, or that woman. Why, even his hair had a streak of yellow dye in it! He is not *sencillo* [simple, honest, straightforward]. His attitudes are very bourgeois and egotistical.

"Others have proletarian souls. People from the country. People who work hard for their livelihood and who care more for others than for themselves. My parents come from the country. They were simple people, who worked hard. My grandmother is an Indian, and I grew up poor. I suppose I have a proletarian soul."

Róger's dichotomized moral framework entailed no analysis of how poor people could become delinquent because of despair or environmental factors. There were, in the end, just two kinds of souls: bourgeois souls, which were sinful, consumerist, and acquisitive; and proletarian souls, which were innocent, simple, and generous.

"But what about people who start out proletarian but end up bourgeois?" I asked. "They really had bourgeois souls all along," he said.

Sometimes Róger discussed his purpose in life with me, his goals, his dreams. These he generally framed in the context of socialism and Christianity. It was his lot to study, to work, and to use his strength and his skills to build a better society and make a better life for himself and his family. "I don't have to be rich to be happy," he said matter-of-factly. "All I want is an education, and a good job, where I can do meaningful work with dignity and respect, and enough money to support myself and my family."

At other times Róger discussed the tribulations of youth with an energy that displayed his romantic temperament. On the week when his girlfriend was turning fifteen, he was preparing to buy her a small, white teddy bear he had seen in one of the stores. When he spoke of the girl, he never talked about how she looked or described her physical beauty; rather, he always said that she was a very special compañera. He wrote her poems and love letters. "I feel close to her because we can feel free to speak our hearts, to speak of our sadness, to each other. But her father doesn't approve of me, so I cannot visit her at her house. I don't understand a man like that; I think he must be a man of the nineteenth century or something. He thinks all youths, just because we're happy, and sometimes a bit *vago* [lazy], are drug addicts, so he wants his daughter to wait until she's twenty to start dating. I think, too, that he believes I'm not good enough for her, because my family is poor, and I'm *negro*. But I have a plan, and I'm going to make it happen. When I get out of the military, I'm going to come back, finish my schooling, and acquire technical training. I'll work, and save money, and become a respectable person with enough money in my pockets to support a family. That is my plan. I know it will take a long time. Probably about seven years. But I know what I'm doing, and I'm very determined. And then I'll ask her to marry me, and how could her father say no to such a presentable young man?"

With a variety of reservations, Róger praised the revolution on several counts: it had opened up the possibility for a collectivist society; it had already given the common people a measure of dignity and respect unthinkable under Somoza; it had offered education and self-improvement for Managua's poor. The fact that it had not achieved all of its goals he attributed to the persistence of the bourgeoisie and bourgeois ideas and to the contra war. There was, however, one thing about the revolution that caused him much anxiety. That was the mandatory military service, the draft. Occasionally he framed his objections to mandatory military service in terms of the teachings of his church; indeed, there had been a period of repression of the Jehovah's Witnesses because of their pacifist teachings. This was a mistake, he said, because while the Jehovah's Witnesses objected to military service, they held many beliefs and encouraged many practices that would be beneficial in reconstructing Nicaraguan society and in building a New Man. And, he pointed out, it was only some church property that was confiscated; the Jehovah's Witnesses continue to meet, and to proselytize, in their homes and meeting houses around the country. "Why should I serve in the military if my conscience tells me not to? I know it's a necessary fight, to stop the contras, but some of us should have the option of not going to war, if that's what we believe." So on various occasions Róger argued that there should be a conscientious objector provision to the draft law that would allow young men like himself to perform medical or social services in support of the war effort but without carrying arms. Usually he framed his arguments in terms of religious freedom, especially the freedom of denominations to object to service if their creeds demanded it, but since his own beliefs were a heady and heterodox mix of beliefs that were scarcely reducible to the standard doctrines of the Jehovah's Witnesses, I sensed that there was more to it than that.

One day Róger read to me a poem by Rubén Darío, "The Blue Bird" (1953)—his favorite, he informed me. The poem tells the story of a poor, sensitive, and artistic boy living in Paris. It is his fate always to be alone, even when he is with other people, Róger added, and always to be misunderstood. One day the boy tells everyone that he has a blue bird living inside his cranium. His parents take him to psychiatrists, who diagnose him as seriously psychotic. Little by little the boy begins composing lines of poetry: sweet, exquisite verses to the bird imprisoned inside his skull. This development only alarms his family more, and no one appreciates his genius. When the death of a childhood girlfriend brings on a serious depression, he pens his last lines, wherein he vows to free the tiny bird imprisoned within his skull. His friends find him in bed the next morning with a hole blown in the side of his head. And the narrator exclaims at the end, "How many more share your sickness!" Róger read this poem with great emotion. His was a moving, theatrical performance, and he frequently lapsed into lengthy recitations, not readings, so well did he know the verses.

Then Róger explained to me his theory of literature. Literature exists to make us more sensitive to other people, more aware of their pain and their feelings. "And then, if you see a boy, sad and preoccupied like this one in the poem, perhaps you will understand him better, and can help him rather than isolate him, and make him feel better rather than worse."

The following day, I mentioned this performance to Jaime, and a story unfolded. "Have you noticed that Róger is a bit temperamental? He is. He sometimes sulks with no reason, he takes offense very easily, and he has a very hot temper. One day he beat up his best friend very badly, over some little slight that was nothing at all. He's very strong, you know, and very quick. You should have seen Juan, walking around for days with swollen eyes and bumps. He once went a full year without talking to Virgilio or me, and then showed up one day as though nothing had happened. Well, there's insanity in his family, and perhaps it's marked him. So there's a reason why he's so temperamental. And there's a reason why he's so abnormally terrified of military service: he's not just opposed to it, he's terrified of it, preoccupied with it, and he thinks about it all the time. And there's a reason why he tries to write poetry. This is the story. Róger had an older brother, and his brother had a passion for literature. He wrote poetry. It was good. The two of them were very close, and Róger admired his brother a great deal. But his brother went very mad serving in Somoza's military, at just about the age that Róger is approaching now. He didn't want to go, but in the last days, the Guardia came around, grabbing boys like Róger's brother, who were tall and strong. So one day his brother committed suicide, and this is how he did it: the autopsy showed that he ate half a pound of nails. It was a horrible way to go. And who do you think found the boy, lying on the floor of the house, dying? It was Róger, who was still a boy, very young and impressionable. And he held his brother in his arms there that day, while he was vomiting blood and dying. Before he died, his brother made Róger make two promises. First, 'Never stop writing,' he told him, and he made Róger promise to go on writing the poetry that he himself so dearly loved. And second, that he would never join any military, and never be a soldier. So how could he renounce his dying brother's request? He couldn't. And so he writes poetry, even though he isn't very good at it. And he dreads the day that he will have to go into the service."

"So that explains 'The Blue Bird'—and vice versa," I said.

"Yes," Jaime agreed. "I worry about Róger's mental health, sometimes. I think he's afraid, in his heart, that he'll do the same thing his brother did. As I say, he's very temperamental and unpredictable. Half crazy, really. And when he gets something into his head, he won't let it go. For example, the love of which he speaks, for the girl who lives down the street: it's an illusion. Truthfully, his obsession with her is almost infantile. It's true that at one time they were a couple. But that was two years ago. They've broken up several times since then, and she sees other boys all the time. I've even been out with her myself. Really, the truth is, she almost hates him. That's the only way she feels about him, and that's what she tells everyone else."

I wondered—and still wonder—whether some old conflict had motivated Jaime's divulgences and whether they could be verified. I corroborated his story with others, and the details were apparently as he had described them.

When the time came, Róger did indeed serve his time in the military.

His was a hard tour of duty; he was stationed away from Managua, near the front lines of the war, and there was a long gap in our contact with each other. Afterwards he severed relations with his friends, Virgilio and Jaime, for reasons I could never quite get to the bottom of, so again, I didn't see him.

In 1988 he looked me up when I was staying in Managua for the summer. Not long out of the service, he was again in school—finishing his last year of *secundaria* (secondary school)—and again making plans. But much of his tone had changed. He had finally seen that his *novia*, his sweetheart, did not care for him and had given up on ever winning her heart. He told me that he was preparing to enter a professional training program, perhaps in engineering.

"But I'm not really very serious about it, because I'm not planning to stay here for long. I'm looking for a way out."

"Why?" I asked.

"The crisis, man, the crisis! I can't stand living in crisis anymore! There's too much tension here. Everything is political, everything is economic, everything is the war. There's not enough money, not enough food. All my friends say they are leaving, too, as soon as they can. The tension is driving me crazy! I want to get out of it. In the United States I could see new things, do new things, have a new life. It would be a good change for me."

I warned him that a voyage to the United States would not be a pleasure vacation and that he'd have to work at low wages doing manual labor.

"Ah," he said. "You're trying to discourage me. That doesn't bother me. The people who go to the United States, they say that they work hard but that they make a lot of money—ample money. I know a couple of people, relatives of mine, and they are doing quite well, working in a factory."

We discussed his options for travel. "I don't want to go illegally, and I don't want to ask for asylum. I want to go legally." I told him that would be difficult, because the U.S. embassy in Managua was no longer granting very many legal residencies anymore, not even visas for visits, least of all to proletarian people from barrios populares. But he persisted: "I know some people who can get them—visas—but they cost a lot. They get stolen papers from the embassy and sell them, stamped and everything."

"It sounds risky to me," I proffered. "Look, what if the papers aren't really official, just forgeries, and you get swindled? Or what if La Migra discovers that the documents are stolen? They'd run you off right away."

"Perhaps you are right," Róger responded. "It would be a terrible thing to go to all that expense and then get thrown out for having illegal papers. It would be best to go legally, like my brother went. Someone asked for him, where he works, and now he makes good money as a car painter and legal resident. Maybe someone could send for me. Maybe you could send for me."

So that's what this is leading up to, I thought. I told him that I could think of no context in which an anthropologist could send for someone, and I doubted that my word would carry very much weight with INS. "You need the recommendation of a factory or something," I told him, "and I don't have any connections with business. All my connections are with labor unions, and they don't really want you under any circumstances, legally, illegally, or whatever." "Why not?" he wondered. "We're all workers, and we're all poor folks." The new immigration laws were being closely followed in Managua, and Róger, like most of my informants, could see no reason for them, other than perhaps the spite and pettiness of a rich country.

"Well, think about it," I told him. "If you work illegally, you'll be working at wages lower than the law would allow or, at any rate, at wages lower than the norm for the industry you're working in. That's bad for North American workers because it has the effect of lowering everybody's wages in the end. At the same time, you'd be providing labor that might have been provided by unemployed people in the States. In essence, you'd be willing to work at lower wages and under worse conditions than North American workers. This means that business has access to a steady supply of cheap labor. As an illegal worker, they'd use you to evade wage and safety laws, to lower wages, and to bust unions. But even as a *legal* worker, with a permit, you'd still be taking a job that might have gone to a native, and you'd probably be willing to do the same or more work at lower wages and without joining a union. So that's why labor unions are in favor of tougher migration laws."

"Perhaps," he responded, "but our problems here are problems of underdevelopment, because the poor countries have been exploited by the rich countries for hundreds of years. And our worst problems here are consequences of the imperialist aggression against Nicaragua. So now everything here is in ruins, and some of us want out. It only seems fair to me that your country should accept us."

I had no real answer to his basic argument. So I tried to get him to see the native's point of view, asking how would he feel if Nicaragua were suddenly flooded by streams of immigrants from a poorer country—say, for example, Haiti—willing to take jobs at wages lower than Nicaraguan workers would accept. But now we had reached the point of jest, and Róger responded, *"Nicaragua para los Nicaragüenses"* (Nicaragua for the Nicaraguans). "And the United States?" I asked. "For everybody," he laughed.

As we examined his options from every angle, it became clear to Róger that I was not able to aid him in his quest. We closed our visit that evening by exchanging addresses and agreeing to keep in touch.

Finally, in 1989, a letter reached me. It was prefaced by a variety of patriotic phrases, and Róger thanked me for helping him to see the issue of immigration more clearly. He informed me that he had elected to stay in Managua, that he was already beginning his studies in engineering, and that he planned to go to work humbly in his own country, to rebuild the devastated economy, and to try to make a reasonable life for himself. Could I send a hundred, perhaps two hundred dollars, to help him through the first year of study? The letter was signed with the familiar slogan *Patria Libre o Morir* (A Free Homeland or Death).

CHAPTER XII

Máximo

With a full stomach or with an empty stomach, we are with
the revolution.

Máximo is a middle-aged man who lives with his wife and only son in
Erasmus Jiménez. He describes himself variously as a Sandinista and as
a socialist. When I first met him in 1984, he was working at a bank as
an information processor. An activist in the local CDS, he quickly rose
into the ranks of the barrio committee.

A garrulous, expansive man of fifty-three (in 1985), Máximo exem-
plified voluntarism in the revolutionary process. Whenever brigades were
mobilized to pick coffee beans or perform communal labor tasks, he
always volunteered. And despite his age, Máximo volunteered for three
tours of duty in the mountainous provinces of Nicaragua, where he
served as a sergeant and saw combat. Of all the soldiers and former
soldiers I met in Nicaragua, Máximo was the only one who gave me the
impression of having liked military service; moreover, he was the only
one who would talk at some length of its details. Most men prefer not
to discuss their military service, especially their own specific exploits. In
this context it seems to me that—contrary to the usual posture of masculinity—most men fear calling attention to themselves lest they appear
egotistical. I have always felt that my informants so loathed the idea of
military service that, although they complied with the law, and although they endorsed the values of bravery, honor, and country, they
secretly feared being seen as someone who loved military life.

Máximo often talked about his war experiences with me while we
drank the bottle of rum his wife invariably produced whenever I showed
up at their house. An excellent specimen for his age, he once displayed

his dexterity at some sort of military maneuver by rolling twice on the ground and coming up on his feet. When he came up, he launched into a discussion of the use of U.S. mercenaries in Nicaragua. "You know," he told me, "all the contras are mercenaries, bought and paid for by the United States. But among the contras there are a number of Yankee mercenaries who were born in the United States. Did you know that? It's true. I've seen them. I even killed one. We came upon him camped in the mountains. His companions fled, but he wasn't fast enough. 'Don't kill me, don't kill me!' he shouted, with his hands up." Máximo mimicked pointing a rifle. He paused. "I shot him." After another pause, he spat out, "Animal." Showing me the olive green canvas hammock he had taken off the "gringo mercenary," he digressed. "This is a beautiful piece of work," he said. "Just look at it. It doesn't leak, it's secure, it sleeps well. It will last forever. Someday perhaps Nicaraguan industry will be able to produce textiles of this quality."

"My parents," Máximo told me on our first meeting, "were workers. I am skilled and well paid now, but really, I have acquired nothing, no property, no durable goods, that I can pass on to my son. And before my present job, I worked for ten years as a day laborer. I was a truck loader, and that's why my back is so strong today. So I am from the working class, and I am with the working class. I have seen class from different perspectives in my life, so I know that it is the most important thing. Popular power and national independence: those are what make the revolution."

From the beginning of our conversations, Máximo took a hard line on the economic complaints of people living in the city. "Look, it is far worse in the country, a thousand times worse in the mountains. People in Managua have little to complain about by comparison. For now, everything should go to the war front, and no one should complain about the inconveniences. The bourgeois parties are trying to capitalize on people's confusion about these things. They say, 'Before, there were never long lines to buy things,' and some of the people will no doubt listen to them. That is because the businessmen want to put everything on the free market, and then instead of seeing lines, we'd go back to the old way, when poor people couldn't buy what they needed to live. Or the bourgeois parties say, 'The draft is bad, we are against the draft,' and some people are willing to listen to this, too, because they don't understand that sacrifice is necessary for the freedom of our country.

But right now we are in a war. It is a war for our freedom, and any country in a war like this has to make sacrifices."

As hard as he was on the everyday grumblings of ordinary Nicaraguans, he was harder by far on Sandinistas who weren't willing to make even more dramatic sacrifices. "One of the problems we have is that of bourgeois elements in the FSLN. Some of those people were Somocistas in the time of Somoza. Yes, they have technical skills, and they might be useful in some ways. But really their outlook is all very bourgeois. Like that man on the corner of the andén where you live: he was a Sandinista, a militant, with a government job. He was caught embezzling money and received a long prison sentence. And now his whole family has passed over to the side of the reaction, and they can't wait to line up at the airport and go to Miami. Out with them! That's fine! That's the sort of party member we don't need. So gradually we are trying to train a whole new generation of skilled workers who can run the state, the banks, the civil service, and who are recruited from the ranks of the working class, not from the bourgeoisie. And little by little the bourgeois elements in the country are being replaced. In the end it is only the working class that is willing to make sacrifices for this country's freedom.

"And it is the Frente itself that must lead the way, setting the example. We should eat like everybody else—no, that is not correct: we should eat *worse* than everybody else if we're going to ask people to make sacrifices. And anybody who fails to live up to the revolutionary ideal of sacrifice should not be a member of the party. They should be thrown out."

Máximo was scathing in his criticisms of the CDS barrio director, Ortíz, who many thought was engaged in featherbedding and corruption (see Lancaster 1988b, 154–59). "A thief and a criminal" was Máximo's epithet. "He is one of those bourgeois elements who puts his own self-interests first. He and the rest of the barrio committee don't like me because I have opposed them and spoken out against them in the past. Come the next election, we are going to throw them all out of office and elect honest people."

When the election came, Máximo was among the twelve candidates for director. I attended a meeting of the barrio CDS at which the candidates were introduced. After some introductory remarks on the seriousness of the election, each candidate was allotted one minute to speak. Actually, most of the candidates were much briefer. On the average, women candidates took about thirty seconds, speaking in soft tones about the need to reform the CDS and get on with the work of safety and health care in the community. Few men strayed many seconds over their one-minute limit. When Ortíz took the stage, a number of people in the audience shouted out, "One minute only!" while others laughed and a few hissed. Ortíz was indeed brief, restricting his remarks to about thirty seconds, in which he said that he felt honored to have been elected to the post in the past and promised to campaign hard to retain his position.

When Máximo took the stage, he spoke for four minutes in a rousing style, lashing out at unnamed corruption, speaking of the need to re-build the mass organizations, and exhorting people to work harder and make sacrifices. When it was over, Máximo had received the most en-thusiastic applause, and I felt confident that he was in the lead. But when I attended smaller meetings of the CDS block committees, I for-mulated a completely different impression. As these smaller groups dis-cussed the various candidates in a neighborhood setting, several people always put forward the thesis that Máximo would be exactly the same as the incumbent director—a thief—and this quickly became a widely held opinion. When I inquired why this was the consensus, most people gave vague answers. "It just seems that way." "He reminds me of Or-tíz." A few said, "Because of the way he talks." As one put it, "He talks like a demagogue, and that's exactly the way Ortíz talked." Clearly, most people were tired of rousing political styles, had had enough sac-rifices, and were suspicious of any politician who promised them more of the same.

The election was actually won by a middle-aged former "Indian beauty queen" living in Erasmus Jiménez. Hers had been the briefest and most unpresuposing statement at the earlier barrio meeting. In general, she employed a very gentle speaking style and emphasized the CDS's role not in the trenches of the battlefield but in the "trench" of health care and hygiene. Máximo was returned to the barrio committee—one of the few incumbents who was returned. No doubt embittered by his defeat, he continued to complain about the rest of the committee's in-eptitude, inactivity, laziness, and presumed corruption, and eventually he resigned his post.

In the summer of 1988 Máximo had just returned from a speaking tour of the United States. It was an unusual situation. He had received an invitation from a radical U.S. college professor who had met him and stayed with his family for several weeks while she was on a political tour of Nicaragua. Apparently judging him a gifted, natural speaker, she set up a schedule that would take him to several cities and universities across the Southeast, where he addressed churches, classes, college anti-interventionist clubs, and even local civic organizations. He had not obtained official approval before making the trip, and at the bank where he worked he was told that he could not take leave for such a visit to the States. He went anyway, touring for two months. I surmised that Máximo was probably considered something of a loose cannon, and his superiors were probably concerned about how he might represent Nicaragua in the States. If there were such concerns, they were not altogether unreasonable. Máximo played for me a tape recording of his meeting with a prominent U.S. congressman—a southern Democrat who had been an important swing vote on contra aid, sometimes voting yes, other times no. Máximo's representations on the political, social, and economic state of affairs in Nicaragua were clear and cogent, but when questioned about the Nicaraguan military, he responded that he had no idea where its arsenal came from. Pressed further on Soviet and Cuban aid, Máximo became increasingly flustered. The congressman actually ended up feeding Máximo the proper and official Sandinista position: that Nicaragua would receive aid from any country that assisted it.

When Máximo returned, not only was he jobless, but *compactación* (streamlining, compacting) was in full swing. Noting his own poor prospects for finding a job in the short term, he said that some former Sandinistas had fallen by the wayside: compactación had been very difficult, and the introduction of the new currency had "hit a lot of people very hard." With compactación, the Sandinista government introduced emergency measures designed to deal with the country's acute fiscal crisis and high level of deficit spending. Compactación merged government ministries, scaled down the size of the government bureaucracy, and laid off large numbers of civil servants in every sector. Sapped by hyperinflation, the old currency had become virtually worthless. The new currency was introduced in February 1988: to combat inflation, black-marketing, and rampant tax evasion and to dry up the contras' reserve funds in córdobas. To prevent cheating, the introduction of the new currency was kept a secret until the very day conversion was to begin—a truly remarkable accomplishment, given that the changeover required the participation of some sixty thousand volunteers. Most people with whom I spoke reported that the new currency briefly improved their standard of living, but that after a few short weeks, the same hyperinflation that had afflicted the old currency set in, and soon things were worse than ever.

"Yes, the new currency has hit people hard," Máximo commented. "But it has hit big business and the contras even harder, so it served its purpose. They lost millions in the changeover, which was staged like a surprise guerrilla attack—and indeed, this loss may have seriously crimped the contras this year. Big business used to evade taxes by holding out unreported income. When the conversion came, they lost all that money, because if they tried to convert more than 10,000 córdobas, they had to provide receipts for that money. If they couldn't provide receipts, and if they hadn't been paying taxes on the money, the government would confiscate it and fine them for delinquent taxes. I myself even lost a few thousand córdobas in the switch because I kept some of the money in a bank account, and I couldn't find the documentation for it. This was the funny thing: rich people tried to get their neighbors and relatives to bring in the money for them, in small amounts under 10,000 córdobas each, and they offered to pay them a fee to do it. But most people would rather see them lose the money than collect the reward. So in the streets of Managua's rich neighborhoods, businessmen held great bonfires and sad little parties in which they burned millions of córdobas.

"At the same time, a substantial percentage of the old currency had fallen into contra hands. It's not clear exactly how much. Perhaps 10 to 15 percent of the córdobas in circulation had been obtained by the contras, who used U.S. dollars to purchase them. This gave them a large bank on which to draw and allowed them to move freely about the countryside, purchasing provisions out of stores and the like. It also sabotaged the national economy. Well, none of them could show up to convert the old currency to the new one, so they lost all that money— millions and millions. This loss may prove decisive, because it already seems to have affected contra operations in the countryside at the same time that we are moving to decisively win the war.

"Yes, with all of this, the last few months, the last few years, have been very hard on my family. But this is a hardship we must endure; it has its purpose, and we are winning the war. The war won't go on forever, and soon we can rebuild. But whatever comes, we are still revolutionaries now, and we will be until the end; we just don't know when the end will be or what it will look like. With a full stomach, or with an empty stomach, we are with the revolution."

I asked Máximo about the special problems affecting households headed by women during the economic crisis. "Most of these houses, 'headed by women,' as you say, are actually supported with money from men who are working in the United States. Well, maybe not all of them, but some. It's not so difficult to tell who's getting money from the United States. Just look up and down this street. Do you see the houses that are adding new rooms, putting up fancy grillwork over the porch, the ones that have fresh paint? That's all bought with U.S. dollars. Now look at the other ones, the ones with old paint, no new rooms, and nothing to protect the porch. Those houses are supported in córdobas. You can see what's what here, it's not mysterious."

Then we discussed the impact of the economic crisis on Sandinista popularity. I said that I heard more and more complaints from people about inflation, shortages, and compactación. "I think I see what you're getting at," he responded, "and I think you're wrong. It's very hard to bring down a government in power. And it's even harder to bring down a revolution. This whole country went through the revolution, an entire people. We created mass organizations that engaged people's energies in the project and affected people's consciousness in important ways. No one can forget the feeling of power we experienced in the literacy brigades, when we virtually wiped out illiteracy, or in the health-care campaigns, when we eliminated most of the preventable childhood diseases, and in the various mass projects of the communities. We took our destiny as a people into our own hands. That is what popular democracy ought to be like in a revolutionary state: the people take the initiative, they rebuild their own society. Most of us remember that. And perhaps we will return to that level of involvement once the war is over. All of us who have worked for the revolution won't turn our backs on it. And in their hearts, most people know that this is the right way to go.

"Now it is true that some former Sandinistas have fallen by the way. A lot of people lost their jobs in compactación, it is true. Do you know who lost their jobs? The people who weren't working. They come to the office, and the women paint their faces, the men comb their hair and talk to the women, and they just sit there all day, talking to each other. If they worked that way in the United States, they couldn't keep their job for even one day! They'd just run them off.

"I'm sick of hearing complaints. [With great exaggeration:] 'Tenemos hambre.... No hay comida aquí en Nicaragua' [We're hungry.... There's no food here in Nicaragua], they say, with their fat bellies sticking out to here. Have you seen malnutrition here in Managua? No. There is enough food. Not in abundance, and not in great variety, but no one here is dropping dead from hunger.

"Some of these people—they used to be with us—thought that independence was going to be an easy road and that the revolution would open up a bounty of wealth and opportunity for them within a matter of years. They never really realized that the revolutionary course is, for the time being, a very hard one, and that first we have to defeat the counterrevolution, and in so doing, deal a blow to U.S. imperialism. Freedom is an arduous course. They heard the word *sacrifice*, but they didn't listen to it. So now they act surprised by the hardship. The heroic people of Vietnam provide our best model. They fought imperialism continuously for twenty years. And there were people who spent two decades underground, in crawl tunnels no more than two feet across. Can you imagine what sort of sacrifices those people made? Would anyone here be willing to make them? Someone has to make sacrifices, heroic sacrifices, to secure national sovereignty. Because imperialism is so strong, there is no other way. And these people, they cry that they're dying of hunger, when they've eaten so many beans that they've swollen their bellies out to here!

"These same people, they obtain their passports from the government and get a visa to go to Mexico, and then they show up in the United States asking for political asylum. 'The Sandinistas are persecuting us,' they say, lying. 'There's a lot of repression in Nicaragua.' Well, I just hope they get sick up there. That'll fix them. They'll see what life in the United States is really like when they have to pay a thousand dollars a day for a hospital visit."

"I've seen your United States, and it doesn't interest me. You can keep it. Yes, you have some very remarkable things: wide highways, well constructed; cars everywhere; tall buildings; beautiful houses. But let me tell you something: I saw the way poor people are treated in your country, and I saw the way black people and Spanish-speaking people are treated. I saw the way some people go to giant, luxurious shopping malls, while in the cities, the secondhand stores are full of black people, poor people, poorly dressed people. I saw the faces on those people. In your cities, among the poor, I saw homelessness, despair, and defeat. Yes, maybe most poor people in the United States live better than most poor people in Nicaragua. That is true. But what sort of life? And what of the life of the soul?

"Better to stay here in my own country, where at least we can fight for dignity."

To what extent does self-sacrifice represent real self-abnegation? And to what extent can it give haven to a distorted egoism of classical machista form—which all the doctrines of Sandinismo, *guerrillerismo*, liberation theology, and Marxism report to abrogate?

I sometimes wonder what sort of world Máximo would build for his utopia. Would his most fondly envisioned world be a socialist bootcamp on a national level? His political discourses are all straightforward, linear narratives about struggle, perseverance, battle. There is something Nietzschean about his sensibility—his pagan delight in the image of Managua's bourgeoisie burning its useless wealth. Perhaps Jack London would have understood him well: the matter-of-fact manner with which he relates his execution of a right-wing terrorist from the United States. War, waged in the mountains, against all odds, is his primary symbol: the metaphor that orients his experience in the world. Notably absent is the other, liberated side of Sandinista political discourse: fat children playing in the streets; poetry as a good thing in and of itself; the laughter of neighbors drinking chicha.

Perhaps the reader will see in Máximo a blundering, swaggering, clumsy fool of a man, or worse yet, something of a jackboot leftist. His words are often hard, his criticisms of others often merciless. His insistence on self-sacrifice has left him unsympathetic to the sufferings of his neighbors. Máximo clings rather singularly to that one dimension of Sandinismo that suits his temperament best. What fails to come through once his words are captured and imprisoned on paper is his warmth. True, he carries on with the zeal of a Protestant missionary, chastising sinners for their sins. But at the same time Máximo is a warm and funny man, hospitable to guests, and amply ready to assist his neighbors when they need advice, when they need help, even when they need money (something of which Máximo himself has little).

And no one can say that Máximo, whether wisely or unwisely, has failed to make the sacrifices he demands of others.

CHAPTER XIII

Jaime

None of this is ideal.

Despite his youth—and he always seemed much older than his late teens—
Jaime proved an astute observer of Nicaraguan social, cultural, and
political life. I often turned to him when I needed a clear, precise explanation of some practice that mystified me. Without being a cynic, he
was often skeptical of people's professed beliefs and public statements.
With equal ease he could describe compadrazgo, color classification,
and machismo as systems. A participant in and partisan of Nicaraguan
culture who sided unambiguously with the Sandinistas, he was also able
to examine his own side—its failures, its shortcomings—more prob-
ingly than most could. Whether we were discussing class structure, religious traditions, folklore, or gender roles, Jaime took little of his own
culture as a priori. He frequently demonstrated an acute double awareness: he knew that people have individual personalities, wills, and desires, but he also knew that they live and act in a world of social conventions, structures, and preexisting ideas that both shape individuals
and resist their efforts to redefine them. For him, practices and structures constituted puzzles, with rationalities and histories of their own.
In short, what made him an ideal informant was that he had a finely
developed sociological imagination.

I do not know the source—if there is ever any one source of such
things—of his unusual ability to think sociologically in the absence of
any formal training. It would be presumptuous to claim to know whence
come such gifts. The experience of social revolution, its mobilizations,
its ongoing analysis of social problems: all these developments pushed

many Nicaraguans toward a more sociological mode of thinking. But some realized the lessons more profoundly, more rapidly, than others did. Although his family was quite poor, his mother's small, sparsely furnished shanty was unusually well stocked with books, especially works of literature, both Nicaraguan and international. His family had an unusual respect for learning. Jaime sometimes asked me about great works of American literature—*Huck Finn, The Great Gatsby*—and he was an avid reader of Simenon's existential detective novels, which he had introduced to a number of his friends.

Jaime was recognized by all his peers as being very bright, and sheer intelligence no doubt accounted for something of his sociological imagination. But intelligence alone rarely predicts that a person will think analytically or critically about the social conventions that surround him or her. Without much evidence, I have sometimes imagined that his perspicacity, his double awareness, flowed from some sense of being simultaneously an insider and an outsider in his society, for Jaime is mildly hunchbacked; his right shoulder and his right eye are slightly elevated. I cannot say, however, that his life experiences have been dramatically marked by stigma or physical imperfection. Jaime's personality has never seemed to me withdrawn or alienated; on the contrary, he is among the most gregarious and extraverted of my informants.

THE DRAFT

In 1986 Jaime and I discussed the political fatigue that was overtaking the mass organizations. "Look," he said finally, "the basic reason for the decline of the CDS, AMNLAE, and other mass organizations is the unpopularity of the draft. Ninety percent of the country fulfills its obligations, but only about 40 percent actually supports the draft. The rest serve, but they resent it. Mothers especially resent it, for who wants to send their boys off to war? We have never had mandatory military service here before. So people still see it as an imposition rather than a necessity or a normal thing."

I suggested that if the economy were functioning better, the draft might be less unpopular.

"That is possible. If the country were richer, it could afford to pay better salaries and benefits to enlisted men, and that would help. As it is now, families lose a great deal of income when a son goes into the military. And if the economy were running better, and people were more prosperous, there'd be less overall complaining. But remember that at the time of the revolution, people's hopes ran very, very high. A sort of triumphalism overtook the people, and now that has given way to pessimism. Many people thought that with Somoza out, everyone would be economically equal right away, and everyone would have more money immediately. And things did improve for a while, as the country recovered from the civil war and the government implemented subsidy programs and redistributed land. So now everyone feels let down—by the war, the cost of the war, the deterioration of the economy. But remember, too, that the cost of living here in Nicaragua is lower than it is in other Central American countries. That is because the government subsidizes basic goods, of course. Why, until recently, when the government started rationing gasoline, Costa Ricans used to cross the border to buy gas because it was so much cheaper here than there. I have relatives in Costa Rica, and good for good, food for food, everything is cheaper here. But do the people say that? No, they complain.

"The government has failed in its task of doing ideological work. People were ready for a revolution, but they weren't prepared for the long struggle. Politics is rapidly becoming demobilized—not because people are counterrevolutionary, but because they are tired of war and sacrifice. This is not a counterrevolutionary trend, but it does give an open window to counterrevolutionary influences unless the government takes things in hand. That is why I say that most people in Nicaragua lack the level of consciousness needed for the longer struggle. And the struggle will be long, anybody can see that. The United States is not going to give up Nicaragua easily, and so far, the contras have been a cheap and cost-effective means of waging war against us.

"We have to be perfectly honest about it and say that no one wants to die. It's as simple as that. Sacrifices are hard to make unless you know absolutely well what the goal is and why the sacrifices are necessary. Some people know what the goal is and what the costs are, but many don't. Here in Nicaragua, as in the United States, it's 'Me first, me second, and me last'—egoism, in a word. People are accustomed to thinking in terms of what benefits them, individually, or their own particular family, but not what's good for the country. That is where the revolution is failing. What is needed is widespread ideological work— not in every barrio or school or block, but house by house. We need an intense, ongoing discussion about the methods and objectives of the revolution and the obstacles to those goals. And, too, we need to insure that the mass organizations and the party function in as democratic a fashion as possible. And that is all the more reason to be alarmed by the collapse of the mass organizations: without them, the discussion ends, and it becomes impossible."

EDUCATION

Once I encountered Jaime walking through the neighborhood during school hours. I asked if he were cutting class. He was indeed, and he added that his mind would be none the poorer for it, which led us into a general discussion of schooling in Nicaragua.

"Education here tends to be of a very poor quality. We are a poor, Third World country, and we haven't had the resources to develop a very good educational system. The work is repetitive and slow because the teachers don't know very much, and they stick as closely as possible to a plan, which is often poorly devised and whose purpose they don't even necessarily understand very well. Most of the teachers can't do anything unless it's in the plan and written out in front of them. So I skip class a lot. Were it not for daily testing, I would attend even less. [A different one of the five classes gives an exam each day.]

"The women teachers who are over forty know absolutely nothing, by and large. Does that sound machista? I guess so. Part of the problem is that they grew up in a very different country than the one we live in today. So they don't understand local events, much less world events. There are exceptions, but as a rule, they are frightfully ignorant. Here, look at this example: this is what I mean." Jaime showed me a geography exam he was carrying with his books. "This teacher misgraded the exam because she thought Florida was Baja California and vice versa. This is the sort of thing I see all the time, and it's very frustrating.

"The new teachers are a little better; they have a better grasp of international events and history, but they don't know a great deal, either, by and large, but are passed on ideology." He showed me some graded English homework; its emphasis was on memorizing the rules of conjugation (not conjugation itself); in a writing exercise, a number of points were counted off for petty inaccuracies that left the meaning of the translation basically intact. "We have teachers teaching English, for instance, who don't speak a word of it; they just go by the plan and have us memorize things, and very often what we memorize is wrong."

A week later, I learned from Jaime's friend Juan that Jaime had received a failing grade on a geometry exam—as had he himself. When I ran into Jaime, I brought up the test and asked how it had happened: had he skipped too many classes? "No, not at all," he responded. "I knew the right answers, I just put down the wrong ones." I doubted this explanation, so he produced the exam from his back pocket and rattled off the correct calculations and answers. "Are you saying that you deliberately failed the exam?" "Yes," he answered. "I've been tutoring Juan in geometry, and he just doesn't understand it at all. He doesn't get it. I knew he was going to fail the exam, so I failed it, too, so he wouldn't be the only one in our group to fail." I wasn't sure whether to believe this explanation or not, but Jaime was absolutely serious about it. When I asked Róger and Virgilio, they said that Jaime's explanation was the only reasonable one, because he had tutored them, too, and they earned A's.

DEMAGOGUERY

I mentioned that one hears the word *demagoguery* a great deal in Nicaragua, and from all sides. I observed that in the United States the word is frequently used by conservatives to indicate the rhetoric of populism, or of mass movement, or of revolutionary governments—that is, anyone who points out how bad things are and says that things can be better than they are, is apt to be accused of demagoguery by people who want to maintain the status quo.

Jaime pointed to a distinction. "The question for us is, Can the speaker deliver, or is he just building up a following to exploit people's hopes?"

"Well," I explained, "in the United States, the historical figure most readily identified with demagoguery is Huey Long, the governor of Louisiana and later the state's senator during the thirties. He attacked the interests of the rich, championed the interests of the poor, and the establishment labeled him a demagogue—even going so far as to call him 'Mussolini of the Backwoods,' 'Hitler of the Bayou.' "

"Did he deliver what he promised?"

"He paved the roads, built schools, taxed the corporations, built hospitals, brought medical care to the state, and improved the life of the poor people. He took his state out of its semifeudal, Third World condition and launched it into the modern world. His ultimate goal was a socialistic agenda called the Share the Wealth program, which would have radically redistributed wealth."

"Then he could not possibly be a demagogue in our sense of the word."

"Not even if he played dirty tricks in politics and extorted money from contributors?"

"Not really; that's not the issue. If he took a firm hand with the rich, and with the political opposition, all the better."

"What if he himself lived relatively well even though he was the leader of a mass movement of poor people?"

"Well, that's more problematic. That would no doubt raise suspicions for us. But for us the question would be whether he was fooling people into supporting him or not and whether he actually helped the poor people, represented their interests, and brought them more power."

"Pretty much the way poor people in Louisiana saw it," I observed.

"I'll give you an example of what we mean by demagoguery," Jaime began. "These two men were in charge of our coffee harvesting brigade. Well, the *chele* [white one] was in charge of the brigade. Do you know how big a brigade is? Well, that means he was in charge of five thousand coffee pickers. The other one, the *moreno* [brown one], was in charge of the hacienda.

"Before we left to do the work, the chele made a long speech, designed to get everyone all motivated and to put the Sandinista Youth to shouting '¡*Viva el Frente!*' and the like. He explained how we were going to suffer through hunger, wet, cold, and diarrhea; how the contras had been attacking coffee brigades; how we, the youth of Nicaragua, had been made into New Men and New Women by the revolution; and how we were going to come through for this country, pick our quota of beans, and look back on our sacrifice with great fondness and satisfaction at having done our duty. And of course, the crowd was moved, and we all yelled slogans.

"Now, when the coffee picking began, our demagogic friend was nowhere to be seen. He didn't pick a single bean, I tell you, not a single one. He got up at eleven o'clock in the morning, every day—both the chele and the moreno. And then, much of the time, they would go into town for lunch in a restaurant instead of eating with the brigade. The last week they spent entirely in bed, claiming diarrhea; all the rest of us, of course, had worked through our diarrhea. And when we were finished, and the party began, who do you think were the first two to dance? Well, these two demagogues had a miraculous recovery from their diarrhea and were the first ones dancing at the fiesta.

"That is what we mean by *demagogue*. Let's say that it's a revolutionary definition of the word, not a conservative one. A demagogue is someone who exhorts you to clean up the street when his own house is dirty. A demagogue is someone who profits from the people, who enriches himself from their hopes and their work, but doesn't give anything other than talk in return.

"Certainly, there are some demagogues among the Sandinistas—people who talk one way and act another; people who are in the party for their own personal advancement; people who were Somocistas in the time of Somoza, and now are Sandinistas. These people are dangerous for the party, and they are dangerous for the revolution. For the most part, though, no one can say that the leaders of the Frente are demagogues. For the most part, they have been to the mountains, they have been in prison, they have been tortured, and they have been in exile. They have made the sacrifices that give them the right to talk about sacrifices."

RELIGION

"Before the revolution, and to some extent today, still, in the countryside, most people used to think that the priests were holy, almost saints themselves. That has changed. Especially in Managua the people are more suspicious of the priests because of political events. At the same time, anticlericalism has long, deep roots in Nicaragua; an important minority has always been skeptical of the priesthood, of its claims to holiness.

"I am religious, I am Catholic, and I believe in God, but I do not go to church, pray, or recite the rosary. Does that make me irreligious? No. I follow the theology of liberation, and in this theology such things are not important. Some people honor God in church. I try to give glory to God in my daily life.

"The present difficulties with the church hierarchy have been growing a long time. Originally, the church was an important backer of Somocismo. As the revolution developed, the official church began to play a mediating role between the Sandinistas and Somoza. Obando was the chief intermediary when the Sandinistas took the National Palace, and also when they took the house of Chema Castillo.[1] The church understood the importance of this role but misunderstood the consequences. The hierarchy believed that the new Sandinista state would be a return to feudalism, and that the church would enjoy a special relationship to the state, and that there would be conservative church officials in the revolutionary junta. As you can see, this was an error, and when they realized it, they began to increasingly oppose the government.

"There were incidents. First, the Sandinistas began expropriating and redividing some of the large landholdings, and in the process they took the land of some priests and bishops. The *clero* [clergy] tended to be rich, and many of them had become landlords. These expropriations cut into their wealth, and no person of wealth likes that.

"Then, later, there was that incident with Bismarck Carballo. There was a lot of confusion about that. Carballo is the second or third in the hierarchy to Obando himself. He was caught sleeping with somebody's wife. The press obtained pictures when somebody called to report a disturbance at the woman's house. For two hours that night, the television announced a special news bulletin that never appeared; people were in a panic, wondering what could possibly be going on. It all came out in the papers the next day, with a picture of the priest running half-naked from the house.

"The church had tried to get the government to run the story on television, so they could claim the government was preparing to repress the church with dirty tactics. But the government refused, even though the information eventually came out in *La prensa,* of all places, and damaged the church's reputation. So this incident further deteriorated relations between church and state. Actually, this is quite ridiculous. It would be as though I caught you sleeping with a woman who wasn't your wife, and then you blamed me for the whole affair, when it was really you who had done the thing. Some people say that the government had laid a trap for Carballo. I don't know; that's possible, but he seemed very willing to fall into the trap, if that was what it was. Well, people have been saying for a long time that Carballo has a problem keeping his vows of celibacy; it's no secret.

"Finally, and most important, there was the pope's visit. Just before he came, there had been a massacre of the reserve battalion Coro de los Angeles [Chorus of Angels] in the mountains: twenty some boys were killed. Coro de los Angeles was one of the most respected battalions in the war.

"Well, the day of the pope's visit was the day of the wake for these youths—a large, public wake, spilling out into the streets with thousands of people. So when the pope appeared in the plaza, the Sandinistas put the mothers of these boys up at the front next to the stage. These mothers asked the pope to say a word for their sons, to give them a benediction, but do you know what the only words he had for them were? '*Tsch. Cállanse.*' [Shh. Be quiet. Shut up.] The mothers grew more and more agitated and eventually began interrupting his homily with chants like 'We want peace.'

"And when the service had ended, the Sandinistas had the band play the Sandinista hymn. So there they were, the pope, cardinal, bishops, and all the priests, standing in front of the crowd to the playing of this revolutionary anthem. It was quite a moment. The pope, Obando, and about half the rest of the priests walked out during the playing. The other half remained standing on the platform. This solidified the split in the church and hardened the position of the official church against both the Popular Church and the government.

"There have been a lot of problems between the church and the government. What else would you expect? We have a revolutionary government, and a very reactionary church hierarchy. We have a poor people, and a rich priesthood. The church is basically a feudal institution, and the Sandinista state is a modern one. The government knows very well that the church hierarchy would like to have Somocismo without Somoza. And the hierarchy believes that the Sandinista government intends to suppress religion eventually, just as it has contained the power and influence of the capitalists in Nicaragua. Of course, the church's own counterrevolutionary actions may in time make it necessary to suppress the hierarchy—but don't confuse that with a repression of religion. Religious belief, conscience—those will always be free here. But that is not to say that the hierarchy can go around, in the middle of war and crisis, urging youths to evade military service and siding with the interests of the rich in a class war. And never forget that the hierarchy of the church is recruited from the wealthiest layers of society. So it acts according to the interests of its office and its class. The dispute between the government and the hierarchy is a political dispute between Left and Right, not a conflict between atheism and Christianity."

On one occasion, I asked Jaime why the Popular Church has drastically reduced the prominence of saints, saints' days, saints' images, and the like. "Because it wants to concentrate people's attention on the task at hand," he explained. "It doesn't want to say, 'This saint says do this,' or 'That saint says do that,' but rather, 'God says do this, the Bible says do that.' Thereby, it can direct people's attention in a more concentrated manner. An earnest reading of the Bible doesn't support the folkloric saints' cults that are traditional here in Nicaragua, nor does it support the hierarchy's ideas about religion.

"An honest reading of the Bible reveals this: that God's word is a calling for the poor to draw themselves closer to Him, and the promise of the Reign of God, which is to say, the reign of justice. To understand what God says, what the Bible says, is more powerful than 'This saint says do this.' And this serves the task at hand."

What is the task at hand?

"To be quite honest and direct, today it is a military purpose. Before the revolution, it was the overthrow of tyranny. Afterwards, and for a long time to come, it is to overthrow imperialism, to defeat imperialism, and to keep it from ever coming back. The Popular Church fortifies the spiritual and ideological state of the people in their popular struggles. And that is why, too, it tries to avoid the distraction of hundreds of saints: to concentrate people's attention on their essentially military orientation against the oppressors.

"The Popular Church, then, is one and the same with the Central American and Latin American revolution. Where revolution spreads, it will spread, and where it spreads, revolution will grow. It is the true church of the people, and it will be the only church in the future."

I offered the example of the Labor Church in England, a very temporary vehicle (according to Eric Hobsbawm's *Primitive Rebels* [1959]) used to encourage the working class to recognize the need for a Labor party. Is it possible that the Popular Church is a similar phenomenon: a vehicle that will be discarded or significantly modified after consolidating an essentially nonreligious or at any rate nontheistic view of the world?

"It is possible, but I don't think so. The roots of the Popular Church go very deep in our history. There is a long anticlerical tradition here—people who distrusted the priests but remained Christians—and a long tradition of the Christ of the Poor. Before it was covert; now it is overt. I think the Popular Church will persist and will eventually replace the official church."

I mentioned that not too many people were attending services these days.

"It is true, there are only a few such churches, and sometimes they are not well attended. But the liberation church continues to grow because more and more young people like myself, who don't go to Mass, are inclined toward its message. Show me where it says in the Bible, 'Go to church on Sunday.' It doesn't. The Bible tells us how to live; it tells us that exploitation is a sin and that God is a partisan of the poor in history. I think the Popular Church now has a majority of the Christians in Nicaragua—not of people going to its services, but of people who understand and agree with its message. And after all, very, very few Catholics go to church, but we are all Catholics nonetheless."

MEN AND WOMEN

"Be careful," Jaime warned one evening while he, Sara, and I were discussing relations between men and women, "that you don't find an unfamiliar doll or trinket in your luggage when you go back to the States." My puzzled expression revealed my ignorance, so Jaime elaborated: "Enchantment! Witchcraft! Several girls on this andén have their eye on you, and they may try to throw a spell on you. So if you find something unfamiliar in your luggage, you'll know you've been enchanted.

"All women are said to know how to enchant, to bewitch," he continued, watching Sara's reaction, "at least a little bit. Usually a woman does this to catch a man or to make him come back to her. The most common traditional version of this is the *oración del puro* [the cigar spell]. I've never seen it; no man ever has, or almost no man. The women keep it very secret, mothers teach their daughters, and only women are supposed to know how to do it." We both looked at Sara, whom we expected to confirm or deny this secret knowledge, and asked if she knew anything about the oración del puro. She replied that she didn't and then added, with a twinkle in her eye, "But of course, if I did, I'd have to deny it in front of you men."

Supposedly, according to Jaime, a woman chants a standard incantation over a cigar, smoked by her at midnight, to make a wandering husband come back home to her. "My cousin," he said, "he claims he saw an aunt of ours one time chanting something over a pig. It was dark, but he could see that the pig had a cigar in its mouth. Now what do you think that means? You're always asking what certain practices symbolize. What do you think that means, to put a cigar in the mouth of a pig, to make your husband come back home? Anyway, almost everyone believes in the effectiveness of this rite. It's a form of white magic—although some people are said to practice black magic as well. But it won't do you any good to ask women about it. They'll all deny any knowledge of it."

Jaime's prediction proved true. Although men universally asserted that all or most women knew how to perform the oración del puro, only a few women would admit that the practice existed, and all denied having ever performed it or even knowing how to perform it. Men's remarks on the subject may indicate any number of things: projection of their own hostility onto women; their fear of resentful women; a collective guilty conscience over men's treatment of their wives; or a factual acknowledgment of women's secret reserve of occult power, obscure practices, pitted against men's more visible power. From the point of view of women, whatever the extent of the practice, it serves their purposes well to deny any secret knowledge: cloaked in denial and secrecy, the threat of enchantment looms all the larger in men's minds.

"Once somebody tried to enchant me. But I," Jaime said, winking, "enacted a counterspell to mitigate its effects."

"Did your counterspell work?" I asked.

"I'm still single, aren't I?"

In 1988 we discussed machismo and ideas of masculinity. I asked, "What is the Nicaraguan idea of a good man? What defines a good man?"

"Do you mean now or before?" Jaime responded. "These ideas have changed a lot, and are still changing, since the revolution. Some people have the old ideal, other people have the new one, so it's hard to say. The new idea of a good man—that is, the revolutionary New Man—is someone who studies to improve himself and his country, who works hard, who is responsible toward his compañera, his children, and is generous with those around him. The old idea of a good man—the ideal of machismo—was someone who could drink, fight, gamble, and have a large number of sexual conquests. It was as simple as that."

I observed that one sees, in practice, some mixing of the two ideals.

"Yes, certainly. Today, I think, young men are apt to be a bit confused by the transition. They don't always know quite what's expected of them. Maybe their father behaves one way, and their older brother behaves another, so they have two conflicting models. Or maybe the revolutionary ideal tells them one thing, but they see another thing in practice. And clearly, some people have changed more than others. For instance, you now have men who help out around the house. This was unthinkable before. No man would be caught washing dishes or cooking or ironing. If his wife asked him to give her a hand, he would just say, 'Yo no soy cochón' ["I'm not a cochón"], and that would be the end of it. Housework and child care, those were women's work. And some men are still like that. But now many mothers are rearing their sons with the expectation that they're supposed to help out around the house. And now, with so many women working, women are saying,

'Look, it's not fair that I work on a job the same as you and then come home and do all the work at the house.' And with the new ideas about cooperation between men and women, there are more and more men who help with the housework and children. Nevertheless, some of these same men sometimes have lapses and do something very machista.

"One interesting thing in all of this is the role of grandmothers in these changes. Most houses have a grandmother in them. She usually ends up doing most of the housework and taking care of the children while both parents are out at work. So it's the grandmother's labor that makes it possible for women to be out holding down a job. And if most young women today are modern, their mothers are more traditional, so the children are going to get traditional ideas and habits from their grandmother, and modern ones from their mother. Who can say what's going to happen when the current generation grows up and the grandmother is dead? Will the women who are working now quit their jobs to take care of their grandchildren and do the housework? Or will men and women have to really share housework, systematically, the way some people do now? And will nurseries and kindergartens become more widely available? Or will people have fewer children, as some are already doing?"

ELECTIONS

When I discussed political events and the impending national elections with Jaime in 1988, I began by saying: "Nicaragua today has hyperinflation and acute shortages of even basic goods. The economic situation is worse than I've ever seen it. A lot of civil servants have lost their jobs in compactación—people who were enthusiastic supporters of the Sandinistas, and many of them are bitter. Now all this must have an effect on party support. The war goes on, despite efforts to bring about a settlement, and that is clearly because Washington will keep the contras alive, at least for a little while longer. And for the time being, it is unthinkable that the United States will lift its trade embargo against Nicaraguan goods."

"Yes," Jaime agreed, "Times have been hard. Very hard. And a lot of people in the party are split now: some because they have lost their jobs, others because they think the party is making errors by being too generous with the opposition and by giving up too much in its negotiations with the contras. Some people, for instance, were very angry when the government started releasing members of the Guardia Nacional from prison. Those guardsmen committed heinous human rights abuses against the people, and they should serve their terms in prison. So, too, a lot of people would like the government to take a firmer hand with the political opposition. And they're very impatient with the compromises being reached with the capitalists. The producers are getting all sorts of incentives and benefits this year, while poor people are losing their subsidies and benefits. Some Sandinistas say, with some justification, that Ortega is presiding over the exploitation of poor people by rich people and that this sort of class compromise is alien to the spirit of the revolution."

"And what do you think?" I asked. Jaime shrugged. "The revolution is under fire. Its leaders are making compromises that go against the goals and spirit of the revolution, but without which the revolution would be destroyed. Do I want to see the Guardia Nacional out walking the streets? No. Do I like the austerity measures or the incentives for rich producers? No. Do I think the political opposition ought to be allowed to play it cozy with the contras and the U.S. imperialists bent on destroying our revolution? Certainly not. None of this is ideal. But pragmatic compromises may be the only way out of the crisis. It's a difficult question. It's a question that can't be answered with a simple answer. But I don't see the point of criticizing the Sandinista leadership at this time. If they are right, then the revolution will at last win peace."

I followed up by broaching the subject of the elections. "So now we are looking at elections down the road. I don't have to tell you that times are hard or that I hear a lot of complaining about conditions here. Under such circumstances, a majority of the electorate may well decide that the best way to insure an end to the contra war and the U.S. boycott that together have destroyed Nicaragua's economy is to elect an opposition ticket and wait for an infusion of U.S. aid." It seemed to me that those were likely to be the real terms of the impending elections, and Jaime agreed. But he would not admit the possibility of a Sandinista electoral defeat. He put it to me this way: "The Sandinistas will probably win, but not by as much as last time." How, I wanted to know? "Because the Sandinistas are the first and only force in Nicaraguan society capable of representing the national interests. And you will see that the opposition to them will always turn out to be stooges of imperialism. So people will vote, in the end, for national honor, not national humiliation."

Jaime's predictions did not prove correct, but I have seen no evidence that the terms of his analysis were anything but to the point.

CHAPTER XIV

Jazmina

Right now I'm poor, and I go around like a bullfrog.

I often visited with Doña Jazmina in the heat of the midafternoon, during a lull in the day when most people on the andén were napping. On these visits, she would sometimes talk at length, without any prompting from me: reviewing the meanders of fortune that happen to us all, discussing her and her children's options in life, and unburdening herself to me. In 1988 Jazmina reflected on her life, her family, the state of the revolution, and the future:

"Everybody in my house is Sandinista. We are not like some houses on the street, where some are Sandinistas and some are reactionaries. Here we all follow the Frente, and we will until the end. But we were not always Sandinistas. Before the insurrection, we were Somocistas, did you know that? My husband was a big Somocista. He had to be, because of his work. A lot of his work came through government contracts, and we thought that what was good for us was good for the whole country. At first we were afraid of the revolution. We became Sandinistas when we saw that the Sandinistas were taking land away from the big landowners and dividing it out to the poor farmers, when we saw that the Sandinistas were for the poor and humble people. We then came to understand the idea of popular power. But the Sandinistas haven't been able to do very much for the people because of the war and the embargo, so times have become very hard for everyone.

"Before, my husband had a good job and a good income. We had plenty. It's a bad thing, a difficult thing, to be left a widow with four children, but we've gotten by, thanks to God.

"My husband worked in construction. He was a contractor, and he built many of the neighborhoods that you walk through now. He built this neighborhood, did you know that? He did. Sometimes I like to go for walks through different parts of Managua and look at all the buildings and houses he built. He made good money, and we used to go out to eat in a restaurant at least once a week. We'd all get into the car—him, myself, the children—and sometimes we'd take a friend along, and go out and eat shrimp, or steaks, or chicken. In those days, we lived in Bello Horizonte [a far more affluent neighborhood]. He was a good provider, and in most ways he was a good husband. But because Nicaraguan men are machistas, they almost all drink too much. He was an alcoholic. He drank a lot, just the way Freddy does now, and that's what killed him. He drank every single day, and on the weekends he was exactly like Rolando, sprawled out in the patio, unconscious. The doctor told him one day, he said, 'You have an ulcer in your stomach. You have to quit drinking or it's going to kill you.' So he quit drinking for nearly a full year. He was doing so well, and everything was going fine. Then one day he started drinking again. He drank bottle after bottle of rum for two days. On the third day he started vomiting blood, and vomiting blood, and he couldn't stop. And then he was dead.

"When my husband died, I was devastated. It was a catastrophe, a total disaster. I loved him, and he was a good man. You can't imagine what I felt when he died. And as sad as I was, it was worse than that, because I was terrified of the future. He left us no money, no insurance. I thought, 'Oh, my God, what's going to become of us now?' I'd been a housewife all my life. My husband was the one who supported us, and I didn't know the first thing about working outside the home.

" 'I am the head of the family now,' I told my children, 'the mother and the father, and what I say goes.' You know, I am a very strong believer in discipline for children. I imagine you still remember the time I beat Virgilio with the flat of the machete. He came home drunk, and he knows that that's prohibited. I don't want him drinking and ending up like his father. And sometimes I still have to spank Sarita, even though she's twenty years old now. You ask her, she'll tell you. I imagine you think, 'Well, that mean little Nicaraguan woman, always scolding and beating everybody.' But I try to give my children a sense of discipline, and they know I love them very much.

"When my husband died, I didn't want my children to quit school and go to work. What kind of future could they have if they quit school? Education is necessary to keep them from becoming *ladrones* [thieves], *vagos* [vagrants], *mariguaneros* [marijuana smokers], or *parásitos* [parasites]. So we sold our house and the car and moved into this neighborhood. I went to work in a factory and did men's work so the children could stay in school. I was a metalworker. I cut tin with these great big shears and wore heavy work gloves. That's why my arms are so big now. And any time I could, I worked extra hours to make more money. Many times I worked twelve hours a day, cutting tin. Ah, I'd come home so exhausted and wouldn't be good for anything around the house. Nora used to massage my arms to make them feel better. And then I'd get up early the next day to take the bus to the factory and do it again. I did that for several years, until Freddy and Nora were old enough to start working.

"Freddy is a sad case, but I don't know what to do. He was close to his father, and I think it hurt him most of all when he died. Now all he does is drink, just like his father. He quit for a while after some thieves stole his pay at the bus stop, because he was drunk then, and that's how he lost all that money. He quit for several months, but now look at him. He's always coming and going with those furious red eyes and slurred speech. He's four years younger than you are, but already he looks old enough to be your father.

"And now that Freddy has lost his job in the compactación, it's even more difficult for us to all get by on La Policía's [Nora's] salary. Let me tell you, there have been many days when we've gotten by on only one meal. There have been times when we've had no food in the house. Sometimes Josué-Luis comes to me and says, 'Mamá, I'm hungry,' and I have to say, 'I'm sorry, my child, but we don't have any food in the house.' Well, he's very young, and he doesn't understand. So he starts yelling that he's hungry and crying, 'I'm hungry!' and I have to spank him and send him to bed. That hurts me a lot. It nearly kills me. But what can you do?

"And poor Nora, she's had bad luck. That husband of hers, he was a very well-beloved man. He was the barrio director in the CDS, but not like some directors, because he really did a lot of work. Everybody loved him because he was generous and friendly and very revolutionary. Sometimes you have asked me about the New Man in Nicaragua; well, he was the New Man. He died in the mountains, assassinated while working in the coffee brigades. When the contras killed him, the people of his neighborhood named the street after him and put up a little monument. Nora can take you there to see it if you like. He left La Policía with Josué-Luis, and I have to look after him now because his mother works. And that was difficult, too, for the longest while. It's a bad thing to be left an orphan. Little Josué was not a healthy baby, as you remember. He kept having those kidney infections, and because of the embargo there was no medicine for him in all of Nicaragua. We had the prescription, and it would have fixed him right up. We went to all the drug stores, every day, but the medicine was never there. The poor little thing was so skinny and sad when he was a baby. You remember the time he had diarrhea for two or three weeks. He was losing weight and getting worse. I don't know what would have happened if you hadn't given us that medicine. It stopped him right up, and he was fine afterwards. Josué-Luis has a delicate constitution; he's very sensitive and requires a lot of care. We all try to protect him as much as possible. But more and more I've been taking a firm hand with him because I don't want him to grow up spoiled. That's a danger when you're a sickly child in a house full of aunts and uncles. I've had to be a mother to him because his own mother is working. So now Josué-Luis calls me 'Mamá,' not his own mother. 'Nora,' he calls her.

"We get a little bit of money each month for Josué-Luis from the fund for orphans of the heroes and martyrs of the revolution. It helps out, but really it's not much. I can't buy Josué-Luis shoes now because I just bought them for Omar. He's going to medical school, so he has to have a good pair of shoes. They cost thirty-five hundred córdobas. Omar is a good young man and very smart. He works hard and studies hard, and he doesn't waste his time drinking and womanizing. Listen, Róger, he's really studying a lot, all night long sometimes, and it's hard work for the brain. Do you know what kind of vitamins he ought to take to strengthen his brain? Maybe you have some ideas.

"Omar will do fine, and so will Virgilio. Virgilio is very intelligent, and I've never even had to tell him to study hard in school. Sara works, and studies, and is a very devoted daughter. I worry about Freddy because of his drinking. And I worry about Nora because of the bad things that have happened to her. I was telling her just the other day, 'Why don't you believe in God? Why did you lose your faith?' She said, 'No, mother, I believe in God in my own way,' and I said, 'Humph. You never *persignarse* [make the sign of the cross], and you never pray. Why don't I ever see you with a rosary? You don't really believe in God anymore.' We all need God.

"Sometimes I think people are losing their faith, gradually. And these military officers! Marx is the holy father and Lenin the holy mother with them. Marx is fine, and I love Comandante Borge, even if he is an atheist. But we need God, too.

"No doubt about it, the reactionary church hierarchy has driven people away from God. They are with the rich and against the poor. This has led to a great loss of faith because the bishops are all men of money and are interested in protecting money and privilege.

"How can you be a good Christian and a rich man at the same time? You can't. Christ told the people, 'Sell everything you have and give to the poor, and share everything equally.' So how can you be a rich man, like the church officials and their wealthy followers, and expect to go to heaven? You can't. The Bible says Christians are to be humble, and not rich. As it is now, the church—the official church—is in the hands of people who are not Christians.

"A good Christian is someone who tries to help people out; he's not an egoist. He gives people things when they need them, and he doesn't talk one way in front of your face and another way behind your back.

"We do try to do things for each other here on this andén. That helps out some. Flora is a very good friend of mine; we help each other out. Virgilio put in a good word for Charlie at the office and helped arrange the paperwork; now the army is going to pay Flora a thousand córdobas a month to help the family while her son is in the service. I bet you didn't know that, did you? We don't talk about what we do the way some people do.

"I've had a lot of friends, close friends, move to the United States. People I talked to every day. Do you think they write? Do you think I've heard from them once? Do you think they've ever sent me even one package? No. It's as though I never knew them. The *zapatero* [shoemaker] that used to live over there, he was very close friends with my husband. Nothing. Doña Olga, we used to talk every day. Not a thing. They send things to their families, but not to their friends, and not even to their compadres. I tell people, the gringo anthropologist is the only one who thinks of us from the United States.

"And so I pray for you every night when I pray. I say, 'Lord, I hope that all should go well with Róger in the United States, that he shouldn't get sick, and that you'll keep the *pandillas* [gangs, gangsters] away from him.' I know you're an atheist, but I say a prayer anyway. Then I say, 'And let him remember us poor folks here in my family.' And I pray for Josué-Luis, for Omar and Nora, for Freddy and Sara and Virgilio, for all my friends and family. Do you think I get bored reciting this long list of people? No. It makes me feel calm and tranquil. After praying I feel serene.

"I'm feeling very old these days. Both of my parents are dead now. My dear mother died this year, and it makes me very sad. I sometimes think about my own death. I don't know what happens to your soul when you die. It is possible that it dies, too. But probably not. I mean, they put your body in the ground, and it eventually rots away, right? But what happens to your soul? We won't know until we die. Some people say that when a mother dies, her soul cannot rest in peace but wanders up and down the earth until her last child is dead. As long as any of her children are alive, her spirit stays on the earth to look after them and see to it that they're all right. I don't know whether this is true or not, but it makes a lot of sense to me.

"Right now, I'm poor, and I go around like a bullfrog, on all fours, and close to the ground. But after a little while, I believe, God will lift me up a little. If I live five more years, I'll see Omar established in his medical practice, Freddy working regularly, and Virgilio and Sara established in their careers. I won't have to go around on all fours anymore. I can rise up just a little bit, and my children will bear me up."

CHAPTER XV

Virgilio

I'm tired of hearing about revolution.

Virgilio had twice been mobilized for the coffee-harvesting brigades. Based on the principle of "moral" as opposed to "economic" incentives, such labor mobilizations have their own important history in the revolutionary process. After the revolution, large numbers of landless peasants received title to land. Land redistribution turned a class of desperate rural day laborers into landowning farmers—and thus created a drastic shortage in farm labor. Given the new rural demographics, even with increased wages it proved difficult to induce people to pick the coffee and cotton that were Nicaragua's major export crops. The Sandinistas organized large mobilizations of voluntary labor to fill the gap. Like the literacy brigades (which mobilized high school and university students to teach reading and writing in rural villages) and the health-care campaigns (which mobilized volunteers to inoculate people living in every corner of the country), labor brigades were promoted as a forging ground for the revolutionary New Man and Woman. The New Man and Woman were to be exemplary people who would discharge their social responsibilities without thought of immediate profit. Voluntary labor brigades were composed largely of students and Sandinista activists who went to the mountains, slept in camps, and harvested coffee beans or cotton without remuneration. As it was explained to the participants, their free labor would lower production and harvesting costs, thus generating greater profits when the coffee or cotton was sold on the international market; the state would reinvest the profits in economic development projects so that in the long run these labor mobilizations would benefit the whole of society.

In previous conversations, Virgilio had always spoken idealistically and positively about the labor mobilizations, the New Man, and the direction of the revolution. In 1988 he spoke differently. At nineteen, with only a few more months of military service left, Virgilio was planning to finish high school and begin college. I asked if he were considering study abroad; he said yes. I asked if he were thinking about study in Cuba or the USSR. "No," he responded, perhaps a little curtly. Based on our previous conversations—Virgilio had in fact considered study in those countries—this surprised me, so I inquired why not. "Because I've heard enough about revolution and politics. I'm tired of hearing about revolution. If it comes down to it, I'll just stay here rather than study in Cuba or the USSR, if it means I'll have to hear a lot of political lectures and political talk." I pressed Virgilio for reasons for this turnaround, and he recited a litany of revolutionary failures.

"The coffee brigades, just look at them. We volunteered to work for free, for the good of the country. But where are the benefits? Did the society benefit? The private farmers pocket incentive pay in dollars, the state sells the coffee on the international market, it all goes somewhere else, and what do we drink here in Nicaragua? The grounds, the trash, the stuff that isn't good enough to sell abroad. We're giving away our labor and produce to foreigners. The same with the sugar. The same with all the best Nicaraguan products. They all go abroad. You say the goal was to raise profits that might be socially reinvested? All right, but where are the development projects? Have there actually been any signs of development? Instead of moving ahead, this country is moving backwards.

"We used to eat something of everything; even poor people used to have a varied diet. Not now. It's just beans and rice—and sometimes not even that.

"And here, what about this?" Virgilio rummaged through the kitchen for a moment, and produced a small package. "What does this say?" NOT FOR SALE was stamped across the front. "*No se vende*, right?" I nodded. "This is *suero* [serum] for oral rehydration. It was donated to Nicaragua by the government of Holland. Why should this be showing up in pharmacies *for sale* if it was a gift, and if it reads 'Not for sale'? I'll tell you why: somebody must be making money on this. If it's not for sale, it should be free."

I agreed with Virgilio that it was a very bad idea to resell medical supplies that had been donated to Nicaragua for free distribution, but I argued that it seemed unlikely that someone in the Ministry of Health was actually pocketing a profit. More likely, this was a misguided—a seriously misguided—attempt at raising funds for a hard-pressed ministry in a virtually bankrupt country. Or perhaps it was an attempt at regulating the distribution of a scarce medicine; the price, after all, had been a very nominal fifteen córdobas. (I suspect that many people were complaining much as Virgilio did about such practices. A few days after our conversation, *Barricada* announced that important infant medicines would henceforth once again be distributed free for all children under the age of six.) Virgilio ultimately agreed that I was probably right. He even volunteered, after all, that the Sandinista program in itself was reasonable and that the Sandinista leadership meant well. But the problem still remained. It had become a question of costs and calories.

"We fought a revolution, and we struggled to build a society that would be free to progress, and where it would all go to the workers and peasants. We are not progressing, we are regressing. And poor people are poorer today than they were before. Why? I suppose it's obvious: because the Sandinistas have crossed the United States. And now we know what the United States can do to a country even without sending in troops. You ask me what's the solution? We have to make peace with the United States. There's no other way that I can see."

Like Virgilio, my informants acted on—and reacted to—their conditions of life in various ways at various times. The discussions and incidents that I record offer divergent and shifting perspectives on the Sandinista revolution through the late 1980s. Virgilio's complaints seem as good a place as any to conclude. They summarize the complaints of many.

For all the various experiences recorded here, it seems to me that four essential conditions proved inescapable—in life as in conversation. These conditions run like threads, sometimes seen, sometimes unseen, through the preceding discussions: the international dimension, and most pointedly, the U.S.-sponsored war; economic scarcity (which sometimes figures, too, as emotional scarcity); the personal politics of gender; and the public politics of revolution. That said, however, I do not wish to categorize each speaker, each discussion, according to a unitary or linear theme, nor do I wish to allocate each discourse to a set position along four narrow dimensions. In my view, such fixed positions do not obtain. Indeed, it might be said that *contradiction* and *ambivalence,* rather than *theme* or *position,* locate my subjects in their own narratives. For example, despite his bitter complaints Virgilio remains to this day a supporter of the Sandinistas. And pursuing the role of ideal mother, Doña Jazmina took a "man's job" and acted as the "father" of the family. I am not even convinced that Rolando left his family with bad intentions from the start. Flora, herself abandoned more than once, "provisioned" her motherhood, and for Osvaldo, this allocation of nurture ultimately meant abandonment.

It is impossible to say where good faith ends and bad faith begins. The conversations I record are mixtures of hope and despair, politics and religion, analysis and passion, conviction and compromise, idealism and self-interest. Traces of each define the other. Through them, people define themselves at any given moment. But the configurations are never the same for any two people, any two moments. And it is not only in Nicaragua that, threading our way through such a fabric, we make our lives.

PART THREE

Power, Politics, and Personal Life

We are most inclined to imagine ideological creation as some inner process of understanding, comprehension, and perception, and do not notice that it in fact unfolds externally, for the eye, the ear, the hand. It is not within us, but between us. . . .

Every ideological product and all its "ideal meaning" is not in the soul, not in the inner world, and not in the detached world of ideas and pure thoughts, but in the objectively accessible ideological material—in the word, in sound, in gesture, in the combination of masses, lines, colors, living bodies, and so on.

—P. N. Medvedev and Mikhail Bakhtin,
The Formal Method of Literary Scholarship

Ideology can no longer be understood as an infrastructural-superstructural relation between a material production (system and relations of production) and a production of signs (culture, etc.), which expresses and masks the contradictions at the "base." Henceforth, all of this comprises, with the same degree of objectivity, a general political economy (its critique), which is traversed throughout by the same form and administered by the same logic. . . . [I]deology is actually *that very form* that traverses both the production of signs and material production.

—Jean Baudrillard,
"For a Critique of the Political Economy of
the Sign"

CHAPTER XVI

Dealing with Danger

Philaster: Oh, but thou dost not know
What 'tis to die.

Bellario: Yes, I do know, my Lord:
'Tis less than to be born; a lasting sleep;
A quiet resting from all jealousy,
A thing we all pursue; I know besides,
It is but giving over of a game,
That must be lost.

> —Francis Beaumont
> and John Fletcher, *Philaster*

"Did you hear it last night? The gunfire: ra-ta-ta-ta-ta-ta-ta!" Virgilio was excited.

"Yes, what was it? Who was shooting?" I asked.

"It was for the *muchacho* [boy] in Rigoberto. He was in the service. The contras ambushed him in the mountains; they cut his throat."

"But why the machine-gun fire?"

"Why, for the wake, of course. His friends were giving him a big send-off." The boy then makes a clenched fist—not the sort that signifies *poder popular* (popular power), but a simpler sort, showing strength. "What a beautiful sound! I hope they send me off that way when I go!"

One day I was discussing current events with some high school students from the neighborhood. A boy asked me if I had seen the movie *Rambo*. "No," I told him, "I haven't." *Rambo* had taken the barrios by storm: Spanish videotapes of the movie were widely available, and although the movie had never been shown in Managua's theaters, nearly all the boys and young men I met had seen it, usually on the VCRs of their family's more affluent friends. I knew this boy well enough: he was from a revolutionary family, he knew perfectly well what imperialism was, and his politics were Sandinista. I told him that I thought *Rambo* embodied the worst aspects of my country: jingoism, national chauvinism, racism. It is the very emblem of the Reagan era, all the way down to a "stabbed in the back" theory of why the United States lost the war in Vietnam. I went on that movies of that sort were useful in whipping up militarist sentiment in the United States and that Nicaragua would be the first victim of such sentiments. Didn't he see that? "No, no," the boy told me, edging toward an aesthetic rather than a political analysis. "It's just a movie. Look at that guy's muscles! And the violence! The way he cuts down his enemies! What a great movie." Feeling rather frustrated, I said, "But don't you see? Rambo is a revanchist: he wants to go back and fight the Vietnam War all over again. And he'll do it in Nicaragua if he has to."

"No," my friend insisted, and then improvised, grinning a bit: "Rambo is like the Nicaraguan soldier. He's a superman. And if the United States invades, we'll cut the marines down like Rambo did. They'll see what we're made of!" And then he mimicked Rambo's famous war howl and mimed his arc of machine-gun fire. We both laughed.

PLAYING WITH DANGER

On an evening stroll down any of the andenes in Erasmus Jiménez, one typically passes by small groups of boys and men, sitting out on the sidewalk in front of a house or clustered on a front porch. Almost invariably, with worn and crinkled decks, they are playing cards: *desmoche,* Nicaragua's most popular card game. Using small bits of wood for chips, or betting a few centavos at a time, they are socializing, passing time, and honing their skills and reflexes for more serious play in other settings.

Desmoche provides a forum for male socializing and camaraderie as well as an arena for male competition. Most Nicaraguan boys learn how to play the game by the age of eleven or twelve—and some learn much younger—either by playing it themselves or by sitting and watching while groups of men or older boys play. The game's importance in masculine culture would be difficult to overstate. On my various trips back and forth between Nicaragua and the United States, my female informants and friends would often ask me to bring them cloth, clothing, material, or toiletries. Men would occasionally ask for articles of clothing or useful things like watches or mechanical pencils, but the request that came up with greatest regularity was for a few fresh, clean, smooth decks of cards.

Desmoche is in Nicaraguan culture what poker is in U.S. culture: a game for men whose rules suggest strong ideas about—and ideals of—masculinity. Each could be counted as its country's national card game.

But as a game, desmoche resembles gin rummy more than poker. Each player is dealt nine cards and then draws by turns from the remaining deck; whenever a player takes a card, he must also throw a card, which other players then have the option of using. The object is to produce a complete hand like that in gin rummy, with three sets of three, three, and four matching cards. It is tempting to count this game as a local variant of gin rummy, bearing some resemblance to other variations of that game. My informants, however, insisted on the distinctly Nicaraguan character of desmoche and minimized its resemblance to gin rummy.

Desmoche's rules, where they differ from those of gin rummy, enhance the dimension of chance. After the deal, play is initiated by a "blind" exchange of cards between participants: each player passes a card facedown to the player to the right (that is, counterclockwise). The circulation of moves is then initiated by the dealer, who takes the first draw from the deck. Whether one can use a card from the stack is more narrowly defined than it is in gin rummy. A player may not draw a card and save it for use at a later time; the drawn card must be laid down as part of a set of at least three matching cards. If the person who draws the card cannot use it, the others then have the option to take it, and the play takes up *after* the person who actually uses the card. Thus, the counterclockwise circulation of moves is frequently interrupted. Finally, any player's sets of cards can be disrupted by other players, who toss matching cards, when they are drawn, onto sets that have been laid down, thus undermining most attempts at set-building strategy.

Before hands are dealt in each game, each player puts up a pre-established stake, the *cuota;* stakes may or may not rise as the night wears on. Unlike an ante, the cuota represents the player's entire stake for the round, and no further bets are made until a new game begins. Because of this method of staking, in desmoche, unlike poker, there is no possibility of folding, no possibility of withdrawing from the betting to conserve one's money. Having definitively lost any chance of winning, a player may either withdraw from play or continue playing in order to block a victory by someone else. With each game the winner takes all, and a new stake is put up for the next game. In this sense, desmoche is a riskier game than poker is. However, because the scope of meaningful planning is so narrowly circumscribed, and because bets cannot be increased once hands are dealt, risk evens out over time. Unless one player is far more skillful than the others are, it is unlikely that he will dominate the winnings night after night: there is too much chance in the play and too many opportunities to scuttle an opponent's plans.

Desmoche produces both friendly, familylike games (with no betting, with chips in lieu of money, or with token amounts of money involved) and aggressive, high-pressure games involving large sums of money. Big-money games with stakes of up to fifteen hundred córdobas per round are played in *casas clandestinas* (illegal betting houses) and at *velas* (wakes). (In late May 1988, fifteen hundred córdobas, roughly fifteen dollars on the black market, was the monthly salary for many of Managua's skilled, white-collar workers.) After the revolution, the Sandinista government closed most of Managua's gambling houses; a few casas clandestinas nonetheless survive. The most typical setting for such high-stakes betting, however, is not the illegal gambling house, but the wake. At Nicaraguan wakes, women stay inside the house, drink black coffee, and pray all night long. Children play games and eat *rosquilla,* a hard, toasted bread made from cornmeal and butter. Men set up tables in the street, drink rum, and play cards until daybreak. Women often leave these occasions feeling elevated; men often leave feeling broke.

Desmoche is played at a rapid pace. Cards are quickly, even sloppily tossed onto the pile. The rapid, disjointed play requires concentration, quick thinking, and a fast eye. Obviously, given the rules, the more players, the more complex the play. More hands mean fewer cards left in the deck, more competition for turned cards, and greater probability of having one's sets disrupted by tossed cards. Yet the play is often most rapid—almost frenetic—precisely when there are more players.

Poker gives us the term *poker face,* meaning "unreadable." It can apply not only to the game of poker but also to business, politics, and any number of other primarily male-male interactions. Success at poker depends on both strategy and the ability to bluff—to keep a "straight" (unreadable) face. This unreadability is the quintessence of the North American idea of masculinity. A man takes risks, but he controls those risks with strategy and an understanding of the probability that a gambit might pay off; above all else, he conceals behind his eyes whatever might make him vulnerable to another. Risk taking in and of itself is scarcely masculine; uninformed risk taking is a sign of compulsion or weakness that betrays a "feminine" personality. With the nerves of a Humphrey Bogart, one aims instead to conceal both one's advantages and disadvantages behind a properly trained face—and that is very much the game of North American masculinity, which is conceived as a *closure* of the personality.

Desmoche's sensibility is completely different. Players are often quite animated and expressive during play. Since many of one's cards are in public view, and since no player can meaningfully plan against the possibility that other players might scuttle one's sequences, there is no advantage to be had by keeping a straight face. Desmoche is a game not of nerves, but of risks.

I was struck by desmoche's formal similarity to gin rummy and wanted to know what my informants thought of that game. Also, I had become tired of losing at desmoche night after night and hankered for a hand of something I knew better, if for no other reason than to display my mastery of something. The truth is that I rather dislike the rules of desmoche: there's too much risk, too much chance, not enough free play for planning. So one evening I asked if the gathering would like to play a hand of gin rummy and offered to teach anyone who did not already know the game. I was surprised by the adamant refusal that came from one of our group. "Why not?" I wondered. "Gin rummy? It's not a game for men," the objector responded. "It's somewhat feminine, really— a game for women," someone else said. "Yes, here, it would be a game for cochones," yet another interjected. And desmoche? "A game for men," the original objector replied. How so? "More risk," Jaime explained, directly to the point.

Risk is very much the essence of desmoche, its dizzying exhilaration, its giddy, jumpy flow. Chance drives the game, and one must move with its random flow: on one's toes, as it were, in a dance with the fate of the draw. Because of the rules of the game, a player is never able to get ahead of the flow of chance before chance produces a winner. Some skills do influence the outcome of the game: a grasp of the probabilities involved, a quick eye, fast reflexes, and a good memory for what cards have come before (and therefore which cards are likely to come after). These skills and trained reflexes aid not so much in strategy as in keeping up with the flow of chance and seeing to it that even minor advantages are capitalized. More than anything else, then, desmoche is a game of risk. And taking risk, displaying bravado in the face of danger, is also very much the essence of machismo's ideal of manhood.

All gambling is playing with danger. Poker and desmoche are both national card games, one distinctly Anglo-American, the other Nicaraguan. They both involve chance, risk, betting, strategy, planning, but the rules of each game are different, the elements are distributed differently, weighted differently. In poker, planning weighs heavily; in desmoche, lightly. In poker, the idea is to conceal one's emotions while weighing one's options and planning one's strategy, to bluff one's opponents, making them think you have what you don't have, or letting them believe that you don't have what you in fact have. In desmoche, the element of bluff scarcely enters at all; it is best to make one's moves with a flourish, as though to embellish one's risk taking and display one's style in the face of danger. Thus, the rules of each game embody the rules of proper masculinity as delineated in different cultures, and although some of the rules are similar, others are different. Each game emphasizes and celebrates what its culture finds commendable in men. For Anglo-American men, the poker ideal is to conceal one's feelings as much as possible, to become unreadable. Risk, yes, but also *caution*, strategic calculation, and an inscrutable position. Nicaraguans understand the element of bluff, and they even see how it operates in machismo, where it becomes bravado, posturing. This is bluffing writ large, extraverted, realized as theatrics rather than the mask of the poker face. And as my informants taught me, desmoche unambiguously underscores and celebrates the element of risk. At the double level of rules of play and style of play, a whole structure of chance and risk underlies the game and makes it quintessentially masculine—as Nicaraguans understand and create masculinity. The idea is to throw oneself into the risks, to take chances, with all the bravado, flair, and even flamboyance that one can muster.

MALE AND FEMALE

In the course of my fieldwork, I have sat with Nicaraguan mothers who took to bed and cried for days when their sons went into the military. Nicaragua has not historically had a military draft, and—despite the culture of *machismo*—most Nicaraguans do not take the sacrifices of war as lightly as many U.S. citizens do, for we have been bred for years on the inhuman calculus of one generation, one war. True, Nicaraguans display bravado in the face of danger; they glorify heroics; they recite the revolutionary hagiography. But they also understand what danger and sacrifice mean. And during the war years, there were tears—ample, often public tears—whenever anyone went into the service.

It has always seemed to me that there is some sort of tacit understanding between men and women in Nicaragua, a division of labor concerning these matters. Charlie, then fifteen, stated the (public) male view succinctly while we watched a neighbor's boy coming down the andén one evening. "Look, there comes José. He's running from the service." That is, he was draft dodging. "He comes here every day about this time to visit his parents," Charlie added. Running from the service was sometimes as simple as that. José was living with his grandparents rather than his parents, in case recruiters came looking for him, but he visited his parents on a daily basis. The Sandinistas had very little capacity to enforce the draft law or keep Nicaragua's citizenry under surveillance. Oddly, no one in the neighborhood ever turned José in, even though many parents had lost sons fighting the contras, and many people resented his open evasion of the draft. Not even the neighborhood CDS involved itself in the matter; José's evasion was not deemed counterrevolutionary.

I asked Charlie what he was going to do when his time came in another year or so. "When it's my time, I'm not going to run. I'd rather stay in school and study, but when I have to, I'll go into the service and do my time. Only the cochones run." Like most men, Charlie (reluctantly) strikes the machista pose: only a faggot would run. The following graffiti, splashed on a prominent wall in Granada, carries the same force; there, neighborhood militants attempted to utilize this machista sentiment: "*Sólo las maricas son evasores*" (Only sissies are evaders).

Men are caught. They have to do the honorable thing, the manly thing—even if it is not what they really want to do—or lose face. And I have heard several family arguments that revolved around the following stereotyped positions: the mothers wanted to hide their sons from the draft or send them abroad; the sons produced all the reasons why it was politically necessary and socially honorable to serve in the military. Although women, too, understand necessity, they are less concerned with male posturing: therein lies the division of labor. And men do not really want to be left to their own devices; they do not want to be caught, without any supports, in the bravado of honor. "Surely the Sandinistas are right, and we all have to make sacrifices to protect the gains of the revolution. But who knows, after all, what sacrifices the government might demand of us, if everyone played that game?" Men cannot normally speak that way: women balance the equation. Women supply them the safety valve. Women cry, and plead, and moan at the prospect of military service. It was adult women, not male youths, who organized the few antidraft demonstrations that occurred in Sandinista Nicaragua. Women supplied the antidote to men's machismo about these matters—and the truth is that the men appreciated it. All along, women provided friction against the possibility of more demands, greater sacrifices.

Maternal sentiment ran so strongly against mandatory military service for a while—especially when the war was very hot—that the government went to great lengths to pacify and flatter mothers into compliance. One long-playing television ad repeated the refrain, "Nicaraguan Mother, A Heroic Mother." Mother's Day became a government extravaganza, eclipsing even dates of revolutionary significance, like Carlos Fonseca's birthday. (Fonseca was the founder and primary theorist of the FSLN.) And whenever cohorts of inductees completed their military service and were demobilized, giant homecomings were held, in stages, first in the Plaza of the Revolution, then across the city in the barrios. "They went out cubs, they came back lions" read the posters for these events, but most of the propaganda showed pictures of young men coming home to their mothers. These homecomings were celebratory and emotional events—hundreds of young men running into their mothers' arms.

When it came time for Virgilio and Charlie to go into the military, their mothers activated their social networks to pull some strings. Virgilio's mother talked to an officer who was a friend of the family, and he saw to it that the boy was stationed in Managua, not sent to the front. Charlie's mother, Doña Flora, even went so far as to beseech Doña Celia—whose house she did not normally enter—to plead Charlie's case with a colonel who was the current boyfriend of Doña Celia's daughter. Charlie, too, was stationed on the outskirts of Managua.

SACRIFICE

One of this book's major themes is how Nicaraguans deal with hardship. Another theme that runs throughout it, explicitly and implicitly, is how they deal with danger. Machismo as a system trades in innumerable risks and dangers: some physical, others psychological. In the culture of machismo, as in any system of power, people are compelled to maneuver their way through its available options. A woman is always at some risk in this system: she might be beaten, she might be abandoned. A man has more options but is no less at risk. In a context where the burdens of manhood weigh heavily, he might fail to maintain an appropriate masculinity.

But the allotment and distribution of danger is not simply a question that begins and ends with Nicaraguan culture, with its conception of proper gender and appropriate sexuality. Danger has had and continues to have an international as well as an interpersonal dimension. The perils of insurrection, revolution, and war were always international in scope. Hardship on the one hand, and war on the other, were Washington's twin strategies for disciplining a people who had the audacity to make a revolution. The transparent aim of U.S. policy was to make life in Nicaragua as precarious as possible, to exact impossible sacrifices, and in so doing, to wear down the political resolve of a people.

Most people made the sacrifices. Noncompliance with mandatory mil itary service probably ran at about 10 to 15 percent for the duration of the war. And I do not want to be misconstrued here: machismo and bravado were not the only motives for compliance. Most of my informants fully understood the necessity of defeating the counterrevolution. No one wanted a return of Somoza's Guardia Nacional. Few people wanted to share power with fragments of the old regime. Few people wanted the bourgeoisie back in power. Adults, and many children, spoke perfectly coherently about the U.S.-sponsored aggression and the need to defend the revolution, as well as their aversion to the horrors of war. "We didn't ask for this fight, but we can't be weak now and lose it."

I attended the wake for one of the neighborhood boys who died fighting the contras. It was the peak of the war, and every week saw a different wake in the barrio; this one was on our andén. The whole neighborhood sat up, all night, with the boy's family. When he had turned draft age, the boy's mother had offered to send him out of the country. "No, mama," he told her, "we have to fight for our country. It would not be right to run." When he was sent to the mountains, he made preparations for his death. He told his mother that he loved her and adjured her not to cry if he did not come home alive; he wrote a pair of patriotic poems to his parents, one of them based on a quote from Augusto Sandino, to have printed on the cards customarily distributed to friends of the family who attend wakes. I still have the card. On the front is a picture of the Sacred Heart of Christ; on the back, the Sacred Heart of the Virgin Mary. Inside it reads:

Padres:

Cuando yo haya muerto
sólo quiero por favor no
lloren. Lo único que más
quiero es que sonrían y
nunca traicionen a la Patria.

Padres:

Su hijo combatiente
Jamás!!! será un traidor

Primero muerto, pero nunca
de rodillas.

                                        Patria Libre!

(Parents:

When I have died
I want only that you please not
cry. The only thing more
I want is for you to smile and
never betray the Homeland.

Parents:

Your combatant son
Never!!! will be a traitor
I would die first, but never
on my knees.

                                        A Free Homeland!)

And from the boy's parents, an acrostic:

Querido Hijo:

Gimen nuestros corazones.
Unico consuelo que nos queda,
Inolvidable hijo, fuiste para nosotros
Los más bellos recuerdos. Hoy se convierte en
Lágrimas, pero de amor, porque para
Esto hemos venido al mundo y te
Recordamos con alegría, ya que Dios te
Mandó a traer y no estás muerto sino,
Ofreciéndonos alegría e iluminando nuestro horizonte . . .
                Tus padres que te quieren y
                recordamos con cariño y amor . . .

(Dearest Son:

Our hearts are crying.
The only consolation left to us,
Unforgettable son, is that you were our
Most beautiful memories. Today they turn to
Tears, but of love, because
That is why we have come to the world and
We remember you with joy, now that God
Has sent for you and you are not dead, but rather,
Bringing us joy and illuminating our horizon . . .
                Your parents who love you and
                remember you with affection and love . . .)

The boy's mother cried at the wake, and his father made a short
speech, saying, among other things: "My son was a good boy, a con-

scientious man. It is tragic that he lost his life this way, but this is a tragedy that we share with all Nicaraguan families, and we know that he is protected in the love of God. His death will not be in vain."

LIFE AND DEATH

But why should desmoche be a standard fixture of the wake? Women pray; this is their way of sending the deceased on to his or her reward, of commending his or her soul into the hands of God. This style asserts transcendent continuity—within the family and community, between life and afterlife, between the human and the divine. Men, too, send off the deceased, but in their own fashion: through the sublime language of desmoche, in games that continue until some of the players are wiped out. The risk of gambling is the risk of engagement in the world, its chance the caprice of fate. A man wrestles with these twists and turns as best he can, not so much getting ahead of the risks as keeping up with them. And in death, the game of risk is the men's last statement on life. It is as though to say: Life is a game, a gamble, full of chance and risks, and it always plays out to the same end.

Doña Flora and Aida were talking about the draft, the war, the sacrifices, the shortages. Doña Flora was weary of it all, and Aida was chiding her for her lack of fortitude. Aida's son, Ervin, is an only child and is rather doted upon—by his mother, his grandmother, and me, his godfather. Doña Flora speculated that when Ervin, then three, reached draft age, his mother would be less cavalier about the prospect of military service than she was at the time. Aida laughed, took her son by the hands, and said, jokingly, "Ervin, you're not going to wait to join the service, you're going to volunteer, right?" "Yes, mama." And then, to complete her self-parody: "You're going to volunteer as soon as you turn six, right?" "Yes, mama."

The night after Yolanda's extraordinary confrontation with Elvis about the course of the revolution, Doña Celia engaged me in a discussion of the war. "You men don't understand how we women feel about the war," she told me. "Yolanda was very hard on Elvis. She shouldn't have spoken to him like that. I know, I know: the war is necessary. Nobody wants the contras to come to power. I know the Sandinistas mean well. I know it's a fight for our homeland. But it's very hard on a mother to send son after son out to battle, not knowing whether he's going to come back alive or not. Why don't you gringos put a stop to the damned war?

"I wish there were a bomb, some sort of bomb, that we had. I've read about the neutron bomb in the newspapers. Perhaps that one. A bomb that would go off one time and kill off all the contras—kill them all, every single one of them, and that would be the end of it."

In the nearby Popular Church, in a special Mother's Day mass, mothers brought pictures of their sons and daughters who had fallen either in the insurrection or in the contra war. The altar was lined with old photographs, some in black and white, others in color. A few of the pictures were pencil drawings made by hired artists. Mothers recited the names of their dead children, and everyone in the congregation shouted out *"Presente!"* after each name. And some mothers recited two, three, even four names.

FIELDWORK DURING WARTIME

Many of my acquaintances in the United States react to my fieldwork in Nicaragua as though I had been constantly subjected to the life-threatening dangers of war. My own experience with the dangers of war were very limited. Managua was far removed from the actual fighting, its barrios more peaceful than many U.S. cities. By comparison with my informants, who faced the perils of war directly, my own risks were rather attenuated. I had but one brush with serious danger, one "close call."

It was time for me to renew my visa, which was, on this occasion, of the tourist variety and expired after three months. Renewal could be accomplished only by leaving the country and then reentering. Of the two possible borders, Honduras seemed more risky: I had heard, by way of internacionalistas, that U.S. citizens were being denied entrance visas to Honduras if they came by way of Nicaragua. Costa Rica seemed more promising. As I had little cash and no desire to tour Costa Rica, I decided to exit and return on the same day. Rather than take a lengthy bus ride to the border, I enlisted the services of a taxi driver who, for a reasonable fee, agreed to take me to the Costa Rican border, wait a couple of hours for me to exit and reenter with a new visa, and then transport me back to Managua.

To prevent border incidents, Nicaragua's government had placed its customs and immigration post a mile or two away from the international border at Peñas Blancas. The resulting stretch of road is an odd thing: a no-man's-land without an apparent government, without commerce, without residents. With Nicaragua on the one side, Costa Rica on the other, this liminal zone is only a place in-between. A more desolate and eerie piece of land would be hard to imagine. I passed a few green-uniformed military guards along the way, but little else. An occasional cart wheeled by, pulled by a burro, bearing passengers across the border. I may have been imagining it, but everyone seemed anxious to complete their appointed rounds. Even the burros seemed uneasy in this odd space where no one lives. I walked this lonesome highway, arriving just in time to find the Costa Rican side closed for lunch. After I had waited an hour, the officials agreed to allow me to enter and exit by paying only the entrance and exit fees and without taking the mandatory malaria test. I hiked back across the border. This time I was the only one on the road. The silence was palpable. I stepped up my pace, reentered on the Nicaraguan side, and was promptly processed and dispatched.

As my taxi pulled away and headed back toward Managua along beautiful Lake Nicaragua, I heard a distant cacophony. Explosions? Could a border skirmish have broken out this very day? No, it was probably just a passing thunderstorm, somewhere nearby, unseen.

The taxi, which had been threatening to overheat all day, completely broke down just outside of Masaya. I paid the driver most of his fee, for taking me most of the way, walked about a mile to Masaya, and then took the bus to Managua, at last arriving in Erasmus Jiménez.

When I arrived at the entrance to the andén, two neighbor children spotted me and ran along ahead shouting, "Róger is all right!" Doña Celia was waiting on her front porch, wringing her hands. "Are you all right? We were so worried about you! Did they shoot at you? Are you all right?"

As we listened to the radio report, Doña Celia informed me that a serious border skirmish had erupted at Peñas Blancas about fifteen minutes after I cleared the area. It lasted several hours and caused several casualties. Had I undergone the malaria test or been delayed for any reason on the Costa Rican side, at the very least I would have been pinned down in the ditch for two or three hours while heavy mortar shelling and even aerial bombardment went on around me.

It was a strange situation for me. I missed this military action by about fifteen minutes. Bombs—Sandinista bombs, contra bombs—were flying, and as we all know, bombs are indiscriminate: they take life and limb without distinguishing between friend and foe, combatant and noncombatant.

I will admit that I was not frightened by this brush with danger. I am not proud of this attitude, and I am not boasting. When I look back at my reaction, I seem like something of a fool to myself. But at the time the situation seemed comic, and I could not help but laugh at the weird contingencies in play. But I laughed because I did not then fully appreciate how precious life is. And because of that, my own life seemed very abstract to me.

BRINGING THE WAR BACK HOME

Since I have probed without modesty into the personal lives of my informants, picking over their tragedies and deceptions, I feel that it would be wrong for me not to discuss my general state of mind when I was beginning the research for this book in 1988. Call it what you will, I see such a discussion as mandated by the need for fairness and reciprocity: part of the necessary requirements for intersubjectivity.

The research for my doctoral dissertation had consumed roughly ten months between late 1984 and mid-1986. Working nonstop an average of twelve hours a day, six days a week, I took roughly nine months to write the dissertation, which I completed in 1987; I then spent several slow, protracted months revising and editing for publication. While writing, I worked with a mania that was not wholesome. My world was narrowed to a fixed and purposeful point: a space no larger than the interior of a tulip, yet into which a universe of writing might comfortably fit. Whatever lay beyond that flower's corolla was treated as a distraction at best. After I left my desk, after I left the library, if anyone spoke to me—even a simple "How are you?"—they had to repeat themselves several times before I could put their words and meaning together. And when I retired late in the evening, my mind would not stop its ceaseless writing, revising, and editing; whole stretches of text would flow through my mind, pools and riffles and cascades of words and meanings forming and reforming themselves against my will. Sleep came only after I poured several shots of bourbon like oil on these troubled waters.

By mid-1988, when I completed *Thanks to God and the Revolution*, the project that directly or indirectly had oriented my activities for five years was finished. In the process, my social life had become almost nonexistent: I had few friends and little human contact. My personal life, too, had deteriorated beyond my comprehension—owing less to overwork and more to my own capacity for self-deception and bad faith; my willingness to put off life's decisions as long as I could keep myself engaged in an all-consuming project; my ability to keep problems and people at arm's length.

Difficulties continued even after I finished the dissertation, as I faced two bouts of unemployment. First, in mid-1987 I graduated with a Ph.D. into an impossibly tight job market for anthropologists. I sent out hundreds of resumes; these produced a half-dozen interviews and no jobs. At the last minute, late in the summer, I got a one-year visiting appointment at a small public liberal arts college. I continued my search for a more permanent position, but to no avail. When my appointment ran out, I was unemployed again and increasingly depressed. Had my unqualified leftism made me unemployable, persona non grata in the academic world? Would I have to devise a new strategy for survival, find a new career? As what? At one end of the spectrum, I know how to perform the farm labor that had kept me occupied as a child, and I know how to wash dishes and wait tables in restaurants—for that was how I put myself through college. At the other end of the spectrum, I know how to teach and write. Between those two poles of manual and academic labor, I know how to do nothing. But that was not the worst of it. Without a task to absorb my energies—indeed, without any re-munerative task at all—I confronted the miserable life I had made for myself.

I went to Nicaragua in 1988, half-heartedly intending to start a new project and hoping at least to lift my spirits a bit—if only vicariously, through Nicaragua's revolution and hope. But things had changed a great deal since 1986. The economy had completely collapsed. People were weary of war and hardship and wary of political promises. It seemed clear to me that the revolution was losing or had already lost peoples' confidence. This atmosphere left me all the more dispirited.

When Máximo and Osvaldo separately approached me to ask if I wanted to volunteer for military duty, I seriously considered doing so. I have no idea whether the Sandinistas would actually have accepted a North American volunteer. I think that Osvaldo was not really serious about the proposition; I am reasonably certain that Máximo was. I am sure that they had in mind the symbolism of the act: a Yankee intellec-tual gives up his comfortable life back home in the defense of the Nic-araguan revolution. The example of Benjamin Linder—a U.S. interna-cionalista assassinated by the contras—was fresh in their minds. Good symbolism—and why not? I was a young man in good health. I had nothing else to do, other than face a humiliating world of unemployment and job searching back in the States. What held me back? The rigors of military discipline? No, my puritanical upbringing had left me with few fears of personal discipline, and military discipline is not particularly taxing: it is mostly a matter of having your body in a certain place at a certain time and of posing your body in certain stereotyped forms—salutes, drills, attention—under particular circumstances. (Military discipline is the easiest sort of discipline in the world because it carries with it no requirement that the disciplined like or pretend to like it.) Physical deprivations? These were not particularly frightening for me; I knew how Nicaraguans live, and a diet of beans and rice is at least filling. Was I afraid of dying in battle? The truth is that I was far more afraid of a life without meaning, and my political commitments were such that the defense of the revolution seemed more compelling than my own personal safety did. Indeed, should I die, I reasoned, it would at least have been for a purpose. All death is tragic—but to lay down one's life for a just cause or for another human being: that is at least a good death, a meaningful death.

In the end, I did not volunteer. My reasons were mixed, but much of it came down to this: If I survived the experience, I would have to become a Nicaraguan, and that terrified me. How would I *be* a Nicaraguan for the rest of my life? How would I *live* as a Nicaraguan? No doubt with my doctorate, and after my military service, I could have secured a position at a Nicaraguan university. Other internacionalistas have taken up more or less permanent residence in Nicaragua, usually laboring in development or technical projects, and their commitment is commendable. Some have even taken Nicaraguan citizenship. Should I have done so, my compadres, my network of friends, would have constituted a sort of Nicaraguan family for me. But I would have been entirely enveloped by the other: by a culture not my own.

I realize that people migrate, that people pass into countries and societies not their own all the time. Perhaps I am more provincial than cosmopolitan, for such migration has always struck me as a very difficult sort of thing. Moreover, what I was toying with was not simply a physical border crossing but an ideological and cultural one. And despite my political sympathies, I have never felt that the Sandinista revolution was in any sense my own. Anthropologists often report the temptation to "go native" and claim the other's culture as their own. But for me, going native has always seemed to constitute the furthest reaches of a peculiar self-deception and artifice: a way of wresting meaning—other people's meaning—to fill a void in one's own life. It is the incongruity here—my void, another's meaning—that evokes in me a whole range of suspicions. No one can really cede one's self to become another—not without resorting to sham, duplicity, bad faith, self-deception, even exploitation. And Nicaragua is a concrete, really existing country, populated by living, breathing people. It is not—or, rather, it should not be—a symbol, an icon, or an escape hatch.

Che Guevara wrote that the revolutionary's real motivation is always love (1968:20). Perhaps this is so, but not necessarily in the idealistic sense of an abstract "love of the people" that Che had in mind. Love of real concrete persons—our families, our spouses, our lovers, our friends—may indeed cause us to take up arms in their defense when they are threatened by cruel economies, despotic regimes, and systematic injustices. Such love may also cause us to lie low when the violence threatens to sever these real human connections.

I dedicated *Thanks to God and the Revolution* to three boys, W, L, and E. As the year of his draft into the military approached, Lenín—the L of the dedication—was sent out of the country by his mother, Doña Celia. She had sent two sons into the military already and could not bear the thought of sending one more, the youngest and her favorite. Lenín is said to be somewhere in Mexico. His mother had her reasons, and I defy anyone to reproach her.

Meanwhile, my lover, who was at the time in the U.S. military, spent four months stationed in Honduras on an involuntary tour of duty. Despite an abundance of Anglo volunteers, he was impressed into this tour—no doubt because he is a native speaker of Spanish, and that is the way an imperial power operates. It serves appearances better to send a few Hispanics to Latin American countries, and besides, it's useful for them to serve as interpreters in subjugated territories. During this period there were various guerrilla attacks on U.S. service personnel stationed in Honduras: ambushes, sniper attacks, mail bombs, bombings. The Honduran guerrillas could not get at the generals, the officers, the bankers, and the businessmen, but they could occasionally strike out at U.S. servicemen—mostly blacks, Hispanics, and poor whites who joined the armed forces not out of ideological commitment but out of the despair bred from poverty and lack of economic opportunity in the United States; who joined because life is hard; who joined because so many of us find no real home in the world.

When my lover was sent off base on missions, I was gripped by a variety of fears.[1] Surely the chances of his being caught in an ambush were remote, but there was always that possibility. In my letters and phone conversations, I began to sound every bit as fearful and cautious as my parents had been when I did fieldwork in Nicaragua. "Don't take any chances." "Be careful." "Remember, your primary responsibilities are to me, not to the military and not to your colleagues." "Be careful."

The day after he returned from a field trip to La Ceiba, someone threw a bomb into a group of servicemen on leave there for the evening, in the entrance of a crowded discotheque. Several North Americans and Hondurans were wounded, some of them quite seriously. I knew my lover was all right because he was safely on base at Comayagua that day; but I also knew that the group he was with had pondered whether to stay an extra day at La Ceiba. I tried to call him on base that evening, just to hear his voice, but the telephone lines were jammed—other families calling their loved ones, too, after a frightening incident. I spent a sleepless night. Contingencies. Chance. The sort of conjunctures that had once seemed amusing to me now gave me sleepless nights and headaches.

This situation put me in a perverse and excruciating predicament. We both knew why the U.S. military presence was so pronounced in Honduras: to menace Nicaragua. Should the United States invade Nicaragua—a scenario that was never, by any means, out of the question—the troops stationed in Honduras—my lover among them—would have been moved forward first. Had God himself wished to punish me for my sins, he could not have devised a more trying existential situation.

And I recalled something written by Christopher Isherwood. In Germany at the beginning of World War II, his lover was drafted into the German army. Isherwood understood, plainly, the nature of fascism. He also understood, very frankly, that real love is always concrete, never abstract. He admits, perhaps injudiciously, that the thought of the entire British Army perishing troubled him little at all, if only his lover would survive the war. I had read those passages, through the eyes of a somewhat naive politico, nearly ten years before, when I was still really a child. I did not understand these sentiments; I could not accept the idea that real love was more concrete than politics, and I even thought the author was something of a moral monster. I would say today that his dilemma was monstrous—as are so many dilemmas in the world.

But now it was I who was fully human. I understood what love is. Not that this experience made me in any sense "soft" on imperialism.

It did not. But I understood the real threat of war and danger. And I understood all too well those poignant passages.

SIGNS OF THE TIMES

> And as he sat upon the mount of Olives, the disciples came unto him privately, saying, Tell us, when shall these things be? and what shall be the sign of thy coming, and of the end of the world? And Jesus answered and said unto them . . . ye shall hear of wars and rumors of wars. . . . For nation shall rise against nation, and kingdom against kingdom: and there shall be famines, and pestilences, and earthquakes in diverse places. All these are the beginning of sorrows.
>
> Matthew 24:3–8

(From my journal, 23 May 1988): *Eben-ezer Church, an Assemblies of God congregation, received a divine prophecy that the world would come to an end last Thursday. Its members locked themselves up on a farm named Filadelfia near Chinandega, where they continue to be holed up. Their refusal to come out apparently stems from their conviction that efforts to dislodge them represent Satan's last temptation of their faith: since the world* must have *come to an end on the appointed date, it really did, and now all that exists beyond the gates of Filadelfia is a netherworld, an emptiness, a nothingness. Authorities who show up outside the gates of the farm, trying to dissuade the congregation from its fantasy, are themselves illusions sent by Satan.*

The congregation has been denounced by the local Baptists, Churches of God, and Apostolics for issuing "false prophecies." And here, through these denunciations, the incident is reenveloped by an apocalyptic vision: Eben-ezer Church itself becomes a sign of the times, for did not Christ warn of false prophecy? In the last days, there shall come false prophets, who will deceive many (Matthew 24:11).

Against the tumultuous landscape of war, hyperinflation, dislocation, and crisis—everywhere, surreal displacements—incidents of this sort seem to have become more and more common. Men under arms, always moving. Rumors of their movements, too, always circulating in advance of and behind them. Drought, followed by floods, followed by drought. Electricity, food, even water: always in short supply. The arms and legs of children thin, while their bellies swell, silent testimony to some diabolical work on the flesh. And who could doubt that these are grave and significant times? Several Nicaraguan congregations, apparently spontaneously, have received revelations of the end of the world on such-and-such an appointed date and acted in accordance with their prophecies. In Erasmus Jiménez, people were talking about the antics of some of the Pentecostal churches—from shifting perspectives, with various interpretations. Flora: "It's just more evangelical madness." Aida: "No, it's a counterrevolutionary plot, a trick to confuse and terrorize the people. That evangelical from the United States—what was his name? the chele—took all those morenos to Guyana and made them drink poison. ¡Qué barbaridad!" Doña Celia: "These are grave and terrifying times." Doña Jazmina: "But imagine, the poor children of those people! The adults have their own free will, to lock themselves up, and go without food and water, and believe in whatever craziness they please. But the children? The children in there don't deserve this."

Apocalyptic revelations go on, in increasingly bizarre form, against the play of light and shadows. Their illuminating effect is both of and not of this world: of, to the extent that prophecy classes real experiences into a schema of divine-historical unfolding and makes sense of a sort out of what very tangibly hurts. *Not of, in that the whole, transparent design of these piercing illuminations is to provide a hasty exit from this vale of suffering. The illumination, and the blindness, is that of one who has stared for too long into the face of the sun. That sun is neither the return of an otherworldly Christ, nor the advent of a human Christ, nor the redemption of revolution: it is instead the fiery maelstrom of a crisis with no apparent exit.*

CHAPTER XVII

The *Negro* of the Family

There is no reality not already classified by men: to be born is nothing but to find this code ready-made and to be obligated to accommodate oneself to it.

—Roland Barthes, *Critical Essays*

It is sometimes stated that Nicaraguan society has historically been relatively free of racism (see T. Walker 1982, 10). And from certain points of view that claim is true. The common forms of racism prevalent in North American history—discrimination, segregation—strike most Nicaraguans with whom I have spoken as both irrational and immoral. Relative to certain other Latin American countries—where racial stratification approaches the form of a caste system—Nicaragua is by no means racially polarized.[1] But I would begin any discussion of skin color, race, and racism by saying that Nicaragua does indeed have a "race problem" or, perhaps more to the point, a "color problem," and this problem manifests itself in insidious and destructive ways. Little that has transpired since the revolution deals directly with this topic, and, indeed, dealing with it will prove difficult because of deep-seated cultural conditioning.

THE ATLANTIC COAST QUESTION

Prejudice against natives of the Atlantic coast—the Costeños—is perhaps the most striking phenomenon (T. Walker 1986, 82–83). In the majority, mestizo (racially mixed), western sector of Nicaragua, Miskitos and African Caribbeans are felt to be "backward" and inferior in various ways. Such prejudicial sentiments, which generally treat the minority sector's "level of culture" or "level of economic development," occasionally take on "racial" forms, as well.

A typical pattern evinced itself in my discussions with ordinary people about the Atlantic coast problem: at an analytical level, almost everyone admits that indigenous Miskitos and African Caribbeans have been the victims of prejudice and misunderstandings by the Spanish-speaking mestizo majority; yet almost no one admits to harboring any personal ill will toward the minority sector. The peculiarity of the ethnic question in Nicaragua is its duplex structure in discourse. Revolutionary ideology recognized the problem of ethnic prejudice; as part of its negotiating position in bringing regional autonomy and peace to the Atlantic coast, the government put dealing with ethnic crisis near the top of its list of concerns. Government representatives spoke openly and frequently about their own "past errors" and the need to overcome chauvinism; in the process, ordinary people took their cues from this governmental discourse. A common refrain went something like this: "We have had our problems with the Atlantic coast, and we have our differences, but we have to learn to live together." True enough. But when individually questioned about racial and ethnic issues, most people have a stereotyped construction: racism exists; mistakes have been made; and no, I am not a racist myself. The density of real, everyday discourse betrays the good intentions of a thin, official discourse.

Elvis was cool and analytical on virtually any topic. A member of the Sandinista Youth, well aware of the status of the ethnic question, and a Marxist trained in materialism, Elvis took it as a matter of personal pride that he was not superstitious. One day I was asking him about his various tours of duty through the mountainous provinces of Nicaragua. He spoke of hunger, isolation, boredom, and danger. "We were in the rain a lot. There were almost no provisions, and I was starving for salt. It was especially bad, having to eat monkeys, because when you skin them, they look like men. But the worst was when they sent me to the Atlantic coast." "Why?" I asked. "Because there are a lot of *gente mala* [evil people] on the coast." "How so?" I wondered. Did he mean counterrevolutionaries? No, *gente mala* was not a political designation at all. "Look, I was never sick in the mountains. But on the Atlantic coast I got a fungus, a skin disease, that covered my whole arm. I still have scars from it." He showed me the patchwork of little scars. "But what's that got to do with bad people?" "Ah," Elvis clarified, "because they all practice witchcraft. A *negra* [black woman] from Bluefields was looking at me, very strange, for a long time, and a couple of days later, I got sick." "And you think she caused it?" "I know she caused it."

"It's doubtful—" I began. "You didn't see her eyes," he retorted. I pressed Elvis a bit further. "I didn't think you believed in witches, the evil eye, black magic and such." "Of course not!" he replied. "Not here. But the Atlantic coast, that's a different thing." Thus, for Elvis the Atlantic coast embodied pure otherness. It was a mysterious zone where all the normal rules of reason were suspended, inverted; a dark land untouched by science, populated by natives known by their rejection of rightness—*gente mala:* bad folks, evil people. As I questioned him further on his characterizations, Elvis grew increasingly uncomfortable and embarrassed; eventually we changed the subject.

Elvis's was a hushed, fearful, and somewhat ashamed discourse on Atlanticity. Sometimes the racism takes a harder, more overt edge. In practice, the basketball courts in Luis Alfonso Park are segregated: mestizos play separately from African Caribbeans, and I have never seen an integrated game. Jaime tells me that once he and some friends were playing a friendly game on one side of the court. A young man from the coast approached and began shooting baskets at the other end of the court. Instead of asking him to join their play, or even going about their game at the other end of the court, Jaime reports, the young men of his group all just walked away. I was surprised, because Jaime is not—or does not seem to be—a racist. Yet rather than try to convince his friends to stay and play ball, he walked away with them. And whenever African Caribbeans enter a bus in Managua, people tend to move away from them—in a country where there is generally little aversion to close physical contact, and on a public transportation system that is heavily overloaded.

The Atlantic coast minorities—African Caribbeans, who speak English, and indigenous peoples, who speak Miskito or English and occasionally Sumo, Rama, or Garífona—are not part of national Nicaraguan culture. Historically colonized by Britain and geographically isolated from the Spanish traditions of the majority sector, they remain both remote and distinct from the mestizo Pacific. No highway links the east coast to the west. Various causes exacerbate the ethnic tensions that already existed in Nicaraguan society. The FSLN was too aggressive in its early attempts to "bring the revolution" to the coast and to its distinctly nonrevolutionary peoples, who tended to see the revolution as a "Spanish thing"—and therefore not good. On the coast, the Sandinistas stimulated the formation of a multiethnic, indigenous mass organization, but Miskito demands soon outstripped the framework of that vehicle, and the organization splintered into increasingly militant and separatist organizations (see Bourgois 1982; Diskin 1987). Various Miskito factions joined the contras and organized their own armed groups. The

Atlantic coast came to be seen as separatist, hostile, counterrevolutionary territory. Many Nicaraguan families from the western majority region lost sons in the fighting. Ultimately, working piece by piece with
various armed groups, the Sandinistas negotiated a gradual peace on
the Atlantic coast that entailed a large measure of economic, political,
and cultural autonomy for that region—indeed, a separate constitution,
with separate laws, education in the native tongue, and guarantees that
youths drafted on the Atlantic coast would be stationed on the Atlantic
coast (see Diskin et al. 1986). In perhaps its boldest move, the FSLN
integrated their former enemies into the Sandinista Army, making what
were formerly armed contra units into the guarantors of peace in the
region. The war is now over, but the wounds remain.

Under such circumstances, even minor events can inflame passionate
hatreds. Virgilio once asked me if I were a racist. I said no; to my
surprise, he asserted that he was. He spoke openly of his hatred of
the African Caribbeans in his high school. "I hate blacks," he told me.
"They are immoral. And black is ugly. Better to just exterminate them
all—cut their throats." Astonished by the vehemence of his remarks, I
pressed Virgilio on his feeling until finally he yielded a "reason": he had
made friends with an African-Caribbean boy at school, and his friend
stole his girlfriend. *"Me traicionó* [he betrayed me], so that's why I hate
blacks. Wouldn't you?" Virgilio concluded, "Whenever black people
touch me, I feel dirty: I want to go wash it off. Black *is* dirty, isn't
it?"

I do not want to give a misleading or one-sided picture here. Such
extreme sentiments are rare. (Virgilio's girlfriend, for example, was clearly
not averse to dating an African Caribbean, nor was Virgilio himself at
first reluctant to befriend the youth.) It seems to me that racism toward
the Atlantic coast minorities is generally less vicious and all-encompassing than racism as I know it in the United States. For instance, I have
never heard anyone assert that these minorities are by nature intellectually inferior to mestizos. No Nicaraguan ever struck up a casual conversation with me around the topic of his contempt for or hatred of
Costeños (nor were any such conversations conducted within my hearing). In many parts of the States—south and north—white people do
just that, employing casual racism and white solidarity as a way of in-
gratiating themselves with white strangers. But this sort of casual racism is not the basis for an easy racial solidarity in Nicaragua. In fact,
none of my informants ever revealed their racism to me—either directly,
as did Virgilio, or indirectly, as did Elvis—until they were confident that

we had already established a solid friendship. Moreover, those African Caribbeans and Miskitos who have migrated from the Atlantic coast to live and work in Managua do not inhabit segregated barrios, and they generally live on good terms with their mestizo neighbors.

After getting to know me, most politically conscious Nicaraguans would eventually ask me if I were a racist, and then (unlike Virgilio) deliver a quick comparative lesson by way of analogy with their own country. "You North Americans have a history of racism starting with slavery," Aida told me, "and even today there is a lot of racism in the States. Your country should treat all its people equally, with respect and dignity. You should learn how to live with your black neighbors. We've had problems with racism in Nicaragua, too. There's a lot of animosity between the Pacific and the Atlantic. But we are learning how to live in peace with our black neighbors on the Atlantic coast." And while it is true that Atlantic coast culture is generally thought to be "inferior" to mestizo culture, this perception did not prevent Dimensión Costeña from becoming Nicaragua's most popular native musical group, nor the Atlantic "Maypole dance" from becoming Managua's biggest dance craze since breakdancing. Finally, people were always telling me that, of the candidates for president in the United States, their favorite was *El Morenito*—Jesse Jackson. He was seen as a Third World candidate, good for minorities in the United States and all nonwhite nations in the world.

Thus, the racial situation in Nicaragua can be summed up as follows: first, racism really does exist in Nicaragua, and it can be detected, its logic diagrammed, in various ways; second, this is not as absolute or all-encompassing a racism as that which one encounters in the United States; and finally, it is nonetheless a significant social problem, posing a range of cultural and political issues that will continue to affect the course of Nicaraguan history.

COLOR SIGNS

But significant though this regionally defined racism may be, prejudice against the Atlantic coast minorities is scarcely the most pervasive form of "racism" in Nicaragua. Indeed, apart from the cultural and political tensions that clearly exist between the western majority and the eastern minority, it seems to me that whatever racism exists toward the Atlantic coast minorities is but an extension of a much deeper-seated pattern *internal* to mestizo culture, not external to it. A more apposite term for this pattern might be *colorism* rather than *racism*.

People put color into discourse in a variety of ways. The ambiguity of Nicaraguan speech about color is perhaps its crucial feature. *Negro* refers to Atlantic coast natives of African heritage, but it may also refer to dark-skinned indigenous peoples such as the Miskitos. It can also refer to dark-skinned mestizos—the majority of Nicaragua's population. For instance, it is common for parents to nickname their darkest-skinned child "Negro" or "Negra." I don't think I've ever been in a house where this was not the practice. When I mentioned this to Virgilio, his first reaction was to deny it—a remarkable thing, because his mother had summoned him to dinner that very afternoon by yelling out "Ne-gro!" at the top of her lungs, as she often does. Virgilio is the *negro* in his house, as is Jaime. In this sense, *negro* is a relative term, marking differences in coloration among the mestizo majority. It is sometimes used to mark very narrow differences indeed. One family in Barrio Sergio Altamirano had a set of twin boys: one had darker brown hair, the other's hair was lighter brown. I had to look closely, at the parents' insistence, to see the difference. One was nicknamed Negro, the other Chele.

Thus, in everyday usage and for most purposes, color terms are *relational* terms. The relativity of this sort of usage turns on the intention of the speaker, comparative assessments, and shifting contexts. Not one but three different, perpetually sliding systems are in use.

It was through an extended series of conversations with Virgilio and Jaime about race, racism, and skin color that this complex system became clear to me. I had seen a variety of perplexing things. On one day, someone would be described to me as negro, on another as moreno, and on yet another as blanco. How to reconcile these apparently contradictory descriptions? After Virgilio proclaimed that he was a racist, he, Jaime, and I discussed the meanings of various terms and usages in some detail. I was, after all, quite confused. Virgilio's skin was darker than that of many African Americans in the United States, although here his indigenous appearance would undoubtedly classify him as either Native American or Hispanic. But for Nicaraguan purposes, what was he? White, brown, or black? And Jaime's dark skin, full lips, and frizzy hair would probably classify him as "black" in the United States. So what was he? The answer is, it all depends on the context.

First, there is the phenotypic system, which is recognized by everyone in at least certain contexts:

Blanco (white)

Moreno (brown)

Negro (black)

This relatively "objective" system of classification is employed to describe the range of possible skin tones. *Blancos* are persons of primarily European ancestry. This is a small minority—by far the smallest of the three categories marked in this system. *Moreno* designates the brown hair and brown skin of the mestizo majority—and here *mestizo* is primarily a cultural, not phenotypic, term. Within fifty years of the Spanish conquest, Nicaragua's indigenous population declined from roughly one million to a few tens of thousands (T. Walker 1986, 10).[2] There were at the same time a few hundred Spanish settlers in the country. Thus, without adequate support for indigenous continuity, Nicaragua's culture developed as a Spanish-speaking mestizo culture; but it is also clear that the vast majority of material in the gene pool was and remains indigenous, not Spanish. Nicaraguan national culture is mestizo; people's physical characteristics are primarily indigenous; and in the terms of this phenotypic system, most people are moreno. In this system, *negro* can denote either persons of African ancestry or sometimes persons of purely indigenous appearance, whether they are culturally classified as Indio or mestizo.

Second, there is the more common polite usage:

Polite terms	Corresponding phenotypic terms
Chele (sometimes *rubio*)	*Blanco* (light hair, blue eyes)
Blanco	*Moreno* (brown hair, brown skin)
Moreno	*Negro* (black or dark brown skin)

In this system, all the color terms are inflated. Europeans are denoted by a special term, *chele* (a Mayan word that literally means "blue," for the eyes of Europeans and Euro-Americans [T. Stephens 1989, 64]), but morenos become blanco and negros become moreno. This is the system normally used in the presence of the person about whom one is speaking. Even persons of African heritage are referred to as moreno in their presence. It is considered a grave and violent offense to refer to a black-skinned person as *negro*. "Never, ever, call a negro *negro*," Jaime warned me, "at least not to his face." "Why not?" I wondered. Virgilio laughed.

"Do you want to die?" Indeed, this inflationary rule extends to a range of circumstances: in the countryside, Indians are called *mestizos* rather than *Indios*.

Finally, there is the pejorative and/or affectionate usage:

Chele   (fairer skin, lighter hair)

Negro   (darker skin, darker hair)

To posit a hostile difference between the speaker and the person spoken about or spoken to, Nicaraguans resort to a simplified dichotomy between white and black. On rare occasions the term *chele* may be thrown out as invective; this usage can occur when someone assumes more familiarity with the target than is socially appropriate.[3] More commonly, *negro* is employed to disparage the victim of one's aggression. "Black as carbon," for instance, asserts the absolute negritude of one's target. Color can also be used to augment the standard invectives. For instance, *hijo de puta* becomes *negro hijo de puta* (black son of a whore). At the same time, these terms are common in affectionate discourse. *Chele* and *Negro* are common family nicknames, and *negrito mio* is a diminutive form commonly exchanged between *novios* (sweethearts). This is not to say that such affectionate nicknames carry with them a directly stigmatizing force. But *negro* or *negrito mio* are affectionate and intimate terms precisely because they are "informal"; and such terms are informal because they violate the rules of polite discourse. Even when motivated by affection rather than anger, such terms can never be innocent of the social relations in which they are embedded. Such terms of intimacy maintain at close range the system of contrasts that is, for other purposes and in other contexts, stigmatizing—and that might, in an argument or in a different tone, carry the force of strong invective.

Both Jaime and Virgilio confidently asserted, on first questioning, that they were blanco, white. After more questioning, they downgraded themselves to moreno. After yet more questioning, they finally admitted, "Well, we're all black from the point of view of rich white people." On the basis of this questioning, drawing out examples and scenarios, Jaime and Virgilio described to me all these various rules of interaction. The three of us sat out on the sidewalk late one night, sometimes talking in low voices, at Jaime's suggestion, lest our neighbors overhear us classifying and reclassifying them. I then drew up the rules of discourse into the three situational systems described above, until I understood the material, and it met with my informants' approval.[4]

Jaime proved very perceptive on the subject and put the entire matter into perspective with one clever sentence. Citing the old aphorism, "In the land of the blind, the one-eyed man shall be king," he observed: "In the land of the negros, the moreno shall be blanco." As Jaime's maxim suggests, something of this very issue—power, status, wealth—clings irrevocably to color distribution and color descriptions. Of poor barrios, it is sometimes said, "They're very black"—and it seems to me that there really is a loose correlation between darkness and poverty. Of wealthier neighborhoods, it is also said, "They're whiter." And in this case there is a very clear connection between affluence, status, power, and whiteness.

Whiteness, then, is a desired quality, and polite discourse inflates its descriptions of people. Well, then, I wondered, how should I respond to Doña Jazmina, when she greets me as "Chele"? Should I respond, "*Buenas tardes, morenita*"? No, not at all, I was informed. A proper and polite greeting would be "*Chela, por cariño*" (more or less, "You, too, are white, in my affection"). When I tried this formula out the following day, the results were exactly as the two had predicted. Doña Jazmina appeared flattered and even remarked on my mastery of polite conversation. Tellingly, she observed that I was speaking good *Castellano* (Castilian Spanish).

Jaime and Virgilio understood perfectly well how color was put into discourse and could describe all the rules for competent performance within the system of color discriminations. Nonetheless, their sociological knowledge of the phenomenon was not enough to permit them to "escape" the system. The competition for a claim to whiteness produces quirky self-deceptions, even among the most astute. At one point, my two best informants on the matter developed for me a Lamarckian, climatic theory of color. Jaime reasoned, and Virgilio agreed, "We would be much whiter than we are, but the sun is very direct, and the climate is very hot. Why, look at the Matagalpeños. They live up in the mountains, where the air is fresh, and they come out much whiter than we do."

As such remarks indicate, a desire to "whiten" oneself pervades the system of color discrimination. Many dark-haired women use manzanilla tea to lighten their hair. *Rubio* (fair) is virtually synonymous with *guapo* (sexy or attractive); indeed, fair-skinned people are considered good catches in a marriage because their children, too, will be lighter-skinned. When one man in the neighborhood learned that I was staying with the Ocampos, he first made various salacious innuendoes about my relationship with Yolanda, the oldest daughter in the household, and then reasoned, "She's a *buena hembra* [a good-looking woman], and a white woman, too." When Doña Flora's sister-in-law had her fourth son, she related the news to me and sympathized with her co-madre's plight: "He came out *varón* [a boy]." The mother had been hoping for a girl. Then she shook her head and added, sympathetically, "And he came out negro, too. All her children came out negros."

One day I watched Doña Flora studying her son Charlie's face. He had been away from home for a couple of months in military training. He had spent much of the time outdoors in training exercises, and his brown skin was a shade darker than it had been before he left home. His first visit home was a festive occasion. Thoughtful and industrious, as usual, he had filled his duffel bag with mangos from a gigantic tree on base. Doña Flora made a pot of pinol, I joked with Charlie about his experiences in boot camp, and we all sat out in the backyard, eating and drinking and catching up on events. After the joy of reunion had passed a bit, Doña Flora examined her son's face, shook her head, and matter-of-factly stated, "*Puro Niquinohomo.*" The boy's father was from Niquinohomo, a small farming community near Masaya. Its residents are considered country bumpkins in Managua; they have very dark skin and strongly indigenous features, and the town is still sometimes considered "indigenous." The point seemed lost on Flora that her son had in fact come out a very handsome young man, with fine bone structure, an appealing face, and a strong, well-proportioned physique. When I asked her what she meant, she responded, as though it were perfectly obvious, "He's very black."

Doña Jazmina once asked me which of her two grandsons was better looking. Josué-Luis was four, and Augusto César was two. For me, the choice was obvious. Josué-Luis had a perfectly proportioned, symmetrical face with even features and large, endearing black eyes. His half-brother had a poorly proportioned, asymmetrical face, uneven features, and small, undistinguished brown eyes; moreover, his bouts with parasites had left him looking sickly. Naturally, I first responded, "Well, they're both such fine-looking young boys." But Doña Jazmina insisted, "Yes, but one of them is much more handsome than the other. Which one?" "Well, Josué-Luis." Doña Jazmina's face showed surprise and disbelief. "No, Róger. Augusto César is much better looking." Now it was I who was incredulous. The difference was so extreme, and my own judgment was so strong in the other direction, that I queried: "How so?" "Well, just look at them!" she responded. "Augusto César is *muy fino* [very fine], rubio. He's clearly the more handsome of the two." She then solicited opinions from her sons and daughters in the house, including the boys' mother, who confirmed her judgment over mine.

Nicaragua's mestizos make a range of assertions about blackness vis-à-vis whiteness. Black is primitive and irrational; it is dirty; it is also less attractive than white. And blackness is clearly associated with evil. The devil is envisioned as black, not red, in Nicaraguan lore, and "black as sin" is a phrase whose meaning would not be lost in the translation from English to Spanish. One young man from a neighboring barrio was referred to by his friends with the nickname *El Diablo* (The Devil). When I asked why he should have such a name, his friends explained, "Why, because he's so black, of course!" In popular discourse, blackness becomes a sort of semiotic sponge, absorbing the entire range of possible negative connotations.

POWER, COLOR, DISCOURSE, AND HISTORY

To return, then, to the question of racism toward the Atlantic coast populations: Nicaraguans apply to Costeños no rules that they do not apply more intimately to themselves. The categories with which they divide up the mestizo world are for them universal framers of experience. The color terms are the same, and the shifting rules of discourse are the same. Moreover, it is not only that many Nicaraguans see their Atlantic coast as a culturally backward region; they apply even that same logic to themselves, relative to other countries. One night at Doña Flora's house, we were watching a series of music videos on Sandinista television. The Mexican group Flans was coming to Nicaragua on a concert tour, and so their videos were getting constant airplay. One video after another depicted very fair-skinned young female singers in a variety of romantic situations, surrounded by opulence and luxury. Then the programming included a video from Nicaragua's own Atlantic coast group, Dimensión Costeña. Produced in Central America, it had simple production values; it was Nicaraguan and Caribbean in flavor. I casually opined that Dimensión Costeña was far superior to Flans. No one in the room agreed with me. Guto interjected, "How? How could *anything* produced here in poor little Nicaragua compare with things produced in Mexico? Or the United States? What good could come out of this poor country?" It was not simply that the band in question reflected the culture of the Atlantic coast; what was really in question was the status of Nicaragua itself. As the Atlantic coast stands to Nicaragua, so Nicaragua stands to the world. Backwardness, poverty, and blackness merge to define the deficient end of a scale.

If whiteness, like wealth, is a "limited good," in George M. Foster's (1965) sense of the term, then blackness, like poverty, is an abundant state of the *absence* of that good. The simultaneously envious and invidious nature of the social setting is clarified if we remember that envy is a state of hostile desire (Foster 1972). Things white are envied, desired; things black are denigrated, shunned. The envy manifests its workings in both centripetal and centrifugal motions. One discursive cycle builds up one's self and one's friends by employing an inflated conception of whiteness. But the countercycle to this is the sometimes teasing, sometimes overtly hostile use of *negro,* in which almost everyone comes out black, and all are drawn back into the color equivalent of shared poverty, shared blackness. People caught in this swirl of envy are thus propelled in two directions: to maximize their own goodness/color/status, and to minimize other people's. "Shared poverty" on the one hand, and the notion of an egalitarian "improvement for all" on the other.

These machinations represent not merely an ideology in the classical sense of the term—for an ideology proper would be easy to contest—but rather a real political economy of the body and its engagement with other bodies in society and history. Such transactions are political and economic in every sense.

Politically, color relations inside Nicaragua reproduce Nicaragua's own history of repression at the hands of other states. Where power and privilege are at stake, *white* implies might and right, as it were. When people employ the ambiguity of color terms to their own advantage, when they shift from one descriptive scale to another, and when they negotiate their own location within a system of contrasts, they are struggling over honor, to be sure, but they are no less struggling over privilege and power.

The transactions I have sketched are no less economic: value is assigned on the basis of exchange, but the values are assigned not to commodities but to human beings. In these daily exchanges, the many words associated with fair skin, with their arbitrary positive connotations, make up an inflated symbolic currency. Whiteness thus serves as a kind of symbolic capital, empowering its claimant to make advantageous exchanges in a host of other symbolic and material realms. Thus, Augusto

César enjoys a social advantage over Josué-Luis, an advantage which will carry across family, neighborhood, and school; a fair-skinned woman will generally be judged more attractive than a dark-skinned woman, and she might parlay her complexion's perceived value into an economically advantageous marriage; a chele in the world of business could readily translate his whiteness into contacts, contracts, and an economic advantage over moreno competitors; Elvis and Virgilio feel intrinsically superior to African Caribbeans; and so on. Such exchanges locate human beings within a system of production that is simultaneously symbolic and material. Color terms constitute, symbolically, a series of representational strata; the people to whom they are applied experience, materially, differential life chances. Although not absolute, the correspondence of economic classes to the representational color scheme is by no means random. From a semiotic point of view, these color relations are ultimately *power* relations, and they constitute, in Marxist terms, a substratum as much as a superstructure.

To speak of a political economy of the body, or to conceive of the body as a field of productive relations, is not to draw rigorous, one-to-one analogies with material production but to reiterate that what is produced in any case is not a good but a "value." What "economy" means in all cases is a system where value is assigned based not on any "intrinsic" worth of an object but rather on that object's position in the system of production and exchange. Thus, the value of a commodity is calculated in relation to other commodities and by the comparative social labor that produced it. Classes, too, are defined relationally: by their relations to each other in the production process. In the political economy of machismo, one's standing as a man is gauged by the execution of certain transactions (drinking, gambling, womanizing) in relation to other men. And in the political economy of colorism, one's value as a person is determined within a system of exchanges and in terms of relations between the lexical clusters around *black* and *white*.

What is always at issue in these daily power plays is the ascent of whiteness over blackness that began with the Spanish conquest. Africanos, Indios, and lower-class mestizos have been lumped together under a single term—*negro*—that signifies defeat. This defeat, however, is not just a "legacy" in the passive sense of the term. It is not a trauma held at a distance on the historical and social horizon. This defeat reproduces itself daily in myriad interactions.

Spanish language and Spanish culture have long been ensconced in the commanding heights of Nicaraguan society. Things Spanish or white are superordinate; things Indian or black are subordinate. This Spanish imposition was one of the bloodiest conquests in history. From extermination, enslavement, forced marches, overwork, and European epidemics, the territory of what is now Nicaragua lost more than 90 percent of its population within fifty years. A more total destruction would be hard to imagine, and the conflicts it engendered remain as more than mere wisps. For most of Nicaragua's population, little remains of pre-Columbian culture. But the conquest has been problematic, uneasy. Traces of indigenous words still remain in the Nicaraguan vocabulary. Historically, in most parts of the country lower-class mestizos assumed the structural positions and cultural characteristics usually reserved for indigenous populations in other Latin American countries: their economic position was defined by patron-client relations with whiter, wealthy landowners; and classical popular culture was defined by participation in religious festivities involving symbolic inversion, economic leveling, and a cargo system (Lancaster 1988b, 27–54)—the very hallmarks of indigenous communities in other parts of Latin America. The politics of this sort of "implicit Indianness" is not lost in real discourse. Upper-class Nicaraguans sometimes refer to lower-class mestizos, especially campesinos, as Indios (as well as negros) and attribute to them all the characteristics that Ladinos in other countries attribute to their own subordinate indigenous populations (laziness, ignorance, poor hygiene). On the other side of the divide, in heated and political moments ordinary people speak of their *sangre india, sangre rebelde* (Indian blood, rebel blood). And every Nicaraguan, save those few ruling class whites of primarily European ancestry, remains at war with himself: Spanish culture, indigenous skin.

Within this simultaneously symbolic and material system, there are moments of reprieve, flashes of rebellion, whose site, too, is the human body. During Carnaval and carnivalesque festivities such as the Coming of Santo Domingo, negritude is symbolically elevated over whiteness, and things indigenous take precedence over things Spanish. Celebrants appear drenched in grease and wearing indigenous costumes. Youths blacken their own and their elders' faces. As though in revenge against white envy and color climbing, blackness thus assaults the entire community, triumphantly asserting itself as a reversal of the people's baptism into a Spanish Catholic Church. But to date, this spirit of rebellion has not much escaped the confines of Carnaval.

Comparisons and contrasts might prove useful. Colonialism's long history, in Nicaragua as in the United States, puts race and color into discourse in subtle and invidious ways. Thus, colonialism can write and rewrite its text anew: in ways of perceiving and treating the human body; in all the ways we talk about ourselves and other people. But the history of colonialism is different in Nicaragua and in the United States. So history is embodied differently, spoken differently, structured differently, in the two countries.

In the United States' race system, at least from the point of view of the white majority, degree of coloration is not an issue: one falls on one side or the other of a boundary whose existence is scarcely subject to negotiation. "Race" is a very definite thing and gives every appearance of a structure. "Race" is no less a structure in those Latin American contexts where phenotypic traits count for nothing, and language, birthplace, and dress count for everything. In Nicaragua, though, "race" is a very different sort of thing. Color discriminations there constitute themselves not so much as solid, permanent structures but as a series of discursive gestures that are contingent and contextual and whose motives are eminently logical and self-interested. The site of these distinctions knows no bounds; they operate equally within the self, the family, the neighborhood, and society at large. Indeed, this system exists always as a practice, never as a structure: there is no race boundary, no line, no stopping point where negotiation and discourse cease. One can play the game with equal amounts of risk and self-interest in any given context. In mestizo company, Costeños, too, play the game, entering the same discourse by the same rules. Not an absolute boundary at all, these color distinctions are best seen as a series of concentric circles, which are in fact power plays, emanating from a highly problematic ego who may win or lose depending on contingent factors. Unlike our own tradition, in Nicaragua race hatred can scarcely be separated from self-hatred. Chauvinism toward the Atlantic coast minorities merely constitutes the furthest reaches of a discourse that ultimately afflicts the majority as severely as it castigates the minority.

THE DOMAIN OF THE SIGN

This line of analysis suggests some of the possibilities for a radical critique of signs. As Roland Barthes (1972b, 9) would say, there can be no semiology that is not at the same time a *semioclasm*—a smashing of signs. It also suggests an approach that dissolves the traditional disciplinary boundaries between political economy, culture studies, and semiotics. Here, both the production and the productivity of language are our targets.

Whenever color takes on meaning and enters into the world of social relations, color constitutes itself as a *sign* (Sahlins 1977; Eco 1985): that is, colors are categories defined by contrast and comparison with other categories, which are themselves defined within a system of contrasts.[5] Color is always a sign, then, in that color categories represent arbitrary inscriptions—imposed discontinuities—marked along the continuous spectrum of light's wavelengths. The "colors" attributed to human beings, too, are always signs (in that they are arbitrary and conventional); moreover, they represent a system of *connotators* continuous with the form of language that Barthes (1972b, 109–58) calls "mythic speech" (signs themselves converted into signifiers, speech at the service of a concept). This is not to say, however, that a synchronic analysis of signs obviates a historical analysis of them or that a semiotic perspective should displace a political one. Indeed, the whole question is how and by way of what practices should color come to be seen in the human body?

Color distinctions in Nicaragua are nothing less than the play of signs in history, for it was in and through history that those signs came to be constituted and became pregnant with all the connotations of conquest, domination, power, morality, wealth, and status.[6] But the historical process is not an "open" one carried out above the board, for color, like myth, takes refuge in the appearances of innocence, objectivity, nature, and biology. Colorized discourse rests on the a priori of its own invention: that color is real, and that color contrasts are natural, not cultural, phenomena. To understand color theoretically, of course, is to critique it: to show it as a social invention, though not necessarily in the sense of classical political economy, with its polarization of practices into an "economic base" and a "cultural superstructure." Thus, there is not some "real" history (of a materialist sort) on the one side and a deceptive "play of signs" on the other. History provides no "base" or backdrop for signs. In a real sense, history *is* the play of signs over time: simultaneously on the body, in economic production, in culture, in ideology.

The domain of the sign, then, is not the domain of the superstructure in classical Marxist analysis, nor is it something "added onto production" as an afterthought. The sign is constitutive in, as well as constituted by, social relations. Marx's method itself used something of this approach: otherwise, why would Marx's analysis of commodity fetishism (1967, 71–83) play such a pivotal role in his analysis of capital? Fetishes are signs, and the role they play is crucial, not epiphenomenal, in the political economy of capitalism. Like the "fetishism of commodities"—which imbues "things" with "life" while draining life from the human subjects who make them and concealing the social labor that produced value—the sign is present from the beginning of production: it is itself both productive and produced. It cannot, then, be banished from the scene, or held at arm's length, or treated as a mere distraction, or relegated to "false consciousness." It may in many cases mask, conceal, distort, or misdirect; in short, it may provide power with an *alibi,* but that in itself is no less an act of production than is economic production itself (in the sense that it is an indispensable element for the mode of production).

To follow Jean Baudrillard's (1988b, 57–97) arguments: Linguistic production, like economic production, is governed by a "code" in the sense that value is always produced within a system of references. Both processes work over materials that have no inherent value (linguistic "substance," perhaps, or "sounds" on the one hand, versus "physical matter" on the other). The process of production, in both cases, is a process of converting empty "matter" into meaningful value. In either case, what is ultimately produced is a "value" (the value of the sign on the one hand, use or exchange value on the other). Moreover, neither form of value is absent where the other is present: with its produced value, significance inheres in economic production from the start; with its produced value, "materiality" is the essence of the sign. Neither, then, can be said to constitute a superstructure for the other's base; rather, language, politics, and economy are coetaneous, and none of the elements of the series (economics-politics-sign) can be arbitrarily distinguished in terms of how it operates, but only by what sort of "matter" it converts.

Production, then, is always governed by a code, and that code ought to be called "power" (Baudrillard 1988b, 19, 76–80). To the extent that power is productive, what does it *produce?* Subordinated, disciplined bodies (Foucault 1979, 25–26; 1980, 92–102, 139–41). (And as Pierre Bourdieu might put it, certain bodies for certain jobs [1984, 191].) The body is perhaps its original working material, and it is to questions of the body that power returns again and again. How to convert the body to value? Power is faced with a series of problems and a series of options regarding the body. To be handled, to be manipulated—in a word, to be both productive and subordinated—the body must first be demarcated. How to demarcate bodies? Gender, sexuality, form, age: these are all possibilities. And color: again and again, color. By the accident of history, lighter-skinned peoples conquered darker-skinned peoples and thus wrote color into history and the body. Just as the colors in the spectrum all intergrade, so, too, do human "colors" intergrade through a narrow range of hues and shades. Power marks those shades, reducing and abstracting them into a scheme of color classifications capable of carrying meaning—for instance, black-brown-white.

Before the age of European expansion, it had never occurred to any civilization to classify people in terms of "color," to evaluate people by "race." Language, culture, religion, lineage: these had provided ample material for earlier civilizations' ethnocentrisms, and it was to such characteristics that the archaic term *race* generally applied. It was with colonialism that color saturated the human form and human races were invented: a new system of meaningful contrasts, a new system of power relations.[7]

Working backwards, then, to a tentative hypothesis: When Spain's colonists began intermarrying and producing children with Nicaragua's indigenous peoples, the problem of bloodlines, of legitimacy versus illegitimacy, and of relative Europeanness became both paramount and ambiguous (hence negotiable). Legitimacy and Spanish descent conferred rights and privileges; whiteness ascended over blackness and brownness, not at the distance of distinct races, but in the proximity of siblings and half-siblings and within the intimacy of the family. Distinctions within groups (*criollos* [creoles] and later mestizos) operated in roughly the same manner as distinctions between groups (Spaniards, mestizos, indigenous peoples). Thus, the system of power was set up. Most of the real privileges of the colonial epoch are today gone, but the ranking and sorting remains, supported less by economic rights and more by the rights and values held to be implicit in the color terms themselves: a colonialism of bodies, trapped by and in discourse; a hegemony not of colonists, nor even of colonialism per se any more, but of the values produced by colonialism.

From this perspective, power is above all else the power to demarcate, to mark, to inscribe, to apportion, to assign and distribute value throughout the system. It is the power to name, and to compel others to name as well. This formula holds true in economics, politics, language, and culture. All are spheres of "production"; all fall under the rule of the code, and that code is power. Was color, its classification and evaluation, a mere excuse for colonialism to extract economic value from subordinated populations? Probably so. But in the sense that the extraction of economic values depended on the production of color values, color's relationship to colonialism is anything but "superstructural."

In the ascent of whiteness over blackness, where color terms act as semiotic sponges, color signs *naturalize* the conquest that still plays itself out in daily interactions. The body itself is both the perfect raw material and the perfect alibi for a power thus constituted—for what could be more real, what could be less negotiable, than the form of the human body? Every speech act about color, whether the speaker is inflating or deflating the scale, thus comes to duplicate the historic practice of conquest: color connotes certain characteristics, and it is "really" and "truly" instantiated in the body. Even tiny distinctions in skin shade can generate ceaseless jabbering about color, because any difference whatsoever is sufficient to be taken up by discourse and made meaningful. Even the difference between twins is adequate to generate the entire range of social and historical connotations.

How Nicaraguans treat their children is a central, not peripheral, issue—for, far from being a refuge against the ravages of history, the family is its driving engine, and power reproduces itself in and through the household. Some children are teased, insulted, and ridiculed while others escape stigma. Based on my observations in various households, it seems to me that *niños negros* are more likely to be taken out of school—for a year, even two—to help out around the house or earn the family extra income. Niños negros are less likely to finish their course of study and are more likely to find their way into manual jobs from an early age. *Niños blancos* are more likely to be encouraged to finish their course of study on time, to go on to study at the university, and to take up professions. Do families also apportion love in the same manner they apportion economic opportunity? That, too, is clearly a temptation, since the connotations of blackness include evil, inferiority, and subordination. It is clear to me that in many families the whitest child is also the favorite child, and the emotional treatment children receive evokes all the colorized associations outlined in this chapter. In other cases, it is the black child who is emotionally favored—but with what sort of love? A love sometimes colored by the sympathy of defeat. And therein lies the imperialism of the sign: long after colonialism ceased to exist as a formal relationship between Spain and Nicaragua, color continues to order the entire range of social relations within Nicaraguan society.

Recall the nature of the linguistic sign (Saussure 1966, 65–70; Barthes

1968, 35–57; Culler 1986, 28–33, 62–64): it is both *arbitrary,* in the
sense that it carries no implicit, necessary meaning, and *contractual,* in
the sense that its meaning represents an agreement within a community
of speakers. Thus, the creation of a sign is always an act of distinction,
for signs may be defined only in opposition to other signs within a system of oppositions. The "value" of the sign is always carved out, as it
were, in opposition to other signs' values, and every act of signification
is thus at the same time an act of production (from raw material) and
an imposition of meaning written on and out of the nothingness of
other signs. As acts of imposition, signification and value are always
simultaneously social, historical, and political in nature. Perhaps in this
sense it is the nature of the sign to be "imperial"—always carving, distinguishing, assigning; always imbuing itself with the fictions of reality,
objectivity, nature, biology; always absorbing yet more signs into discourse and hence colonizing yet more territory into elaborate systems
of connotation; in short, always producing, always subordinating, always masking. And perhaps this critical and interrogative picture of the
sign suggests the proper lines of analysis into those colonial signs that
mask themselves with the objective or innocent appearances of color.
Color signs translate imperiality, colonialism, into practices at the level
of the body—and it is the body, after all, that is power's first and last
recourse. In this case, it is the body, and our experience of the body,
that is ultimately being created.

Nicaraguans themselves remain trapped in a discourse not of their
own invention, unable to break the circuit of logorrhea.[8]

POLITICS?

What is the prospectus for changing Nicaragua's political economy of
the body? How to translate dignity and sovereignty into body and discourse? Writ into the body and carried out in myriad daily transactions,
such practices cannot be suppressed by decree. Making them taboo might
well drive them underground and render them all the more powerful. A
massive consciousness-raising effort might at least bring these practices
to the level of self-consciousness, but even the most sociologically minded
of my informants were still fully subject to the logic of this system. The
always negotiable nature of the system; the fact that any given person
may always defer a final judgment on his or her location within the
system of contrasts; the presence of racial thinking combined with the
absence of corporate races: these factors distribute the weight of color

in Nicaragua in a subtle and pernicious manner and militate against efforts to address—or even perceive—the issue as a problem, as an issue of power.

When I attempted to discuss the politics of color with my informants, I was often charged with racism. Why? First, because I pointed out the political implications of everyday discourses deemed apolitical and thus was accused of having an unhealthy interest in the subject. And, more often than not, because people felt that I was relegating them to an inferior color status. "I see, chele," I was told on more than one occasion: "You want to be the only blanco in the room!" Granted, the interpersonal dynamics of such discussions were less than ideal (and it is not my business to meddle, only to report), but they do point up the special constraints of the system. Nicaraguans are personally invested in the values of a system that rarely pays off, except in the little daily exchanges that validate the system.

Nicaraguans do develop a different way of appreciating racism when they come to visit or work in or live in the United States, for they then inhabit a solid "structure" of race (where to be Hispanic is to be brown), and not the sliding practices of their own color discourse. On the Nicaraguan terrain, a "negro" or "moreno" pride movement might be helpful, but the sliding of signifiers and signifieds would prove slippery soil indeed. Most people would have the option of resisting such a revolution in connotators, and they could take tactical refuge in their own "whiteness," unless it could be proven that they would come out ahead by changing the game. Worse yet, systematic consciousness raising might well resort to the "objectivity" of phenotypic variation and tactically freeze the sliding signs, but still fail to erase the stigma that clings to color's history. In so doing, the best of efforts might transform the color code into a truly totalitarian scheme of race classification.

The form, scope, and play of power analyzed here obviously recall Foucault's descriptions of power as decentered and nonbinary. Other than language itself, there is no "center" to this system of power. In most cases it would be hard to say who is dominated and who is dominating. It is not so much that white people dominate black and brown people; rather, *whiteness* dominates *blackness*. And someone is always whiter than any given speaker, just as someone is always blacker. Although color clearly participates in each generation's construction of economic hierarchy, the cleavage into white elites and dark subjects is by no means sharp. The original colonialism that sorted people into rulers and ruled is gone; the discourse of power—and the power of

discourse—remains. This discourse feeds less on the energy of domination than on the despair of defeat. One could hypothesize that, although
the original colonialism that invented the color terms and invested them
in the human body is gone, its power/discourse has remained, supported by subsequent U.S. colonialism.

Attractive as this thesis is, it shares the weakness of the classically
Marxist analysis of base and superstructure: it cannot specify in any
detail the links whereby U.S. colonialism produces discourse. The thesis
rests, ultimately, on its attractiveness alone, and it mystifies more than
it illuminates. The Spanish origin is not mysterious. Spain imposed a
language, a religion, and a culture on the territory of what is now Nicaragua; its colonists lived among, dominated, and intermarried with the
indigenous natives and thereby created a mestizo culture. Its values established hegemony: white over black and brown, Christian over non-
Christian, Spanish over Indian, and so on. Today's North American
conquerors might occasionally refer to the land as "Niggeragua," but
their colonialism has no power to compel Nicaraguans to call each other
"nigger." And were that power/discourse supported only by the interests of the local, affluent, white elites, it could not compel the active
participation of people in every household. Its overthrow would be a
relatively simple matter.

Consequently, I have pursued a "how," not a "who," of power. This
power "is not something that is acquired, seized, or shared, something
that one holds on to or allows to slip away; power is exercised from
innumerable points, in the interplay of nonegalitarian and mobile relations" (Foucault 1980, 94). Surely, its play is "strategic," "intentional,"
and "nonsubjective"; and just as surely, the system already accounts
for "resistances" and diversionary tactics by its targets (ibid., 94–96),
which by no means constitute a threat to the power that is ultimately
held by no one, owned by no one, but firmly implanted in both discourse and body.

Even though the prospects for change seem remote, I do not want to
construct a "winner loses" argument (Hoy 1986, 11) of the sort critiqued by Fredric Jameson in his analysis of postmodernism:

What happens is that the more powerful the vision of some increasingly total
system or logic—the Foucault of the prisons book is the obvious example—
the more powerless the reader comes to feel. Insofar as the theorist wins,
therefore, by constructing an increasingly closed and terrifying machine, to
that very degree he loses, since the critical capacity of his work is thereby
paralyzed, and the impulses of negation and revolt, not to speak of those of

social transformation, are increasingly perceived as vain and trivial. (Jameson 1984, 57)

There is more pathos than terror in the machineries at hand, and while their operation exacts a very real human cost, the results for any particular individual are more often mundane than tragic. Perhaps this power resists politicization because it is so diffuse. Almost everyone suffers somewhat; almost everyone inflicts some pain on others; few suffer very greatly, and those who do are apt to redouble their efforts to exact vengeance on others *within* the system of values. The tragedy, of course, is cumulative: that this ceaseless whirligig should go on, ranking and sorting ad nauseam; that this monster of colonialism should endure as an internal and psychological colonialism.

Nor do I want to suggest that the situation is as bleak as that described by Vincent Crapanzano in South Africa, where "the tyranny of language," no matter how narrowly we inscribe it, "offers no escape" (1986, 29). Freedom is always, in Sartre's sense, the freedom to affirm or negate, the freedom to say yes or no—collectively, individually, and at every level of the question. Carnaval, the Coming and Going of Santo Domingo, and other carnivalesque festivities provide symbolic revolt against the system of values entailed by and reproduced within this system of power; they support the form of color discourse (black/white, Indio/Ladino) but scramble and invert the values of the discourse. That is one way of negating. Some people refuse to participate in the ranking or use only the color terms of "polite" discourse; that is another, partial way of negating. Leftist political discourse often draws on "Indianness" and "Indian blood" to contest colonialism in all its dimensions. That is yet another way of negating. What was made by history can also be unmade by history; what is affirmed by language may also be negated by language.

One of Foucault's aphorisms states, "People know what they do; they frequently know why they do what they do; but what they don't know is what what they do does" (in Dreyfus and Rabinow 1982, 187). Therein lies the problem, and therein lie the seeds for a more systematic and explicit way of negating. To get a handle on any given system of power, one must first stop negotiating one's way through its series of mazes and options and realize it in its totality of consequences. Consciousness raising, change, social transformation: these are difficult, but possible.

A thoughtful *fotonovela* (photographic comic book) published by the Centro Valdivieso (the coordinating center for liberation theology in Nicaragua) follows the plight of a young working-class girl, teased by her peers and finally tormented to tears by the term *negra* and its associated abuses. When her mother finds her, weeping and distraught, she draws the story out of her and consoles her: black is the color of the soil; black is the color of your mother; black is beautiful. It is nothing to be ashamed of. Simple and direct, a child's tears suggest the bitter legacy of a colorized history and the lived realities of a present-day system of power. The words of consolation spoken by a loving mother offer a humane politicization of language and suggest a different way of living.

CHAPTER XVIII

Subject Honor, Object Shame

Before the wide use of the word heterosexual, I suggest, women and men did not mutually lust with the same profound, sure sense of normalcy that followed the distribution of "heterosexual" as a universal sanctifier.

According to this proposal, women and men make their own sexual histories. But they do not produce their sex lives just as they please. They make their sexualities within a particular mode of organization given by the past and altered by their changing desire, their present power and activity, and their vision of a better world.

—Jonathan Ned Katz,
"The Invention of Heterosexuality"

What is machismo? Why do Nicaraguan men behave as they do (as Nicaraguan women vigorously complain): beating their wives, simultaneously fathering children in multiple households, abandoning compañeras and children, gambling away hard-earned money, and drinking to excess? And why did a decade of efforts to roll back the culture of machismo achieve so few tangible results?

An easy answer would be that the strain on Nicaragua's economic resources has made social restructuring impossible for the time being. That is indeed a partial answer. For those men already engaged in the culture of machismo, what AMNLAE and the Sandinistas call "responsibility" would prove costly even under the best of circumstances. Under the current economy of scarcity, such restructuring is probably prohibitively costly. Perhaps under a recovered economy, men might be more likely to support the children they father, and perhaps under better circumstances, sex education and contraception might make alternatives to the status quo available. But amid the dislocations of war and hyperinflation, and among all the personal turmoils thus engendered, it is difficult to speak realistically of any systematic restructuring of the personal life and of personal relations. Richard Adams's survey of Nicaraguan society suggests that its "loose family structure" is in part the outcome of the same sort of social and historical dislocations that are occurring today (1956, 892; 1957, 189–95). In the earlier instance, these dislocations revolved around the rise of *latifundismo* (the concentration of land into fewer and fewer hands), the uprooting of traditional peasants, and the emergence of mobile rural labor patterns. In the present instance, the dislocations center around the destruction of Nicaragua's economy and the emergence of labor mobility on a global scale. The real extent to which war and economic collapse perpetuate the status quo in gender relations is at present an open question; the answer will await the social and economic recovery of Nicaragua.

But there is more to the matter than that, for the arrangement of interpersonal relations depends on far more than the immediate state of the economy. A certain kind of standard Marxist political economy—itself a critique and revision of classical political economy—would perhaps relegate machismo to the level of an ideological or cultural superstructure. But the question of machismo cannot be addressed adequately if it is viewed as an ideology in the classical sense of the term. Machismo is not a set of erroneous ideas that somehow got lodged in people's heads. Rather, it is an organization of social relations that generates ideas. Machismo, therefore, is more than an "effect" produced by other material relations. It has its own materiality, its own power to produce effects. The resilience of machismo as a system has nothing to do with the tendency of ideological systems to "lag" behind changes in the system of economic production, for machismo is more than a "reflection" of economic practices. It is its own economy.

As in the case of colorism, and no less than in economic production proper, machismo produces and circulates values: the value of men and women. What is ultimately produced—in all three systems—is one's social standing. Machismo is more, too, than a political conceit of the body politic. It conceives myriad politics and inscribes all bodies with power. Machismo is a real political economy of the body, a field of power entailing every bit as much force as economic production.

Nor can the question of machismo be fully addressed as a matter of relations between men and women. It is that, but it is also more. Machismo (no less than Anglo-American concepts of masculinity and appropriate sexuality) is not exclusively or even primarily a means of structuring power relations between men and women. It is a means of structuring power between and among *men*. Like drinking, gambling, risk taking, asserting one's opinion, and fighting, the conquest of women is a feat performed with two audiences in mind: first, other men, to whom one must constantly prove one's masculinity and virility; and second, oneself, to whom one must also show all the signs of masculinity. Machismo, then, is a matter of constantly asserting one's masculinity by way of practices that show the self to be "active," not "passive" (as defined in a given milieu). On the surface, it is a primarily gestural system, for it is only through the competent performance of certain stereotyped gestures that machismo may be read, both by others and by the actor himself. Every gesture, every posture, every stance, every way of acting in the world is immediately seen as "masculine" or "feminine," depending on whether it connotes activity or passivity. Every action is governed by a relational system—a code—that produces its meanings out of the subject matter of the body, its form, its engagement with other bodies. As a gestural system, machismo has a steep temporal dimension, and yesterday's victories count for little tomorrow. Every act is, effectively, part of an ongoing exchange system between men in which women figure as intermediaries. To maintain one's masculinity, one must successfully come out on top of these exchanges. To lose in this ongoing exchange system entails a loss of face and thus a loss of masculinity. The threat is a total loss of status, whereby one descends to the zero point of the game and either literally or effectively becomes a cochón.

The cochón, itself a product of machismo, thus grounds the system of machismo and holds it in its place—just as machismo grounds the cochón and holds him in his place.

THE SOCIAL CONSTRUCTION
OF SEXUAL PRACTICES

The cochón, at first glance, might be interpreted as a Nicaraguan "folk category." The noun itself appears in both masculine (el cochón) and feminine (la cochón, la cochona) genders; either case typically refers to a male. The term is loosely translated as "queer" or "faggot" by English-speaking visitors; educated Nicaraguans, if they are fluent in international terminologies, are apt to translate the term in a similar (but more polite) fashion, giving "gay" or "homosexual" as its English equivalents. It becomes clear on closer inspection, however, that the term differs markedly from its Anglo-American counterparts of whatever shade. (And therein lies the danger of treating it as a folk category, which suggests that it is simply the rural version of some larger cosmopolitan concept.) In the first place, the term is not always as derogatory as the slanderous English versions are. Of course, it can be derogatory, and it almost always is. However, it can also be neutral and descriptive. I have even heard it employed in a particular sort of praising manner by ordinary Nicaraguan men: for instance, "We must go to Carnaval this year and see the cochones. The cochones there are very, very beautiful."[1]

Second, and more important, the term marks and delimits a set of sexual practices that partially overlaps but is clearly not identical to our own notion of the homosexual. The term specifies only certain practices in certain contexts. Some acts that we would describe as homosexual bear neither stigma nor an accompanying identity of any special sort whatsoever; others clearly mark their practitioner as a cochón.

If homosexuality in the United States is most characteristically regarded as an oral phenomenon, Nicaraguan homosexual practice is understood in terms of an anal emphasis. The lexicon of male insult clearly reflects this anal emphasis in Nicaraguan culture, even as the North American lexicon generally reflects an oral orientation. *Cocksucker* is the most common sexually explicit pejorative in the United States. Although equivalents to this term are sometimes used in Nicaragua, men there are more likely to be insulted in reference to anal intercourse. The dominant assumptions of everyday discourse, too, reflect the assumption of privileged, primary, and defining routes of intercourse in each case. That is, in Anglo-American culture, orality defines the homosexual; whatever else he might or might not do, a gay man is understood as someone who engages in oral intercourse with other men. In Nicaragua, anal intercourse defines the cochón; whatever else he might or might not do, a cochón is tacitly understood as someone who engages in anal intercourse with other men. But more is involved here than a mere shifting of the dominant sites of erotic practice or a casting of stigma with reference to different body parts. With the exception of a few well-defined contexts (e.g., prisons) where the rule may be suspended, homosexual activity of any sort defines the Anglo-American homosexual. In Nicaragua, by contrast, it is the passive role in anal intercourse that defines the cochón. Oral or manual practices receive scant social attention; everyday speech does not treat them in great detail, and non-anal practices appear far less significant in the repertoire of actually practiced homosexual activities.

The term *cochón* itself appears to indicate the nature of that status and role. None of my informants was certain about the origin of the term; it is *Nica*, a word peculiar to the Nicaraguan dialect of Spanish. Moreover, one encounters different pronunciations in various neighborhoods, classes, and regions, so there can really be no agreed spelling of the word: I have heard it rendered *cuchón, culchón,* and even *colchón.*[2] The last suggests a possible origin of the word: *colchón* means "mattress." As one of my informants suggested when prompted to speculate on the origin of the word, "You get on top of him like a mattress."

In neighboring Honduras, the point is made with even greater linguistic precision. There, "passive" partners in anal intercourse are known as *culeros,* from the term *culo,* meaning "ass," with the standard ending *-ero.* A *zapatero* is a man who works with shoes (*zapatos*); a *culero* is a man whose sexual activity and identity are defined as anal. As in Nicaragua, the act of insertion carries with it no special identity, much less stigma.

"You get on top of him like a mattress" summarizes the nature of the cochón's status as well as any phrase could, but it also points to the question, *Who* gets on top of him like a mattress? The answer is, Not only other cochones. Indeed, relationships between cochones seem relatively rare and, when they occur, are generally short-term. It is typically a noncochón male who plays the active role in sexual intercourse: a machista or an *hombre-hombre,* a "manly man." Both terms designate a "masculine man" in the popular lexicon; cochones frequently use either term to designate potential sexual partners. Relationships of this type, between cochones and hombres-hombres, may be of any number of varieties: one-time-only affairs; purchased sex, with the purchase running in either direction (although most typically it is the cochón who pays); protracted relationships running weeks or months; or full-scale emotional commitments lasting years.

The last sort is preferred but carries its own type of difficulties, its own particular sadness. As one of my informants related, "I once had a lover for five continuous years. He was a sergeant in the military, an hombre-hombre. During this period of time he had at least fifteen girlfriends, but I was his only male lover. He visited me and we made love almost every day. You have asked me if there is love and romance in these relations; yes, there is. He was very romantic, very tender, and very jealous. But he is married now and I rarely see him."

The actual range of sexual practices employed by cochones may be wider than the prevailing sexual ideology would suggest. My research did not involve extensive or numerous interviews with members of this sexual minority; rather, my strategy was to explore the general social conception of sexual categories and practices, primarily as maintained by my usual network of informants. Systematic investigation of the lives, beliefs, and practices of cochones might well yield very different results. It goes almost without saying that the stigmatized and oppressed resist, reinterpret, and recode the social conventions they find around them (Certeau 1984). Notwithstanding, from a sociological point of view, it would seem necessary first to understand the social conventions—the entrenched code—that situate resistance before understanding strategies and tactics of resistance proper.[3]

In spite of my research strategy, and in settings as diverse as the marketplace and the school, I did meet and interview a number of men classified as cochones.[4] In our discussions, many of them told me that they were really comfortable only in the anal-passive position. Others alternate between active and passive roles, depending on whether they are having relations with an hombre-hombre (almost always passive) or with another cochón (passive or active). Some reported practicing oral sex, though not as frequently as anal intercourse. Several of my noncochón informants denied having any knowledge of oral techniques. Nicaraguans in general express revulsion at the idea of oral intercourse, whether heterosexual or homosexual. "Oral sexual relations? What's that?" was a common response to my queries about varied sexual positions in heterosexual intercourse. "*Me disgusta*" (That's disgusting) was the typical response to my descriptions of cunnilingus and fellatio. A series of (not necessarily sexual) aversions and prohibitions concerning the mouth seems to be involved here. The mouth is seen as the primary route of contamination, the major path whereby illness enters the body, and sex is quintessentially *sucio* (dirty). This conception is socialized into children from infancy onward. Parents are always scolding their small children for putting things in their mouths. This oral prohibition curbs the possibilities of oral intercourse.

The resultant anal emphasis suggests a significant constraint on the nature of homoerotic practices. Unlike oral intercourse, which may lend itself to reciprocal sexual practices, anal intercourse invariably produces an active partner and a passive partner. It already speaks the language of "activity" and "passivity," as it were.[5] If oral intercourse suggests the possibility of an equal sign between partners, anal intercourse in rigidly defined contexts most likely produces an unequal relationship: a "masculine" and a "feminine" partner, as seen in the context of a highly gendered ordering of the world. But this anal emphasis is not merely a negative restraint on the independent variable (homosexuality); positively, it produces a whole field of practices and relations.

THE SPECIFIC ROUTES OF STIGMA

There is clearly stigma in Nicaraguan homosexual practice, but it is not a stigma of the sort that clings equally to both partners. Only the anal-passive cochón is stigmatized. His partner, the active hombre-hombre, is not stigmatized at all; moreover, no clear category exists in the popular language to classify him. For all purposes, he is just a normal Nicaraguan male. The term *heterosexual* is inappropriate here. First, neither it nor any equivalent of it appears in the popular language. Second, it is not really the issue. One is either a cochón or one is not. If one is not, it scarcely matters that one sleeps with cochones, regularly or irregularly. Indeed, a man can gain status among his peers as a vigorous machista by sleeping with cochones in much the same manner that one gains prestige by sleeping with many women. I once heard a Nicaraguan youth of nineteen boast to his younger friends "I am very sexually experienced. I have had a lot of women, especially when I was in the army, over on the Atlantic coast. I have done everything. I have even done it with cochones." No one in the group thought this a damning confession, and all present were impressed with their friend's sexual experience and prowess. This sort of sexual boasting is not unusual in male drinking talk.

For that matter, desire is not at issue here, and it is irrelevant to what degree one is attracted sexually to members of one's own sex, as long as that attraction does not compromise one's masculinity, defined as activity. What matters is the *manner* in which one is attracted to other males. It is expected that one would naturally be aroused by the idea of anally penetrating another male. (In neighboring Honduras, it is sometimes said that to become a man, one must sleep with a culero and two women.)

This is not to say that active homosexual pursuits are encouraged or even approved in all social contexts. Like adultery and heterosexual promiscuity, the active role in homosexual intercourse is seen as an infraction. That is, from the point of view of civil-religious authority, and from the point of view of women, it is indeed a "sin" (*pecado* or *mal*). But like its equivalent forms of adultery and promiscuity, the sodomizing act is a relatively minor sin. And in male-male social relations, any number of peccadillos (heavy drinking, promiscuity, the active role in same-sex intercourse) become status markers of male honor.

Nicaraguans exhibit no true horror of homosexuality in the North American style; their responses to the cochón tend rather toward amusement or contempt. The laughter of women often follows him down the street—discreet derision, perhaps, and behind his back, but the amusement of the community is ever present for the cochón. For men, the cochón is simultaneously an object of desire and reproach—but that opprobrium knows tacit limits, community bounds. A reasonably discreet cochón—one who dresses conservatively and keeps his affairs relatively discreet—will rarely be harassed or ridiculed in public, although he may be the target of private jokes. If he is very discreet, his status may never even be publicly acknowledged in his presence, and his practices will occupy the ambiguous category of a public secret.

The stigma involved here is not at all the same as the stigma implied in the Western or North American concept of "the perverse," meaning "mis-use." It is certainly not the stigma of the fully rationalized, medicalized system of sexual meaning that elaborates a category, "the homosexual," to identify both practice and identity. Rather, it is anal passivity alone that is stigmatized, and it is anal passivity that defines the status identity in question. Moreover, the social definition of the person and his sexual stigma derive from culturally shared meanings not just of anal passivity and penile activity in particular but of passivity and activity in general. While the lexicon involved varies, its meanings are neither plural nor ambiguous. Thus, "to give" (*dar, meter, poner*) is to be masculine; "to receive" (*recibir, aceptar, tomar*) is to be feminine. At the same time, however, when the idiom of violence or coercion comes into play—as the word *verga* (cock) most frequently connotes (*hacer verga, verguiar*)—"to take by force," "to seize," or "to grab hold of" (*coger;* sometimes *tomar*) is to be masculine, whereas "to surrender," "to yield," or "to give up" (*rendirse;* sometimes *dar*), is to be feminine. In any case, the one who initiates action, dominates, or enters is masculine; whoever is acted upon, dominated, or entered is feminine. This relationship holds as the ideal in all spheres of transaction between the genders. It is symbolized by the popular interpretation of the male sexual organ as active in intercourse and the female sexual organ (or male anus) as passive.

Cochones are therefore feminine men, or, more accurately, feminized men, not fully male men. They are men who are "used" by other men. Their stigma flows from this concept of use. Used by other men, the cochón is not a complete man. His "passive" acquiescence to the active drive of other men's sexual desires both defines and stigmatizes his status. Consequently, when one "uses" a cochón, one acquires masculinity; when one is "used" as a cochón, one expends it. The nature of the homosexual transaction, then, is that the act makes one man a machista and the other a cochón. The machista's honor and the cochón's shame are opposite sides of the same coin. The line that this transaction draws is not between those who practice homosexual intercourse and those who do not (for this is not a meaningful distinction at all in Nicaragua's popular classes) but between two standardized roles in that intercourse. Machistas make cochones out of other men, and each is necessary to the definition of the other in a dynamic sense that is very different from the way North American categories of the heterosexual and homosexual define each other. Although each is defined by his exclusion from membership in some normative category, the cochón is defined by his inclusion in the sexual practices of ordinary men, albeit in a standardized and stigmatized role, and the homosexual by his exclusion from the sexual practices of ordinary men.

This inclusive aspect of sex also has implications for the cochón's status as a political concept, for that category lacks the theoretical independence attributed to Western homosexuality as a distinct category of activity and personal identity. A cochón requires ordinary men, and his activity and identity can never be quite independent of them. Defined by its passivity, the status is ever a dependent one.

The stigma of the cochón applies, in its strictest and most limited sense, to a relatively small minority of men: those who are the "passive" participants in anal intercourse. In its broadest sense, however, the stigma threatens, even taints, all men.

The circulation of stigma implies a complex economy, an ambiguous discourse, and incessant power struggles. In the words of Erving Goffman, stigma requires of us a carefully staged "presentation of self in everyday life" (1959); it entails multiple levels of public, private, and intermediate transactions. To extend the dramaturgic metaphor, it brings into play many stages, many backstages, and many choruses. Or, to employ a game analogy: everyone wishes to pass the stigma along; no one wishes to be left holding it. As cunning and artful as are those who dodge it, by that very token must the invocation of stigma be coarse, generalized, and to some degree nondiscriminating. Thus, although the system of stigma produces certain distinct categories, its operation is never entirely categorical, for stigma is necessarily "sticky."

In the culture of machismo, the cochón is narrowly defined as anal-passive, but the concept of anal passivity serves more loosely as a sort of extreme case of "passivity." The term cochón may thus be invoked in both a strict and a loose sense. Which aspect of the concept is emphasized—anality or passivity—will determine whether it encompasses a small minority or a potentially large majority of men. Therein lies the peculiar power of stigma to regulate conduct and generate effects: it ultimately threatens all men who fail to maintain a proper public face. In machismo, as in colorism, the ambiguity of discourse is a highly productive feature of the system.

Thus, the hombre-hombre's exemption from stigma is never entirely secure. He might find his honor tainted under certain circumstances. If an hombre-hombre's sexual engagement with a cochón comes to light, for example, and if the nature of that relationship is seen as compromising the former's strength and power—in other words, if he is seen as being emotionally vulnerable to another man—his own masculinity would be undermined, regardless of his physical role in intercourse, and he might well be enveloped within the cochón's stigma. Or if the *activo*'s attraction to men is perceived as being so great as to define a clear preference for men, and if this preference is understood to mitigate his social and sexual dominion over women, he would be seen as forgoing his masculine privileges and would undoubtedly be stigmatized. However, the Nicaraguan hombre-hombre retains the tools and strategies to ward off such stigma, both within and even *through* his sexual relationships with other men, and his arsenal is not much less than that which is available to other men who are not sleeping with cochones.

This is a crucial point. These kinds of circumstances are perhaps not exceptions at all but simply applications of the rules in their most general sense. Such rules apply not only to those men who engage in sexual intercourse with other men but also to men who have sex only with women. The sound of stigma is the clatter of a malicious gossip that targets others' vulnerabilities. Thus, if a man fails to maintain the upper hand in his relations with women, his demeanor might well be judged passive, and he may be stigmatized, by degrees, as a *cabrón* (cuckold), *maricón* (effeminate man), and cochón. Whoever fails to maintain an aggressively masculine front will be teased, ridiculed, and, ultimately, stigmatized. In this regard, accusations that one is a cochón are bandied about in an almost random manner: as a jest between friends, as an incitement between rivals, as a violent insult between enemies. Cats that fail to catch mice, dogs that fail to bark, boys who fail to fight, and men who fail in their pursuit of a woman: all are reproached with the term. And sometimes, against all this background noise, the charge is leveled as an earnest accusation.

That is the peculiar and extravagant power of the stigmatizing category: like Nietzsche's "prison-house of language" (Jameson 1972), it indeed confines those to whom it is most strictly applied; but ambiguously used, it conjures a terror that rules all men, all actions, all relationships.

DISCOURSE, DOMINATION, SEX

During my fieldwork in Erasmus Jiménez I observed, over a period of several years, the interaction of boys in the neighborhood with Miguel, a child who was already labeled a cochón. This label was in very common use. Other children, including his older brother, Guto, teased him with the name, and on occasion even adults would taunt him.

In 1984–85, when he was twelve, Miguel bore few characteristics that would distinguish him from other boys his age. He was unusually small, giving the impression of being a much younger child of perhaps eight or nine. He was also quite intelligent and received good marks in school but not to such a degree that he had set himself apart from his peers. Mischievous and always getting into trouble, Miguel was by no means what one would think of as a "sissy" or "mama's boy."

Miguel's torment was an everyday affair. A typical interaction between Miguel and the other boys would go as follows. They are all playing some game on the sidewalk out front or in the yard back behind the house. The competition becomes acute and an argument develops. The argument eventually centers on Miguel versus some other boy or group of boys. Miguel's claim in the dispute is answered by the charge that he is a cochón. He insists, "Yo no soy cochón" (I am not a cochón), and fighting ensues, with Miguel typically throwing the first punches. The other boys eventually subdue Miguel and mimic sodomizing him. The marking of Miguel as a cochón dissipates whatever original dispute gave rise to conflict between the boys.

In public, Miguel resisted the label; in private, he was less adamant. It is premature to say whether Miguel will in fact grow up to be a cochón, and I have no way of knowing the personal "truth" of his sexuality, only the manner in which community discourse produced its own "truths" about personalities, sizes, apparent strengths and weaknesses, and practices. It appeared to me that public opinion in the neighborhood was attempting to socialize him in that direction. But note that, unlike an Anglo-American counterpart labeled homosexual, the boy Miguel, though labeled a cochón, was not thereby completely barred from social activities with other boys his age. He played games and sports with them and fought with them; at this stage, the only thing that distinguished him from the others was the fact that they called him cochón and piled on top of him in mock intercourse.

Of course, other readings of these actions are possible. Perhaps, seeing that he was small and vulnerable and fearing that he might grow up to be a cochón, the community was attempting to avert him from that dishonorable fate by punishing him whenever he showed signs of weakness, dependence, or passivity. It seemed to me, however, that he was most likely to be punished by his peers when, as a small person, he attempted to assert his equality with much larger boys. At any rate, the argument is not that this particular child will indeed go on to become a cochón, but that such interactions exemplify something of the rules of that status and its production.

The same sort of ambiguous status—stigmatized yet not fully marginal—obtains for adults. One incident in particular will illustrate this situation. I was sitting and talking with Carlos in front of his repair shop one afternoon when a young man passed by on the street, riding in the back of a pickup that was hauling mechanical equipment. Carlos made obscene gestures at the other man, in effect offering to sodomize him. The man answered with his own gesticulations as the truck drove away. Carlos grinned and said, by way of explanation, that the man in the truck was a cochón, that he had fucked the man before, and that he would probably soon fuck the man again.

In 1986, after a series of particularly cruel attacks on Miguel by other boys in the neighborhood (which I interrupted), I took Miguel aside and had a talk with him. "Listen," I said, "first of all, it doesn't matter to me what people say about you, or what they think, but you're taking a lot of abuse because you're small and because you don't know how to defend yourself." "You think I'm a cochón, too, don't you?" he demanded. "No," I responded, "I didn't say that. I meant that it wouldn't make any difference to me if you were or weren't. But my real point is that you're small, you aren't fighting very well, and everyone knows it." I offered to teach him how to better defend himself. Over the next few weeks, I proceeded to give Miguel a few elementary lessons in fighting and to teach him a few dirty tricks: guard with one hand, punch with the other. Anyone can take a punch to the arm or shoulder; hit spots that hurt, like the stomach, the face, even the groin. Finally we practiced his delivery of blows, and I showed him how he could substantially augment the force of his punches by enclosing a large pebble or solid object in his palm.

Boyhood brawls in Erasmus Jiménez are not terribly aggressive affairs. For the most part, they involve wrestling, light punches. Most boys of the neighborhood lack the serious fighting skills that might be observed in poorer neighborhoods. The outcome of these encounters is usually decided by size, and in all the altercations I observed, there was a substantial size discrepancy. Despite his size, Miguel became a good fighter. Soon I saw him turn away bullies with two or three harder-than-expected punches. The game in which his neighborhood peers had tormented him gradually diminished. By 1988 no one taunted Miguel anymore, and at his school Miguel warded off bullies and defended his weaker friends.

"The Siege," a short story by Sergio Ramírez (1986, 27–35), narrates the plight of Septimio and Avelino, two cochones living together in a small Nicaraguan town. Tormented and harassed by mostly unseen, offstage townspeople, the two are reduced to a state of fearful siege in their house. When they report their predicament to the local police captain, his response is short: they don't behave like men. (By definition, the men harassing them are behaving like men.) Ramírez's story dramatizes Nicaraguan culture's intolerance and bigotry toward cochones and machismo's implicit violence. Tellingly, the story ends not in murder, or even in violence alone, but in the gang rape of Avelino by the couple's tormenters.

The question of violence is paramount. Every system of exploitation and oppression both *is* violent (by definition) and *requires* violence (force, coercion, compulsion) to continue operating. But this is not to say that all inequalities are the same. Violence, force, and coercion are distributed differently, elaborated variously, in different power systems. When questioned, my informants could not imagine a Nicaraguan equivalent of gay-bashing—and this situation seems logical enough. Bullying, yes; intimidation, sometimes; blackmail, certainly; rough play, frequently. But neither organized, lethal violence nor panicked attacks. In the United States, gay-bashing—physical attacks against homosexuals—bolsters the fragile masculinity and heterosexuality of insecure men. "Homosexual panic," in the context of gay-bashing, has been a legal defense in several trials in the United States (including murder trials), and I suppose we can acknowledge that such a state of panic really does exist: ap-

proached by a homosexual (or imagining that they have been approached by one), some men do experience "panic." The panic rests on
the principle of homology: a man who has sex with a man is like that
man, who is a homosexual. The "panic" erupts when the approached
realizes that he is indeed capable of same-sex coitus and is then confronted by the label his actions would impose. Confronted, and doubly
so: to be desired by a man raises the question of what that man saw,
what he read, in the man who becomes constituted as the object of
homosexual desire. And at the same time, if the man realizes that he is
capable of performing a homosexual act: to desire a man is to be like
the man desired. (Another variation on this: desirable men are apt to be
labeled homosexual, a strategy that points desire's arrow in the other
direction.) To brutalize what one inwardly, secretly, or subconsciously
desires is, of course, a denial.

This state of panic would be impossible in Nicaragua, where assumptions about the nature of intercourse carry no principle of homology
and where it is not especially problematic that men are capable of coitus
with members of their own sex. Violence is indeed possible—in the form
of harassment, censure, stigma, physical intimidation, even rape—but
not in the same "panicked" context as in the United States. In Nicaragua, insecurity about one's masculinity or sexuality could be dispelled
by mounting—thus sexually subordinating—a cochón. Intercourse in
the proper position, more than physical violence, can be a nonthreaten-
ing means of subordinating another, hence solidifying one's own masculinity: recall that the penis *(verga)* is itself already seen as a "violent"
organ; its operation in intercourse necessarily exercises both pleasure
and power principles.

These obscene gestures, offers, and childhood games provide insight
into the nature of the sexual practices in question and throw light on
the social creation of the cochón. The cochón is but a necessary precip-
itant of the culture of machismo, or aggressive, competitive masculinity.
One man offers to sodomize another, in effect, to make of him a cochón, or if he already is one, to use his services. Thus, men desire to
sodomize other men and fear being sodomized by them (Suárez-Orozco
1982). In the same manner, they desire to claim status and prestige and
avoid being stigmatized. The routes of sexual use and pleasure thereby
illuminate the pathways of male status and sexual power. In a fiction-
alized version of the same dynamic, Avelino was harassed and gang-
raped, stigmatized and desired. Boys likewise exhibit their virility by

labeling one of their members and mimicking anal intercourse with him. The object of sex/power is the same in either case. Those who consistently lose out in the competition for male status, or who can be convinced to dispose themselves to the sexual urges and status plays of other men, or who dissent from the strictures of manhood, or who, in spite of the stigma, discover pleasure in the passive sexual role or its social status: these men are made into cochones. And those who master the rules of conventional masculinity, or who desire pleasure through their *use* of another (stigmatized by that very pleasure in a sexual position defined as subordinate), are made into machistas.

It is most difficult to get reliable long-range material on the life cycles of cochones. Wrapped in an ambiguous public secrecy, they are both protected and maligned by community gossip. In practice, at the level of neighborhood rumors, this secrecy lends itself to both admissions and denials, accusations and defenses. Some men are clearly defined by that status; others are only tainted with suspicion. Some apparently live out their entire lives in that status; others successfully masculinize themselves by taking a wife and rearing children—though in practice they may (or may not) continue having covert affairs with men. Some develop longstanding covert relationships with particular men. Many live within the closure of secrecy and are not suspected by their neighbors, families, wives, and children. Others become known in male gossip as someone to visit for sexual favors.

RULES IN THE SOCIAL CONSTRUCTION OF SEXUALITY

These processes in the production of sexuality do indeed bear some resemblance to U.S. practices, where male power and status are bound around sexual themes, but the resemblance holds only to a point. Both the homosexual and the cochón are objects in a sexual discourse whose real subject is sexual power. But the structure of that discourse, the meaning of its categories, and the language in which it speaks are decidedly different in each case. To the extent that these processes may be seen at work in our own culture, we may summarize that the object is to label without being labeled, but not to use without being used, for it is the homosexual act itself that is prohibited and not any particular role within the act. Some males in our own milieu, especially adolescents, do in fact attempt to label without being labeled and also use without being used. The difference is that in Anglo-American contexts such conduct is seen as a breach of the rule (or, sometimes, an adolescent suspension of the rule), since homosexual desire itself, without any qualifications, stigmatizes one as a homosexual.

The nature of homosexual transaction in Nicaragua's popular classes seems to bear much greater resemblance to the sexual economy of U.S. prison populations (Blake 1971)—and, by extension, to the milieu of truckstops (Corzine and Kirby 1977) and some types of encounters in public toilets (Humphreys 1970)—where one may indeed both label without being labeled and use without being used. (See also Chauncey's historical account [1989] of sailors in Newport.) Similar rules seem to be in play in either context: passive partners are labeled and stigmatized; active partners are not. The act of intercourse assigns honor to one man, shame to the other. In North American prisons, sex between men becomes a means of exchange because it signifies both pleasure and power in the absence of access to either by other means. But this comparison, although suggestive, should not be overstated or underqualified. Whereas the rules of prison sexuality reflect a deviant and stigmatized subculture, where "normal" rules are suspended or even inverted, the rules of sexuality and stigma in Nicaragua reflect the dominant culture of the popular classes and are thus a normative rather than deviant set of rules and categories.

Thus, the dominant Anglo-American rule would read as follows. A man gains sexual status and honor among other men through and only through his sexual transactions with women. Homosexuals appear as the active refuseniks of that system. In Nicaragua, the rule is built around different principles. A man gains sexual status and honor among other men through his active role in sexual intercourse (either with women or with other men). Cochones are (passive) participants in that system.

As in Anglo-American and Northern European stereotypes of the homosexual, the cochón is commonly ascribed (and sometimes exhibits) such personal characteristics as "effeminacy" and "flamboyance." (I should hasten to add that many cochones exhibit the same temperament as noncochones around them and thus remain as invisible as the majority of homosexuals in the United States.) Feminized by more masculine men, some cochones act out their role in the more extreme form of transvestism. Many others appropriate semitransvestic forms of dress: a shirt just a little too blousy, pants slightly too feminine in color, fit, or texture. Normally, transvestism and near-transvestism receive the reproach of the community. (I once saw a Nicaraguan girl throw dishwater on a cochón who passed by her house in just such a state of near-transvestism.) However, on the special occasions of certain popular religious celebrations, cochones may publicly exhibit their cross-dressing with the goodwill and even encouragement of the whole community.

These festivities represent a special niche in the religious life of the lower classes: like Mikhail Bakhtin's (1984) carnival, they project the image of a libidinous popular insurrection (Davis 1978) through a spree of stylized rule breaking. For these ritual occasions, the feminization of men semiotically corresponds to the themes of inversion and reversal that are the core of several popular religious festivities; men dress as women, people take on the costumes of animals, animals challenge human authority, lower classes challenge elite power, and so on (Lancaster 1988b, 38–51). In Masaya's Carnaval, Managua's Coming and Going of Santo Domingo, and other such rituals, the cochón is granted a reprieve from his secrecy and surreption, given a "political" voice, and cast in a central role in popular religious festivities. The transvestic cochones' appearance in these festivities in no sense "scandalizes" public opinion (as does the "coming out" of homosexuals in the United States), for the cochón is supported there by a wider language of travesty, reversal, and parody.

The popular imagination, then, takes up the cochón in an ambiguous way that imbues him with two different meanings. He is usually an object of amusement and contempt, a passive participant put to the use of others. On special occasions, though, the cochón becomes a subject who offers his parodic commentary on a whole array of social and sexual relations. Frequently taunting machistas and mocking civil-religious authority along the way, the transvestic cochón becomes the polysemic voice of discontent in these processions. In his inversion, object becomes subject, and silence bursts out with a voice that discerns the real powers of the powerless and the used. Through the alchemy of popular ritual, the cochón represents the larger point of view of the dispossessed classes in revolt against established authority.

Again, this representative quality of the cochón points to a striking contrast with Anglo-American homosexuals. At their most politically conscious, homosexuals organize themselves into a subculture, a subeconomy, a single-issue politics, all of whose logic is quite singular. Although Managua's cochones pass in and out of an urban demimonde, it can hardly be said that they inhabit a subculture. At his most political, the cochón also represents a very different sort of being than the homosexual: through the polymorphousness of metaphor, carnival speaks to a multiplication of meanings and social entanglements, not to their compartmentalization and impoverishment.

Where Nicaragua's sex categories and sexual transactions most strikingly parallel Western European and North American rules is not in any deviant subculture of the present but in sexual categories and practices widespread in the past, before progressive rationalization in the institutions of religion, law, medicine, and psychiatry had refined a category, the homosexual, out of traditional folk constructs (Trumbach 1977; Weeks 1977). Like its traditional Western parallels (e.g., "bugger," "sodomite," "faggot"), the cochón represents a stigmatized sexual identity, as yet still minimally administered by the institutions of rational sexual categorization and control, still more or less under the rule of popular categories and controls. But even here the cultural tradition in which we encounter the cochón is different from the Anglo-European tradition, whose folk terms often designate the *active,* not passive, category of practice, identity, and stigma. Even as a traditional or nonrationalized construct, the cochón lives in a different cultural stream than do "buggers" and "sodomites."

COCHONES, HOMOSEXUALITY, AND THE REVOLUTION

From the beginning, revolutionary sectors proved divided on sexual and moral questions. Before the Sandinista triumph of 1979, Christian base communities sometimes held criticism and self-criticism sessions—in the style of the early Christian church—when members were under suspicion of "sexual sins." Nothing could have seemed more bizarre than these "sex trials" to young Sandinista militants drawn from college campuses and influenced by the international New Left of the 1960s. After the revolution, AMNLAE and its feminist supporters were frequently at loggerheads with the Popular Church on issues such as abortion, sterilization, and contraception. And within the Frente Sandinista itself, there were wide divergences of opinion: one could subscribe to a more puritanical current (influenced by local conventionality as well as by Soviet and Cuban Marxism) or to a relatively cosmopolitan leftist current (influenced by New Left Marxism as well as by a more militant reading of revolutionary Christianity).

The Sandinista revolution and its accompanying changes introduced a variety of contradictory changes in the culture's understanding of sexual practices. It may be that the image of Carnaval captures and perpetuates the image of revolt so necessary in the imagination of the populace that would be revolutionary, but the consolidation of a revolutionary state is anything but an extended carnival. Certainly, in its early years the revolution constrained homosexual practice. The nature of socialist revolution, and perhaps particularly that variety influenced by liberation theology, entails a strong normative or corporatist component. The "New Man" and the "New Society" are envisioned as hardworking, diligent, and studious, pure and without corruption. The aspect of machismo that the New Man embodies is the ascetic side, not the hedonistic one. The cult of the New Man, then, produced a cultural atmosphere in which homosexual practice (and sexual transgression in general) was at least publicly regarded as more suspect than before, tainted with the image of indulgence or corruption, and was perhaps even somewhat less readily available.

More concretely, the revolution for a time tried to strengthen the moral force of the community, especially through the neighborhood CDS. Through such organizations, and through the sensibility of revolution generally, the gaze of the community was particularly strong. At the peak of CDS activism, the semiprivate, semipublic status of the cochón was rendered more problematic. Especially in areas of public morality and public order, a variety of activities, such as prostitution, were actively curbed by the Sandinista Police and the CDS. According to some of my informants, Managua once sported an elite and tourist-oriented nightlife, including perhaps a dozen assorted homosexual bars, exclusive gay clubs, drag shows, and male stripper acts. These apparently serviced Managua's middle-class homosexuals, some of its lower-class cochones, and gay tourists from other countries. They are gone now, and what remains is a small handful of much more discreet bars.

Such closures have affected the traditional cochón much less than the Western-oriented gay or homosexual of professional or middle-class origins. (The rationale for my distinction between these categories will become apparent shortly.) As one Sandinista activist from a working-class barrio (who alternately and in his mind synonymously described himself as a cochón, homosexual, or gay) put it, "It is true that there are fewer bars now, but most of the ones that existed before served only the affluent, not the poor. You had to be rich to get into those nightclubs. It is not so much that they have been closed down by the police or the CDS as that they have moved to Miami with the rich people."

More alienated and less revolutionary cochones spoke of going to live in Miami or especially San Francisco; others spoke of carving out a

broader tolerance within the revolutionary process. Not all of the effects of the revolution on cochones were restrictive. While maintaining
a discreet sexual profile, many participated in the revolutionary process,
some rising to positions of great authority in the CDS, the FSLN, and
even the government proper. The informant quoted above, for instance,
was elected to the post of barrio director in his community—the highest
position in the local CDS. Having fewer family responsibilities and dependents appears to have freed many politically conscious cochones to
work for the revolution. In the process, some have gained recognition
and status in the community, much as priests derive charisma from a
life of celibacy and service. As another informant—a schoolteacher—
pointed out: "Cochones were very active in the Sandinista movement
from the very beginning. Some people say it's because we're smarter
than other people. I don't think it's that. I think it's because we have a
different perspective, and we see things differently." How so, I wondered? "We experience oppression more intensely and more intimately
than most people. So naturally we identified with the vanguard of the
oppressed."

In Nicaragua, the traditional categories remain the dominant popular
ones, but they are now coexisting and competing with Western perceptions of homosexuality. Sexual education in the schools, social contact
with internacionalistas from the United States and Western Europe, and
greater access to international ideas and philosophies all facilitate the
acquisition of Western sexual models, especially in the urban, middle-
class sectors that look to the United States and Western Europe for
educational and cultural values. But changes are also under way—at a
slower pace, and in uncharted directions—for a broader section of the
urban working class.

In some sections of Managua one now hears such terms as *homosexual* and *heterosexual*. For certain members of a narrow stratum of urban elites, these terms are not so misleading. Many of Managua's sexually active youth, even some of working-class origins (like the barrio
director quoted above), also now call themselves "homosexual," "bisexual," or "gay." New syncretisms are indeed slowly emerging, but in
practice the dominant logic of the sexual system remains traditional,
native, and popular. That is, despite a trend toward greater politicization and organization among a loose network of urban cochones, in
popular discourse a cochón remains defined by anal-passive sexual
practices (and is, moreover, strongly associated with transvestism).
Moreover, the social bearing and political direction of even politicized

cochones is to some extent an open question. Greater pride and self-esteem are indeed expressed, and it is often called "gay pride" (*orgullo gay*). But the casual importation of scientific and even political sexual terminologies confuses casual foreign observers in much the same way that the casual use of those terms in social science confuses issues and assimilates real differences. What a Nicaraguan most probably means when he calls himself "gay" is very different from what a homosexual in the United States has in mind when he uses the same term, even though the two may find themselves in broad agreement on certain narrow particulars. New words such as *homosexual* and *gay* typically enter the popular vocabulary as synonyms for familiar categories and practices rather than as new concepts in themselves. This is especially true in the popular classes; and many Nicaraguans, even in Managua, remain quite unfamiliar with these newly introduced words. The frequent misuse of such terms, when they occur, indicates that traditional values still prevail. "Es dicho que él es un *sexual*" (They say that he is a *sexual*) was the way one informant put it to me, referring to a man many thought to be a cochón.

The remarkable conservatism of culture lies in its ability to animate new words with old ideas.[6] Although it is doubtful that one could speak of a "purely" native model anymore in Managua, it is clear that the traditional logic of sexuality remains intact for the massive lower classes. It is not enough to say that most urban cochones call themselves "gay," "homosexual," or "bisexual." (As one informant put it, when asked for definitions, "A homosexual is a cochón; a heterosexual is an hombre-hombre. That means he can fuck women or men.") It would be more compelling evidence of systematic culture change if men who prefer homosexual intercourse but were previously defined as hombres-hombres took up new self-labeling strategies. More compelling yet would be the appropriation of new terms *and* new logics by the population at large. And a real sea change in Nicaragua's sexual culture would be marked not by the importation of a new sexual lexicon—which might just as easily be imbued with "archaic" as with "modern" meanings—but by the introduction of new terms along with the proliferation of specialized bureaucratic instruments of sexual regulation to which those terms correspond (e.g., psychology, sex education) and the development of a homosexual subculture based on a wider variety of less stereotyped roles and practices. But these conditions clearly have not been met.

It is sometimes asserted that even if the various modes of sexual economy amount to something more than folkloric variations on a single universal type (heterosexual/homosexual), the global AIDS epidemic is rapidly changing all configurations toward a Western type—or, more appropriately, an Anglo-American and Northern European model. (See, for instance, Arguelles and Rich 1986, 193.) This notion rightly deserves consideration and scrutiny. In the West, the language of disease and health figures prominently in the history of sexual mores. Illness is a convenient metaphor—for danger, disorder, evil—which can soak up a range of possible meanings (Sontag 1979; Sontag 1989). The cholera epidemics of nineteenth-century America provided the context for both modern hygienic practices *and* a body of assumptions that wedded public health and popular puritanism into something resembling its present configuration (Rosenberg 1962). And persons were first designated as either homosexual or heterosexual by the medical/psychological health establishment, which, using the language of illness and health, reworked conventional religious taboos into a modern, "scientific" system (Lancaster 1983).

The issue of AIDS was posed most dramatically in Nicaraguan discourse in 1985—by way of a decidedly quirky route. Rock Hudson's death from the disease was vigorously covered by Nicaragua's three newspapers. After much sensational reportage of Hudson's death, *El nuevo diario* touched off a round of debates on the scope of the problem in Central America and began running AIDS caseloads for various countries in the hemisphere. On 13 August 1985, its front-page headline queried: "Does AIDS Threaten Nicaraguans? Two Suspicious Cases under Investigation." And within its pages, the same issue reported ("AIDS Advances in Latin America" [p. 3]), investigated ("AIDS Alarm in Costa Rica, Yankees and Ticos Accuse Each Other" [p. 7]), and warned ("AIDS, Venereal Diseases, and Sexual Dangers" [p. 7]). The following day, *Barricada* castigated *El nuevo diario* for "alarmism," "superficial reportage," "pseudoscience," and even "disinformation" (p. 3), while running its own piece by Gregorio Selser asserting that "Yankee Marines Are Carriers of AIDS" (p. 4). *El nuevo diario* backtracked somewhat with another front-page headline, "There Is No AIDS in Nicaragua," and argued that the campaign against dengue was Nicaragua's most pressing health issue. *La prensa* ventured into the foray by opining, "Central America Does Not Have AIDS, Regional Health Centers Affirm"—a piece that indicated, contrary to its headline, that an AIDS epidemic was already advancing in the region. The following day (15 August), *El nuevo diario* lapsed once again into sensationalism with the front-page headline, "Do Mosquitoes Transmit AIDS?" (which indicated, to a mosquito-beleaguered population, that they might), followed by "Teardrops Might Carry AIDS" (17 August). (During the same period, *La prensa* maintained its usual U.S. slant on the news: "Burt Reynolds Asserts He Doesn't Suffer from AIDS" [14 August] and "Sexual Revolution Ends in the United States" [14 August].)

Subsequently, *El nuevo diario* carried out a vigorous debate not only on AIDS but also on homosexuality. In an editorial of 8 November 1985 on garbage disposal, Alfonso Miranda Saenz wrote, by way of introduction: "The levels of drug addiction and homosexuality [in Nicaragua] are low in comparison with the decadent societies in the vicinity. All this is reason to be proud. But this does not justify the other kind of filth" (tossing garbage into the streets). It came as a surprise to many Sandinistas and Sandinista supporters to read such casually invoked hatred in a progovernment publication—even if it had been authored by Miranda (whose marked puritanism had earned him the label "Stalinist" in some circles, despite the fact that he was a Baptist). *Barricada*'s reportage on AIDS, for instance, while warning against the dangers of unprotected intercourse (with homosexuals, with prostitutes), trod very lightly on the homosexual angle; for *Barricada*, AIDS was a disease carried by the U.S. military forces invading Central America. In a response titled "Homosexuality and Garbage" (13 November), *El nuevo diario* columnist Pablo Juárez Calvo took public issue with Miranda's cavalier equation of homosexuality with trash.

> Is this affirmation not the product of a rigorous education in a machista society? Is such a statement in keeping with the future constitution of Nicaragua, which rejects all discrimination against people on the basis of religion, race, etc.? . . . Or is the author the victim of a world of prejudices that escape scientific analysis?
>
> Today, it is roundly admitted that homosexuality, the same as heterosexuality, are two different forms of living human sexuality. . . . There are authors who opine that heterosexuality or homosexuality is decided in the mother's womb. . . . According to some opinions, Latin American machismo could be the case of people born to be homosexual, who put all their efforts into not appearing to be so, within a society that condemns this tendency: Nobody, by God, is going to suspect that of him! That is why he will deflower every woman he can, will man-handle them, will have an obsession with numbers, with the repetition of acts.

Juárez rounded out his argument by citing evidence that the pre-Columbian cultures of America had not discriminated against sodomy, transvestism, and various other practices that would today be seen as sexual nonconformism and concluded that the intolerance of different sexualities was part of an "imperializing heterosexist paradigm" introduced by colonialism.

Miranda responded on November 19 with a more pointed reaffirmation of his position:

> Please, Mr. Juárez! Just to mention such things revolts me. And it's not that I'm a product of a "machista" society as you say. Honestly, I cannot view as natural what is unnatural. And everything that is unnatural or against nature is revolting.
>
> Mankind was created male and female, to reproduce themselves through sexuality, and the sexual instinct has its end: reproduction. . . . Since male-male or female-female sexual relations never lead to reproduction, they cannot be considered more than a deviation from nature. I can agree that such deviations in boys can be considered, not as cases of perversion, but of sickness. In such cases it will always be a deviation and it must be fought, like diseases are fought.

Having established his argument within a discourse on Nature, Miranda concluded that, although some homosexuals are indeed sick and incurable, the real danger is that rich homosexuals corrupt and pervert young boys.

Continuing the debate, and trying to "understand the issue intellectually," Pablo Juárez Calvo responded with "Is Homosexuality Garbage?" (21 November):

> That the reproduction of the human species is one end of sexuality, anyone can see. That it is the only end, now that is not such a clear thing. . . . Is human sexuality "unnatural" in those more or less 20 days a month when the woman isn't fertile? Is it always "unnatural" when a woman or man uses contraceptives? All these cases exclude conception. If all those who live their sexuality in this manner are "against nature," we don't need to envision a future of homosexual clubs and marriage between members of the same sex. "Unnaturalness" and "immorality" reign today in our society.

Pointing out the religious origins of the taboo against homosexuality, the author goes on to distinguish "sins of the flesh" from the social sin of exploitation and argues that the task at hand is to focus on the *social* dimension of evil. "Even though it isn't 'unnatural,' it's a great sin to leave a little girl pregnant, or to not look after the children one procreated in a 'natural' style—sins that go without treatment by many men in Nicaragua."

The following day, *El nuevo diario* printed a letter from Miguel Otelo Bonilla, titled "To What Drug Addicts Is Mr. Miranda Referring?"

> Poor Plato with his beloved and peripatetic philosophers. Miranda doesn't need books, serious studies and documents, or the scientific opinion of hu-

man psychology, and even the opinion of Catholic episcopates in the world, not to say—as more concrete proof—he doesn't need the life and homosexual experience of millions of human beings.

It delights Miranda that in our country there aren't very many homosexuals, like there also aren't very many drug addicts. But to what drug addicts is he referring? Heroin addicts, cocaine addicts, marijuana addicts, alcoholics? Do you know that in Nicaragua the consumption of cigarettes and rum has increased? Have you seen how many Toyota jeeps are parked early in the morning by the side of the road [selling liquor]?

Perhaps it would make Mr. Miranda less happy to know that a good part—the majority—of homosexuals maintain an absolutely "normal" life, have their wife or husband, children, etc.

Otelo concludes by reiterating that the ultimate end of sex is not procreation, but love: "And what of the sweetness of two old people, who continue living their sexuality even though they've lost the capacity to procreate?"

A final response from Miranda (29 November) was illustrated with a cartoon of a skeleton writing "AIDS" on a grim-reaper sickle. Its caption read, "AIDS: according to some, God's lash for homosexuality." Miranda reiterated his position a final time, with a minor difference: he distinguished between people who are homosexual because of hormonal, nervous, or physiological deficiencies and "those who are homosexual by their own free choice, owing to a degenerate and depraved environment with which they've consciously surrounded themselves." Apparently because they seek to pervert others, these latter homosexuals are "trash," no better than heterosexual rapists.

Finally, on 6 December *El nuevo diario* printed a letter from Esperanza Sandino (a name rich in political resonances), accompanied by an editorial by José Manuel Ruiz Marcos.

A Mother and Homosexuality

A mother wrote to us from Somoto about homosexuality, and the supposition that it's trash:

With deep pain I read your article about homosexuality.

No mother wants to have children of that nature, but if you were a great scientist and you knew which of your sperms were machos, you would breed them immediately, while on the other hand, if you knew which ones were homosexuals, you wouldn't dare to breed that "trash," as you call them. It would seem that you don't have your feet planted on the ground.

Dear readers of that article, beware, because what you hate the most is what pursues you the hardest. Like the Nicaraguan saying goes, "When you spit into the wind, it falls back into your own face." Those beings aren't responsible for the way they are. They are men and women who think and feel like everyone else, and when they give their friendship, it's very real.

Dear reader, if you are still young, I beg you to devote your life to scientific investigation, to learn when these beings are going to be born, and to exterminate them before they're born, and then all you'll have to worry about are the men who are very macho—even though you say you're not machista, you are.

Those of you who are still immaculate, don't get married, but if you do, don't have children, because you might end up breeding "trash," as you say.

Are we mothers responsible because you men give us those genes? Or is it that you think we are factories, and you can manage us? I will say with all my pride: we, the mothers, love that trash, my beloved macho, and they are more responsible toward their mothers than the real machos who, when they grow up, don't even remember the woman who gave them life.

Fraternally,
Esperanza Saŋdino,
A Mother

Apartheid for Homosexuals
José Manuel Ruiz Marcos

Today we published a letter in this same issue, the letter of a mother. It is strong, and it appears to be sincere.

Will that end here the interesting discussion of this subject?

We have received in *El nuevo diario* various opinions, and even pressures . . . no doubt, all very well intended, although it's never possible to judge intentions.

We grappled with the following arguments: There are more urgent subjects to be discussed, like production, the aggression, military service, shortages.

To those arguments we say that that is all true, but we cannot put everything on hold because we're in a war. There is still time for love, for example. For the arts, music, and literature. Why don't we ask our poets to go and pick coffee, or demand that the ink and paper that are wasted in poetry and literary supplements be used in school texts?

There are other underlying subjects that are not discussed by these objections; sometimes they get talked about, and sometimes they fall through the cracks: Why waste time with "cochones"! I've heard that these days, in different variations. And that makes me indignant, in a country where we are trying to advance a revolution. Like it or not, we are talking about an oppressed minority, like women, children, Jews, strangers. They are worthy subjects of a revolution. We don't have to put them aside until we have peace, just like we don't have to leave trash out uglifying the streets.

Whoever says so proves that we are dealing with a taboo which is very sensitive in this society. Something that is very deeply rooted in our way of thinking and *discriminating*.

Within a revolution that the whole world is watching and observing and

criticizing, we cannot, just like that, say that "it's not an urgent subject."
Where anyone is suffering, is feeling oppressed, is disempowered by a capri-
cious "legality," there will be the changing and powerful fist of revolution,
to bring hope and love. And to bring justice.

It would be sad if, in our revolutionary Nicaragua, we had some sort of
apartheid . . . for those who are different. To say that "they are not normal"
or that "they are trash" is to put the branding iron to their skin, as was done
to lord Somoza's cattle.

These debates—between well-educated, middle- to upper-class Nicaraguans—were carried out largely in the language of a basically Anglo-
American paradigm. Everyone—except Esperanza Sandino—claims the
lessons of Science and Education. Both sides depict heterosexuality and
homosexuality as distinct sexual orientations; on the Right, the former
is grounded in nature, the latter a digression from nature; on the Left,
each is equally well grounded in a human physiology of pleasure and
an ecology of love. Ruiz puts *cochones* in quotation marks, setting it
aside as slang or invective and opposing it to proper, scientific terms
such as *homosexual*. That is, in the educated discourse of elites, *cochón*
has already become the vernacular-pejorative and folkloristic version of
homosexual (which may be either stigmatizing or neutral). On many
counts, the overall structure and sensibility of the arguments are much
the same as those in North American debates on sexuality. At the same
time, however, Miranda's distinction between those homosexuals "who
can't help the way they are" and those who can suggests a syncretism,
a manipulation of Nicaraguan and non-Nicaraguan categories: for the
author, the image of congenital and effeminate homosexuals fills the
void left in his lexicon by the disappearance of the cochón. To differ-
entiate them from "homosexuals of free choice"—depraved products of
personal and social decadence—suggests that some machistas or hombres-
hombres might, under freer circumstances, redefine themselves in the
light of which sexual activity they prefer—that redefinition being a
product of various social changes beyond the pale of either traditional
society or a truncated ideology: urbanization, education, access to international models.

For urban elites, including a relatively broad sector of the educated
middle class, it is clear that traditional sexual configurations have changed
and are changing. It is possible—though not probable—that such changes
could become more generalized and systematic in Nicaraguan society
at large. If, for instance, the AIDS epidemic resulted in the rapid importation of medical and sexual terminologies and the implementation of

intensive sex education projects conceived along Anglo-American and Northern European lines, accompanied by a whole package of assumptions about the designation of pleasures, then the response to the AIDS epidemic might well bring about a systematic reconfiguration of Nicaragua's sexual economy. Yet AIDS itself has no inherent power to project such a model. (AIDS in Nicaragua does not even appear to be spread primarily by way of unprotected homosexual intercourse.) Moreover, if AIDS prevention education is undertaken within the framework of assumptions and values alien to the target population, it will be far less effective than it might be.

Rather than reconstituting Nicaragua's sexual economy along the lines of an Anglo-American model, AIDS is more likely to enter as one more element into an ongoing syncretism and synthesis of models. To the extent that Nicaraguan conceptions have changed and continue changing, it seems to me that cochones have undergone a process of political intensification *as cochones* (not as something else) and that the public in general has become more aware of sexual-political issues as framed by and through popular traditional understandings of sexuality.[7]

By 1986 most of my adult informants knew more or less how AIDS was transmitted: sexual intercourse with either sex, blood transfusions, contaminated needles. They also knew that anal intercourse was a particularly risky practice. On various occasions, when the topic of AIDS arose, I heard mothers warning their older sons, "Don't fool around with prostitutes, and don't have sex with cochones." Not "Don't be a cochón," not "Don't be homosexual," but rather "Don't fuck cochones." Whatever the public discourse on homosexuality had maintained—in *El nuevo diario*'s pages, in Sandinista-sponsored sex education classes, and in television programs—the working assumption in popular neighborhoods was still that copulating with a cochón did not make one a cochón, and that since any man was capable of intercourse with a cochón, the only proper form of instruction was to tell one's children to avoid cochones just as one would avoid prostitutes.

RIGHTS

Some Sandinista leaders have been more or less outspoken on the topic of sexuality. A few make no secret of their own sexual preferences in international gatherings. Others have visibly supported homosexual liberation in an international context. On a tour of the United States, Omar

Cabezas—in some ways the paragon of revolutionary machismo—wore a pink triangle in solidarity with North American gay organizations. And for its solidarity work in the United States, Gay People for Nicaragua received an official letter of gratitude from the Sandinista government. AMNLAE has taken public positions on the matter, endorsing full civil and legal rights for all persons regardless of their sexual preference. An officially produced sex education program on television dealt with homosexual intercourse (as well as pregnancy, masturbation, etc.) in a matter-of-fact and nonstigmatizing way. The republic's vice president under the Sandinistas was Sergio Ramírez, author of "The Siege"; his point of view can scarcely be considered machista or intolerant.

Although clearly not malicious, the Sandinistas' record was by no means spotless with regard to cochones. Police harassment does not appear to have been official policy, but there were sporadic cases carried out under the public order laws. And in some instances neighborhood mass organizations defined their mission not in terms of revolutionary goals but in terms of a traditional and conservative morality and thus spied on the goings and comings of suspected cochones in their communities. To say that the Sandinistas' record was either exemplary or abhorrent on this issue would be to exaggerate the terms of their real engagement with the matter. Concretely, one could say that the Sandinista government did not make a priority of the issue of homosexual intercourse one way or the other. In fairness, one should also add that the Sandinista revolution never systematically obstructed political participation on the basis of sexual preference and that the Sandinista revolution was the first social revolution of the twentieth century *not* to persecute or scapegoat a sexual minority defined as deviant in its society.

Complaints that the government was not doing enough, or not moving quickly enough, to destigmatize passive homosexuality were the staple of my conversations with cochones. At the same time, even the most politicized of Managua's sexual nonconformists realized the dangers for the revolution of broaching a cultural war with the conservative church on so sensitive an issue. The political risks here were not imaginary. The Sandinistas had tentatively confronted the reactionary church on the abortion issue only to find that its own ranks were split. The leftist Popular Church sided with the conservative church—against AMNLAE and the Sandinistas—on legalizing abortion. A compromise was reached: a prerevolutionary law banning abortion remained on the books, but no one was ever prosecuted for performing an abortion. On

another front, the New Family Laws (and the legal recognition of illegitimate children) had been roundly criticized as antifamily by the conservative church. Taking its cues from the religious New Right in the
United States, the political and religious Right in Nicaragua frequently
invoked "the sanctity of the family," "the elevated status of woman/
mother," and the subordination of children to their parents in polemics
against Sandinismo.

Because abortion and illegitimacy had proved so divisive, the Sandinistas were not eager to tackle a question potentially even more explo-
sive. So many people consigned themselves to wait for better times.

Verifiable word of only one major abuse of human rights came my way
during my conversations with people.[8] Not surprisingly, it involved AIDS.

Sitting together on the wall that enclosed her family's porch, María-
Teresa and I had been making small talk and discussing her work as a
nurse. I asked her if she had seen many cases of AIDS in Nicaragua.
"There are some cases—a few, not too many yet. I've seen only one. He
was in the hospital for more than a year before he died."

"More than a year? That's a long time."

"Yes. Well, he didn't want to stay in the hospital, so they locked him
up in it. They never let him leave: the doctors and the health authorities
said it was both to protect him from infections and because he might
spread AIDS by having sex with someone. He was a *co*—How do you
say it? A homosexual.

"Now, if you ask me, I think he was too sick to have sex with anyone. All he wanted was to go outside, to be at home, to feel the earth
under his feet and the sun on his face. That was his only wish, but he
never got to leave the hospital, not even once. Maybe if he'd had family,
they would have released him to the care of his family. But his parents
had disowned him, and nobody ever came to visit him.

"A lot of the nurses were afraid to take care of him, to touch him,
even to be in the room with him. You could see it in the way they acted.
I wasn't afraid, because I know you can't get AIDS that way.

"The doctors used to ask him for the names of people that he'd slept
with. They told him, 'Don't you realize, they might get AIDS, too,' and
'They need medical treatment,' and so forth. But he never would say a
word to them. He never gave them any names.

"And why should he, if you think about it? So the doctors could have
his friends locked up, too, the way he had been locked up? Those doc-

tors meant well, I suppose, but they did a very cruel thing to that poor young man."

WHAT IS A HOMOSEXUAL?

There is no *essence* of homosexuality whose historical unfolding can be illuminated. There are only changing patterns in the organization of desire whose specific configuration can be decoded.

—Jeffrey Weeks,
Sexuality and Its Discontents

Marilyn Strathern (1981, 682) uses the phrase "No such thing as a woman" to stress certain theoretical points on the nature of gender studies: if womanhood is conceived in terms of fundamentally different logics in different cultures, then the universal category *woman*, taken as an already known universal, hinders any anthropological attempt at understanding the definition, construction, and meaning of womanness in those cultures. Quite literally, then, for anthropology there can be no such thing as a priori woman or a priori man; rather, anthropology's task is to inquire into the various ways cultures elaborate meaning and practice. Here, I follow Strathern's lead and attempt to make similar points in treating the nature and construction of the traditional Nicaraguan category of the cochón. We may speculate that this category is the result of a syncretism between Iberian and indigenous sexual role systems. Moreover, based on my conversations with other Latin Americanists, it seems that the cochón exemplifies something of the sexual rules that are generally found in many Latin American countries, where the essential elements of the cochón appear under different names and with somewhat different definitions (Carrier 1976; Parker 1984; Parker 1985; Parker 1991; Williams 1986, 147–51).

Labels such as *homosexual* or *heterosexual,* along with Northern European and Anglo-American assumptions about stigma, fail to account for the Nicaraguan sexual constructs that ultimately produce the cochón. Theoretically, this sort of difficulty crimps attempts at writing a general history or anthropology of homosexuality (or, for that matter, of heterosexuality and even sexuality in general), for such projects must be hedged from the outset with myriad qualifications and circumlocutions (Weeks 1981, 97). Perhaps it does not seem so astonishing anymore to point out that the term *homosexual* (or some immediate equivalent), used to define a person's identity, does not translate into every language. It might still seem more scandalous to point out that *heterosexual* is itself by no means a universal category. But with these realizations come an even more systematic dislodging of Western categorical assumptions. Deprived of the easy language of our own sexual system, and dealing with practices culturally remote from our own, the analyst might find himself or herself compelled to take up various ellipses and periphrases. Thus, in an empirical description of what two people were doing with their bodies, instead of an unproblematic reference to "homosexual acts," the analyst might substitute "what we would call 'homosexual acts.' " Ungainly? No doubt. But having deconstructed the homosexual or heterosexual as persons, the acts themselves have also been undone. What is (what we would call) a homosexual act? The almost tautological answer: Two men engaging in (what we would call) intercourse. That is, a penis in another man's mouth, or anus, or hand or stationed at some other strategic location on the body; at any rate, two male bodies engaged in some activity defined by one or both as pleasurable in a carnal sense. But indeed, what do the two bodies mean, how are they conceived and understood? What does the act mean to them in the context of their culture? Is it taboo, and if so, what sort of infraction does it entail? Or is it mandatory, and if so, by what code? Moreover: What is a man? How is he defined? Is he defined simply by the presence of a penis, or by a web of practices and meanings that locate him in the male sphere? Indeed, what is a penis? Is it an instrument of pleasure, of power, or is it not an instrument at all? Such interrogations take us beyond "the misleading light of the obvious" (Matthieu 1978)—which turns out to be our own common sense, reified as Nature.

Such a calculated circumlocution—"what we would call homosexual"—at least permits a more self-conscious discourse: with relative economy, it allows the bundling of types of sex acts across cultures for comparison and contrast with each other; simultaneously, this operation provides us with critical leverage to understand our own practices as relative and produced; finally, it reminds us that the interest in types is, after all, our own, and that whatever the benefits of this typological analysis by us and for us, the distinctions may not be meaningful (or may not carry the same meaning) in the cultures in question.

At every turn, then, we are always running up against the unintelligibility of foreign practices to our concepts and categories—and vice versa. The best that can be done is to write a limited, circumscribed, and qualified history or anthropology of homosexuality. To write the alternative, a general history or anthropology of homosexuality, one has to posit at least one of two propositions: either (1) that homosexuality and heterosexuality are secured in Nature as distinct biological entities (the difference grounded, presumably, in genetic, hormonal, or developmental differences between homosexuals and heterosexuals), or (2) that culture everywhere and always defines sexual pleasure, sexual practices, and sexual identity in pretty much the same terms, categories, and meanings, *and,* moreover, that some interaction between culture and biology everywhere thus secures the same essential rules of personal development from infancy to adulthood.

Some practitioners of gay studies take the position that homosexuals exist, a priori, across human cultures and throughout human history, *even in cultures that do not necessarily recognize them as such.* It seems to me that one cannot maintain such a position without positing a homosexual/heterosexual distinction in nature, in biology, as an irreducible and eternal essence. And that nature, that biology, must be understood not as an "open" system (e.g., pleasure may be defined and produced in the human body by innumerable strategies) but as a "closed" one (human bodies come prewired: a majority can really appreciate only the arousal of the other sex; a minority can really enjoy only homosexual pleasure).[9]

The majority of biological research on homosexuality traffics in its own mystification—most strikingly, the old-fashioned assumption that male homosexuals are (genetically, hormonally, physiologically, dispositionally) more female than nonhomosexual men are, and lesbians more male than nonlesbian women are. (Thus the search for female hormones in homosexual men and male hormones in lesbians.) Since no significant innate, genetic, hormonal, or biological differences have ever been demonstrated between homosexuals and heterosexuals (where those terms are in currency), and since even the hypothetical discovery of some minor difference would fail to establish cause and effect (biology? socialization?), to posit a "natural" distinction between homosexuality and heterosexuality is to fall prey to the very cultural logic (and its naturalistic alibi) that produces such a categorical distinction in the first place.[10] The second proposition, on closer inspection, is ultimately grounded in the first: it apprehends culture as a reflection of biology, folkloristically understood.[11] If the historical and cross-cultural data demonstrate anything, it is that the distinction between heterosexuality and homosexuality—like the idea of "sexuality" itself as an uncontextualized biological pleasure—is a relatively recent Western cultural product. And these difficulties cannot be resolved by distinguishing identity from orientation—with orientation as essential and biological, and identity as secondary and cultural—for in practice one finds not one orientation, not two, but dozens. Even if we confine ourselves to Western societies, there is no reason to assume that all men reach their homosexuality or heterosexuality by means of the same psychological-developmental route; as Kenneth Lewes (1988, 69–94) argues in his reinterpretation of Freud, not all homosexualities are necessarily the same, just as not all heterosexualities are identical. Lewes discerns at least a dozen possible destinations of sexual development, a dozen distinct, successful modes of resolving the conflicts of the Oedipus complex, six of which are heterosexual and six of which are homosexual. If it is no longer possible to speak of a monistic homosexuality or heterosexuality in the West, what, then, is one to make of persons whose sexual experience is not grouped under a rubric that arbitrarily discerns two modes of intercourse and assigns everyone an identity as either heterosexual or homosexual? Of cultures whose family organization is based on different principles? Of cultures that prescribe (and proscribe) lists of sexual practices very different from our own, and do so by different logics?

Other cultures *are* different. They maintain different understandings of masculinity and femininity, different conceptions of the body and its engagement in the world and with other bodies. But the cochón is by no means as exotic a phenomenon as the cross-gendered (Whitehead 1981) or gender-mixed (Callender and Kochems 1983) Native American *berdache,* nor are his practices as far from Anglo-American and Northern European notions of homosexuality as are the mandatory homosexual initiation rites practiced in parts of Melanesia (Herdt 1981; Herdt 1982). Indeed, it is the very similarity between the cochón and the Anglo-American homosexual that makes the two appear, at first glance, to be readily interchangeable: both are adult males with a stigmatized sexual identity. Only on close inspection can we see that the processes of producing identity and stigma differ radically: governed by different rules, each case produces a markedly different existential state. We could say, in Wittgensteinian terms, that machismo is a different game, governed by different rules; or we could say, in Marxist terms, that it represents a different sexual economy, a different mode in the production of sex/gender; or, in Foucauldian terms, we could say that

Nicaraguan sexuality represents a discursive (and intercursive) practice radically different from Anglo-American sexuality.

The necessity of drawing such distinctions is far from settled in the current literature. John Boswell (1980) discerns "gay people" in premodern Europe, Gilbert Herdt (1981, 3, 321) finds "homosexual adults" in the highlands of Papua New Guinea, and Walter Williams (1986) has more recently reiterated the old thesis that the berdache is a Native American gay in drag. Nonetheless, anthropology and sociology have been growing more sensitive to phenomenological differences when they exist at these great historical and cultural distances (see especially Greenberg 1988). Until now, though, the nuances that distinguish, say, the cochón from the homosexual, typically have been glossed over by the misleading terminologies of the latter. June Nash (1979, 141) identifies persons who appear to be the Bolivian equivalents of Nicaraguan cochones as "men with homosexual tendencies," and Cuba's Santería cult is sometimes described as a native niche for an otherwise unproblematic Cuban homosexuality (Arguelles and Rich 1984, 688). At best, modifications of that terminology have been suggested: for instance, "selective homophobia" to identify the stigmatization of the "passive homosexual" (Murphy 1984), or, in Barry Adam's (1987) description of Nicaraguan practices, "homosexuality without a gay world." (See also Brandes's discussion of the passive role in homosexual intercourse in Andalusia [1981, 232–34].)

Such terminology, even when modified, obscures more than it clarifies. Nicaragua's cochones are ontologically different from Anglo-American homosexuals. Both are clearly stigmatized, but they are stigmatized in different ways, according to different rules. Nor is it, as it is often maintained, that in Latin America homophobia is substantially the same as that which one encounters in Northern Europe and the United States, though more severe in its operations. It is not that homophobia is more intense in a culture of machismo, but that it is a different sort of thing altogether. Indeed, the word *homophobia,* meaning a fear of homosexuals or homosexual intercourse, is quite inappropriate in a milieu where unlabeled men desire and actively seek intercourse with labeled men. An altogether different word is necessary to identify the praxis implicit in machismo, whereby men may simultaneously desire to use, fear being used by, and stigmatize other men.

No inner psychology, no desiring subject, no autonomous individual—in short, no a priori entity, sexual or otherwise—precedes social intercourse and awaits its influence. However it is defined, desire—like gender, color, or class—exists not *within* us, but *between* us. Desire is not part of "nature," nor is it "opposed to" or "beyond" meaning; it is always meaningful, and it operates no less semiotically than language itself does. That it is often felt as an "inner," "subjective" experience by no means diminishes its "outer," "social" character, for desire is always a relation between two *relata;* as such it is constitutive of as well as constituted by the subject of desire. And in this constitution of subjectivity, the desiring subject is traversed, even in his innermost experience of desire, by social forces: not simply (at the most superficial level) by the prohibitions, rules, and recommendations of sanctioned desire, but more significantly, by values, erotics, and evaluations that are part of and made possible by *social language* and by conflicts over them that are no less social in nature. "Inner desire," then, no less than "thinking to oneself," is a social act carried out in and through a social language.[12] Desire is thus always part of the cultural, economic, and ideological world of social relations and social conflicts. It is not simply that these relations and conflicts act on some interior and preexisting sexuality "from the outside" but that they constitute it "from the inside" as well. Which is to say (contrary to common sense): sexual history is possible only to the extent that desire is thoroughly historicized, and sexual anthropology only to the extent that its subject is effectively relativized.[13]

If these criteria allow us to distinguish various systems of sexual signification and power, they may also allow us to generalize a limited (though potentially endless) number of systems based on the operation of similar rules (Greenberg 1988, 25). Nicaragua's sexual system, with its active-honor and passive-shame dichotomy, exemplifies rules governing male sexual relations not only for much of Latin America generally but also for cultures throughout the Mediterranean and the Middle East. Numerous and widely variegated subtypes no doubt obtain, but with its series of dichotomies—penile-anal, active-passive, honor-stigma— this sexual pattern, which is found in peasant societies across much of the world, clearly stands opposed to the system of sexuality predominant in Northern Europe and its offspring cultures, especially in the Anglophone world.[14] Although the Northern European system has undergone successive degrees of intensification and rationalization, its original peculiarity seems to rest on its blanket condemnation of all same-sex practices and, perhaps, active ones in particular (Trumbach 1977).

The provisional models offered here (and elaborated elsewhere [Lancaster 1988a, 121–22]) do not directly address female same-sex practices. In Nicaragua, as in many peasant societies throughout the world, there is little popular interest in categorizing or regulating female same-sex relations, and little exists in the popular lexicon to account for it. There were scattered references to lesbianism in the various newspaper articles I have cited, but in all my conversations the subject of lesbianism never came up unless I raised it. (And even when the subject was raised, some of my informants—men and women—genuinely appeared to know nothing about the matter.) Surely, Nicaraguans can censure female same-sex improprieties, but without the refined and specialized vocabulary through which they speak of the cochón. The culture of machismo, which speaks so directly to male practices, can speak only indirectly or inversely of female ones.

SEXUAL POLITICS? SEXUAL COMMUNITIES?

Resentment, bitterness, alienation; a recognition of the arbitrariness of power and privilege: such sentiments underlie all oppositional politics, all states of outsiderness and marginality. Those underpinnings are indeed equally present among Nicaragua's cochones and Anglo-American homosexuals. "Things are not always what they seem" is as good a maxim as any for characterizing the double awareness of the oppositional personality. Certainly, it is a maxim that has long characterized the homosexual sensibility in America. And that sensibility is by no means absent from discussions and small talk among Nicaragua's cochones. These oppositions to power, this awareness of the density of oppression, dispersed across the system of social relations, *might* provide the basis for a self-conscious politicized movement of cochones on a significant scale, as they did for U.S. homosexuals. However, they have not yet, and it is not clear whether, when, or how they shall. As I have attempted to show, the very construction of machismo and sexual practices in Nicaragua disables that possibility, and by a logic different from that which constructs masculinity and sexuality in the United States. In the United States, the type of sexual community that provides the social base for homosexual politics is predicated on two social premises: (1) that all homosexual acts of whatever sort are equally stigmatized, and (2) that all men who participate in those acts are defined and stigmatized as homosexual. Such premises are not only absent from

Nicaragua but are also quite alien to Nicaraguan popular cultural assumptions.

At the peak of revolutionary tourism in Nicaragua, gay and lesbian activists were numerous among the internacionalistas visiting from the United States and Western Europe. On more than one occasion (and with various degrees of success), some activists attempted to stimulate the formation of a variety of gay self-help groups, educational clubs, and political organizations. Such efforts have always seemed suspect to me: duplicating the logic of colonialism, they invariably posit the U.S. or Western European activist as "teacher" (and never as "student") of some dependent population. As a consequence, such efforts proceed from the peculiar assumption that cochones need a "vanguard from without" to plant the seeds of radical political organization and to clarify, represent, and refine *for them* their implicit political point of view. One of the key limitations of these efforts was the essentialist assumption that homosexuality and lesbianism (somehow merrily integrated by sleight of hand) constitute an international fabric, a universal phenomenon affected by only minor variations in style and expression and afflicted to various degrees by the same homophobia. The task of the teacher, then, would always be to reveal the Truth of (homo/hetero)sexuality, as imported from beyond the borders of Nicaraguan culture. Now I am not saying that gays are not in a unique position, among North Americans and Europeans, to sympathize with and understand the plight of cochones in Nicaragua (it seems to me that they are, though not in any exclusive way), but sympathy, sensitivity, and understanding need not envelop the cochón within the boundaries of Western homosexuality, unreflexively understood. Such activist efforts, and my skepticism toward them, prompted this chapter, with its emphasis on the distinction between cochones and homosexuals; only much later did I come to realize the crucial role of the cochón in centering and grounding machismo as a system. These considerations imply yet more open-ended interrogations: on the question of homosexuality in the United States; on the successes and failures of gay rights politics here; and on the applicability of such gay rights politics in Nicaragua. For if it is agreed that the injurious treatment of the cochón demands a political response, the question becomes, What politics? How defined?

In broad strokes, the possibilities for a radical politicization of the cochón in Nicaragua are not so different from the possibilities of radically politicizing homosexuality in the United States. What is required in either case is a revolution in connotators. On the U.S. side: By what logic and for what reasons does one act belong to the Natural, the other to the Unnatural? How is privilege inscribed by an arbitrary marking of human beings, and how might that system of writing be undone? On the Nicaraguan side: By what necessity is the penis "active" and the anus (or vagina) "passive" in sexual intercourse? Intercourse could just as easily be imagined the other way around. Or any participant in any position could be seen as an "active" partner in intercourse. And why should the feminine be associated with passivity in general, and why should both be denigrated by comparison with masculinity/activity? Indeed, why should risk taking be masculine and planning feminine, if that description distorts each? How is it that the penis is a *violent* organ, and what system of social relations does this conception support?

In narrower strokes: There is no reason why the politicization of the cochón should follow a path resembling the politicization of the homosexual, with its history- and culture-bound definition, identity, and subculture, either as that politicization has already occurred or as it might occur in the future. The cochón's milieu is different; his history is different; the rules that govern the system are different and require different approaches.

THE COCHON, MACHISMO, AND THE POLITICS OF GENDER

A rule is best preserved in its infractions. And a structure, a system of practices, is most readily defined not by what is central to it but by what is apparently marginal to it (Scheper-Hughes 1979, 13). The cochón, by violating the standards of appropriate male behavior, defines appropriate masculinity in Nicaragua. His passivity, as the opposite of activity, defines the latter, even as it is in turn defined by the former. His status constitutes the ultimate sanction within a political economy of the body, its practices, its instrumentalities.

The image of the cochón, for most purposes, is clear enough. When I was discussing the difference between North American homosexuals and Nicaraguan cochones with Jaime, he had already formulated—from news accounts, international publications, and contact with internacionalistas—a strong opinion on the matter. "Well, your homosexuals are something like our machistas," he reasoned, "whereas our cochones are basically *masoquistas* [masochists]." Jaime's insight was his rare perception of cultural difference—his understanding that other understandings of sexual activity are possible. His limitation was his inability to see the cochón in any terms other than those framed by machismo itself. In the cultural code of machismo, a series of couplings deploy themselves and define reality: masculinity/femininity, activity/passivity, violence/abuse, domination/subordination. Decoupling such a chain of associations would have to entail a political program far more radical than anything AMNLAE proposed or the Sandinistas actually tried.

Very much to the point of this chapter: when I interviewed Nicaraguan men on the New Family Laws (with their stipulation that paternity entail economic responsibility, both inside and outside marriage) and their intention (to minimize irresponsible sex, irresponsible parenting, and familial dislocation), my informants very frequently took recourse to the same standard constructs. First the interrogative: "What do the Sandinistas want from us? That we should all become cochones?" And then the tautological: "A man has to be a man." That is, a man is defined by what he is not—a cochón.

From one angle, the distinction between men and women might seem enough to keep machismo's dynamics in play. Not so. For men do not "fall" to the status of *women* when they fail to maintain their predefined masculinity; they become something else: not quite men, not quite women. It could be said, then, that they fall both farther and less far than women's station. Less far because for some purposes and in some contexts, despite his stigma, a cochón can usually maintain some masculine prerogatives. Farther, because a woman is not stigmatized for being a woman per se, not even for being a strong woman; the cochón is, however, stigmatized for being less than a man. Machismo's ultimate reinforcement is the threat that one might be seen as, or become stigmatized as, or become a cochón if one fails to maintain one's proper masculinity as defined by machismo. If the New Family Laws, the project of the New Man, and attempts to roll back the culture of machismo have largely failed, they have done so because such attempts at cultural reconstruction left undeconstructed the grounding oppositions of the system, and thus left machismo's driving engine largely untouched.

THE DOUBLE GESTURE

Jacques Derrida describes as the general strategy of deconstruction "to avoid both simply *neutralizing* the binary oppositions of metaphysics and simply *residing* within the closed field of these oppositions, thereby confirming it." He goes on to describe deconstructive writing as a "double gesture," a "double science":

> On the one hand, we must traverse a phase of *overturning*. To do justice to
> this necessity is to recognize that in a classical philosophical opposition we
> are not dealing with the peaceful coexistence of a *vis-à-vis*, but rather with
> a violent hierarchy. One of the two terms governs the other (axiologically,
> logically, etc.), or has the upper hand. To deconstruct the opposition, first of
> all, is to overturn the hierarchy at a given moment. To overlook this phase
> of overturning is to forget the conflictual and subordinating structure of
> opposition. Therefore one might proceed too quickly to a *neutralization* that
> *in practice* would leave the previous field untouched, leaving one no hold on
> the previous opposition, thereby preventing any means of *intervening* in the
> field effectively. We know what always have been the *practical* (particularly
> *political*) effects of *immediately* jumping *beyond* oppositions, and of protests
> in the simple form of *neither* this *nor* that. When I say that this phase is
> necessary, the word *phase* is perhaps not the most rigorous one. It is not a
> question of chronological phase, a given moment, or a page that one day
> simply will be turned, in order to get on with things. The necessity of this
> phase is structural; it is the necessity of interminable analysis: the hierarchy
> of dual oppositions always reestablishes itself. Unlike those authors whose
> death does not await their demise, the time for overturning is never a dead
> letter.
>   That being said—and on the other hand—to remain in this phase is still
> to operate on the terrain of and from within the deconstructed system. By
> means of this double, and precisely stratified, dislodged and dislodging, writ-
> ing, we must also mark the interval between inversion, which brings low
> what was high, and the irruptive emergence of a new "concept," a concept
> that can no longer be, and never could be, included in the previous regime.
> (Derrida 1981, 41–42)

Obscurantism is often a danger of deconstructionist projects, especially those that emphasize the second gesture over the first. I do not
wish to declare, hastily, the negation of hetero/homo, which is, after all,
very much a lived reality *for us*. Nor do I wish to leave us with a language by means of which it would be impossible to speak economically
of homosexual acts in other cultures—for the project of radical deconstruction *requires* other configurations, other meanings, to provide the
critical leverage by means of which we cast our own meanings, practices, structures, and systems into relief. One cannot even readily identify *sexuality as a system* in the West until its categories and operations
have been relativized by contact with other systems, other possibilities.

This chapter differentiates apparent similarities in two sexual systems; it diagrams the rules that define the stigmatized Nicaraguan sexual category, the cochón, and contrasts it with the North American
homosexual. The cochón is not just one refraction of a larger, universal
homosexual category (embedded in Nature—or perhaps, in Unnature),

nor is the English term *homosexual* an appropriate translation of that concept—which must, indeed, remain fundamentally untranslatable. This method of semiotic differentiation is in keeping with prevailing deconstructionist and Marxist approaches in sexuality studies (D'Emilio 1983, 4; Weeks 1985; Greenberg 1988), but it also represents a straightforward application of basic Boasian principles to the question of sex: to wit, that what is meaningful about culture is internal, not external, and that cultural meaning resides in specific milieus, not in aggregations of cultures assembled in the light of unproblematic commonsense categories. Indeed, considered this way, cultural relativism was from its inception a doubly deconstructive practice: we can see readily enough that the beliefs and practices of other people are in a sense arbitrary (since they are not like our own); by studying them in some detail, we come to see that our own understandings and practices are no more privileged by Nature. Thus, to study the cochón—as a category, as a discourse, as a practice of machismo—is also to deconstruct our own universalized category, the homosexual; an act may be called *homosexual* if it involves two men (if labeling such things is what we do), but what is significant and meaningful about that act lies beyond any a priori assumptions about the nature of homosexual activity.

Seen in these terms, the specific configuration of sex, power, and stigma traced in Nicaragua's popular classes is indeed jarringly different from the predominant configuration in the United States. But it is not dissimilar from other configurations. Our critical method need not lend itself only to the endless production of distinctions; it can also elaborate typologies based on the operation of similar rules. For instance, I have provisionally proposed an Anglo–Northern European or bourgeois sexuality and a circum-Mediterranean/Latin American or peasant sexuality.

To renounce abstract universalism, to thus articulate differences, and to thereby generalize limited typologies is, of course, not a passive duplication of reality. The construction of models is always a *motivated* activity. Typologies become dangerous when they are reified and when the motivated nature of their construction is forgotten. I hope that my analysis has pushed the principles of neither differentiation nor similarity past the point of their intelligibility and utility. Surely, meaning lives in given, distinct cultural milieus that are wondrously varied; certainly, some milieus are more like each other than they are like certain others. But cultures, although distinct, are not altogether discrete; they do not come in hermetically sealed tubes. Living cultural systems, like language systems, interact at their margins with the many other systems on their horizon. No culture has ever been unaware of other cultures, and this awareness allows its members both to portray themselves as unique and to borrow practices from abroad. Nicaragua's traditional sexual system—like that of the United States, and like all others—is itself a cultural hybrid (in this case, Spanish and indigenous: that is, mestizo), and the process of borrowing while remaining distinct continues. This syncretism supports a sometimes open, sometimes closed arena of disagreement, conflict, and change. And as a field of power, the sexual system is not arbitrarily separable from other arenas of power. So, while maintaining a picture of the traditional and still conventional mode of sexuality in Nicaragua, I have also attempted to describe today's situation as a configuration of power and resistance, tradition and change, internal agreements and conflicts in the context of a class system, a gender system, and a revolution, and at the confluence of various interacting and competing sexual modes.

This analysis of the cochón and the concomitant typology it draws differ from previous typologies on another significant count. Earlier typologies have classified same-sex practices in terms of simple variations on the repressive principle. For instance, Vern Bullough (1976, 25) accounts for the presence of role-differentiated homosexual activity in the Mediterranean by the relative absence of available heterosexual outlets.[15] His logic is very simple: sexuality, like water, is an a priori force; dammed up in one outlet, it will invariably seek out another. In contrast to such simple hydraulic models of sexuality, my analysis of the cochón, and my elaboration of a broader cochón type, flows from my emphasis on a productive (not repressive) paradigm (Foucault 1980, 3–13). That is, something in machismo other than "scarcity of women" (which hardly obtains in Nicaragua), and certainly other than extreme homophobia, precipitates the cochón (as opposed to masturbation or abstinence), shapes his behavior, defines his identity. That something is a configuration of sex/power along the active/passive dimension. It renders certain organs and roles "active" and other body passages and roles "passive," and it assigns honor/shame and status/stigma accordingly. And, indeed, this mapping is critical to the operation of machismo as a system of produced identities, desires, and practices: it defines what a man is, and what he isn't; what he should want, and what he shouldn't; what he may do, and what he may not do.

This topography of the body, its accesses and privileges, is at once a map of pleasure and power. And the relationship of the cochón to power, as to the grammar of sex, constitutes a cultural ensemble different from that configuration which we call the homosexual. The object choice of the homosexual isolates him from male power, except insofar as he can serve as a negative example and thus mark off the circuitry of power; a breaker of rules, he is positioned outside the operational rules of normative (hetero)sexuality. The object choice of the cochón casts him in the role of object to machismo's subjectivity; that is, it puts him in a stigmatized but by no means marginal relation to sex/power. Each is defined by a play of sex/power, but the homosexual is a marginalized subject, divested of power, around whom power flows, whereas the cochón is an object through whom power flows and who is therefore, paradoxically, the locus of power's investment in itself.

Conclusion

To throw Nicaragua into the same bag as the Eastern European countries is a mistake. It is—as Eduardo Galeano says—like attending a fu-
neral that is not ours.

—*Barricada internacional*

A book on power, resistance, and hardship should not conclude with
everything neatly tied up, all the issues cleverly resolved. It should not
be written in the format of a "solved mystery"—the theoretical equivalent of a "happy ending"—in which complex and disturbing surfaces
give way to an elegant statement on the simplicity of depth. Everybody
knows that happy endings and solved mysteries belong to the genre of
writer's tricks, sleight of hand. Such endings are dangerous, not because
they are happy, but because, in tying up all loose ends, they are false.

The sources of hardship and suffering in Nicaragua are many. Underdevelopment, dependency, and dictatorship; exploitation and poverty: these intersections of class exploitation and neocolonial domination
are historically the most obvious causes of distress, and it was in response to these that the Nicaraguan people brought about the Sandinista Popular Revolution of 1979. Each of the preceding chapters treats
hardship and suffering in the context of but also in excess of the dimensions of class and neocolonialism. More specifically, this book treats
those dimensions of power and domination whose engines can be located in the family: gender relations, color, and sexuality.

In summing up, it might seem tempting either to totalize all such
forms of power into a single, given, closed "system of power" or to
grant everything its own autonomy, its own independent space. In attempting to come to terms with the multiplicity of oppressions, radical
social theory has pursued each of these strategies by various degrees.
The former approach has the appeal of finality, as complex material at

last gives up its secrets in a simplified form. Such a method has governed
Marxist discourse since the wide dissemination of a base/superstructure
paradigm, in which cultural and ideological "superstructures" are visualized as resting atop an economic "base" (Marx in Marx and Engels
1968, 182). Marx and Engels's comments on the subject are cursory at
best, and such slight remarks have been imbued with far more significance than they merit. Certainly, the base/superstructure paradigm is in
no sense a synecdoche for Marxist methods, and it could be argued that
Marxism has no theory of the base and superstructure. Even in their
own lifetimes, Marx and Engels were unhappy with the simplistic and
vulgar uses to which such a schematic conception was already being put
(Marx 1965, 86; Engels in Marx and Engels 1968, 692–93). And Engels (1972), for example, attempted to locate gender relations, sexuality, and family structure somewhere in the "economic base": a little
higher (less determining) than property relations proper, a little lower
(less determined) than the ideological superstructure itself. Debates within
Marxism ever since have revolved around the various and necessary
conundrums of this base/superstructure template.[1]

Marxist criticism has become increasingly sensitive to the deficiencies of such a model. Whether the relationship between base and superstructure is viewed as mechanical or dialectical, the paradigm remains inherently hierarchical and reductionist (Roseberry 1989, 37).
Even when complicated by other factors (such as "power relations"),
this model provides poor theoretical armature for understanding even
class relations (Roseberry 1989, 30–54; Donham 1990, 8–12, 66–77),
much less racial-ethnic (Bourgois 1989, xiv–xv, 213–27), gender (Benería and Roldán 1987, 8–11), or sexual (Greenberg 1988, 493–94)
relations. Therefore, the models I have proposed have no "base" or
"superstructure." The analyses I offer pursue a different strategy, in
which "mode of production" refers not simply to economic or material
production in its usual sense but to that concern for real people in real
life sketched out by Marx and Engels in *The German Ideology:* to wit,
that people, in producing their conditions of existence, also produce
themselves. "This mode of production must not be considered simply
as being the production of the physical existence of the individuals.
Rather it is a definite form of activity of these individuals, a definite
form of expressing their life, a definite mode of life on their part"
(Marx 1977, 161). In such a conception, further elaborated in *Theories
of Surplus Value,* "Man himself is the basis of his material production,
as of any other production that he carries on" (my emphasis). And

even if one considers directly economic production, "it can in fact be shown that *all* human relations and functions, however and in whatever form they may appear, influence material production and have a more or less decisive influence on it" (Marx 1963, 280; emphasis in the original).

Two possible analytical strategies suggest themselves from this point of departure, and I have pursued them both to various degrees. One is a political economy in which production in general (of goods, commodities, signs, genders, sexualities, persons, etc.) works over whatever material is at hand in a process that cannot be arbitrarily separated into deterministic hierarchies or distinct spheres of activity. Alternatively, one could view each "activity" or "relation" as its own mode of production—analytically distinct, yet practically intertwined with other modes of production.[2] I would argue that both approaches are necessary if we wish to account for specific forms of exploitation as well as oppression in its global sense—that is, if we wish to link the "micro" to the "macro" (Scheper-Hughes and Lock 1987) while retaining a distinct and defensible conception of each. Thus, instead of conceiving machismo or colorism or sexuality in terms of preexisting Marxist categories of base and superstructure, I have attempted instead to reconceive them, in Marxist terms, as plural modes of production, as systems of power covering different symbolic and material terrains.[3] And instead of "getting down to the bottom of things" by establishing a series of determinations, I have attempted to suggest how the various practices of power and resistance are intertwined.

Although these plural systems of power cannot credibly be traced to any one given "source" or be made to rest on any one determinant "economic base," neither can they be arbitrarily disconnected from each other. Class stratification in Nicaragua already entails a prominent dimension of gender inequality, in that the ranks of the poor and disenfranchised are disproportionately female. Gender inequalities, like color differences, are felt most sharply in terms of income. The stigma of Nicaragua's sexual minority, too, is by no means unrelated to the system of gender norms and gender sanctions, for sexuality as a system is most directly tied to the gender system (Rubin 1975). All these systems—gender, color, sexuality—are "economic": they produce value out of some material; they order human inequalities in the process of symbolic and material production; each system produces both a "product" and the corresponding consciousness to receive it. In a very real sense, each "system of power," each "mode of production" secures the intelligibility and reproduction of the others, without any one of them occupying either a determinant or determined position.

The danger of depositing some of these factors into the "infrastructure" and others into the "superstructure" of a given mode of production or system of power is that this maneuver diminishes the productive side of gender, sexuality, and color while slighting the role of class in reproducing the others. This conception is indeed dangerous (for everyone whose interests are allocated to the superstructure) if it leads to the belief that the superstructure will sooner or later rectify itself in alignment with transformations in the base. The alternative conceit—that is, to hypostatize oppressions—carries its own dangers. One danger of granting all systems of oppression complete autonomy is that this schema enshrines them each as autonomous "facts." In the density of real life experience, such systems are always mutually complicit. The other danger is that such a happy pluralism, in replacing macropolitics with micropolitics, diminishes the significance of class—with all the political consequences that follow. The class dimension *is* privileged, if only circumstantially and politically (not analytically), and by this index: class exploitation necessarily produces an exploiting minority and an exploited majority. The same cannot be said of other dimensions of oppression. Whether one is seeking to reform or to overthrow *any* system of exploitation, the dynamics of class and class resistance remain, in Marx's sense, strategic and paramount.[4]

THE DECLINE OF SANDINISMO

No book is ever entirely about what its author set out to write. Again, my aim was to trace, in a Marxist vein, those fields of power not normally treated by Marxists. I also trace, however, the decline of a revolution whose hopes were ground down in the day-to-day hardships of existence. Whether my informants were validating or denying the political and moral qualifications of the FSLN, whether they were endorsing or criticizing the revolutionary process, their discourses in 1988 all registered a diminution of political hope and the decline of revolutionary commitment.

In retrospect, I would plot the decline of the revolution into the following periods. In 1984 and well into 1985 Sandinista popularity and authority remained high (as indicated in that country's first free elections, conducted in November 1984, when the Sandinistas gained 63 percent of the vote in a large and varied political field, with 75 percent of the voting-age public casting ballots). By 1986 the worsening economy presented a different situation: the revolution—and the Sandinistas who governed it—maintained authority despite the hardships of war, inflation, and recession that were clearly eroding the popularity of the Sandinistas and the enthusiasm of their supporters. For another two years, the war and the economic crisis continued with no letup in sight, so that by 1988 the Sandinistas were already approaching the bedrock of their active political support (represented by the 41 percent of the vote they garnered in 1990—a critical drop of 22 percent).

Without imminent elections, held during an economic crisis, the Sandinistas could no doubt have continued to govern for some time. And had the war definitively ended and the economy improved perceptibly, the Sandinistas would probably have won elections held under more normal circumstances. But that is all hypothetical: history rarely affords such test cases that would render the social sciences "experimental" and hence "predictive." What is not hypothetical is this: what Marxists call "a revolutionary situation" (and what in this case might be termed more accurately a genuinely "counterrevolutionary situation") showed no signs of developing at any point in the 1980s, despite the acute, protracted crisis. The war against the counterrevolution was never seriously hampered by draft resistance—despite the wide unpopularity of the draft in a country with no history of mandatory military service. The type of insurrections that brought the Sandinistas to power never developed against them under their rule, despite the ease with which they might have been mounted, under the circumstances. Large caches of weapons were deposited in every barrio and town as part of Nicaragua's strategy of popular self-defense. These weapons were never turned against the Sandinista government; on the contrary, they were used to defend villages and hamlets against the contras. The contra war itself never posed a serious threat to Sandinista rule, as evinced by the fact that, unlike El Salvador's poorly outfitted leftist guerrillas (who controlled between a quarter and a third of that country's territory at various times in El Salvador's civil war), the heavily financed, well-armed, and generously supplied contras never captured and held a single foot of Nicaraguan territory.

VOTING FOR RELIEF

Real political pluralism, and genuinely free elections, were part of the original Sandinista platform, long before the FSLN came to power in the 1979 revolution. As everyone knows, elections always provide choice, and no one wins such elections in perpetuity. In their commitment to formal democracy, the Sandinistas underwrote the terms of their own removal from office. International comparisons make good sense here: what incumbent government could maintain an adequate base of popular support to weather free elections under such conditions of economic crisis? It is not really counterintuitive that the Sandinistas would lose elections held under such circumstances. Perhaps the remarkable thing is that the FSLN maintained support in its heavily politicized bases and captured more than four of every ten votes.

Times grew hard after the Sandinistas won their elections in 1984—extremely and increasingly hard, and plenty of people voiced complaints. War, dislocation, and crisis rendered most of the revolution's promises null and void. Important social gains of the 1979–84 period—in health care, consumption, and standard of living for the poor—were eaten up by inflation, shortages, and, ultimately, the austerity measures adopted in attempts to revive the prostrate economy. The prospects for a more equitable reconstruction of Nicaraguan society receded. Instead of voicing political optimism about the future, by 1988 most of my informants were expressing a personal and pessimistic view of the world. "La vida es dura"; "Es dura, la vida . . . ."

Neutral polls conducted in the months leading up to the 1990 elections were unanimous in showing a large Sandinista lead—generally two to one—over the opposition. Neutral polling also showed (1) that Daniel Ortega's personal popularity ran high, while Violeta Chamorro's was low; (2) that Ortega was seen as being on the side of the common people, whereas Chamorro was not; and (3) that large sectors of the public believed that Chamorro would be unable or unwilling to maintain her political independence from the United States. Chamorro led, and Ortega lost, on only two counts: first, the public perceived that Chamorro would be able to normalize relations with the United States; and second, the public was confident that she would eliminate military conscription. And thereby hangs the real tale of the election—as well as the failure of opinion polls to predict the election results.[5]

To explain the obvious failure of polling, various analysts and commentators have cited the "intimidation factor" in Nicaragua's preelection polling, and that explanation has come to permeate media coverage here. In a *New York Times* editorial, Norman Ornstein stresses the intimidation factor. "Nicaragua has lived for years with an authoritarian (at best) government and in a state of war. . . . [V]oters in such circumstances are easily intimidated. To imagine that they would eagerly open up to strangers coming to interview them defies belief" (7 March 1990). Accompanying Ornstein's editorial was a complementary article by Howard Schuman of the Survey Research Center at the University of Michigan. He offers what he calls a "test" of the "intimidation factor" hypothesis: in an experiment, three hundred interviews were conducted in Managua and its vicinities. One-third of the respondents were interviewed by pollsters who held red-and-black pens bearing the slogan "Daniel Presidente." Another third of the interviewers held blue-and-white pens marked with the "UNO" label; the remaining third held pens that were politically unmarked and neutral in color. Both the Sandinista pen and the neutral pen recorded a large Sandinista lead; only the interviewers holding the UNO pen predicted a Chamorro victory (by roughly the actual margin of victory). Schuman concludes that "distrust" of the pollsters—including the neutral pollsters—was thus the main factor that skewed results in favor of the Sandinistas—an extension of the "intimidation factor."

I am reasonably certain that of my primary network of informants, a substantial percentage voted for UNO. I am also reasonably certain that those who voted for UNO would not, for the most part, open up to strangers coming to interview them. Their reluctance would have nothing to do with intimidation or fear.

There is an alternative explanation for the discrepancy between polling and voting. It covers all the known facts—including those attitudes toward the candidates revealed in the polls—and does so rather more compellingly than Ornstein's intimidation scenario. As Schuman himself notes, "Polls had proved accurate in even more repressive Central American countries than in Nicaragua." Indeed, were intimidation so prominent a feature of Nicaraguan political life, then respondents might well prove as unlikely to speak forthrightly to an UNO pollster as to a neutral pollster. (Under the circumstances imagined by Ornstein and Schuman, the presumed UNO pollster might just as easily be a Sandinista activist in disguise, gathering intelligence on the dominated population and marking for police harassment those so foolhardy as to express an opinion unfriendly to the government in power.) The charge of intense intimidation also fails to explain the presence of a substantial number of Chamorro supporters in every poll—rarely much less than the conservative third of voters who cast conservative anti-Sandinista ballots in 1984.

Quite simply, the more compelling explanation is this: Nicaraguans who supported the Sandinistas in 1984 but defected in 1990 (more than a fifth of the electorate) were not proud of their choice and were thus unlikely to discuss their intentions beyond their own family and close friends. Troubled by a difficult decision, they might reveal their choice to a presumed UNO supporter, but not to either a Sandinista supporter or a neutral pollster.[6] Thus, intimidation was not the main factor. Rather, shame was. In a significant sense, voters still responded to the ideas, ideals, and ideology of the revolution; revolutionary discourse continued to monopolize the "public" and "honorable" sphere. But politics alone failed to carry the day. Without even minimal material rewards for ideology, a fifth of previous Sandinista supporters—what has been described as the "mixed middles"—cast ballots on the basis of private and pragmatic concerns.[7]

The election was held on exactly the terms outlined by Jaime in 1988, but not with the results he anticipated. Voters were faced with a difficult choice. The Sandinistas offered national independence, but at a high price: military conscription would probably continue as part of a national self-defense policy necessitated by Washington's belligerence. With good reason, well grounded in experience, Nicaraguans widely believed that both the contra war and U.S. boycott would continue indefinitely in the event of a Sandinista victory. UNO offered the certainty of an end to the contra war, the draft, and the U.S. embargo, as well as the promise of generous U.S. aid to rebuild the shattered economy. And in the end Chamorro took the political vows that made her coalition palatable (promises that themselves proved unpopular with her own strongest supporters on the Right, who had rallied against the Sandinistas in 1984): among them, that land and property granted to peasants under the agrarian reform would not be confiscated and returned to its original owners.

After years of war and hardship imposed by the superpower to the north, people voted for relief. But they were neither proud of their choice nor festive afterwards. (The atmosphere in Nicaragua in the aftermath of the elections has often been described as "funereal.") Voters knew and understood the terms of the election quite well. They understood the nature of Washington's ultimatum—and who could mistake it? Nicaraguans had been looking down the barrel of a gun for more than a decade: "Cry 'uncle' (in Ronald Reagan's words), or we will continue inflicting war and hardship on you." They could also hope that the revolution's gains would be preserved, despite a transfer of power, and they relied on a strong Sandinista opposition to protect popular interests in the new national assembly. Conservatives now speak of "a return to democracy in Nicaragua" or—throwing Nicaragua into the same bag as Eastern Europe and the Soviet Union—use events there to refute Marxism, revolution, and radical politics in general. What events really demonstrate is that even the class consciousness, political commitments, and national will of a revolution can be undercut by a long enough crisis. The economic and military resources of the United States can bring a proud and heroic—but poor and small—country to its knees. And one need not adhere to a classical base/superstructure paradigm to understand the vulgar side of materialism. Power, in its most arrogant and vulgar form, is the power to make people say uncle. Life indeed conditions consciousness.

I do not mean to say that people who really supported the Sandinistas defected at the last minute (as a literal reading of the polls would suggest). And although many people, never suspecting that UNO might actually win, unwittingly cast protest votes to teach the Sandinistas a lesson in humility (by lowering their margin of victory), that is not the real nature of politics, and such protest votes cannot account for UNO's margin of victory. Nor do I mean to imply that people resorted to bad faith or self-deception in making their choices. That is not for me to say. The calculated choice people made in the voting booths was both rational and informed, in this sense: whose victory will more likely end the crisis in the short term? I do mean to say that politics gradually became not just "demobilized" but "depoliticized." The ideology that grew out of people's real experience before the revolution was gradually demoted to a minor concern in most people's lived experience during the crisis. At some level, people knew that the Sandinistas represented an independent Nicaragua, but they downgraded their appreciation of national autonomy. They could remember that the revolution had once brought the popular classes a higher standard of living and enhanced working-class power in various measurable ways—and they might even believe that its policies could do so again—but the immediacy of the crisis, the nature of the outside threat, and the austerity measures forced by the war: these neutralized the class issues—and the class loyalties— that were the original bedrock of Sandinista support.

Some Sandinista policies proved especially unpopular: mandatory military service, draconian austerity, and the monetary stabilization efforts. Despite the unpopularity of the draft, the Sandinistas might have prevailed (as they did in 1984) had the economy not collapsed. The most visible signs of a collapsed economy, however, were the government's austerity policies: the elimination of consumer subsidies, currency devaluations, anti-inflationary measures, and massive layoffs of government workers. Such government policies were scarcely consonant with the politics of socialism or the rhetoric of popular democracy and people's will. Many Sandinista supporters and even some Sandinistas themselves were demoralized by the economic stabilization efforts of the late 1980s. But it makes little sense to point to military service and austerity policies as the "causes" of the electoral loss: these policies were direct responses to the war, embargo, and subsequent crisis.

Finally, the issues of "arrogance" and "corruption" played a part in the long-term decline of Sandinismo and—I have no doubt—in the election results. Pressed by war, insulated from public criticism, and enjoying the closed authority of the revolution, some members of the Frente gradually developed a presumptuous and even arrogant style of leadership. Sometimes, party members employed terms of political derision—*vendepatria* (national sellout), *reaccionario* (reactionary)—in a manner designed to silence dissent, even the constructive criticisms of fellow revolutionaries. The burdens of austerity were sometimes presented as the patriotic duty of every citizen—with little or no acknowledgment that such emergency measures departed from the mandate of the revolution.[8] Party patronage, the politics of spoils, and low levels of party corruption provided for many working-class people the final reason they needed to vote for UNO—especially in the context of dire hardship for the masses. But even these factors cannot be readily divorced from the international context, nor should their ultimate weight be overstated. By comparison with historical precedent in Nicaragua, and by comparison with their regional neighbors, the Sandinistas were paragons of good government. Most of the hostile gossip about corruption that circulated in Managua's working-class neighborhoods seems trivial, even frivolous (especially in comparison with scandals concerning corruption and abuse of power in U.S. political life).

Placing these issues in their proper context requires, first, an understanding of the sensibility of the revolution and, second, an appreciation of its predicament: encirclement by a hostile superpower. In Nicaragua's aggressively egalitarian political culture, *any* level of haughtiness, corruption, malfeasance, featherbedding, or trafficking in privilege would have provoked murmurings and discontent. Carlos Fonseca's maxim had provided the model for Sandinista political practice during the struggle against the Somoza dictatorship: "Those who give of their all,

including their lives, have the right to demand sacrifices." In the guerrilla struggle and in the insurrectionary period, the Sandinistas and their
partisans suffered imprisonment, torture, execution, and death on the
battlefield, thus securing for the Frente a position of revolutionary leadership. This conception of exemplary authority also implied a new egalitarian political culture: the political authority of revolutionaries was
necessarily contingent on their acceptance of sacrifice in the name of a
cause. Fonseca's formula would come to haunt the FSLN after the mid-
1980s, as the war dragged on, as the economy collapsed, as draconian
austerity measures were imposed, and as the masses of people experienced extraordinary hardships. To the extent that the political elite was
perceived as enjoying special privileges, its authority was undermined.

Was it all—the Sandinista revolution, the revolutionary process, the
mobilization of hope and activism—just an exercise in bad faith? Judged
in the light of subsequent developments, was it a collective self-deception
for Nicaragua's people to believe that they could achieve a real measure
of national autonomy? Was the goal of social justice—through popular
participation and a socialist mixed economy—another impossible dream?
In today's disillusioned era, marked by what some have called an "inverted millenarianism" (Jameson 1991, 1), such questions pose themselves and demand answers. How one answers such questions, of course,
will depend a good deal less on the ambiguous "facts" than on one's
selection and interpretation of them (which, in any event, produce and
determine the "facts"). From one angle, the utopian hopes of the revolution might seem like a function of desperation. The absence of conditions under which even a minimal revolutionary agenda might have
been realized makes the whole thing appear improbable and ill conceived. Politically, economically, and geographically, Nicaragua's was
not an advantageous position: "So far from God, so close to the United
States . . ." But revolutions are rarely undertaken by advantageously
situated peoples. They are undertaken most frequently by people who
feel that they have nothing to lose and everything to gain. The class
struggles, the political positions and utopian yearnings of the people,
the revolution itself: all these, too, were real. It seems to me still, even
after its apparent failure—and *failure* is only one way of saying what
happened—that the revolution and its subsequent revolutionary process were made in good faith. And I cannot bring myself to conclude
that even a modest conception of social justice is inherently impossible—for if we all convince ourselves of that, then most assuredly it will

be. And the consequences of such an illusion will not simply be that utopia has become impossible.

It is not my purpose to impose a weary, tragic model of social and political change on Nicaragua's history, whereby every revolution begins with euphoria, proceeds through disillusionment and cynicism, and culminates in despair, corruption, and monstrous crimes. That was not the tale I witnessed, and it was not the course of the developments that led to the Sandinistas' electoral defeat in 1990. The Nicaraguan tragedy was of another sort. It seems to me that, with few exceptions, the Sandinistas did the best they could do, given the dilemmas with which they were faced. The austerity policies of the late 1980s were inevitable, given the war and the embargo. Given a chance, their overall strategy (a socialist mixed economy) might have worked—not in the sense of delivering a heaven on earth, but at least in the sense of constructing a more equitable society. If a more equitable society was not constructed, that failure was caused much less by Sandinista errors, miscalculations, and failures than by the persistence of U.S. imperialism in the region.

Surreal inflationary rates; bizarre currency distortions; precipitous declines in family incomes; hunger, malnutrition, uprootedness: these were all effects of Washington's belligerence. Washington's unmistakable message, communicated to Nicaraguans by a variety of means—speeches by Reagan and Bush, congressional votes on contra funding, the tenor of U.S. political discourse, and not least the 1989 invasion of Panama—was that such belligerence and such dislocations would continue as long as the Sandinistas held power.

Nicaragua's poor, the peasants, and the working class absorbed the brunt of hardships, and the class base of Sandinismo ultimately eroded. Within the popular classes, women and children were especially disadvantaged. Never adequately adjusted in the light of revolutionary intentions, and never absent in the protracted sufferings of the 1980s, the gender dimension was powerfully present in the 1990 elections.

VIOLETA, MADRE DE NICARAGUA?

There is ample space in Nicaraguan culture for this sort of gesture, ample supports for this image of Violeta Chamorro as Madre de Nicaragua. María, Madre de Dios, the patron saint of Nicaragua, also constitutes an apotheosis of the real mother who, through her children, affects a this-worldly saintliness of nurturing, caring, protection, and self-sacrifice.

And this is the whole psychological appeal of "Doña Violeta," as her admirers call her ("La Vieja"—the Old Woman—as her detractors refer to her): she seems to represent a dreamy ideal of Nicaraguan mother-hood. Like Nicaragua itself, hers is a squabbling family—two of her children are Sandinistas, and two are reactionaries—yet the family matriarch (a synecdoche for the Nicaraguan matriarch) brings children and grandchildren together for peaceful dinners where they put politics aside. Could she, then, for all her conservatism, privilege, and aristocracy, turn Nicaragua into a banquet, where Left and Right, poor and rich, Sandinista and contra, dine together in tranquility? And how could she, as a mother, retaliate against her own children?

Never mind that she lacked political experience, or that she was in daily communication with her martyred husband, or that her only response to questions about economic policy was "God will guide my hand." In the course of the campaign, such foibles served only to humanize her and caused her supporters to savor these motherly eccentricities. (In the same way, the U.S. electorate was always protective of the avuncular Ronald Reagan: they made allowances for his obvious deficiencies and wrote generous exceptions to his frequent misstatements. Eventually, anyone who held Reagan to even minimal standards of coherence, competence, and performance seemed to be picking on a handicapped relative.) The savvy of running Chamorro against Ortega—no, we should be clear: the U.S. State Department *imposed* her on a fractious, divided, and reluctant Nicaraguan opposition—was the genius of obviousness. The packaging, the symbolism, reflected a theater of sublime "lowness" that borrowed from Nicaraguan family culture and the traditional cult of motherhood. Ortega could not directly attack Chamorro, a mother, a grandmother, without appearing to be a bully. And no one could survey the CDS election results during the mid to late 1980s without detecting the trend. At every turn, blustering, ideological male candidates were unseated by maternal, nonideological women who spoke softly (Lancaster 1988b, 157).[9] And even if some listeners failed to appreciate the neighborhood murmurings, no one could misapprehend the polls. Disaffected with the draft and the high cost of living, poorer housewives and mothers composed the largest block of sentiment against the Sandinistas.[10]

Was the packaging of Doña Violeta media hype? No doubt. Obvious? That, too. Subtlety has a low rate of return in electoral politics. And advertising is never more effective than when it taps deep cultural roots.

THE DIMENSION OF GENDER

If this discussion of Chamorro's victory is correct—and if it is possible to speak of "error" or "miscalculation" in the context of superpower encirclement—then the Sandinistas' "big mistake" might have been their failure to appreciate the gender dimension of politics, as defined by their own culture and as contextualized by the revolution. For the 1990 presidential campaign, Daniel Ortega shed his familiar green fatigues, but he could never shed the baggage of war. The male, aggressive, macho trappings remained everywhere. In jeans, cowboy boots, and a leather jacket—"the Danny look"—his appearance was more like that of a young rancher, cowboy, or rebellious teenager than president of the republic. If Chamorro was an older candidate, then Ortega's image shapers targeted a younger audience. And when his supporters dubbed him *el gallo ennavajado* (the knife-wielding fighting cock), they, too, drew on the deep reserves of Nicaraguan culture, but from the other side: young against old, male against female. Politically and organizationally, Ortega's campaign had migrated far from the forms and norms of revolutionary mobilization. Perhaps its most enduring images were the massive gift distributions that occurred at campaign appearances, along with the candidate entertaining specific requests for specific intercessions from various individuals and constituencies. Ortega presented himself as a Big Man (Hombre Grande) dispensing largesse to all the little people. Aesthetically, Ortega's campaign was indeed unbridled machismo, but its distance from traditional Sandinista politics, its independence from party organization, and the relative absence of class analysis in its rhetoric also suggested, as Carlos Vilas (1990a; 1990c) has put it, an attempt to build his own power base: caudillismo, in a sense not unfamiliar to Nicaraguan history.

Whereas Chamorro's supporters carried her in parades in the same fashion one might carry the Virgin Mary in a religious procession, Ortega entered town on horseback. In a war of styles, the two sides drew on different sides of traditional symbology. What Sandinista strategists failed to calculate was that Chamorro appeared to be a beleaguered, sympathetic mother and grandmother, while Ortega appeared machista in a society grown weary of machismo.[11]

Perhaps it was an unavoidable mistake: the same sets of rules that pushed women toward an oppositional stance also reduced their overt political expression of that opposition. On the one hand, in their role as mothers and nurturers, women indeed felt the brunt of the war and the shortages. They came to resent the draft and to wish only for an end to the immediate causes of distress: draft, war, embargo. That same role—subordinate wife, caregiving mother—reduced women to virtual silence in the public sphere. On the other hand, the revolution politicized women, brought them into the public sphere, and gave them a political voice—a voice with which they could not speak in good faith against the very politics that gave them a voice.

AMNLAE, whose charter was to defend women's rights within the revolution, emphasized defense of the revolution (to some extent at the expense of women's issues) early on: a perfectly logical position, despite critiques by some feminists in the United States, since the Sandinista revolution and its perpetuation provided the only real context for radically advancing women's rights and meaningful political participation. A duplex discourse ensued: publicly, working-class women defended the revolution, its accomplishments, its necessary sacrifices; privately, in smaller numbers, they hid their children from military service; semi-privately, in larger numbers, they murmured in increasingly sharp tones about the draft, the shortages, and the whole revolutionary project.

Chamorro actively campaigned for women's votes: with her promise to end the war and the draft, and with her appeal both to and through Nicaraguan women as domestic peacemakers. The vague campaign promise to "restore the true dignity of womanhood and motherhood" can be taken as flattery, but it is also the threat of a retrograde politics of gender to come (De Santis 1990). Chamorro was the publisher of the same La prensa that depicted every Sandinista effort to improve women's and children's legal and social positions as "an attack on the institution of the family." Chamorro's election was both a triumph and a perversion of feminism in Nicaragua: a triumph in that a majority of the electorate should vote for a woman for president; a perversion in that her entire appeal was couched in the most unfeminist of terms.

AFTER THE REVOLUTION—WHAT?

On my return visit to Erasmus Jiménez in 1991, I encountered a Nicaragua I hardly knew. UNO held power, the Sandinistas were on the sidelines, the war was over, and the embargo had ended. But the political situation had by no means "stabilized." On the contrary, social conflicts had reached a new level of barely restrained anarchy. Goods were available in abundant supply, the shelves in new, modern supermarkets were amply stocked, and the rate of inflation had come down to manageable levels; yet the unemployment rate in Managua was over 50 percent. Few could enjoy the apparent boom in consumer items. As tidal waves of government and industrial layoffs swept the economic landscape, a pattern had become chillingly clear: unemployment disproportionately afflicted Sandinista partisans. There was much talk in the press about Sandinista and UNO "cogovernment," "democratization," and "normalization," yet neighborhoods were tensely divided, and some neighbors were engaged in violent political feuds. Indeed, violence had become a normal occurrence: some of it political, some of it criminal, some of it ambiguous.

In Doña Flora's family, only Clara and Osvaldo held jobs. Osvaldo had left the army immediately after the peace treaty and had secured a position as office manager in a government enterprise. Aida, after facilitating a series of strikes in defense of jobs and wages, had lost her job in a round of layoffs earlier in the year. Charlie had been unable to find work since being demobilized. Guto had been robbed and stabbed by muggers on his way to the market and was still recovering from his injuries. In Doña Jazmina's family, only Sara remained employed. In Doña Celia's family, Yolanda had retained her job, Gustavo had been unemployed since leaving the service, and Marco-Polo and Lenín had gone to Miami in search of work. Elvis had retained his job and started a family, but Máximo had been unemployed since his return from the United States. Máximo's wife had gone to the United States—first to Washington, D.C., then to Miami, to work as a domestic. Máximo was planning to follow her as soon as they had saved enough money for him to make the trip. Jaime graduated into a depressed job market but stumbled into an open high school teaching position. Esperanza was unemployed, but her spouse, Pedro, still retained his unionized position at a government-owned factory. Onix was serving a long prison term: in a moment of desperation, she had stolen jewelry from a neighbor's house. Róger had eventually quit school and smuggled his way into the States; he is now living in the Bronx.

Three events from that visit to Nicaragua summarize the present situation for me. The first reveals ongoing and brutal conflicts; the second, the sense of political disillusionment that has set in in some quarters; the third, a sense of remaining, though tempered, optimism.

Early in my return visit, Aida, Flora, Ervin, and I went to Esperanza and Pedro's house for a Sunday lunch. The pair's house was still prominently painted with Sandinista electoral slogans; their neighbor's house was just as aggressively painted in UNO messages. While Pedro lit the charcoal and discussed his union's strategy in its ongoing negotiations with the government over privatization, a drunken Unista neighbor began haranguing us from across the barbed-wire fence that separated his yard from Pedro's. "Hey, Pedro, see to it that you don't give us all AIDS by putting that gringo out on the patio like that. He looks sick to me, man! Hey, you'd better take him indoors: there's a breeze blowing and we might catch something." When such baiting failed to elicit a response, the neighbor upped the ante. "Hey, Pedro, I've seen this guy coming around to your house to visit your wife while you're away at work. Did you know that he's been fucking your woman? I imagine you did, *cabrón* [cuckold]." Eventually he picked up a board and began threatening us. "Hey, don't hide behind your mother's skirts over there. Come on out, you and the gringo: we're going to have at it before you leave." The man's brothers and cousins, who were playing baseball in the street, gathered around the front of the house, carrying boards and baseball bats. Esperanza had slipped out of the house only moments before the situation became threatening and called the police from a nearby phone. The police arrived within minutes. When the drunk man began berating them, they arrested him and told the crowd to go home.

My presence that day kindled an ongoing conflict between neighbors. Accounts of such neighborhood conflicts—sometimes verbal, sometimes violent, sometimes lethal—were commonplace across Nicaragua in 1991. (These feuds continue with no sign of abatement in 1992.) Sandinista partisans remained convinced that the terms of the 1990 election had been unfair, that the United States had used all its might to compel an UNO victory, and that the election had in effect been stolen. The most conservative UNO supporters, too, were bitter. They had imagined that after UNO's victory, Sandinismo would be expunged from Nicaragua, that strong-arm tactics would guide Nicaragua toward a restoration of Somocista-style government, and that in the retributive aftermath there would be substantial political spoils for lower-level UNO partisans.

Like many other Sandinista partisans, Esperanza and Pedro are in the process of moving into a new barrio that sprang up in the wake of the elections on the eastern side of Managua. What was once a vast open field is now a bustling shantytown, overwhelmingly pro-Sandinista, and many of the residents have moved there to escape unbearable squabbling in polarized neighborhoods.

It might seem odd, but Máximo, once the severest of revolutionaries, had become the most pessimistic and dispirited of my informants. Or perhaps that is not so peculiar after all. "This is a disorganized, chaotic, undisciplined country," Máximo began, "but even so, nobody deserves the kind of governments we've had. I voted for the Frente, and I'd do it again, but not without some sense of loss. The revolution was in the early years more than what it became. It reached an impasse. The Sandinistas, the leadership: they talked in a good, political, romantic language, they said things that were correct, but all the while they were lining their pockets. It's an old tradition in this country. And this UNO government: they know nothing. They're hopelessly inept. They make promises but don't follow through on anything. They respond to the people's union demands, and to the campesinos, and to the students, but then they break all their promises and make everyone angry in the process. I tell you, it would come to civil war if people weren't so tired of war . . . And it might yet come to that."

At the same time, what seems to me most remarkable is that the majority of my informants who had a revolutionary vision of a New Nicaragua still retain that vision and are, to a large extent, imparting it to their children. No doubt this vision is now less apocalyptic and utopian, but it nonetheless implies a radically different imagination of Nicaragua than that which existed before the revolution or is projected under the present regime. Ervin, now five, was showing me some of the things he had learned at home and in school; he was reciting the alphabet, counting to twenty, and beginning to write. Proud of her son's skills, Aida requested, "Now sing the national anthem." Instead, Ervin began the Sandinista hymn: "*Adelante, marchemos compañeros. . . .*" Aida watched, apparently embarrassed that her son had mistaken the one song for the other, but proud that he knew all of the lyrics. Midway we both joined in and sang along.

It would be foolhardy to venture predictions at this tense and conflict-ridden moment in history. Everything is now an open question. Perhaps the revolution, and all that it signifies, is really over; perhaps it is not. Populist movements everywhere are motivated by a certain ideal of stability, and millenarian movements of whatever sort take permanence, timelessness, as their image of social good. Since in the modern world no one rules in perpetuity, it might seem that such movements are hopeless from the beginning. But the success of a revolution is not best measured by whether the party of the revolution holds formal political power. Rather, the question is whether a revolution systematically implements key elements of its class, structural, political, and ideological agenda and whether its supporters retain the organizational base and the energy to defend their accomplishments. Judged in those terms, the 1979 revolution is still an ongoing, undecided revolution.

After their defeat, the Sandinistas claimed that Sandinismo would continue to govern Nicaragua and that the Sandinistas would "rule from below." The immediate response of Chamorro's new government—and the U.S. press—was to scoff at such claims and to predict the imminent demise of Sandinismo as a political movement. The Sandinistas have not exactly continued to set the agenda, but through a variety of mass organizations, and calling on their popular base of activists, they have prevented others from unilaterally setting it. Moreover, the mass organizations—farm organizations, labor unions, student fronts—have effectively vetoed policies set by the Chamorro government that were interpreted as attacks on the revolution's most popular achievements. It is safe to say that these mass organizations—far more so than the Sandinista leadership—have taken the political initiative since the elections. The rank and file, not the leadership, have been the most active defenders of popular interests. Many of the people about whose lives I have written here have participated in strikes, hunger strikes, sit-ins, and demonstrations since the elections: renewing their commitments to various mass organizations, establishing new popular organizations, and setting the terms of engagement in postrevolutionary Nicaragua. The ongoing political contests, not the 1990 elections, will decide whether the Sandinista revolution is scrapped or whether it will be substantively preserved.

Chamorro's electoral campaign was framed neither as an attack on the revolution's most popular accomplishments nor as a crusade to erase Sandinismo from the political map. Concretely, Chamorro promised to abolish the draft, and that was the only programmatic issue on which she campaigned. Should her government interpret its margin of victory as a mandate for full-scale reaction, it would find its own position precarious, and Nicaragua could become ungovernable.

Nicaragua remains under a revolutionary constitution, and UNO lacks the two-thirds majority it would need in the national assembly to amend it or rewrite any of its provisions. UNO's efforts to privatize all public property and its attacks on various forms of cooperative ownership have already met strong, organized resistance. The series of strikes that followed in the wake of UNO's victory at the polls demonstrate the new vitality of Sandinista unions and mass organizations. Underscoring the volatility of the present situation, these strikes also hold out the prospect of accelerated class struggles and a violent counterreaction by UNO's partisans. At this writing, the Nicaraguan economy continues to decline, and Nicaraguan society is roiling with class, political, and social conflicts whose outcomes are anything but clear. Much depends on the courses of action and reaction decided by the Chamorro government, the FSLN, the mass organizations, and, naturally, Washington. National and international reconciliation, on terms acceptable to all parties; a bitter, tense peace, devoid of spirit or enthusiasm; outright civil war: these are all possibilities. New errors will no doubt be made on all sides, but we may hope that no one will repeat past errors.

The Sandinistas still remain the largest, best-organized, and most disciplined political force in Nicaragua, and they are not likely to give over complete control of the armed forces to a government they see as invented in Washington (and likely to turn its arms against the Sandinistas and their supporters in some future season of turmoil). The question of the contras remains paramount. Their reintegration into Nicaraguan social life is possible, though problematic; should contra remnants reconstitute themselves in sufficient numbers, formally or informally, as an armed force, such a move would raise the specter of right-wing terror, death squads, and ultimately civil war.[12] If UNO proves conciliatory, moderate, and nominally progressive, a power-sharing arrangement may prove workable.

The Sandinistas will probably survive their electoral defeat, and they may come out of the experience better able to wage the fight. Party consultations have already begun a process of reviewing Sandinismo's errors and failures, and the self-criticism has not been sparing (see "Resolutions of the FSLN Assembly," *Barricada internacional,* 14 July 1990). Clearly, after a decade in power—removed from the daily struggles of ordinary people and remote from working-class experiences—elements of the FSLN leadership lost touch with the revolution's popular base. It remains to be seen whether the electoral debacle will prod those elements back toward a more populist-leftist orientation, or whether the leadership will continue to drift toward a more elite-managerial style of politics. It remains, too, to be seen whether the Frente will operate as a strong opposition or whether it will "cogovern" with UNO moderates; whether it will rediscover its voice in and for the poor or whether political compromises will ultimately compromise its popular charter. The Sandinistas could use this respite from governmental office to undergo systematic reassessment of their agenda and to shed those members whose presence in the party always suggested narrow self-interest. Or, embittered by defeat, a pervasive cynicism may set in and ultimately convert the Sandinistas to a very different political style. Indeed, under precipitous enough conditions and given sharp enough internal disagreements over strategy and goals, the Sandinistas could again split into factions, as they did in 1975; or, alternatively, the rank and file could split, leaving the leadership with an empty shell of a party.

Either way, the national and international dilemmas that led to a Sandinista victory in 1979 largely remain. Neocolonial domination of Central America continues, as does the resistance it engenders. To paraphrase Eric Hobsbawm (1984, 32), classes exist, and they remain conscious of themselves as classes. Politics remains. Class struggles go on. So, too, the struggles of women—and of every oppressed group denied human dignity by persistent systems of inequality. Hope, though tempered in the midst of so much despair, has not been completely extinguished. And of course, in that sense, the largest question pertains not to political parties but to popular will and the engagement of the popular classes in a history not always of their own making, but which must nonetheless reckon with them.

One truth is as good as any other. Life is hard, the saying goes. But then, too, life goes on.

Notes

THIS BOOK AND ITS TITLE

1. Walter Benjamin (1969; 1983; 1986) often employs proverbs in the service of a revolutionary aesthetic. In Benjamin's work, proverbs (like parables) bring together two recurring themes: the "politics of memory" (see Jameson 1971, 62) and "crude" or "coarse thinking" (see Arendt in Benjamin 1969, 15; Benjamin 1986, 199–200).

2. On this point, my work belongs to a dialogical conception of anthropology in which ethnography represents a conversation between peoples and cultures. See Crapanzano 1980; Crapanzano 1986; Clifford 1986, 14–15; Clifford 1988, 41–44; and Rabinow 1986, 245–47.

INTRODUCTION

1. Guatemala's present torment has its roots in the U.S.-sponsored coup of 1954, which overthrew the reformist Arbenz government and installed a regime friendly to the interests of the United Fruit Company (Schlesinger and Kinzer 1983). The CIA coup foreclosed the possibility of social and economic reforms and sowed the seeds for subsequent conflicts between the rich oligarchy and the poor masses, between urban Ladinos and Maya peasants, and between the military and radical Christians (Black et al. 1984). Some hundred thousand people have been killed and some million people uprooted and dislocated in the political violence of recent years, mostly between 1982 and 1986—largely by government security forces prosecuting an anti-insurgency war against the Maya Indians. Despite the present veneer of a civilian government, Guatemala's problems of land, power, and race are no nearer a solution today than when the violence began (see Carmack 1988).

El Salvador, at the time of this writing, gropes its way toward an uncertain peace as a long civil war winds down. Seventy thousand people have been killed, mostly by government security forces and military-affiliated death squads pursuing their war against the FMLN (Frente Farabundo Martí para la Liberación Nacional), a rural guerrilla movement. Across the border in Honduras, where the United States maintained an ominous military presence after losing its puppet regime in Nicaragua, there has been a degree of political stability. However, since the early 1980s Honduran death squads, modeled after those in neighboring countries, have carried out assassination campaigns against radicals, trade unionists, *campesino* leaders, and human rights activists. The local economy has not been well served by generous U.S. military aid: the influx of dollars has spawned massive corruption in the Honduran military and encouraged land grabs by moneyed generals and businesspersons. Native peasants were uprooted both by these land acquisitions and by the large contra presence which once camped along Nicaragua's border. Throughout the 1980s the U.S. military conducted large-scale maneuvers on Honduran soil; as a result, "prostitution" has become more than a convenient metaphor for describing Honduran social and economic relations with the United States. Honduras has the unhappy distinction of carrying Central America's largest AIDS case load. And as a predictable consequence of the situation, guerrillas have made their first substantial appearance on the Honduran political scene.

2. Financed by American industrialists and adept at power politics, was Walker a cynical operator, a con man and pirate? Or was he genuinely motivated by the various, contradictory, and often ignoble "noble causes" he espoused: the manifest destiny of the United States to rule the Americas; the preservation of slavery as an institution; democracy; and the white man's burden of bringing progress and modernization to the mestizos and indigenous peoples of Central America? Or was he simply a very capable madman, caught up in some unexpected combination of his own lunacy and the cross-currents of his day? The Walker episode (Carr 1963) is less enigmatic than paradigmatic of American entanglements in Central America; each of these questions could again be posed—and left similarly unanswered—with regard to key players in the Iran-Contra scandal.

3. For more detailed information on the history I have been recounting, including a history of the Somoza period, see T. Walker 1982, 13–14; T. Walker 1986, 13–34; Booth and Walker 1989, 28–31; LaFeber 1984. For excellent surveys of Sandino's ideology and its relationship to the later Sandinista movement, see Ramírez 1990; Hodges 1986.

4. On the Sandinista revolution, see T. Walker, ed., 1982; T. Walker 1986; Rosset and Vandermeer 1983; Rosset and Vandermeer 1986.

5. Indeed, in 1975 there was so much disagreement within the FSLN over strategy that the organization temporarily split into three factions. As its name indicated, the Prolonged Popular War tendency saw extended guerrilla warfare as the proper course for both educating the populace and defeating the Guardia Nacional; with a mobile army of guerrilla fighters, this faction concentrated its efforts in rural areas, developed peasant strongholds of support, and maintained close ties to the Christian base communities. The Proletarian Tendency held a more or less classical Marxist view that the urban, industrial,

unionized proletariat was the revolutionary class, and it concentrated its efforts in that field. The insurrectionist or Tercerista (Third Way—that is, between the other two options) tendency predicted—accurately—that urban, neighborhood-based uprisings would bring down the Somoza regime; it concentrated on neighborhood organizing and developed relations with leftist European social-democratic parties. Each successful in its own field, the three tendencies continued to work in concert and were formally reunited only months before coming to power.

6. UNO's campaign was financed in large part by the Washington-based, federally funded private corporation the National Endowment for Democracy (NED) and, according to reports in *Newsweek* and the *New York Times,* the CIA. In directly funding the apparatus of the opposition coalition, the NED departed from its charter, which specifies that it is only to encourage and assist the holding of free elections and prohibits it from taking partisan sides in those contests; instead, the NED operated more or less straightforwardly as an international conservative political action committee. See MacMichael 1990.

7. The urban insurrections that brought the Sandinistas to power were orchestrated not in the industrial workplace but in a range of poor to middle-income neighborhoods. Because of such organizational demographics, many have argued that the revolution itself was popular and nationalist, not socialist or proletarian. However, no one has actually demonstrated that the popular classes mobilized in the Sandinista revolution were substantially more heterogeneous or less proletarian than those that have participated in other revolutions of the twentieth century. (See Gould's [1990] arguments about the class base of the Sandinista revolution, especially pp. 292–305.) Whatever the demographics of its revolution, I realize that it is problematic to refer to Nicaragua's mixed economy as "socialist." Judged in the light of other economies normally called socialist, it was not. (See Vilas and Harris 1985; Vilas 1986, 263–69; Gonzalez 1990, 108–16.) I would say instead that the revolutionary polity was broadly socialist: Sandinismo's activist base was popular (in a context where it makes little sense to speak of a classical Marxist "proletariat"); its economic policies—especially its early policies—were markedly redistributive, in a vigorously egalitarian spirit; and, although the revolution indeed attempted to secure class coexistence (rather than a classless society), it did so in the context of working-class political power. Plainly, the socialist aspect of the revolution faded as the war and economic crisis dragged on, and emergency economic measures increasingly favored medium to large producers after 1988.

8. On the political economy of revolutionary Nicaragua, see Harris and Vilas 1985; Vilas 1986; Spalding 1987.

9. For a broad sampling of social science research at the intersection of class and gender in Latin America, see Nash and Safa 1980; Nash and Safa 1986; Benería and Roldán 1987; Bergmann et al. 1990. Scheper-Hughes's (1992) ethnography provides a multifaceted treatment of gender, reproduction, and work in Brazil. For works that examine class and gender in the context of the world economic system, see Afshar 1985; Afshar 1987; Brydon and Chant 1989; Nash and Fernández-Kelly 1984; and Ward 1984.

10. "Luisa Amanda Espinosa, a seamstress by trade, was the first woman member of the Frente Sandinista to fall in combat—a symbol of the struggle of the Nicaraguan Women" (AMNLAE 1983, 324).

11. For more extensive material on the legal reforms I am surveying here, see Collinson 1990, 109–21; Dirección Nacional, FSLN 1987; Dirección de Orientación y Protección Familiar 1983; IHCA 1984; Molyneux 1985; Molyneux 1986a; Molyneux 1986b; Ramírez-Horton 1982; B. Stephens 1990.

12. In 1988, assisted by Erika Obrietan and Jaime (see chapter 15), I conducted an informal census in a section of Barrio San Lucas (also a pseudonym) and another in a section of Erasmus Jiménez. Barrio San Lucas is a sprawling, lower-working-class community on Managua's perimeter. Of the 63 households surveyed, children under 18 were present in the vast majority—61 houses, or 97 percent. Of those 61 households where children were present, 44 percent (27) contained at least one single mother; single fathers were present in an additional 7 percent (4 households). Only in 30 households—49 percent—were both parents present.

Erasmus Jiménez is by no means as poor as San Lucas. Predictably, economic dislocations had left fewer mothers single. Still, the percentage of households with single mothers was roughly the national average in the neighborhood surveyed. Children under 18 were present in 90 percent (45) of the 50 surveyed households. Of those households where children were present, 36 percent (16) contained single mothers; another 4 percent (2) contained single fathers. In the remaining 27 households (60 percent), both parents were present with the children.

13. This much seems clear: the socialist camp's existence facilitated the activities of a wide range of anti-imperialist and popular social movements throughout the less developed world. Between World War II and the disintegration of Soviet control over Eastern Europe, the socialist camp provided material aid, military assistance, international protection, and moral support for progressive, anti-imperialist, and leftist movements in settings as diverse as Vietnam, Cuba, Zimbabwe, South Africa, and Nicaragua—to name only a few. Such aid, of course, could be a curse as well as a blessing. Like Western assistance, Eastern bloc aid often came with strings attached, and Eastern bloc assistance tended to steer its beneficiaries toward a Leninist political model and a Soviet-style command economy, whether those were applicable to local conditions or not. Assessments made and strategies planned in Moscow were often presumptuous, self-interested, and uninformed about local conditions. And in the context of pursuing its own national interests, the Soviet Union was as likely to curb assistance to revolutionary movements at critical moments—for the sake of peaceful superpower coexistence—as it was to accelerate assistance. Plainly, the USSR urged the FSLN to make broad concessions to the contras and manipulated the flow of economic and military assistance to pressure the Sandinistas toward a "peaceful settlement" of the conflict rather than an outright military victory.

Thus, one could argue many points about Soviet influence on revolutionary movements (including Nicaragua's): it accelerated them, it decelerated them; it aided, it compromised. In short, the sharp edge of Soviet influence cut many ways. The point is that these movements themselves were by no means "orchestrated" by or "directed" from Moscow. They had domestic origins, and—as well as they could in an international world—they pursued domestic agendas. We should avoid lumping together nationalist and leftist revolutionary movements of the period into a uniform "Soviet bloc," no matter how politically tempting that explanation is under present conditions. Outside of Eastern Europe (where a definable and coercive "bloc" indeed really existed), such a monolithic bloc existed primarily in the rhetoric of U.S. conservatives as a means of condemning a wide variety of anti-imperialist and anticapitalist movements. An occasional subsidy by the socialist camp was in many ways the only substantial link between these diverse movements. What drew such movements toward a greater or lesser degree of alliance with the Soviet Union were, as I see it, two considerations, one practical, the other ideological. On the practical side, revolutionary movements in impoverished and underdeveloped countries, opposed by local oligarchies and U.S. foreign policy, needed military and economic assistance from a source whose preconditions did not preclude a revolutionary transformation of the domestic political economy. Whatever preconditions were part of Soviet aid, they rarely precluded economic redistribution. Western capitalist states—even the more or less social-democratic ones—were scarcely disposed to finance radical projects, and the United States was likely to intervene against them. Practically, and despite limitations in the quantity and quality of Soviet aid, a working relationship with the Soviet Union was necessary for any political project seeking to alter the capitalist and neocolonial status quo. On the ideological—some would say mythical—side, leftists were heartened to perceive that the bolshevik revolution had inaugurated a course of history that was irreversible and unstoppable, a course whose terminus would be a global socialism substantively different from any of its really existing variations. Whatever monstrous "deformations" had been born in the USSR and its Eastern European satellites, one could hope (1) that these deformations would eventually be corrected within the system of socialist production and (2) that for the working class, the socialization of production still signified an absolute advance over capitalist relations of production. Leftists, of course, defined themselves along a broad continuum of positions on the Soviet Union: the USSR could appear as a beacon of progress, a flawed but functional alternative to capitalism, a deformed workers' state, or a monstrous deformation of socialist principles. Still, it signified the existence of a possible alternative to capitalism in the world, and certainly its presence provided a counterweight to capitalist and imperialist hegemony.

Finally, in terms of the prospectus for future anti-imperialist and socialist movements, the collapse of the socialist bloc and the demise of the USSR mean that short-term conditions for success are bleak indeed. Without some level of subsidy from *somewhere,* revolutionary movements and governments in less developed countries are likely to wither. Moreover, the United States remains the last superpower standing, and little in the way of an international structure remains to prevent it from articulating its perceived interests against movements and governments not to its liking.

I. JUNKYARDS

1. I do not mean that gender relations are any happier or less conflictive in the United States than they are in Nicaragua. I simply observe that many Nicaraguan women expressed a belief that this was so.

2. Emigration to escape poverty and underdevelopment in Nicaragua is nothing new. Internal rural migration and rural-to-urban migration are old patterns there. Indeed, a limited pattern of migration to the United States pre-dates the Sandinista revolution: some families migrated permanently; others sent laborers abroad for a few years, with the understanding that they would return home with savings. That much is not altogether new. But with the economic crisis of the 1980s, this trickle became a human torrent. By some estimates, up to 15 percent of Nicaraguans took up permanent residency abroad, mostly in the United States. The scope of economic dependency structured by this large-scale emigration was unprecedented.

3. This is not to say that Nicaragua has no long-term environmental crisis. The deceptively beautiful Lake Managua is virtually dead. During the Somoza period, chlorine factories in the hills around the lake and industrial runoff from the city contaminated the lake with various chemical toxins, including mercury. The lake has also provided a huge open sewer for parts of Managua. It is quite possibly beyond rehabilitation. During the same period, the lumber industry stripped extensive mountainous areas of their trees, leaving behind all the problems of soil erosion and flooding that accompany deforestation. Reforesting those fragile ecosystems will be a costly and time-consuming project, if it ever occurs. And the long-term use of dangerous insecticides on Nicaragua's latifundios has left that country's people with high levels of carcinogens in their water, in their food, and in their bodies.

II. BEATING ONE'S WIFE

1. See B. Stephens 1990, 73 n. 53.

2. "The conquest of women" (Mörner 1967, 21–29) was a generalized feature of the Spanish conquest of the Americas. To take a territory, a land, a world, was to take its women. Rape, concubinage, and polygynous patterns of intermarriage formed the gridwork of early *criollo* [creole] and mestizo society. Thus, the medium of sex inescapably expressed themes of male, white, military, and upper-class domination, as against female, indigenous, civilian, and lower-class defeat. The forms of family life that emerged in colonial society and the gender norms constructed in the postconquest world (MacLachlan and Rodríguez 1980, 229–48) bore the cultural and psychological marks of the traumatic event of conquest (Paz 1985, 82; Goldwert 1983).

This connection—between the importance of sexual conquest in the present-day culture of machismo and the historical processes of the Spanish conquest—has been noted so often that it has become commonplace. Too generic a version of this connection no doubt conceals and distorts the differences between cultures spanning two continents. There is no reason to suppose that all the culturally and ethnically diverse peoples of Latin America, each with their own distinct history, developed a uniform sexual culture. I do not want to propose, prematurely, a generic model of machismo in Latin America. Yet the essential structure of encounter and conquest was remarkably similar from region to region. The signal processes of colonization and mestizoization in the emergent societies, too, were similar. It remains for historical and ethnographic research to establish degrees of similarity and parameters of variation in the gender and sexual cultures of Latin America.

3. The language of sex thus reflects the language of violence and power through an idiom which bears much in common with Paz's description of the place of the verb *chingar* in Mexican machismo. *Chingar* (like the Nicaraguan *verguiar*) is prohibited speech, a "secret word" without clear meaning (Paz 1985, 73); yet it is nonetheless frequently used and altogether meaningful.

> In Mexico, the word [*chingar*] has innumerable meanings. . . . But in this plurality of meanings the ultimate meaning always contains the idea of aggression, whether it is the simple act of molesting, pricking or censuring, or the violent act of wounding or killing. The verb denotes violence, an emergence from oneself to penetrate another by force. It also means to injure, to lacerate, to violate—bodies, souls, objects—and to destroy. . . .
>
> The idea of breaking, of ripping open, appears in a great many of these expressions. The word has sexual connotations but is not a synonym for the sexual act: one may *chingar* a woman without actually possessing her. And when it does allude to the sexual act, violation and deception gives it a particular shading. The man who commits it never does so with the consent of the *chingada*. *Chingar*, then, is to do violence to another. The verb is masculine, active, cruel: it stings, wounds, gashes, stains. And it provokes a bitter, resentful satisfaction.
>
> The person who suffers this action is passive, inert and open, in contrast to the active, aggressive and closed person who inflicts it. The *chingón* is the *macho*, the male; he rips open the *chingada*, the female, who is pure passivity, defenseless against the exterior world. The relationship between them is violent and it is determined by the cynical power of the first and the impotence of the second. The idea of violence rules darkly over all meanings of the word, and the dialectic of the "closed" and the "open" thus fulfills itself with an almost ferocious precision.
>
> . . . The *macho* is the *gran chingón*. One word sums up the aggressiveness, insensitivity, invulnerability and other attributes of the *macho:* power. It is force without the discipline of any notion of order: arbitrary power, the will without reins and without a set course. (Paz 1985, 76–81)

4. Working in a feminist vein, Nancy Chodorow has developed a body of psychological literature on the implications of gendered socialization routines. If small children identify with their primary caregivers, then all small children, male and female, identify with their mothers. The personality development of boys must entail a traumatic "break" with their primary caregiver in order to establish an independent, male identity; the maturation of girls is more "continuous" and less traumatic since girls grow up to be women and caregivers, like their mothers. Trauma—the active solicitation of masculinity and independence—would seem to be built into the socialization routine for boys. See Chodorow 1974; Chodorow 1978; Chodorow 1989. See also Gilligan 1982.

5. Marriage itself, as opposed to free union, is a complicated affair. In the past, Nicaraguan law stipulated that marriage be performed as a civil ceremony before it could be performed as a religious ritual (Adams 1957, 189). Although it is no longer required by law, some couples continue to observe

this two-stage marriage practice. Others opt for either a civil or religious ceremony. Poor people, at least those who live in the Pacific belt, still prefer informal union. (See Adams 1957, 189–95.)

6. Such a perspective contrasts with and complements the usual economic analysis of the prevalence of informal unions in Central America. It is generally maintained that the need for a highly mobile (male) labor force facilitated the present pattern of unstable informal unions. Informal unions do indeed predominate in the regions where large-scale agriculture has required seasonal and mobile labor (see Adams 1957, 189–95, 457–58; Anderson 1971, 13). Undoubtedly, male labor mobility in the context of Catholic prohibitions on divorce facilitated the development of the present norm. At the same time, however, I would argue that other social norms and gender conflicts played their part as well. What this discussion brings to the fore is how gender norms and gender concepts in a culture of machismo have affected the development of the Nicaraguan family. Oddly enough, men actually seem more in favor of marriage than women do. And as difficult as it is to be an abandoned mother, most of my informants thought it a far worse fate to be trapped in a bad marriage.

7. It is widely maintained in Managua's working-class neighborhoods that Protestants are more likely than Catholics to implement Christian teachings in their daily life. See Lancaster 1988b, 104–15.

IV. COPING WITH LESS

1. "Nicaragua Libre: The Praxis of a Popular Revolution," session at the eighty-seventh annual meeting of the American Anthropological Association, 1988.

2. See Aburto 1988, 33; see also Stahler-Sholk 1988, 47.

3. Reliable statistics on this point are not available, and I would be skeptical of any method that claimed to gauge the real level of support provided by laborers abroad. Community gossip asserts that various people receive large amounts of such income; people, however, always demur to discuss their own income sent from abroad and either deny receiving any or minimize its scope when questioned by their neighbors. Families are under considerable pressure to obtain such income, as this chapter documents; they are also under considerable pressure to conceal such income, as the following chapter shows.

4. For a detailed examination of the economics and logic of gift exchange versus commodity exchange, see Gregory 1982.

5. In Nicaragua, most people measure liquids in the metric system (*litros*, liters) and solids in the English system (*libras*, pounds). Although one occasionally encounters the reverse—*onzas* (ounces) for liquids and *kilos* for solids—most vendors sell items in the standard units I record.

6. Seeing food and being entitled to a share of it are inextricably linked in various beliefs and practices. Although not many Nicaraguans appear to believe in the "evil eye" per se, it is assumed that bad luck follows from stinginess that is seen by others. The following example is typical: We were eating watermelon; I dropped my slice and looked up, embarrassed at my clumsiness.

Doña Jazmina commented, "Don't look at me, Róger. I didn't want your watermelon; I have my own right here."

7. See Sidney Mintz and Eric Wolf's comprehensive essay, "An Analysis of Ritual Co-Parenthood (Compadrazgo)" (1950), as well as George Foster's "Cofradía and Compadrazgo in Spain and Spanish America" (1953). Obviously, my analysis of compadrazgo owes much to these classic essays, and to Carol Stack's study (1974).

8. Carol Stack's ethnography, *All Our Kin* (1974), traces the circulation of gifts in an African-American community in a U.S. city. Her thesis there, like mine here, is that such gift circulation is an important means by which poor people—especially families headed by women—survive adversity and scarcity. See also Judith Stacey's engaging study (1990) of the postmodern family in America.

V. CHICKEN SOUP

1. It might be imagined that the storekeepers knew my vitae so well because they were CDS members and therefore kept tabs on me, but I think that political vigilance was not the source of their detailed information: (1) they were not members of the barrio committee, which oversaw the barrio CDS, and thus were not especially informed on surveillance matters; (2) I had similar encounters with others who were neither CDS members nor acquaintances yet who were rather well informed about me; (3) when I later asked Doña Carmen the source of her information about me, she responded simply that she had "heard it" from neighbors.

2. There are alternative explanations. Perhaps at the beginning my informants were all having a collective joke on me by feigning ignorance of the chicken soup remedy. Although gossip is often conspiratorial, I very much doubt that the entire community had either the will or the energy to pull my leg on so trivial a matter. Or, perhaps, chicken soup was a "traditional remedy" for some Nicaraguan families in some parts of the country, but not in others. The absence of any apparent knowledge of the remedy by any of my informants on the early visit, however, makes this explanation very doubtful. Or, finally, while not having seen my chicken soup remedy, perhaps Doña Flora had heard detailed accounts of it and wished to make me feel at home by my own culture's known rules and so feigned ignorance of my remedy and pretended that chicken soup was a tradition of her own. Such a scenario would complicate but still confirm my argument about gossip and tradition. Nicaraguan standards of hospitality are indeed capable of such minor (dis)simulations, but Flora vigorously and repeatedly maintained her representations to me as accurate.

VI. CENSORING *LA SEMANA COMICA*

1. The term *marianismo* itself has been sharply debated. At best, it is an analytic category proposed by social scientists, not an indigenous concept per se; the term does not occur in popular usage in any Latin American country.

As a heuristic device, the term presents many problems. The couplet *machismo/marianismo* suggests a certain complementarity, reciprocity, and equilibrium. Thus, the marianismo model suggests that men exercise power in their spheres, and women in theirs—without any clear sense of how unequal those spheres themselves might be. In its rounded wholeness, the couplet also suggests coetaneous origins for both sides of the equation: machismo, the male side of domination and conquest; marianismo, the elevated spiritual and martyrlike compensation for suffering. Silvia Arrom (1985) argues that in Mexico City the cultural ideas and practices that might be glossed "the *marianismo* complex" were introduced after the middle of the nineteenth century—a Victorian import, not a long-standing feature of the Latin American heritage. Tracy Ehlers (1991) sets out to debunk the concept of marianismo altogether: if women endure male domination and spousal abuse, it is less because they mistake their status for elevated purity and more because they have few options in coping with male and class power.

Because my informants used the term *machismo* and were very consistent in their usage of it, I use that term to describe traditional ideas and ideals of masculinity. However, because my informants did not use the term *marianismo* or any equivalent, I do not use it. I might note that when I discussed the matter with several key informants, they rejected the term outright for the simple reason that María was a virgin; "sexual purity" in the sense of virginity is not and never has been an important element of the Nicaraguan ideal of proper womanhood.

2. The series indeed generated an uproar and was suspended before it had run its course. See Collinson 1990, 22–23, 168–71, for another account of the *Semana cómica*–AMNLAE dispute and the uproar around "Sex and Youth."

3. For a somewhat different perspective on public discourse, see Post 1990; Post 1991. Post locates speech as a special form of action (1991, 285)—as I do—and depicts certain paradoxes in the regulation of public discourse. We would both agree that speech can (and perhaps should) be regulated in certain arenas (e.g., the workplace) and that its regulation is far more problematic in others (e.g., newspapers, political debate). Our analysis differs to the degree that he begins from the premise of free individuals, whereas I begin with constrained groups and social categories of people; we therefore differ to the degree that we see power, coercion, and force operating in and through discourse.

4. For various legal perspectives on the issue of hate speech, see Delgado 1982; Borovoy et al. 1989; Massaro 1991; and Post 1991.

5. Since every representation "objectifies" what it represents, we need to exercise some care in specifying what sorts of representations are actually oppressive, which ones commit actual violence, and precisely how they do so. Only if we see the body itself as shameful, and only if we understand sex itself as debasing, could simple depictions of nudity and intercourse be labeled oppressive. The essays in Vance 1984 explore the liberatory side of sexuality and representation; these essays provide a useful corrective to what might justifiably be described as a puritanical antisex current in feminist analysis.

VII. ROLANDO

1. I have translated Rolando's words in keeping with his written style: erratic capitalization, virtually no punctuation, occasional misspellings, and run-on sentences.

XIII. JAIME

1. Obando was an archbishop when the Sandinistas seized the National Palace in 1978, holding the national assembly hostage; later he became a cardinal. Castillo was minister of agriculture under the Somoza regime; the Sandinistas kidnapped a party of Somoza's cronies at his house in 1974.

XVI. DEALING WITH DANGER

1. I should say *surplus* fears. As an institution, the U.S. military maintains surveillance over its members and remains the largest outpost of absolutist antigay discrimination in American society. My primary fear for the duration of my partner's enlistment was that our relationship would be discovered and that he would receive a dishonorable discharge—or even a prison sentence— for the "crime" of loving me. We had to be especially careful during those long months of separation, for phone lines were monitored and mail might be opened. Beyond the standard fear of exposure (a fear shared by hundreds of thousands of homosexuals and lesbians in the military) and the anxiety of separation and concern about physical safety (discomforts shared by all families who have a member in the military), then, there was this additional injury to human dignity: that two thirty-year-old men should have to resort to circumlocutions, pseudonyms, and periphrases in even their most intimate communications with each other.

XVII. THE *NEGRO* OF THE FAMILY

1. Racial and ethnic problems would seem inevitable in a context shaped by a long history of conquest, colonialism, and neocolonialism (Stein and Stein 1970; Mörner 1970). Studies as diverse as Wolf's (1959) and Taussig's (1987) show how the colonial experience produced and continues to produce dislocations and power struggles that are at once ethnic, racial, and class conflicts. The bulk of anthropological works on race and ethnicity in Latin America highlights specifically Latin American conceptions of race and analyzes the maintenance of racial identity and subordination in systems of stratification where social position takes precedence over phenotypic characteristics (Harris 1964; Wagley 1965; Pitt-Rivers 1971; Brintnall 1979; Warren 1979; Hawkins 1984; Bourgois 1989). These ethnographic studies treat societies in which socially constructed and rigidly defined groups (indigenous peoples, Ladinos, and sometimes African Americans) live in close proximity, with no two groups enjoying social and economic equality.

Nicaragua provides a case very different from the type of society generally considered in the existing literature. By the early twentieth century, the overwhelming majority of Nicaragua's population had been linguistically, culturally, and ethnically "mestizoized" (mixed). Persons of indigenous or African identity today constitute only a tiny fraction of the population and are heavily concentrated along the Atlantic coast. Owing no doubt to the geographical separation of mestizos and minorities, as well as a tradition of governmental disinterest in Atlantic coast affairs, violent racial-ethnic conflicts have been relatively rare in modern Nicaraguan history.

2. There is much disagreement on the size of Nicaragua's preconquest population. Some estimates have put it at less than 500,000. Newson (1987, 84–88, 117–24) reviews the literature and incorporates information on technology and land fertility, concluding that the entire territory of Nicaragua may well have supported a population of up to 1.6 million.

3. This use of *chele* almost always calls attention to a power inequality, as experienced by the person being dominated. It offers, effectively, a curt insult to power. The wealthier, more powerful, better-dressed, or better-educated person in a dispute—that is, the person who is perceived as having the upper hand—will be called *chele*. In this context, the chele might actually be just as dark skinned as the person who labels him. Such a colorized discourse supports innumerable forms of power relationships. In the countryside, for example, campesinos often referred to union organizers and Frente militants from the city as "those cheles." (Jim Quesada, pers. comm.)

4. Years later, Jaime and Virgilio recalled this exercise as both enjoyable and educational. "I think I see how anthropology works," observed Virgilio. "You forced us to think systematically about what everyone usually takes for granted," added Jaime.

5. Different cultures and different languages recognize a range of between two and eleven "primary" color categories. Historically, anthropologists have cited the diversity of color categories as evidence for the diversity—hence arbitrariness—of culture itself and as a demonstration of cultural relativism. That is (as an extension of the Sapir-Whorf hypothesis), if a language endorses only three color categories, its members' perceptions will be "wired" to see or discriminate only three colors. Berlin and Kay's (1970) cross-cultural study found a regular progression of basic color terms: whether a culture recognizes two or eleven terms, the categories follow a regular sequence. Some took this finding as hard evidence against the assumptions of cultural relativism. Sahlins argues that Berlin and Kay's results show that the eye operates semiotically: color categories structure "distinctive features" (Jakobson and Halle 1956) of perception; the sequence of categories described by Berlin and Kay "*are not terms but relations between terms*" (Sahlins 1977, 175; his emphasis). The regularity of the color sequence is "constrained" not by anything natural or universal about color but by the requirements of minimal distinctive features.

> Because colors subserve this *cultural significance*, only certain color percepts are appropriately singled out as "basic," namely those that by their distinctive features and relations can serve as signifiers in informational systems. . . . *It is not, then, that color*

terms have their meanings imposed by the constraints of human and physical nature; it is that they take on such constraints insofar as they are meaningful. (Sahlins 1977, 167; his emphasis)

6. I am not arguing that before the age of colonialism individual human beings were incapable of recognizing a range of human colors, within as well as beyond their own societies. Such a position would be a banal trivialization of the issues that are at stake here. What I am arguing is that with colonialism it became necessary to *socially* mark and maintain color categories as biological and moral categories of people.

7. See Forbes 1988; Montagu 1974. On the particular instantiation of racial/colorized thinking in Latin America and the process of *mestijaze* ("ethnic mixing" or "mestizoization") especially in Mexico, see Mörner 1967 and the various essays in Mörner 1970.

8. Logorrhea, which is Barthes's (1972b) neologism, brings together *logo-* (word, speech) with *-rrhea* (flow) to suggest an uncontrolled torrent of speech.

XVIII.   SUBJECT HONOR, OBJECT SHAME

This chapter represents something of an ethnography within an ethnography. Its earliest draft was presented at the 1986, 85th Annual Meeting of the American Anthropological Association in Philadelphia. An outline of my arguments appeared in *Signs* 12, no. 1 (1986): 188–92, and a version substantially shorter than the present chapter appeared in *Ethnology* 27, no. 2 (1988): 111–25. For their comments on earlier drafts, I am grateful to Marie Boutte, Samuel Colón, Sue Estroff, Robert Fernea, Byron Good, Richard Parker, Leonard Plotnicov, Jim Quesada, Nancy Scheper-Hughes, and Marilyn Strathern.

1. Called "the festival of disguises," Carnaval is a religious celebration held annually in the large agricultural market town of Masaya. It marks the climax of a series of religious festivals in that town, and not the approach of Lent. An important presence among the elaborate masks and disguises of Carnaval is that of the cochones, who don female attire and parade alongside other participants in the day's procession.

2. My spelling throughout conforms to the only spelling I have ever seen in print, in a *Nuevo diario* editorial (6 Dec. 1985).

3. Working with a network of *pasivos* or cochones, Adam (1987) provides an overview very similar to the analysis I am developing here.

4. I was not "out"—openly gay—in Erasmus Jiménez. At first, this strategy was to ensure that I could establish good relations with my informants, who, I imagined, would not approve. Later, it became problematic to me just how I would articulate my own understanding of my own sexuality to my informants—as this chapter demonstrates. Covertly, and through various circumlocutions, a few men from the neighborhood attempted to establish sexual liaisons with me; more generally, I encountered cochones in "neutral" and relatively "anonymous" settings such as the marketplace. In either case, for the most part these men assumed that I was an hombre-hombre. If I described

myself to them as homosexual or gay, their sexual interest was generally diminished greatly.

5. As Boswell observes (1989, 33–34), fellatio can be considered an "active" behavior; if anything, it is the fellated who is "passive."

6. For example, Potter and Potter (1990, 251–69) show in some detail how the patrilineal system reproduced itself (in its specifically patriarchal form) in China during—and despite—forty years of revolutionary, collectivist efforts designed to eliminate it.

7. See Lucinda Broadbent's 1991 video, *Sex and the Sandinistas*.

8. I do not claim to be a human rights expert or a human rights investigator. Human rights abuses, although not systematic among the Sandinistas (as they were among the contras), did occur, especially in the war zones. See the Introduction to this volume.

9. For theoretical discussions of "innatist" versus "constructionist" positions, see Boswell 1989; Halperin 1989; and Padgug 1989.

10. For instance, assuming some general correlation were soundly demonstrated (which is not the case; this example remains hypothetical), would we conclude that men with lower-than-average levels of testosterone (or, perhaps, men who were exposed to lower-than-average prenatal levels of androgen, or men whose hypothalami were smaller than average, or whatever the prevailing biomythology of a given decade) were biologically predisposed toward homosexual acts by way of some physiologically determined process, or would we conclude that a complex socialization process perceives and marks those men as "homosexual" and systematically prods them in that direction? Or might it be that the cumulative social, cultural, and sexual experiences of being heterosexual versus being homosexual produce minor physiological variations between these two socially and culturally produced populations? The remarkable thing about sociobiological rubbish on homosexuality is its absolute reification and naturalization of categories: as though a very large percentage of "heterosexuals" had not had homosexual experiences (and vice versa); as though even in our own society Kinsey had not demonstrated that sexual practices and sexual desires run along a spectrum and are not divided into distinct populations; as though human society could not do without some contrast between homosexual and heterosexual acts and persons.

One does find the most remarkable rubbish in this literature. By manipulating the prenatal and postnatal hormonal levels of some rats, a certain "Dr. Frankenstein" (Katz's [1990] term, applied to a different doctor) has produced what he calls "homosexual rats"—that is, male rats who routinely show a "feminine" lordosis response (squatting, allowing penetration) when other male rats mount them (Ruse 1988, 103–12). But just who is displaying homosexual behavior? The mounted? The mounting? Or both? And if ordinary, untreated male rats will routinely attempt to mount other male rats, altered or unaltered, how could it be said that these ordinary rats are "heterosexual"? If one wants to play the game, one might more justifiably say—with a straight face, and in their defense—that the altered rats are not homosexuals at all, but transsexuals: female rats trapped in the bodies of male rats.

We go on to read not only of rat sexualities but also of rat attitudes, of rat desires, and of rat freedoms (Ruse 1988, 119)—no doubt rat fantasies shall come next, at the very moment when human beings are shown to *lack* attitudes, desires, freedoms, and fantasies. After having learned that male homosexuals, whether rats or humans, are in some biological sense "more feminine" than male heterosexuals, we go on to learn that the profligate sexuality of the homosexual subculture is a function of men behaving straightforwardly like men, rather than like women (Ruse 1988, 137). Social structures, cultural meanings, and human volition are all reduced to the status of superficial, secondary constraints on an essential, primary biology, and anything in human homosexual behavior that deviates from the model of the altered-male-rat-lordosis response is casually brushed aside as "a matter of learning, imitation, and so forth" (122). Ruse goes on to argue that critiques of the hormonal and sociobiological paradigms make "linguistic points" motivated by a moral and political perspective (138–39). The real point is that language and science cannot be readily extricated from moral and political concerns. Words and concepts have been naively employed, and it is not just that this confusion exists as a bad writing practice, but that it undergirds the hormonal studies and sociobiological science fiction at deep, methodological levels: the studies in question analogize between rats and humans precisely by imbuing rats with extraordinary human powers and depriving humans of even minimal human powers.

Of course, the hormonal and sociobiological literature is not the only place one can find various naturalistic groundings of sexuality; the idea that one encounters Nature at the bottom of Sex—an idea that compels us to "seek the Truth in sex" (Foucault 1980, 53–73, 79)—is widespread. Even in anthropology, one encounters bizarre arguments: Kardiner (1954, 168) was terrified by, and attempted to terrify his readers with, the lavender menace (see Lewes 1988, 168). In an uncharacteristic moment of bigotry in *Sex and Temperament in Three Primitive Societies,* Margaret Mead (1963, 290–322, esp. 293–95, 318–19) concludes that if only our society would provide people more leeway in terms of gender and the expression of *temperament,* it would curb the production of sexual inversion.

11. At the bottom of naturalistic heterosexism lies a series of premises, each more fallacious than the last:

a. A paramount project of both biology and culture is to secure the reproduction of the species or the group and (more to the point) the reproduction of one's own genetic material. Stated this way, the idea of some inner "biologic" of culture would seem straightforward and innocent enough. It would seem to place some conception of "material needs" at the heart of culture. But we are already well on the way to a series of other planks: competition for maximization as a biological principle; survival of the fittest as an evolutionary fact rather than business dogma; evolution as "progress" (toward a goal); cultural change as a form of evolution; and so on, ad nauseam. Traveling a similar path, Malinowski ultimately arrived at a conception of culture as an extended gut. But this manifestly social "naturalism" reads into both biology and culture a Darwinian imperative, an active force, a metaphysical drive. Thus reified, natural selection becomes an active process rather than a contingent result: the telos of history, the logos underlying culture. In such an idealist biology and metaphysical materialism, culture becomes nothing more than biology's afterthought: a means of securing for biology what biology cannot secure for itself.

b. Homosexual acts proper do not produce offspring. This is true enough, but neither do most heterosexual acts.

c. Homosexual (and heterosexual) *persons* really do exist, in a cross-cultural and transhistorical sense, defined by their preference for homosexual (or heterosexual) intercourse. This plank has no evidence whatsoever, and the bulk of sophisticated ethnographic data weighs against it. Indeed, what of societies where homosexual practice is conceived as a normal (classical Greece) or even mandatory (parts of Melanesia) aspect of every man's life experience?

d. Homosexual persons, then, are less likely to reproduce themselves than heterosexual persons are. This coupling of (b) and (c) ignores all sorts of possibilities and must be considered unimaginative at best. True enough: in our society, self-identified homosexuals (and lesbians) are less likely to bear offspring than are persons not self-identified as gay. But the bulk of closeted homosexuals *are* married and *do* produce children. And at the same time, self-identified gays (and lesbians) who want children have availed themselves of a variety of means of producing them, outside (as well as within) the confines of heterosexual marriage. In the end, the simple fact that one prefers intercourse of a homosexual sort by no means obviates the possibilities of reproduction—in this or any other society.

e. This vital reproductive project requires (or, rather, historically *required*) that everyone (or at least most people) be engaged in a heterosexual union organized for the purposes of reproduction—a biological and material necessity that means that culture everywhere has expressed a preference for heterosexual over homosexual. Actually, as Greenberg (1988, 10) has pointed out, "Even if sexual partners were chosen entirely at random at each mating, without regard to sex, birthrates would remain high enough to sustain population growth." It may well be the case that *most* societies prefer heterosexual union to homosexual union—although (1) the question of union (marriage) is distinct from sexual intercourse preferences, and (2) this presumed "preference" for heterosexual union depends in large part on how one raises the question. As Lévi-Strauss (1969) has shown, marriage does not exist to secure the production of children but to extend the field of one's social and political alliances *between* men *through* women. And as Rubin (1975), following Lévi-Strauss, has argued, one could explain the apparent preference of cultures for heterosexual marriage, then, without any recourse whatsoever to biology; that is, it becomes an entirely social and political question. Departing from Rubin, one might question whether cultures' apparent preference for heterosexual marriage implicitly entails a preference for heterosexual over homosexual intercourse. There is no reason to assume it would, unless one defaults to the series of deductions outlined here, which are really a modernized reading of Leviticus and which would no doubt make the pope glad, since at every step it assumes that sex exists for purposes of procreation and that any other sexual activity is a misuse of what Nature (God) has given us.

12. Here I am applying the linguistic methods of the Bakhtin school to the problem of desire. See Medvedev and Bakhtin 1978; Vološinov 1986.

13. Misunderstandings and misrepresentations of this principle (sexual relativism) abound—as much on the "constructionist" side of the debate as on the "essentialist" one. On the constructionist side: it has been altogether too tempting a gesture to reify "social acts" as "social facts," thus capitulating to the totalitarian logic of functionalism (Weeks 1981, 8). Peculiar statements frequently center on the principle of *rules* versus *violations of the rule*, with scenarios that presuppose a view of culture more absolutist than creative, more programmed than practical. On the other side, rule violations are sometimes cited by those holding an "essentialist" view as evidence of an innate propensity—a natural tendency—in some distinct (if unlabeled) minority toward a homosexual orientation.

Much of the debate has revolved around the misleading question of "sexual plasticity" (see Greenberg 1988, 486–87), with allied disputes regarding all the familiar antinomies: biology versus culture, individual behavior versus social conventions, and subjective desires versus cultural rules. At stake ultimately—and from various and contradictory angles—is the question of freedom versus determinism. "Constructionists" have sometimes implicitly rested their theoretical arguments on the assumption that human sexuality is inherently polymorphous and malleable. If sexual response is infinitely plastic, then it can be shaped only by culture. "Culture," thus abstracted from practice and reified, becomes an active and dictatorial force in human affairs rather than an arena of practice, conflict, and change. If the relativist/constructionist position maintains that all human beings are inherently malleable and that culture is a "program" that controls perception and experience, it remains far behind theoretical advances in semiotics. That erotic response in the human race is highly varied is undeniable; that erotic response in any given human being—who necessarily lives in his or her own time, his or her own society, his or her own life, and his or her own existential dilemmas—is highly plastic: that is a completely different idea, and it is not a secure proposition at all. To blur these propositions is to confuse analytical domains.

Actually, sexuality as a social system needs to be theorized as neither more nor less "plastic" than language is (understood as a Bakhtinian "dialogue," not as a Saussurean "structure"). To argue by analogy: the facility for language is made possible by the human brain and connected with the physiology of the vocal apparatus. The human brain is most decidedly a biological organ instantiated in each individual human being; the vocal cords, tongue, and palate, too, belong to our anatomy. Is language, therefore, "rooted" in individual biology? Is it in any significant sense "constrained" by anatomy? Is it the expression of biological or individual essences? Certainly not. As a social-practical phenomenon, language cannot be reduced to biology, anatomy, or the individual. Questions of language are questions of meaning. The biological and anatomical mechanics of speech are not relevant to the meaning of any given speech act or any given discourse, text, or language. Even though the capacity for and necessity of language are both "wired" into the grooves of the brain, no language is explicable in terms of biological imperatives. However, as inadequate as are biological and essentialist views of language, the structuralist or functionalist view of language merely replaces one determinism with another. Its determinism, too, is inadequate—for whatever else language is, it is more a zone of "dialogue" than of homogenous "structure." Even though each language entails normative rules, a stable syntax, a logical grammar—in short, a hypothetical "structure"—speech acts may indeed violate all the tenets of linguistic structure and still remain intelligible linguistic phenomena. Language, though structured, naturally entails disagreements, conflicts, misunderstandings, and ambiguities; though regular, it is very much an *open* (not closed) system; though rulelike, it is not rendered unintelligible by the breaking of rules. The rules of language, then, do not determine what we say; they only circumscribe it. Nor, for that matter, does knowing a language (and thinking in it) preclude learning a second language (although some will have more trouble than others) or even losing one's facility in the first language (given enough time).

The same holds true for sex. The anatomy of the conscious body affords the potential for a large but theoretically limited range of sexual acts. This range of sex acts might be viewed as the sexual equivalent of phones in language. Sexual acts in themselves, like phonetic sounds in and of themselves, are meaningless. Sexual meaning occurs when sexual acts are grouped into vocabularies, are imbued with other associations, are appropriated by a sexual grammar. In short, they are meaningful only in a social context—but this is not to say that they are necessarily under the totalitarian control of a cultural program, for what could be more "dialogical," more "interdiscursive," than sex? One could imagine, instead, a series of concentric circles (rather than a hierarchical or deterministic scheme): (a) an individual's sexual practices and narratives, which represent both a lifetime of social intercourse with other people *and* an engagement with and *within* (b) a wider horizon, not of a specific narrative, but of plural, competing, and often conflicting social narratives about sexual practices, which is itself engaged in a dialectical relationship with (c) a larger political economy of gender and sexuality. (And, of course, even this third sphere is embedded in a larger social environment.) Meaning in any of these spheres is never either entirely "determined" or "free"; rather, the meaning of any individual or collective erotic life is precisely the living process of exchange between these zones, which range from the "micro" to the "macro"—and which are traversed by various degrees of autonomy and control, freedom and determinism, rebellion and conformity, power and love. (See Medvedev and Bakhtin 1978, 26–28.)

It should not surprise us that we are still at a stage of misunderstanding and misrepresentation. Anthropology is much older than gay studies, and anthropologists still sometimes confuse "culture" with an "inventory of rules." The debates between "constructionists" and "essentialists" recapitulate many of the features of the stale arguments around the Sapir-Whorf hypothesis (see Sahlins 1977, 166): Does language/culture *control* perception or *reflect* it? It is time to move on to a more dialogical and practical approach. I would reiterate what I said in chapter 5 about tradition and apply it to the question of sexuality. People do indeed play with, manipulate, blur, make recourse to, take refuge in, and transgress sexual rules, prohibitions, and other social boundaries—that is, they employ their conventions practically and often cynically. These, of course, are social acts, too.

14. For instance, some Middle Eastern cultures cast these active-passive rules in terms of active adults and passive youths (Trumbach 1977, 8). (See also Foucault's discussion of "the antinomy of the boy" in Greek antiquity [1986, 221].) The cochón is an adult though stigmatized male. Nicaraguan and Middle Eastern practices could be seen as variations on the larger type (active-passive rules), or each could be classified as an independent type. The typologies one draws up, then, will depend on one's purpose in classifying practices and what features one deems important (see Greenberg 1988, 490–93).

15. This premise has become so widespread that it can be recited without providing any substantial historical citations or ethnographic evidence. Ruse, cheerfully drawing lessons from anthropology and history, asserts that "when homosexual behavior is accepted and practiced by all as part of culture, it is generally associated with the unavailability of heterosexual contacts" (1988, 122).

CONCLUSION

1. For years the debates within Marxism—especially those between Marxist humanism and Marxist structuralism—revolved around such issues: To what extent can one speak of "structure" (as opposed to "practice") in human social life? To what extent is the ideological superstructure determined by an economic base—and should one understand this "determinism" broadly or narrowly? For a Marxist-humanist and existentialist perspective on such issues, see Sartre 1963; Sartre 1976. For a summary of the structuralist position, see Althusser and Balibar 1970. For a highly productive reworking of Marxist categories and analyses, see Donham 1990, esp. 8–12, 66–77.

2. Even on the economic terrain alone, Rey (1982) views modern capitalism as the articulation of various and plural modes of production.

3. Keeping strictly to Marx's remarks (which I have quoted from *The German Ideology* [1964] and *Theories of Surplus Value* [1963]), to speak of gender, sexuality, and color as "modes of production" is neither more nor less allegorical than to speak of an "economic mode of (material) production."

4. To reread carefully what Marx actually said (Marx and Engels 1948, esp. 20–21): it is not that the proletariat is the only oppressed group or even that class stratification is the only form of oppression under capitalism, but rather that the proletariat is the only group whose position in production pits its interests against the system of class stratification in general *and*, just as important, whose numbers give it the social weight to lead the way in overthrowing all systems of oppression.

5. For a review of the polling results, see IHCA 1990a, 8–9; 1990b, 10–16.

6. It is worth observing that the preelection polls were not far off in predicting the level of actual support for the FSLN—which was generally gauged at well under 50 percent—in the elections. Large numbers of "undecideds" showed up in every poll. Generally, when public opinion surveys detect large numbers of undecideds and the incumbent party falls short of a majority, such results are considered an ominous sign for the party in power, even if the

incumbent holds a considerable advantage over the opposition. Thus, rather than showing the Sandinistas with a comfortable lead, these polls, properly read, indicated that a majority of the electorate was unwilling to state a preference for the Frente.

7. For general discussions of the election and the failure of preelection polling, see IHCA 1990a; 1990b; 1990c; Barnes 1991.

8. See, for example, "Sandinistas Explain New Pay Policy," *Intercontinental Press,* 9 Sept. 1985, 528–33.

9. In a sense, the CDS elections of 1985–86 (Lancaster 1988b, 151–59) proved paradigmatic of the 1990 national elections. In those elections, older women with little or no political experience who were not FSLN members defeated incumbent younger men who were FSLN members. In 1986, as in 1990, the gender of the candidates was anything but insignificant. My informants in Erasmus Jiménez felt that women—especially older women, who were also mothers or grandmothers—were less likely than men to grandstand, to engage in demagoguery, or to make unreasonable demands on people's time and energy. Thus, within the arena of the declining CDS (as echoed in the national arena in 1990), maternal, practical, and nonideological rhetoric displaced masculine, exemplary, and revolutionary rhetoric. Although acute, the contradictions of 1986 were still manageable within a revolutionary framework that validated the effective leadership of the FSLN, and, I have no doubt, political consensus still operated in much the manner that I have described. By 1990, those contradictions had deepened to the point that Sandinista authority itself collapsed. The draft's unpopularity became more acute as the contra war dragged on; shortages, inflation, and recession produced not only political exhaustion within the framework of the revolution but increasingly cynicism concerning the revolutionary framework itself; resentments—fueled by ample tales of petty corruption, party patronage, malfeasance, and haughtiness—increasingly targeted not just particular Sandinistas, particular officials, but Sandinista leadership in general. However, despite the problems that beleaguered the Sandinistas, it seems unlikely that a standard male conservative candidate heading any of the existing political parties could have prevailed in national elections.

10. For the results of Nicaragua's first preelection public opinion poll, see IHCA 1988b.

11. As some of my informants put it in 1991, "*La gallina come el gallo*" (The hen ate the rooster).

12. In late 1991 and into 1992, various contra units have regrouped themselves on a small scale: the *recontras.* Violent conflicts, political assassinations, and kidnappings continue throughout the countryside. In response, small numbers of demobilized Sandinista soldiers have also regrouped into irregular units: the *recompas* (from *compañero,* or comrade). Chamorro's executive branch and the FSLN leadership have cooperated in attempting to demobilize the recontras and recompas. In some cases, however, recontras and recompas have combined forces: the *revueltos,* "mixed" or "scrambled" guerrilla units. Such developments underscore the desperation and volatility of the present situation.

References

Aburto, Roger. 1988. "El *boom* en la economía informal en Nicaragua." *Boletín socioeconómico,* June–July, 26–38.

Adam, Barry D. 1987. "Homosexuality Without a Gay World: The Case of Nicaragua." *ARGOH Newsletter* 9, no. 3:6–10.

Adams, Richard N. 1956. "Cultural Components of Central America." *American Anthropologist* 58:881–907.

———. 1957. *Cultural Surveys of Panama-Nicaragua-Guatemala–El Salvador–Honduras.* Scientific Publications no. 33. Washington, D.C.: Pan American Sanitary Bureau, Regional Office of the World Health Organization.

Afshar, Haleh, ed. 1985. *Women, Work, and Ideology in the Third World.* London: Tavistock.

———, ed. 1987. *Women, State, and Ideology: Studies from Africa and Asia.* Albany: State University of New York Press.

Althusser, Louis, and Etienne Balibar. [1968] 1970. *Reading Capital.* Translated by Ben Brewster. London: New Left Books.

AMNLAE (Asociación de Mujeres Nicaragüenses "Luisa Amanda Espinoza"). 1983. "From AMPRONAC to AMNLAE." In Rosset and Vandermeer, *Nicaragua Reader,* 323–24.

Anderson, Thomas P. 1971. *Matanza: El Salvador's Communist Revolt of 1932.* Lincoln: University of Nebraska Press.

Arguelles, Lourdes, and B. Ruby Rich. 1984. "Homosexuality, Homophobia, and Revolution: Notes Toward an Understanding of the Cuban Lesbian and Gay Male Experience, Part I." *Signs* 9, no. 4:683–99.

———. 1985. "Homosexuality, Homophobia, and Revolution: Notes Toward an Understanding of the Cuban Lesbian and Gay Male Experience, Part II." *Signs* 11, no. 1:120–36.

———. 1986. "Reply to Lancaster." *Signs* 12, no. 1:192–94.

Arrom, Silvia Marina. 1985. *The Women of Mexico City, 1790–1857*. Stanford: Stanford University Press.

Bakhtin, Mikhail M. 1984. *Rabelais and His World*. Bloomington: Indiana University Press.

———. 1986. *Speech Genres and Other Late Essays*. Translated by Vern W. McGee. Edited by Caryl Emerson and Michael Holquist. Austin: University of Texas Press.

Barnes, William A. 1991. "Rereading the Nicaraguan Pre-Election Polls in the Light of the Election Results (And What Can Be Learned about the Fate of the Nicaraguan Election Thereby)." Memo for the LASA (Latin American Studies Association) Commission on Nicaraguan Pre-Election Polls. Typescript.

Barthes, Roland. [1964] 1968. *Elements of Semiology*. Translated by Annette Lavers and Colin Smith. New York: Hill and Wang.

———. 1972a. *Critical Essays*. Evanston: Northwestern University Press.

———. [1957] 1972b. *Mythologies*. Translated by Annette Lavers. New York: Hill and Wang.

———. 1982. *A Barthes Reader*. Edited by Susan Sontag. New York: Hill and Wang.

Baudrillard, Jean. [1986] 1988a. *America*. Translated by Chris Turner. London: Verso.

———. 1988b. *Selected Writings*. Edited by Mark Poster. Stanford: Stanford University Press.

Benería, Lourdes, and Martha Roldán. 1987. *The Crossroads of Class and Gender: Industrial Homework, Subcontracting, and Household Dynamics in Mexico City*. Chicago: University of Chicago Press.

Benjamin, Walter. [1955] 1969. *Illuminations*. Edited by Hannah Arendt. Translated by Harry Zohn. New York: Schocken.

———. 1983. "N (Theoretics of Knowledge: Theory of Progress)." *Philosophical Forum* 15, nos. 1–2:1–40.

———. [1978] 1986. *Reflections: Essays, Aphorisms, Autobiographical Writings*. Edited by Peter Demetz. Translated by Edmund Jephcott. New York: Schocken.

Bergmann, Emilie, et al. 1990. *Women, Culture, and Politics in Latin America: Seminar on Feminism and Culture in Latin America*. Berkeley and Los Angeles: University of California Press.

Berlin, Brent, and Paul Kay. 1970. *Basic Color Terms*. Berkeley and Los Angeles: University of California Press.

Black, George, with Milton Jamail and Norma Stoltz Chinchilla. 1984. *Garrison Guatemala*. New York: Monthly Review Press.

Blake, James. 1971. *The Joint*. New York: Doubleday.

Blonsky, Marshall, ed. 1985. *On Signs*. Baltimore: Johns Hopkins University Press.

Booth, John, and Thomas W. Walker. 1989. *Understanding Central America*. Boulder: Westview.

Borovoy, Alan, Kathleen Mahoney (speakers), Barry Brown, Jamie Cameron, David Goldberger, and Mari Matsuda (commentators). 1989. "Language as

Violence Versus Freedom of Expression: Canadian and American Perspectives on Group Defamation. The James McCormick Mitchell Lecture." *Buffalo Law Review* 37, no. 2:337–73.

Boswell, John. 1980. *Christianity, Social Tolerance, and Homosexuality: Gay People in Western History from the Beginning of the Christian Era to the Fourteenth Century*. Chicago: University of Chicago Press.

———. 1989. "Revolutions, Universals, and Sexual Categories." In Duberman et al., *Hidden from History*, 17–36.

Bourdieu, Pierre. [1972] 1977. *Outline of a Theory of Practice*. Translated by Richard Nice. Cambridge: Cambridge University Press.

———. [1979] 1984. *Distinction: A Social Critique of the Judgment of Taste*. Translated by Richard Nice. Cambridge: Harvard University Press.

Bourgois, Philippe I. 1982. "The Problematic of Nicaragua's Indigenous Minorities." In T. Walker, *Nicaragua in Revolution*, 303–18.

———. 1989. *Ethnicity at Work: Divided Labor on a Central American Banana Plantation*. Baltimore: Johns Hopkins University Press.

Brandes, Stanley. 1981. "Like Wounded Stags: Male Sexual Ideology in an Andalusian Town." In Ortner and Whitehead, *Sexual Meanings*, 216–39.

Brintnall, Douglas. 1979. "Race Relations in the Southeastern Highlands of Mesoamerica." *American Ethnologist* 6:638–52.

Broadbent, Lucinda. 1991. *Sex and the Sandinistas* (videotape). Oakum Productions. Distributed by Women Make Movies, New York.

Brydon, Lynne, and Sylvia Chant. 1989. *Women in the Third World: Gender Issues in Rural and Urban Areas*. New Brunswick: Rutgers University Press.

Bullough, Vern L. 1976. *Sexual Variance in Society and History*. New York: John Wiley.

Callender, Charles, and Lee M. Kochems. 1983. "The North American Berdache." *Current Anthropology* 24, no. 4:1–76.

Carmack, Robert M., ed. 1988. *Harvest of Violence: The Maya Indians and the Guatemalan Crisis*. Norman: University of Oklahoma Press.

Carr, Albert Z. 1963. *The World of William Walker*. New York: Harper and Row.

Carrier, J. M. 1976. "Family Attitudes and Mexican Male Homosexuality." *Urban Life* 5, no. 3:359–75.

Certeau, Michel de. 1984. *The Practice of Everyday Life*. Berkeley and Los Angeles: University of California Press.

Chauncey, George, Jr. 1989. "Christian Brotherhood or Sexual Perversion? Homosexual Identities and the Construction of Sexual Boundaries in the World War I Era." In Duberman et al., *Hidden from History*, 294–317.

Chodorow, Nancy. 1974. "Family Structure and Feminine Personality." In Michelle Zimbalist Rosaldo and Louise Lamphere, eds., *Woman, Culture and Society*, 43–66. Stanford: Stanford University Press.

———. 1978. *The Reproduction of Mothering: Psychoanalysis and the Sociology of Gender*. Berkeley and Los Angeles: University of California Press.

———. 1989. *Feminism and Psychoanalytic Theory*. New Haven: Yale University Press.

Clifford, James. 1986. "Introduction: Partial Truths." In Clifford and Marcus, *Writing Culture*, 1–26.

———. 1988. *The Predicament of Culture: Twentieth-Century Ethnography, Literature, and Art.* Cambridge: Harvard University Press.

Clifford, James, and George E. Marcus, eds. 1986. *Writing Culture: The Poetics and Politics of Ethnography.* Berkeley and Los Angeles: University of California Press.

Colburn, Forrest D. 1986. *Post-Revolutionary Nicaragua: State, Class, and the Dilemmas of Agrarian Policy.* Berkeley and Los Angeles: University of California Press.

Collins, Joseph, with Frances Moore Lappé and Nick Allen. 1982. *Nicaragua: What Difference Could a Revolution Make?* San Francisco: Food First.

Collinson, Helen, ed. 1990. *Women and Revolution in Nicaragua.* London: Zed Books.

Condominas, Georges. 1973. "Ethics and Comfort: An Ethnographer's View of His Profession." *American Anthropological Association Annual Report, 1972,* 1–17. Washington, D.C.: AAA.

Conroy, Michael E. 1990. "The Political Economy of the 1990 Nicaraguan Elections." *International Journal of Political Economy,* Fall, 5–33.

Cooke, Nick, and Mariuca Lomba. 1988. "Hay que abrir la Caja de Pandora del sexismo y el machismo." *Pensamiento propio,* April–May, 15–18.

Corzine, Jay, and Richard Kirby. 1977. "Cruising and Truckers: Sexual Encounters in a Highway Rest Area." *Urban Life* 6, no. 2:171–92.

Crapanzano, Vincent. 1980. *Tuhami: Portrait of a Moroccan.* Chicago: University of Chicago Press.

———. 1986. *Waiting: The Whites of South Africa.* New York: Random House, Vintage Books.

Culler, Jonathan. 1986. *Ferdinand de Saussure.* Rev. ed. Ithaca: Cornell University Press.

Darío, Rubén. 1953. "El pájaro azul." In *Obras Completas,* vol. 5, *Poesía.* 678–83. Madrid: Afrodisio Aguado.

Davis, Natalie Zemon. 1978. "Women on Top: Symbolic Inversion and Political Disorder in Early Modern Europe." In Barbara A. Babcock, ed., *The Reversible World: Symbolic Inversion in Art and Society,* 147–90. Ithaca: Cornell University Press.

Delgado, Richard. 1982. "Words That Wound: A Tort Action for Racial Insults, Epithets, and Name-Calling." *Harvard Civil Rights–Civil Liberties Law Review* 17, no. 1:133–81.

D'Emilio, John. 1983. *Sexual Politics, Sexual Communities: The Making of a Homosexual Minority in the United States, 1940–1970.* Chicago: University of Chicago Press.

Dening, Greg. 1988. *History's Anthropology: The Death of William Gooch.* Lanham, Maryland: University Press of America.

Derrida, Jacques. 1981. *Positions.* Translated by Alan Bass. Chicago: University of Chicago Press.

De Santis, Marie. 1990. "Nicaragua Rolls Back Reproductive Rights." *Off Our Backs* 5 Aug., 3.

Dirección de Orientación y Protección Familiar. 1983. "Informe sobre la familia en Nicaragua." *Instituto Nicaragüense de Seguridad Social y Bienestar, Oficina de la Mujer, Secretaria de la Junta del Gobierno de Reconstrucción Nacional.* Managua: Nicaragua.

Dirección Nacional, FSLN. 1987. *El FSLN y la mujer.* Managua: Editorial Vanguardia.

Diskin, Martin. 1987. "The Manipulation of Indigenous Struggles." In T. Walker, *Reagan Versus the Sandinistas,* 80–96.

Diskin, Martin, Thomas Bossert, Salomón Nahmad S., and Stéfano Varese. 1986. *Peace and Autonomy on the Atlantic Coast of Nicaragua: A Report of the LASA Task Force on Human Rights and Academic Freedom.* Pittsburgh: Latin American Studies Association Secretariat.

Dolgin, Janet L., David S. Kemnitzer, and David M. Schneider, eds. 1977. *Symbolic Anthropology: A Reader in the Study of Symbols and Meanings.* New York: Columbia University Press.

Donham, Donald L. 1990. *History, Power, Ideology: Central Issues in Marxism and Anthropology.* Cambridge: Cambridge University Press.

Dreyfus, Hubert, and Paul Rabinow. 1982. *Michel Foucault: Beyond Structuralism and Hermeneutics.* Chicago: University of Chicago Press.

Duberman, Martin, Martha Vicinus, and George Chauncey, Jr. 1989. *Hidden from History: Reclaiming the Gay and Lesbian Past.* New York: Meridian.

Dworkin, Andrea. 1987. *Intercourse.* New York: Free Press.

———. 1989. *Pornography: Men Possessing Women.* With a new introduction by the author. New York: Dutton.

Eagleton, Terry. 1983. *Literary Theory: An Introduction.* Minneapolis: University of Minnesota Press.

Eco, Umberto. 1985. "How Culture Conditions the Colors We See." In Blonsky, *On Signs,* 157–75.

Ehlers, Tracy Bachrach. 1991. "Debunking Marianismo: Economic Vulnerability and Survival Strategies Among Guatemalan Wives." *Ethnology* 30, no. 1:1–16.

Engels, Frederick. [1942] 1972. *The Origins of the Family, Private Property, and the State.* Edited by Eleanor Burke Leacock. New York: International Publishers.

Fagen, Richard R., Carmen Diana Deere, and José Luis Coraggio, eds. 1986. *Transition and Development: Problems of Third World Socialism.* New York: Monthly Review Press.

Forbes, Jack. 1988. *Black Africans and Native Americans: Color, Race, and Caste in the Evolution of Red-Black Peoples.* New York: Basil Blackwell.

Foster, George M. 1953. "Cofradía and Compadrazgo in Spain and Spanish America." *Southwest Journal of Anthropology* 9, no. 1:1–28.

———. 1965. "Peasant Society and the Image of Limited Good." *American Anthropologist* 67:293–315.

———. 1972. "The Anatomy of Envy: A Study in Symbolic Behavior." *Current Anthropology* 13, no. 2:164–202.

Foucault, Michel. [1975] 1979. *Discipline and Punish: The Birth of the Prison.* Translated by Alan Sheridan. New York: Random House, Vintage Books.

———. [1976] 1980. *The History of Sexuality*. Vol. 1, *An Introduction*. Translated by R. Hurley. New York: Random House, Vintage Books.

———. [1984] 1986. *The Use of Pleasure*. Vol. 2 of *The History of Sexuality*. Translated by R. Hurley. New York: Random House, Vintage Books.

Gilligan, Carol. 1982. *In a Different Voice: Psychological Theory and Women's Development*. Cambridge: Harvard University Press.

Goffman, Erving. 1959. *The Presentation of Self in Everyday Life*. Garden City, N.Y.: Doubleday.

Goldwert, Marvin. 1983. *Machismo and Conquest: The Case of Mexico*. Lanham, Md.: University Press of America.

Gonzalez, Mike. 1990. *Nicaragua: What Went Wrong?* London: Bookmarks.

Gould, Jeffrey L. 1990. *To Lead As Equals: Rural Protest and Political Consciousness in Chinandega, Nicaragua, 1912–1979*. Chapel Hill: University of North Carolina Press.

Greenberg, David F. 1988. *The Construction of Homosexuality*. Chicago: University of Chicago Press.

Gregory, Chris A. 1982. *Gifts and Commodities*. London: Academic Press.

Guevara, Che. 1968. *Socialism and Man*. New York: Pathfinder.

Halperin, David M. 1989. "Sex Before Sexuality: Pederasty, Politics, and Power in Classical Athens." In Duberman et al., *Hidden from History*, 37–53.

Hanson, Allan. 1989. "The Making of the Maori: Culture Invention and Its Logic." *American Anthropologist* 91:890–902.

Harris, Marvin. 1964. *Patterns of Race in the Americas*. New York: Walker and Company.

Harris, Richard L., and Carlos M. Vilas, eds. 1985. *Nicaragua: A Revolution under Siege*. Avon: Zed.

Hawkins, John. 1984. *Inverse Images: The Meaning of Culture, Ethnicity, and Family in Postcolonial Guatemala*. Albuquerque: University of New Mexico Press.

Herdt, Gilbert H. 1981. *Guardians of the Flutes: Idioms of Masculinity*. New York: McGraw-Hill.

———. 1982. "Fetish and Fantasy in Sambia Initiation." In Gilbert H. Herdt, ed., *Rituals of Manhood: Male Initiation in Papua New Guinea*, 44–98. Berkeley and Los Angeles: University of California Press.

Hobsbawm, Eric. 1959. *Primitive Rebels: Studies in Archaic Forms of Social Movement in the Nineteenth and Twentieth Centuries*. New York: Norton.

———. 1984. *Workers: Worlds of Labor*. New York: Random House, Pantheon Books.

Hobsbawm, Eric, and Terence Ranger, eds. 1983. *The Invention of Tradition*. Cambridge: Cambridge University Press.

Hodges, Donald C. 1986. *Intellectual Foundations of the Nicaraguan Revolution*. Austin: University of Texas Press.

Hoy, David Couzens. 1986. *Foucault: A Critical Reader*. Oxford: Basil Blackwell.

Humphreys, Laud. 1970. *Tearoom Trade: Impersonal Sex in Public Places*. Chicago: Aldine.

IHCA (Instituto Histórico Centroamericano). 1984. "La Familia Nicaragüense en Proceso de Cambio." *Envío,* Apr., 1–12.

———. 1988a. "Economic Reform: Taking It to the Streets." *Envío,* Apr., 14–39.

———. 1988b. "Sandinistas Surviving in a Percentage Game." *Envío,* Dec., 10–23.

———. 1990a. "FSLN Scoreboard—Esquipulas 1:4, Elections 3:2." *Envío,* Feb., 3–9.

———. 1990b. "Media Watch: Nicaragua's Poll Wars." *Envío,* Feb., 10–16.

———. 1990c. "After the Polling Wars: Explaining the Upset." *Envío,* Mar.–Apr., 30–35.

Jakobson, Roman, and Morris Halle. 1956. *Fundamentals of Language.* The Hague: Mouton.

Jameson, Fredric. 1971. *Marxism and Form: Twentieth-Century Dialectical Theories of Literature.* Princeton: Princeton University Press.

———. 1972. *The Prison-House of Language: A Critical Account of Structuralism and Russian Formalism.* Princeton: Princeton University Press.

———. 1984. "Postmodernism, Or, The Cultural Logic of Late Capitalism." *New Left Review* 146 (July–August):53–92.

———. 1991. *Postmodernism; or, The Cultural Logic of Late Capitalism.* Durham: Duke University Press.

Kardiner, Abram. 1954. "The Flight from Masculinity." In *Sex and Morality.* New York: Bobbs-Merrill.

Katz, Jonathan Ned. 1990. "The Invention of Heterosexuality." *Socialist Review* 20, no. 1:7–33.

LaFeber, Walter. 1984. *Inevitable Revolutions: The United States in Central America.* Expanded ed. New York: Norton.

Lancaster, Roger N. 1983. "What AIDS Is Doing to Us." *Christopher Street,* no. 75:48–54.

———. 1986. "Comment on Arguelles and Rich's 'Homosexuality, Homophobia, and Revolution: Notes Toward an Understanding of the Cuban Lesbian and Gay Male Experience, Part II.' " *Signs* 12, no. 1:188–92.

———. 1988a. "Subject Honor and Object Shame: The Construction of Male Homosexuality and Stigma in Nicaragua." *Ethnology* 27, no. 2:111–25.

———. 1988b. *Thanks to God and the Revolution: Popular Religion and Class Consciousness in the New Nicaragua.* New York: Columbia University Press.

Landau, Saul. 1991. "The East Joins the South." *Barricada internacional,* Jan., 19–22.

Lévi-Strauss, Claude. 1969. *The Elementary Structures of Kinship.* Boston: Beacon.

Lewes, Kenneth. 1988. *The Psychoanalytic Theory of Male Homosexuality.* New York: New American Library.

MacKinnon, Catherine A. 1983. "Feminism, Marxism, Method, and the State: Toward Feminist Jurisprudence." *Signs* 8, no. 4:635–58.

MacLachlan, Colin M., and Jaime E. Rodríguez O. 1980. *The Forging of the Cosmic Race: A Reinterpretation of Colonial Mexico.* Berkeley and Los Angeles: University of California Press.

MacMichael, David. 1990. "Nicaraguan Elections: The U.S. Plays the Contra Card." *Nation*, 5 Feb., 162–67.

Malinowski, Bronislaw. [1922] 1961. *Argonauts of the Western Pacific*. New York: Dutton.

Marx, Karl. 1963. *Theories of Surplus Value, Part I*. Vol. 4 of *Capital*. Moscow: Foreign Languages Publishing House.

———. 1965. *Pre-Capitalist Economic Formations*. Introduction by Eric J. Hobsbawm. New York: International Publishers.

———. [1867] 1967. *Capital: A Critique of Political Economy*. Vol. 1, *The Process of Capitalist Accumulation*. Edited by Frederick Engels. New York: International Publishers.

———. 1977. *Selected Writings*. Edited by David McLellan. Oxford: Oxford University Press.

Marx, Karl, and Frederick Engels. [1848] 1948. *The Communist Manifesto*. New York: International Publishers.

———. 1964. *The German Ideology*. Moscow: Progress Publishers.

———. 1968. *Selected Works*. New York: International Publishers.

Massaro, Toni M. 1991. "Equality and Freedom of Expression: The Hate Speech Dilemma." *William and Mary Law Review* 32, no. 2:211–65.

Matthieu, Nicole-Claude. 1978. "Man-Culture and Woman-Nature?" *Feminist Studies International Quarterly* 1:55–65.

Mauss, Marcel. [1925] 1967. *The Gift: Forms and Functions of Exchange in Archaic Societies*. Introduction by E. E. Evans-Pritchard. New York: Norton.

Mead, Margaret. [1935] 1963. *Sex and Temperament in Three Primitive Societies*. New York: Morrow Quill.

Medvedev, P. N., and Mikhail M. Bakhtin. [1928] 1978. *The Formal Method of Literary Scholarship: A Critical Introduction to Sociological Poetics*. Translated by Albert J. Wehrle. Baltimore: Johns Hopkins University Press.

Mintz, Sidney. 1973. "A Note on the Definition of Peasantries." *Journal of Peasant Studies* 1:91–106.

Mintz, Sidney, and Eric Wolf. 1950. "An Analysis of Ritual Co-Parenthood (Compadrazgo)." *Southwest Journal of Anthropology* 6:341–68.

Molyneux, Maxine. 1985. "Mobilization Without Emancipation? Women's Interests, The State, and Revolution in Nicaragua." *Feminist Studies* 11, no. 2:227–54.

———. 1986a. "Mobilization Without Emancipation? Women's Interests, State, and Revolution." In Fagen et al., *Transition and Development*, 280–302.

———. 1986b. "Women: Activism Without Liberation?" In Rosset and Vandermeer, *Nicaragua*, 478–81.

Montagu, Ashley. 1974. *Man's Most Dangerous Myth: The Fallacy of Race*. 5th ed. New York: Oxford University Press.

Mörner, Magnus. 1967. *Race Mixture in the History of Latin America*. Boston: Little.

———, ed. 1970. *Race and Class in Latin America*. New York: Columbia University Press.

Murphy, M. 1984. "Masculinity and Selective Homophobia: A Case from Spain." *ARGOH Newsletter* 5:6–12.

Nash, June. 1979. *We Eat the Mines and the Mines Eat Us: Dependency and Exploitation in Bolivian Tin Mines*. New York: Columbia University Press.

Nash, June, and María P. Fernández-Kelly, eds. 1984. *Women, Men, and the International Division of Labor*. Albany: State University of New York Press.

Nash, June, and Helen Safa, eds. 1980. *Sex and Class in Latin America: Women's Perspectives on Economics, Politics, and the Family in the Third World*. South Hadley, Mass.: Bergin and Garvey.

———. 1986. *Women and Change in Latin America: New Directions in Sex and Class*. South Hadley, Mass.: Bergin and Garvey.

Newson, Linda A. 1987. *Indian Survival in Colonial Nicaragua*. Norman: University of Oklahoma Press.

Ortner, Sherry, and Harriet Whitehead, eds. 1981. *Sexual Meanings: The Cultural Construction of Gender and Sexuality*. Cambridge: Cambridge University Press.

Padgug, Robert. 1989. "Sexual Matters: Rethinking Sexuality in History." In Duberman et al., *Hidden from History*, 54–64.

Parker, Richard. 1984. "The Body and the Self: Aspects of Male Sexual Ideology in Brazil." Paper presented at the Eighty-third annual meeting of the American Anthropological Association, Denver.

———. 1985. "Masculinity, Femininity, and Homosexuality: On the Anthropological Interpretation of Sexual Meanings in Brazil." *Journal of Homosexuality* 11:155–63.

———. 1991. *Bodies, Pleasures, and Passions: Sexual Culture in Contemporary Brazil*. Boston: Beacon.

Paz, Octavio. [1961, 1972] 1985. *The Labyrinth of Solitude (and The Other Mexico, Return to the Labyrinth of Solitude, Mexico and the United States, The Philanthropic Ogre)*. Translated from the Spanish by Lysander Kemp, Yara Milos, and Rachel Phillips Belash. New York: Grove Press.

Pitt-Rivers, Julian. 1971. "The Colors of Race." In James P. Spradley and David W. McCurdy, eds., *Conformity and Conflict: Readings in Cultural Anthropology*, 171–84. Boston: Little, Brown.

Post, Robert C. 1990. "The Constitutional Concept of Public Discourse: Outrageous Opinion, Democratic Deliberation, and *Hustler Magazine* v. Falwell." *Harvard Law Review* 103:603–86.

———. 1991. "Racist Speech, Democracy, and the First Amendment." *William and Mary Law Review* 32, no. 2:267–327.

Potter, Sulamith Heins, and Jack M. Potter. 1990. *China's Peasants: The Anthropology of a Revolution*. Cambridge: Cambridge University Press.

Rabinow, Paul. 1986. "Representations Are Social Facts." In Clifford and Marcus, *Writing Culture*, 234–61.

Ramírez, Sergio. [1976] 1986. *Stories*. Translated by Nick Caistor. London: Readers International.

———, ed. [1984] 1990. *Sandino: The Testimony of a Nicaraguan Patriot: 1921–1934*. Edited and translated by Robert Edgar Conrad. Princeton: Princeton University Press.

Ramírez-Horton, Susan E. 1982. "The Role of Women in the Nicaraguan Revolution." In T. Walker, *Nicaragua in Revolution*, 147–59.

Rey, Pierre-Philippe. 1982. "Class Alliances." *International Journal of Sociology* 12, no. 2:1–120.

Roseberry, William. 1989. *Anthropologies and Histories: Essays in Culture, History, and Political Economy*. New Brunswick: Rutgers University Press.

Rosenberg, Charles E. 1962. *The Cholera Years: The United States in 1832, 1849, and 1866*. Chicago: University of Chicago Press.

Rosset, Peter, and John Vandermeer, eds. 1983. *The Nicaragua Reader: Documents of a Revolution under Fire*. Rev. ed. New York: Grove.

———, eds. 1986. *Nicaragua: Unfinished Revolution*. New York: Grove.

Rubin, Gayle. 1975. "The Traffic in Women: Notes on the 'Political Economy' of Sex." In Rayna N. Reiter, ed., *Toward an Anthropology of Women*, 157–210. New York: Monthly Review Press.

Ruse, Michael. 1988. *Homosexuality: A Philosophical Inquiry*. Oxford: Basil Blackwell.

Sahlins, Marshall. 1968. *Tribesmen*. Englewood Cliffs, N.J.: Prentice-Hall.

———. 1972. *Stone Age Economics*. Chicago: Aldine-Atherton.

———. 1977. "Colors and Cultures." In Dolgin et al., *Symbolic Anthropology*, 165–80.

Said, Edward. 1978. *Orientalism*. New York: Random House, Vintage Books.

Sartre, Jean-Paul. [1960] 1963. *Search for a Method*. Translated by Hazel E. Barnes. New York: Knopf.

———. [1960] 1976. *Critique of Dialectical Reason: Theory of Political Ensembles*. Translated by Alan Sheridan-Smith. Edited by Jonathan Rée. London: NLB.

Saussure, Ferdinand de. [1915] 1966. *Course in General Linguistics*. Edited by Charles Bally and Albert Sechehaye. New York: McGraw-Hill.

Scheper-Hughes, Nancy. 1979. *Saints, Scholars, and Schizophrenics: Mental Illness in Rural Ireland*. Berkeley and Los Angeles: University of California Press.

———. 1992. *Death Without Weeping: The Violence of Everyday Life in Brazil*. Berkeley and Los Angeles: University of California Press.

Scheper-Hughes, Nancy, and Margaret Lock. 1987. "The Mindful Body: A Prolegomenon to Future Work in Medical Anthropology." *Medical Anthropology Quarterly*, n.s., 1, no. 1:6–41.

Schlesinger, Stephen, and Stephen Kinzer. 1983. *Bitter Fruit: The Untold Story of the American Coup in Guatemala*. Introduction by Harrison Salisbury. Garden City, N.Y.: Doubleday, Anchor Books.

Smith-Rosenberg, Carroll. 1985. *Disorderly Conduct: Visions of Gender in Victorian America*. New York: Oxford University Press.

Sontag, Susan. 1979. *Illness as Metaphor*. New York: Random House, Vintage Books.

———. 1989. *AIDS and Its Metaphors*. New York: Farrar, Straus and Giroux.

Spalding, Rose J., ed. 1987. *The Political Economy of Revolutionary Nicaragua*. Boston: Allen and Unwin.

Stacey, Judith. 1990. *Brave New Families: Stories of Domestic Upheaval in Late Twentieth Century America*. New York: Basic.

Stack, Carol. 1974. *All Our Kin: Strategies for Survival in a Black Community*. New York: Harper and Row, Torchbooks.

Stahler-Sholk, Richard. 1988. "Un tratamiento 'shock' para la economía." *Pensamiento propio*, Mar., 45–48.

Stein, Stanley, and Barbara Stein. 1970. *The Colonial Heritage of Latin America: Essays on Economic Dependence in Perspective*. New York: Oxford University Press.

Stephens, Beth. 1990. "A Developing Legal System Grapples with an Ancient Problem: Rape in Nicaragua." *Women's Rights Law Reporter* 12, no. 2:69–88.

Stephens, Thomas. 1989. *Dictionary of Latin American Racial and Ethnic Terminology*. Gainesville: University of Florida Press.

Stevens, Evelyn P. 1973. "*Marianismo:* The Other Face of *Machismo* in Latin America." In Ann Pescatello, ed., *Female and Male in Latin America*, 89–101. Pittsburgh: University of Pittsburgh Press.

Strathern, Marilyn. 1981. "Culture in a Netbag: The Manufacture of a Subdiscipline in Anthropology." *Man*, n.s. 16:665–88.

Suárez-Orozco, Marcelo M. 1982. "A Study of Argentine Soccer: The Dynamics of Fans and Their Folklore." *Journal of Psychoanalytic Anthropology* 5:7–28.

Taussig, Michael. 1987. *Shamanism, Colonialism, and the Wild Man: A Study in Terror and Healing*. Chicago: University of Chicago Press.

Tribe, Laurence. 1988. *American Constitutional Law*. 2d ed. Mineola, N.Y.: Foundation Press.

Trinh T. Minh-ha. 1989. *Woman, Native, Other: Writing Postcoloniality and Feminism.* Bloomington: Indiana University Press.

Trumbach, Randolph. 1977. "London's Sodomites: Homosexual Behavior and Western Culture in the Eighteenth Century." *Journal of Social History* 11:1–33.

Vance, Carole, ed. 1984. *Pleasure and Danger: Exploring Female Sexuality*. Boston: Routledge and Kegan Paul.

Vickers, George R. 1990. "A Spider's Web." *NACLA Report on the Americas* 24, no. 1:19–27.

Vilas, Carlos M. 1986. *The Sandinista Revolution: National Liberation and Social Transformation in Central America*. New York: Monthly Review Press.

———. 1987. "Troubles Everywhere: An Economic Perspective on the Sandinista Revolution." In Spalding, *Political Economy*, 233–46.

———. 1990a. "What Went Wrong." *NACLA Report on the Americas* 24, no. 1:10–18.

———. 1990b. "Is Socialism Still an Alternative for the Third World?" *Monthly Review*, July/Aug., 93–109.

———. 1990c. "Nicaragua After the Elections: The First 100 Days." *Z Magazine*, Nov., 91–97.

Vilas, Carlos M., and Richard L. Harris. 1985. "National Liberation, Popular

Democracy, and the Transition to Socialism." In Harris and Vilas, *Nicaragua: A Revolution under Siege*, 216–34.

Vološinov, V. N. [1929] 1986. *Marxism and the Philosophy of Language*. Translated by Ladislav Matejka and I. R. Titunik. Cambridge: Harvard University Press.

Wagley, Charles. 1965. "On the Concept of Social Race in the Americas." In Dwight B. Heath and Richard N. Adams, eds., *Contemporary Cultures and Societies of Latin America*, 531–45. New York: Random House.

Walker, Thomas W. 1982. "Introduction." In T. Walker, *Nicaragua in Revolution*, 1–22.

———. 1986. *Nicaragua: The Land of Sandino*. 2d ed. Boulder: Westview.

———, ed. 1982. *Nicaragua in Revolution*. New York: Praeger.

———, ed. 1987. *Reagan Versus the Sandinistas: The Undeclared War on Nicaragua*. Boulder: Westview.

Walker, William. [1860] 1985. *The War in Nicaragua*. Foreword by Robert Houston. Tucson: University of Arizona Press.

Ward, Kathryn B. 1984. *Women in the World-System: Its Impact on Status and Fertility*. New York: Praeger.

Warren, Kay. 1979. *The Symbolism of Subordination: Indian Identity in a Guatemalan Town*. Austin: University of Texas Press.

Weeks, Jeffrey. 1977. *Coming Out: Homosexual Politics in Britain from the Nineteenth Century to the Present*. London: Quartet.

———. 1981. *Sex, Politics, and Society: The Regulation of Sexuality since 1800*. New York: Longman.

———. 1985. *Sexuality and Its Discontents: Meanings, Myths, and Modern Sexualities*. London: Routledge and Kegan Paul.

Whitehead, Harriet. 1981. "The Bow and the Burden Strap: A New Look at Institutionalized Homosexuality in Native North America." In Ortner and Whitehead, *Sexual Meanings*, 80–115.

Williams, Walter L. 1986. *The Spirit and the Flesh: Sexual Diversity in American Indian Culture*. Boston: Beacon.

Wolf, Eric. 1959. *Sons of the Shaking Earth*. Chicago: University of Chicago Press.

Index

Compositor: Maple-Vail Book Mfg. Group
Text: 10/13 Sabon
Display: Sabon
Printer: Maple-Vail Book Mfg. Group
Binder: Maple-Vail Book Mfg. Group

CPSIA information can be obtained
at www.ICGtesting.com
Printed in the USA
LVHW031434231218
601536LV00004B/344/P

9 780520 089297